THE AGE OF
AMERICAN UNREASON

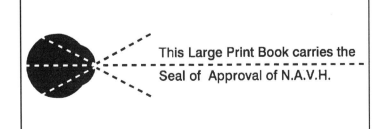

This Large Print Book carries the
Seal of Approval of N.A.V.H.

THE AGE OF
AMERICAN UNREASON

SUSAN JACOBY

WHEELER PUBLISHING
A part of Gale, Cengage Learning

GALE
CENGAGE Learning™

Detroit • New York • San Francisco • New Haven, Conn • Waterville, Maine • London

GALE
CENGAGE Learning

LIBRARY OF CONGRESS CATALOGING-IN-PUBLICATION DATA

Jacoby, Susan, 1945–
  The age of American unreason / By Susan Jacoby.
    p. cm.
  "Wheeler Publishing large print hardcover" — T.p. verso.
  Includes bibliographical references.
  ISBN-13: 978-1-59722-793-3 (hardcover : alk. paper)
  ISBN-10: 1-59722-793-5 (hardcover : alk. paper)
  1. United States — Civilization — 1945– 2. United States — Social conditions — 1945– 3. Mass media — Social aspects — United States. 4. Popular culture — United States. 5. Reason — Social aspects — United States. 6. Social values — United States. 7. Social psychology — United States. 8. National characteristics, American. 9. Large type books. I. Title.
E169.Z83J33 2008a
973.9—dc22   2008015844

Published in 2008 by arrangement with Pantheon Books, a division of Random House, Inc.

For Aaron Asher

If a nation expects to be ignorant and free, in a state of civilization, it expects what never was and never will be.

— Thomas Jefferson, 1816

CONTENTS

INTRODUCTION

It is the dream of every historian to produce a work that endures and provides the foundation for insights that may lie decades or centuries in the future. Such a book is Richard Hofstadter's *Anti-Intellectualism in American Life,* published in early 1963 on the hopeful cusp between the McCarthy era and the social convulsions of the late sixties. "One of the major virtues of liberal society in the past," Hofstadter wrote in an elegaic yet guardedly optimistic conclusion, "was that it made possible such a variety of styles of intellectual life — one can find men notable for being passionate and rebellious, others for being elegant and sumptuous, or spare and astringent, clever and complex, patient and wise, and some equipped mainly to observe and endure. What matters is the openness and generosity needed to comprehend the varieties of excellence that could be found even in a single rather parochial society. . . . It is possible, of course, that the avenues of choice are being closed, and that the culture of the future will be dominated by single-minded men of one persuasion or another. It is possible; but in so far as the weight of one's will is thrown onto the scales of history, one lives in the belief that it is not to be so."

I was moved by those words when I first read them as a college student more than forty years ago, and I am still moved by them. Yet it is difficult to suppress the fear that the scales of American history have shifted heavily against the vibrant and varied intellectual life so essential to functional democracy. During the past four decades, America's endemic anti-intellectual tendencies have been grievously exacerbated by a new species of semiconscious anti-rationalism, feeding on and fed by an ignorant popular culture of video images and unremitting noise that leaves no room for contemplation or logic. This new form of anti-rationalism, at odds not only with the nation's heritage of eighteenth-century Enlightenment reason but with modern scientific knowledge, has propelled a surge of anti-intellectualism capable of inflicting vastly greater damage than its historical predecessors inflicted on American culture and politics. Indeed, popular anti-rationalism and anti-intellectualism are now synonymous. I cannot call myself a cultural conservative, because that term, hijacked by the religious right and propagated by the media, is customarily used to describe a person preoccupied with such matters as the preservation of the phrase "under God" in the Pledge of Allegiance; the defense of marriage as an institution for heterosexuals only; the promotion of premarital chastity; and the protection of cancer patients from marijuana addiction. I do, however, consider myself a cultural conservationist, committed, in the strict dictionary sense, to the preservation of culture "from destructive influences, natural decay, or waste; preservation in being, life, health, perfection, etc."

Hofstadter's examination of American anti-intellectualism, an exemplary specimen of cultural conservationism, appeared at a time when the nation was taking a more critical look at the entire array of self-congratulatory pieties connected with the Pax Americana after the Second World War. The three years between the election and assassination of President John F. Kennedy generated considerable optimism among most Americans, but no group had greater reason for hope than the intellectual community. Intellectuals had become accustomed during the late forties and early fifties to a political climate that equated academic and scholarly interests with communist and socialist leanings or, at the very least, with a dangerous tolerance toward those who *did* harbor left-wing sympathies. Even when "eggheads" were not being portrayed as potential traitors, they were often dismissed as incompetents. In 1954, President Dwight D. Eisenhower, speaking at a Republican fund-raiser, described an intellectual as "a man who takes more words than are necessary to tell more than he knows."

When the Soviet Union bruised the nation's ego by launching Sputnik in 1957, it dawned on Americans that intellectuals might actually have some practical value. Public interest and money, however, were largely reserved for scientific endeavor — with its obvious importance for both national defense and bragging rights. Intellectuals who devoted themselves to scholarship or ideas with no obvious utilitarian purpose had little stature or status as far as the general public was concerned. When I moved to New York in the early seventies, I was astonished to meet intellectuals who, in the fifties, had actually believed that Adlai

Stevenson could defeat Eisenhower for the presidency — a wishful misconception that was surely a measure of their psychological and social distance from ordinary Americans in the nation's heartland. My parents, grandparents, and most of their friends had voted for both Franklin Roosevelt and Harry Truman, but all I ever heard about Stevenson when I was growing up in a small town in Michigan was that he was too much of an egghead to have any understanding of ordinary people and their problems. Stevenson's cultivated speech, such a strong point in his favor among his fellow intellectuals, was seen as a liability by most of the adults who inhabited my childhood world. My grandmother, who before her death at age ninety-nine boasted that she had never voted for a Republican, was able to overcome her distaste for Stevenson's syntax and elevated vocabulary only by recalling the Depression and her beloved FDR. "Adlai talked down to people," she recalled, "and he didn't have the common touch. Ike had the common touch and I loved him, but in the end, remembering which party gave us Social Security and which party couldn't care less about starving old people, I just couldn't bring myself to vote Republican."

Kennedy, by contrast, managed the tricky feat of displaying his intelligence and education — his manner of speaking was every bit as polished and erudite as Stevenson's — without being seen by the public as a snooty intellectual. The public was right: Kennedy was no intellectual, if an intellectual is, to borrow Hofstadter's definition, someone who "in some sense lives for ideas — which means he has a sense of dedication to the life of the mind which is very much like a religious commitment." Few politicians of any era, in any country, could qualify as intellectuals by that strict standard. One of the most remarkable characteristics of America's revolutionary generation was the presence and influence of so many genuine intellectuals (although the term had not been coined in the eighteenth century). Men of extraordinary learning and intellect were disproportionately represented among the politicians who wrote the Declaration of Independence and the Constitution and led the republic during its formative decades. True to Enlightenment values, they saw no contradiction between their roles as thinkers and actors on the public stage: the founders would have been astonished by the subsequent development of what Lionel Trilling would describe in 1942 as "the chronic American belief that there exists an opposition between reality and mind and that one must enlist oneself in the party of reality."*

Kennedy spoke and wrote frequently — and had done so long before he became president — of the need for American society to abandon its parochial twentieth-century image of an inevitable division between thought and action and return to an eighteenth-century model in which learning and a philosophical bent were thought to enhance political leadership. His government appointments reflected that philosophy; when it came time to fill important jobs in his administration, Kennedy hired prominent academics in numbers that provided clear evidence of his comfort in the presence of men (though not women) of ideas. The knowledge that the new president had sought out such undeniable egg-heads as John Kenneth Galbraith, Richard Neustadt, Richard Goodwin, Arthur Schlesinger, Jr., and Walter Heller did much to elevate public respect for the intellectual

* This lecture, originally delivered at Columbia University, was reprinted in Trilling's influential collection of essays, *The Liberal Imagination,* in 1950.

community, and intellectuals themselves were sometimes overwhelmed by simultaneous sensations of gratification and guilt at the newly apparent possibilities of power and its attendant material rewards.

In his 1978 memoir *New York Jew,* the literary critic Alfred Kazin, with his characteristic mixture of malice and good humor, captured the mood in a description of summers spent in increasingly fashionable and prosperous intellectual havens on Cape Cod, where everyone basked in the glory of the Kennedy connection. "The woods . . . were suddenly full of White House detail in incongruous business suits . . . Arthur Schlesinger and Richard Goodwin, released from academic constraints and just in from the Kennedy compound at Hyannis, gamboled and gossiped. . . . Young men in rustic beards sat cross-legged on the floor humming and strumming folk rock to their own guitars. There was a cocktail-party sense of everybody's ability to move fluently anywhere. Power from Washington seemed to be stored up in the cells of Kennedy's executive assistants and advisers even on a weekend romp in Wellfleet among their old colleagues from Harvard, M.I.T, and the Institute for Advanced Study."

At this moment of cultural equipoise, Hofstadter's *Anti-Intellectualism* was published. In one important sense, the book is very much a product of the McCarthy era: Hofstadter was determined to examine the fierce postwar melding of anti-intellectualism and prosecutorial anti-Communism within the broader long-term context of American cultural propensities that declared themselves soon after the first Puritan settlers landed at Plymouth Rock. "Our anti-intellectualism is, in fact, older than our national identity and has a long historical background," Hofstadter argued. "An examination of this background suggests that regard for intellectuals in the United States has not moved steadily downward and has not gone into a sudden, recent decline, but is subject to cyclical fluctuations; it suggests, too, that the resentment from which the intellectual has suffered in our time is a manifestation not of a decline in his position but of his increasing prominence." In this view, American anti-intellectualism represented the flip side of America's democratic impulses in religion and education. Fundamentalist religion, grounded in the belief in a personal relationship between man and God and resistance to orthodox ecclesiastical hierarchies, was also resistant to the modernizing and secu-

19

larizing trends long associated with intellectualism — including the religious intellectualism of many of the early Puritan clerics. The democratization of education, which greatly expanded the number of high school students beginning in the late nineteenth century and did the same for college enrollment in the twentieth century, inevitably relaxed the more rigorous standards prevailing in societies in which only a minuscule fraction of students was destined for instruction beyond basic reading, writing, and arithmetic. Finally, America's idealization of the self-made man — one who succeeds by his own wit and industriousness without advantages conferred by either a privileged family background or formal education — did not easily accommodate respect for those who devoted their lives to teaching and learning.

Ironically, the denigration of professional educators did not really take hold until the middle of the twentieth century, when a college degree first became a necessary passport to success not only in professions like law and medicine but in the world of business, once seen as the domain of the self-made. "Those who can, do; those who can't, teach" is an adage that would have seemed ridiculous to Americans in the eighteenth and nineteenth centuries, when the hiring of a schoolteacher was one of the two fundamental markers of civilization in frontier communities (the other being the presence of a minister). Of course, the ubiquitous and indispensable community schoolteacher, often deficient in formal educational credentials, was a very different cultural and social animal from the credentialed "experts" who, especially after the Second World War, increasingly dominated business, government, and education, and were frequently viewed as enemies of the common sense that is supposedly the special virtue of ordinary people.

Rereading Hofstadter at the end of the nineties, I was struck by the old-fashioned fairness of his scholarship — not the bogus "objectivity" or bland centrism that always locates truth equidistant from two points, but a serious attempt to engage the arguments of opponents and to acknowledge evidence that runs counter to one's own biases. I could not have possessed a full appreciation of this quality when I read the book for the first time, because fairness was, to a considerable degree, taken for granted as an ideal for aspiring young scholars and writers during the first half of the sixties. If intellectuals are now beginning to look back on the work of mid-twentieth-century "consensus historians" — of whom Hofstadter was an eminent example — with a renewed esteem, their respect may be the scholarly equivalent of the general public's weariness with ideological polarization that has sanctioned not only the demonization of opponents but the trivialization of all opposing opinions.

The denigration of fairness has infected both political and intellectual life and has now produced a culture in which disproportionate influence is exercised by the loud and relentless voices of single-minded men and women of one persuasion or another. Political polarization is often depicted by the press as the expression of irreconcilable moral values and styles of living — blue states versus red states, moral relativism (the latter a demonized word) versus moral absolutism, secularism (another dirty word) versus traditional religion. After the 2004 election, the hucksters of conventional wisdom declared that "values issues," narrowly defined in the contemporary cultural conservative manner, trumped everything else. But the conventional wisdom did an instant about-face, as it so often does, after Democrats — many combining an image of cultural traditionalism with opposition to the war in Iraq — regained control of both houses of Congress in 2006. Hurrah! The "vital center" was back! The congressional power shift in the midterm elections was, however, determined by a few thousand votes in a few states — as was President George W. Bush's election in both 2000 and 2004. Even though, for the moment, the real war in Iraq has eclipsed the culture wars in political importance, there is no reason to believe that the American center has suddenly become immune to polarizing appeals to fear and self-righteousness, accompanied by disdain for reason and evidence. It remains to be seen, as the current presidential campaign unfolds, whether Americans are willing to consider what the flight from reason has cost us as a people and whether any candidate has the will or the courage to talk about ignorance as a political issue affecting everything from scientific research to decisions about war and peace.

To cite just one example, Americans are alone in the developed world in their view of evolution by means of natural selection as "controversial" rather than as settled mainstream science. The continuing strength of religious fundamentalism in America (again, unique in the developed world) is generally cited as the sole reason for the bizarre persistence of anti-evolutionism. But that simple answer does not address the larger question of why so many nonfundamentalist Americans are willing to dismiss scientific consensus. The real and more complex explanation may lie not in America's brand of faith but in the public's ignorance about science in general as well as evolution in particular. More than two thirds of Americans, according to surveys conducted for the National Science Foundation over the past two decades, are unable to identify DNA as the key to heredity. Nine out of ten Americans do not understand radiation and what it can do to the body. One in five adults is convinced that the sun revolves around the earth. Such responses point to a stunning failure of American public schooling at the elementary and secondary levels, and it is easy to understand why a public with such a shaky grasp of the most rudimentary scientific facts would be unable or unwilling to comprehend the theory of evolution. One should not have to be an intellectual or, for that matter, a college graduate to understand that the sun does not revolve around the earth or that DNA contains the biological instructions that make each of us a unique member of the human species. This level of scientific illiteracy provides fertile soil for political appeals based on sheer ignorance.

The current American relationship to reading and writing, by contrast, is best described not as illiterate but as a-literate. In 2002, the National Endowment for the Arts released a survey indicating that fewer than half of adult Americans had read any work of fiction or poetry in the preceding year — not even detective novels, bodice-ripper romances, or the "rapture" novels based on the Book of Revelation. Only 57 percent had read a nonfiction book. In this increasingly a-literate America, not only the enjoyment of reading but critical thinking itself is at risk. That Americans inhabit a less contemplative and judicious society than they did just four decades ago is arguable only to the ever-expanding group of infotainment marketers who stand to profit from the videoization of everything. The greater accessibility of information through computers and the Internet serves to foster the illusion that the ability to retrieve words and numbers with the click of a mouse also confers the capacity to judge whether those words and numbers represent truth, lies, or something in between. This illusion is not of course confined to America, but its effects are especially deleterious in a culture (unlike, say, that of France or Japan) with an endemic predilection for technological answers to nontechnological questions and an endemic suspicion of anything that smacks of intellectual elitism.

One important element of the resurgent anti-intellectualism in American life is the popular equation of intellectualism with a liberalism supposedly at odds with traditional American values. The entire concept is summed up by the right-wing rubric "the elites." Prominent right-wing intellectuals, who themselves constitute a prosperous and politically powerful elite, have succeeded brilliantly at masking their own privileged class status and pinning the label "elites" only on liberals. The neoconservative patriarch Irving Kristol, in *Reflections of a Neoconservative* (1983), observed that although "intellectuals" were alienated from "the American way of life," the American people were not. "It is the self-imposed assignment of neoconservatism to explain to the American people why they are right," Kristol explained, "and to the intellectuals why they are wrong." One would never guess from this passage that Kristol himself was a New York Jewish intellectual through and through and that what separated him from those wrongheaded other intellectuals, so at odds with the American Way of Life, was his embrace of the Republican Party. An "intellectual," by this selective definition, is any intellectual who disagrees with conservatives; people like Kristol can no longer openly call themselves intellectuals because they have been so effective at turning the once honorable word into a political pejorative. The right wing has been able to get away with this disingenuous logic — and with putting it in the mouths of genuinely anti-intellectual right-wing politicians — because nonreading Americans know less and less about their nation's political and intellectual history.

The most ominous and obvious manifestation of this ignorance, serving as both cause and effect, is an absence of curiosity about other points of view. After the publication in 2004 of my book *Freethinkers: A History of American Secularism,* I began to receive invitations to lecture in many parts of the country, and I welcomed what I thought would be an opportunity to educate a broader and more diverse audience about America's secular traditions. Instead, I have found myself preaching almost entirely to the converted. With the exception of certain university appearances where student attendance was required for course credit, my audiences were composed almost entirely of people who already agreed with me. Serious conservatives report exactly the same experience on the lecture circuit.

The unwillingness to give a hearing to contradictory viewpoints, or to imagine that one might learn anything from an ideological or cultural opponent, represents a departure from the best side of American popular and elite intellectual traditions. Throughout the last quarter of the nineteenth century, millions of Americans — many of them devoutly religious — packed lecture halls around the country to hear Robert Green Ingersoll, known as "the Great Agnostic," excoriate conventional religion and any involvement between church and state. When Thomas Henry Huxley, the British naturalist and preeminent popularizer of Darwin's theory of evolution, made his first trip to the United States in 1876, he spoke to standing-room-only crowds even though many members of his audiences were genuinely shocked by his views on the descent of man. Americans in the 1800s, regardless of their level of formal education, wanted to make up their own minds about what men like Ingersoll and Huxley had to say. That kind of curiosity, which demands firsthand evidence of whether the devil really has horns, is essential to the intellectual and political health of any society. In today's America, intellectuals and nonintellectuals alike, whether on the left or right, tend to tune out any voice that is not an echo. This obduracy is both a manifestation of mental laziness and the essence of anti-intellectualism.

If, as I will argue in this book, America is now ill with a powerful mutant strain of intertwined ignorance, anti-rationalism, and anti-intellectualism — as opposed to the recognizable cyclical strains of the past — the virulence of the current outbreak is inseparable from an unmindfulness that is, paradoxically, both aggressive and passive. This condition is aggressively promoted by everyone, from politicians to media executives, whose livelihood depends on a public that derives its opinions from sound bites and blogs, and it is passively accepted by a public in thrall to the serpent promising effortless enjoyment from the fruit of the tree of infotainment. Is there still time and will for cultural conservationists to ameliorate the degenerative effects of the poisoned apple? Insofar as the weight of one's will is thrown onto the scales of history, one lives in the stubborn hope that it might be so.

CHAPTER ONE:
THE WAY WE LIVE NOW:
JUST US FOLKS

The word is everywhere, a plague spread by the President of the United States, television anchors, radio talk show hosts, preachers in megachurches, self-help gurus, and anyone else attempting to demonstrate his or her identification with ordinary, presumably wholesome American values. Only a few decades ago, Americans were addressed as people or, in the more distant past, ladies and gentlemen. Now we are all folks. Television commentators, apparently confusing themselves with the clergy, routinely declare that "our prayers go out to those folks" — whether the folks are victims of drought, hurricane, flood, child molestation, corporate layoffs, identity theft, or the war in Iraq (as long as the victims are American and not Iraqi). Irony is reserved for fiction. Philip Roth, in *The Plot Against America* — a dark historical reimagining of a nation in which Charles Lindbergh defeats Franklin

D. Roosevelt in the 1940 presidential election — confers the title "Just Folks" on a Lindbergh program designed to de-Judaize young urban Jews by sending them off to spend their summers in wholesome rural and Christian settings.

While the word "folks" was once a colloquialism with no political meaning, there is no escaping the political meaning of the term when it is reverently invoked by public officials in twenty-first-century America. After the terrorist bombings in London on July 7, 2005, President Bush assured Americans, "I've been in contact with our homeland security folks and I instructed them to be in touch with local and state officials about the facts of what took place here and in London and to be extra vigilant as our folks start heading to work." Bush went on to observe that "the contrast couldn't be clearer, between the intentions of those of us who care deeply about human rights and human liberty, and those who've got such evil in their heart that they will take the lives of innocent folks." Those evil terrorists. Our innocent folks. Even homeland security officials, who — one lives in hope — are supposed to be highly trained experts, cannot escape the folkish designation. All of the 2008 presidential contenders pepper their speeches with appeals to folks, but only John Edwards, who grew up poor in North Carolina, sounds as if he was raised around people who actually used the word in everyday conversation. Every time Hillary Rodham Clinton, brought up in a conservative Republican household in an upper-middle-class suburb of Chicago, utters the word "folks," she sounds like a hovering parent trying to ingratiate herself with her children's friends by using teenage slang.

The specific political use of folks as an exclusionary and inclusionary signal, designed to make the speaker sound like one of the boys or girls, is symptomatic of a debasement of public speech inseparable from a more general erosion of American cultural standards. Casual, colloquial language also conveys an implicit denial of the seriousness of whatever issue is being debated: talking about folks going off to war is the equivalent of describing rape victims as girls (unless the victims are, in fact, little girls and not grown women). Look up any important presidential speech in the history of the United States before 1980, and you will not find one patronizing appeal to folks. Imagine: *We here highly resolve that these folks shall not have died in vain . . . and that government of the folks, by the folks, for the folks, shall not perish from the earth.* In the 1950s, even though there were no orators of Lincoln's eloquence on the political scene, voters still expected their leaders to employ dignified, if not necessarily erudite, speech. Adlai Stevenson may have sounded too much like an intellectual to suit the taste of average Americans, but proper grammar and respectful forms of address were mandatory for anyone seeking high office.

The gold standard of presidential oratory for adult Americans in the fifties was the memory of Roosevelt, whose patrician accent in no way detracted from his extraordinary ability to make a direct connection with ordinary people. It is impossible to read the transcripts of FDR's famous fireside chats and not mourn the passing of a civic culture that appealed to Americans to expand their knowledge and understanding instead of pandering to the lowest common denominator. Calling for sacrifice and altruism in perilous times, Roosevelt would no more have addressed his fellow citizens as folks than he would have uttered an obscenity over the radio. At the end of 1940, attempting to prepare his countrymen for the coming of war, the president spoke in characteristic terms to the public.

Tonight, in the presence of a world crisis, my mind goes back eight years to a night in the midst of a domestic crisis . . . I well remember that while I sat in my study in the White House, preparing to talk to the people of the United States, I had before my eyes the picture of all those Americans with whom I was talking. I saw the workmen in the mills, the mines, the factories; the girl behind the counter; the small shopkeeper; the farmer doing his spring plowing; the widows and the old men wondering about their life's savings. I tried to convey to the great mass of the American people what the banking crisis meant to them in their daily lives.

Tonight I want to do the same thing, with the same people, in this new crisis which faces America. . . .

We must be the great arsenal of democracy. For us this is an emergency as serious as war itself. We must apply ourselves to the task with the same resolution, the same sense of urgency, the same spirit of patriotism and sacrifice as we would show were we at war. . . .

As president of the United States I call for that national effort. I call for it in the name of this nation which we love and honor and which we are privileged and proud to serve. I call upon our people with absolute confidence that our common cause will greatly succeed.[1]

Substitute folks for people, farmer, old men, and widows, and the relationship between the abandonment of dignified public speech and the degradation of the political process becomes clear. To call for resolution and a spirit of patriotism and sacrifice is to call upon people to rise above their everyday selves and to behave as true citizens. To keep telling Americans that they are just folks is to expect nothing special — a ratification and exaltation of the quotidian that is one of the distinguishing marks of anti-intellectualism in any era.

The debasement of the nation's speech is evident in virtually everything broadcast and podcast on radio, television, and the Internet. In this true, all-encompassing public square, homogenized language and homogenized thought reinforce each other in circular fashion. As George Orwell noted in 1946, "A man may take to drink because he feels himself a failure, and then fail all the more completely because he drinks. It is rather the same thing that is happening to the English language. It becomes ugly and inaccurate because our thoughts are foolish, but the slovenliness of our language makes it easier for us to have foolish thoughts."[2] In this continuous blurring of clarity and intellectual discrimination, political speech is always ahead of the curve — especially because today's media possess the power to amplify and spread error with an efficiency that might have astonished even Orwell. Consider the near-universal substitution, by the media and politicians, of "troop" and "troops" for "soldier" and "soldiers." As every dictionary makes plain, the word "troop" is always a collective noun; the "s" is added when referring to a particularly large military force. Yet each night on the television news, correspondents report that "X troops were killed in Iraq today." This is more than a grammatical error; turning a soldier — an individual with whom one may identify — into an anonymous-sounding troop encourages the public to think about war and its casualties in a more abstract way. Who lays a wreath at the Tomb of the Unknown Troop? It is difficult to determine exactly how, why, or when this locution began to enter the common language. Soldiers were almost never described as troops during the Second World War, except when a large military operation (like the Allied landing on D-Day) was being discussed, and the term remained extremely uncommon throughout the Vietnam era. My guess is that some dimwits in the military and the media (perhaps the military media) decided, at some point in the 1980s, that the word "soldier" implied the masculine gender and that all soldiers, out of respect for the growing presence of women in the military, must henceforth be called troops. Like unremitting appeals to folks, the victory of troops over soldiers offers an impressive illustration of the relationship between fuzzy thinking and the debasement of everyday speech.

By debased speech, I do not mean bad grammar, although there is plenty of that on every street corner and talk show, or the prevalence of obscene language, so widespread as to be deprived of force and meaning at those rare times when only an epithet will do. Nor am I talking about Spanglish and so-called Black English, those favorite targets of cultural conservatives — although I share the conservatives' belief that public schools ought to concentrate on teaching standard English. But the standard of standard American English, and the ways in which private speech now mirrors the public speech emanating from electronic and digital media, is precisely the problem. Debased speech in the public square functions as a kind of low-level toxin, imperceptibly coarsening our concept of what is and is not acceptable until someone says something so revolting — Don Imus's notorious description of female African-American college basketball players as "nappy-headed hos" is the perfect example — that it produces a rare, and always brief, moment of public consciousness about the meaning and power of words. Predictably, the Imus affair proved to be a missed opportunity for a larger cultural conversation about the level of all American public discourse and language. People only wanted to talk about bigotry — a worthy and vital conversation, to be sure, but one that quickly degenerated into a comparative lexicon of racial and ethnic victimology. Would Imus have been fired for calling someone a faggot or a dyke? What if he had only called the women hos, without the additional racial insult of nappy-headed? And how about Muslims? Didn't Ann Coulter denigrate them as "ragheads" (a slur of which I was blissfully unaware until an indignant multiculturalist reported it on the op-ed page of *The New York Times*).[3] The awful reality is that all of these epithets, often accompanied by the F-word, are the common currency of public and private speech in today's America. They are used not only because many Americans are infected by various degrees of bigotry but because nearly all Americans are afflicted by a poverty of language that cheapens humor and serious discourse alike. The hapless Imus unintentionally made this point when he defended his remarks on grounds that they had been made within a humorous context. "This is a comedy show," he said, "not a racial rant." Wrong on both counts. Nothing reveals a lack of comic inventiveness more reliably than the presence of reflexive epithets, eliciting snickers not because they exist within any intentional "context" but simply because they are crass words that someone is saying out loud.

Part of Imus's audience was undoubtedly composed of hard-core racists and misogynists, but many more who found his rants amusing were responding in the spirit of eight-year-olds laughing at farts. Imus's "serious" political commentary was equally pedestrian. He frequently enjoined officials who had incurred his displeasure to "just shut up," displaying approximately the same level of sophistication as Vice President Dick Cheney when he told Senator Patrick J. Leahy on the Senate floor, "Go fuck yourself." As the genuinely humorous Russell

Baker observes, previous generations of politicians (even if they had felt free to issue the physically impossible Anglo-Saxon injunction in a public forum) would have been shamed by their lack of verbal inventiveness. In the 1890s, Speaker of the House Thomas Reed took care of one opponent by observing that "with a few more brains he could be a halfwit." Of another politician, Reed remarked, "He never opens his mouth without subtracting from the sum of human intelligence."[4] Americans once heard (or rather, read) such genuinely witty remarks and tried to emulate that wit. Today we parrot the witless and halfwitted language used by politicians and radio shock jocks alike.

The mirroring process extends far beyond political language, which has always existed at a certain remove from colloquial speech. The toxin of commercially standardized speech now stocks the private vault of words and images we draw on to think about and to describe everything from the ridiculous to the sublime. One of the most frequently butchered sentences on television programs, for instance, is the incomparable Liberace's cynically funny, "I cried all the way to the bank" — a line he trotted out whenever serious critics lambasted his candelabra-lit performances as kitsch.[*] The witty observation has been transformed into the senseless catchphrase, "I laughed all the way to the bank" — often used as a non sequitur after news stories about lottery winners. In their dual role as creators of public language and as microphones amplifying and disseminating the language many Americans already use in their daily lives, the media constitute a *perpetuum mobile,* the perfect example of a machine in which cause and effect can never be separated. A sports broadcaster, speaking of an athlete who just signed a multi-year, multi-million-dollar contract, says, "He laughed all the way to the bank." A child idly listening — perhaps playing a video game on a computer at the same time — absorbs the meaningless statement without thinking and repeats it,

[*] Liberace first used this line in 1957, when he won a libel judgment against the British tabloid *Daily Mirror,* which published a column calling the entertainer a "deadly, winking, sniggering, snuggling, chromium-plated, scent-impregnated, luminous, giggling, fruit-flavored, mincing, ice-covered heap of mother love." The British court concluded that the article had libelously implied that Liberace was a homosexual (which of course he was, but there was no proof).

spreading it to others who might one day be interviewed on television and say, "I laughed all the way to the bank," thereby transmitting the virus to new listeners. It is all reminiscent of the exchange among Alice, the March Hare, and the Mad Hatter in *Alice's Adventures in Wonderland.* "Then you should say what you mean," the March Hare tells Alice. " 'I do,' Alice hastily replied; 'at least — at least I mean what I say — that's the same thing, you know.' " The Hatter chimes in, "Not the same thing a bit! Why, you might just as well say that 'I see what I eat' is the same thing as 'I eat what I see'!" In an ignorant and anti-intellectual culture, people eat mainly what they see.

It is impossible to define anti-intellectualism as a historical force, or a continuing American reality, in a manner as precise or useful as the kind of definition that might be supplied for, say, abolitionism or feminism. In Hofstadter's view, anti-intellectualism is not an independent historical or social phenomenon but the consequence of some other goal — such as the desire to extend educational opportunities to a broader population or to wrest control of religious life from ecclesiastical hierarchies. "Hardly anyone believes himself to be against thought and culture," Hofstadter writes. "Men do not rise in the morning, grin at themselves in their mirrors, and say: 'Ah, today I shall torment an intellectual and strangle an idea!' "[5] This seems to me an overly charitable portrait of anti-intellectualism — then and now. It is surely true that few people like to consider themselves enemies of thought and culture. Bush, after all, called himself the "education president" with a straight face while simultaneously declaring, without a trace of self-consciousness or self-criticism, that he rarely read newspapers because that would expose him to "opinions."[*]

However, there are ways of trying to strangle ideas that do not involve straightforward attempts at censorship or intimidation. The suggestion that there is something sinister, even un-American, about intense devotion to ideas, reason, logic, evidence, and precise language is one of them. Just before the 2004 presidential election, the

[*] On September 22, 2003, the Associated Press reported that President Bush scans headlines but rarely reads entire newspaper stories, which would expose him to nonobjective "opinions." He prefers that White House staffers provide him with a more "objective" digest of the daily news.

journalist Ron Suskind reported a chilling conversation with a senior Bush aide, who told Suskind that members of the press were part of what the Bush administration considers "the reality-based community" — those who "believe that solutions emerge from judicious study of discernible reality." But, the aide emphasized, "That's not the way the world really works anymore. We're an empire now, and when we act, we create our own reality. And while you're studying that reality — judiciously, as you will — we'll act again, creating other new realities, which you can study too. . . . We're history's actors . . . and you, all of you, will be left to just study what we do."[6] The explicit distinction between those who are fit only to study and those who are history's actors not only expresses contempt for intellectuals but also denigrates anyone who requires evidence, rather than power and emotion, as justification for public policy.

Anti-intellectualism in any era can best be understood as a complex of symptoms with multiple causes, and the persistence of symptoms over time possesses the potential to turn a treatable, livable condition into a morbid disease affecting the entire body politic. It is certainly easy to point to a wide variety of causes — some old and some new

— for the resurgent American anti-intellectualism of the past twenty years. First and foremost among the vectors of anti-intellectualism are the mass media. On the surface, today's media seem to offer consumers an unprecedented variety of choices — television programs on hundreds of channels; movies; video games; music; and the Internet versions of those products, available in so many portable electronic packages that it is entirely possible to go through an entire day without being deprived for a second of commercial entertainment. And it should not be forgotten that all of the video entertainment is accompanied by a soundtrack, usually in the form of ear-shattering music and special effects that would obviate concentration and reflection even in the absence of visual images. Leaving aside the question of whether it is a good thing to be entertained twenty-four hours a day, the variety of the entertainment, given that all of the media outlets and programming divisions are controlled by a few major corporations, is largely an illusion.

But the absence of genuine choice is a relatively minor factor in the relationship between the mass media and the decline of intellectual life in America. It is not that television, or any of its successors in the world of video, was designed as an enemy of active intellectual endeavor but that the media, while they may not actually be the message, inevitably reshape content to fit a form that subordinates both the spoken and the written word to visual images. In doing so, the media restrict their audience's intellectual parameters not only by providing information in a highly condensed form but by filling time — a huge amount of time — that used to be occupied by engagement with the written word.

It is easy with hindsight to view the present saturation of our culture by video images and all-encompassing noise as an inevitable progression from the early days of television. But that is not how things looked in the early fifties, when many intellectuals had great hopes for television as an educational medium and as a general force for good. Television coverage had, after all, spelled the beginning of the end for Senator Joseph R. McCarthy in the spring of 1954, when ABC devoted 188 hours of broadcast time to live coverage of the Army-McCarthy Hearings. Seeing and hearing McCarthy, who came across as a petty thug, turned the tide of public opinion against abuses of power that had not seemed nearly as abusive when reported by the print media. The hearings pitted the bushy-browed McCarthy and his chief counsel, the vulpine Roy Cohn, against the U.S. Army and its special outside counsel, the well-mannered Joseph Welch. The most famous sound bite of the hearings came after McCarthy, reneging on an earlier agreement, accused a young lawyer at Welch's firm of being a Communist sympathizer. Welch, turning in an instant from a kindly uncle into an avenging angel, thundered at McCarthy, "Until this moment, senator, I think I never gauged your cruelty or your recklessness. . . . Have you no sense of decency, sir, at long last?" Although ABC televised the hearings live, the other networks provided a foretaste of the commercial priorities that now completely control network television. CBS, fearful of losing revenue through the preemption of its popular daytime soap operas, declined to cover the hearings at all. NBC opted out early on, when it became clear that there was no drama to be had in the initial sessions. In their fifteen-minute evening news programs, both CBS and NBC presented snippets of the hearings, edited from ABC's live broadcasts. But by the time the climax of the hearings came with the confrontation between McCarthy and Welch, millions of Americans had gained context by watching at least some of the live committee sessions; that context ensured that the Welch-McCarthy exchange would not become a five-second wonder.

Optimism about the civic educational value of television — at least among those who had favored the election of John Kennedy — was bolstered again by the broadcast of the first presidential debates in the fall of 1960. Yet Kennedy's victory in the initial debate was based more on his appearance than on his words or policies; the pasty-faced Nixon, with his five o'clock shadow, projected an image not unlike that of Joe McCarthy, while the tanned Kennedy, with his thick shock of hair, seemed the very essence of youth, energy, and virility. The potential civic danger of determining a presidential election on the basis of a telegenic appearance was largely ignored at the time. Later polls showed that those who had listened to the debate on radio thought Nixon had won, while those who saw the debate on television judged Kennedy the winner. This finding might have raised a red flag among more farsighted members of the intellectual community, but it was largely ignored — possibly because no politician, until the rise of Bush *fils,* was more despised by American intellectuals than Nixon.

In spite of the growing influence of television on public affairs, the overall power and presence of television were less pervasive throughout the fifties and the first half of the sixties than they would become by the beginning of the seventies — let alone with the rise of cable in the eighties. This was true even though the number of American households with television jumped from 9 percent in 1950 to nearly 90 percent in 1960. Although television had ceased to be a novelty by the mid-fifties, it still offered only a limited number of programs and did not broadcast around the clock. Moreover, the relatively small number of home television sets at the start of the decade meant that for older baby boomers, born before 1950, television was a treat rather than the metronome of everyday life — at least in their formative preschool years. Americans born in the late forties might well be viewed as a different cultural generation from the younger boomers, because a great many, if not most, members of the elder cohort learned to read before television entered their homes. People now in their early sixties, unless they came from the tiny minority of families affluent enough to afford a television set in the 1940s, spent the first five to seven years of their lives in much the same fashion as their parents had — playing outdoors, listening to a favorite radio program, learning their ABCs from parents and books and not from *Sesame Street*. But adults now in their early fifties were being schooled in front of the television set long before entering a real school. And boomers now in their forties, like their own children today, were exposed to television from infancy — though few parents in the 1960s were foolish enough to put television sets in front of their babies' cribs.

It is sobering to reflect that during the next decade, as the oldest baby boomers enter retirement beginning in 2011, the political and cultural leadership of the nation will inevitably pass to the first generation raised on television from Day 1. The prospect is especially depressing to those of us who doubt that any attempts at adding more "quality" programming to the video menu can ever offset the negative intellectual impact of sheer quantity. This view was first expressed by Neil Postman in his prescient 1985 jeremiad, *Amusing Ourselves to Death*. "I raise no objection to television's junk," Postman declared unequivocally. "The best things on television *are* its junk, and no one and nothing is seriously threatened by it. Besides, we do not measure a culture by its output of undisguised trivialities but by what it claims as significant. Therein is our problem, for television is at its most trivial and, therefore, most dangerous when its aspirations are high, when it presents itself as a carrier of important cultural conversations."[7]

Postman was writing at the dawn of the era of personal computers and just before various taping devices, beginning with the VCR, became a fixture in homes and made it possible for entertainment consumers to acquire a virtually limitless stock of visual images for home viewing at their leisure. Everything he had to say about the implications of the shift from a print to a video culture is valid today — only more so. Well-off professionals, including a fair number of intellectuals, have proved especially vulnerable to the bromide that there is no harm, and may be great benefit, from video consumption as a way of life — as long as the videos are "educational." But medical research does not support the comforting notion that a regular diet of videos, educational or otherwise, is good for the developing brains of infants and toddlers. A growing body of pediatric research does indicate that frequent exposure to any form of video in the early years of life produces older children with shortened attention spans. It does not matter whether the images are produced by a television network, a film studio, or a computer software company: what matters is the amount of time children spend staring at a monitor. The American Academy of Pediatrics has concluded that there is no safe level of viewing for children under age two, but whatever the Academy may recommend, the battle against videos for infants is already lost.

One of the most common statements made on blogs by anxious parents, fearful that too much viewing is bad for their children but eager for the convenience supplied by an electronic babysitter, is: "We never let our child watch TV, only videos." A comical example of this widespread rationalization is the enthusiasm of ambitious, time-starved upper-middle-class parents for the *Baby Einstein* series, which force-feeds toddlers with a series of educational films designed to introduce them to everything from Monet's water lilies to the poetry of Wordsworth. Infants are next in line. Home Box Office's *Classical Baby,* which premiered in the spring of 2005, is a perfect illustration of the genre. The half-hour film consists of musical excerpts from

Tchaikovsky, Bach, Duke Ellington, and Irving Berlin, all accompanied by animated images of clowns, fairies, and animals, and irritating, flashing glimpses of famous paintings by the likes of Jackson Pollock, Vincent van Gogh, and Claude Monet. When groups opposed to marketing television programs to infants objected, Dr. Eugene Beresin, a child psychiatrist on the staff of the Harvard Medical School and a consultant to HBO, declared that "to say that this kind of TV is bad is tantamount to saying art is bad."[8]

This statement should be considered prima facie evidence of video's capacity to dull the wits of highly educated professionals as well as innocent babies. How pathetic it is that such products now appeal to a huge market of people who do not understand that the way to introduce children to music is by playing good music, uninterrupted by video clowns, at home; the way to introduce poetry is by reciting or reading it at bedtime; and the way to instill an appreciation of beauty is not to bombard a toddler with screen images of Monet's Giverny but to introduce her to the real sights and scents of a garden. It is a fine thing for tired parents to gain a quiet hour for themselves by mesmerizing small children with videos — who would be stuffy enough to suggest that the occasional hour in front of animals dancing to Tchaikovsky can do a baby any real harm? — but let us not delude ourselves that education is what is going on. Or rather, education is going on — but it is the kind of education that wires young brains to focus attention on prepackaged visual stimuli, accompanied by a considerable amount of noise.

Only a Luddite would claim that the video culture, whether displayed on television screens or computer monitors, has nothing to contribute to individual intellectual development or the intellectual life of society. Certainly the promotion of anti-intellectualism is not the intent of *Baby Einstein,* which, after all, is designed to cater to both the competitive anxieties and the intellectual pretensions of upper-middle-class parents. Yet there is little question that the intrusion of video into the psyches of Americans at ever earlier ages is not only making it unnecessary for young children to entertain themselves but is also discouraging them from thinking and fantasizing outside the box, in the most literal as well as a figurative sense. Predictably, the video culture has spawned an electronic cottage industry of scholars and writers taking up the cudgels in defense of a multi-billion-dollar conglomerate and pooh-poohing old-fashioned intellectuals (a.k.a. curmudgeons) for their reservations about sucking at the video tit from cradle to grave. Only in today's America could a book titled *Everything Bad Is Good for You: How Today's Popular Culture Is Actually Making Us Smarter* have received respectful reviews. The author, Steven Johnson, writes the "Emerging Technology" column for *Discover* magazine and, by his own account, spends a fair amount of time immersed in video games. "Parents can sometimes be appalled at the hypnotic effect that television has on toddlers," Johnson writes. "They see their otherwise vibrant and active children gazing silently, mouth agape at the screen, and they assume the worst: the television is turning their child into a zombie." Not to worry, Johnson assures us. The glazed stares at the television — and later, at video games — "are not signs of mental atrophy. They're signs of *focus*."[9]

The real point is not what children are focusing *on* but what they are screening *out* with their intense focus, most likely directed at a video already viewed scores of times. Johnson then goes on to declare that studies demonstrating the decline of reading and writing skills are deeply flawed because they "ignore the huge explosion of reading (not to mention writing) that has happened thanks to the rise of the Internet." While conceding that e-mail exchanges or Web-based dissections of the television show *The Apprentice* are "not the same as literary novels," Johnson notes approvingly that both are "equally text-driven."[10] Such self-referential codswallop is only to be expected from a self-referential digital and video culture; one might as well make the statement that kiddie porn and Titian nudes are "equally image-driven." The appeal of such rationalizations in an acquisitive, technology-dependent society is obvious: parents can rest assured that their money is being well spent because electronic media toys all have educational value; that there is really nothing wrong with not having made time to read a book for the past six months; and that their children are actually getting smarter as they watch the action on their various monitors.

What kind of reading has exploded on the Internet? Certainly not the reading of serious books, whether fiction or nonfiction. The failure of e-books to appeal to more than a niche market is one of the worst kept secrets in publishing, in spite of the reluctance of publishers to issue specific sales figures. Even a popular mass-market novelist like Stephen King has flopped on the Web. In 2001, King attempted to serialize one of his supernatural thrillers online, with the proviso that readers pay $1 for the first three installments and $2 for subsequent portions. Those who downloaded the installments were to pay on an honor system, and King pledged to continue the serialization as long as 75 percent of readers paid for the downloads. By the fourth installment, the proportion of paid-up readers dropped to 46 percent, and King canceled the series at the end of the year. King's idea of serialization had of course been tried before, and it was a huge success — in the nineteenth century. London readers used to get up early and wait in line for the newest installment of a novel by Charles Dickens; in New York, Dickens fans would meet the boats known to be carrying copies of the tantalizing chapters. The Web, however, is all about the quickest possible gratification; it may well be that people most disposed to read online are least disposed to wait any length of time for a new chapter of a work by their favorite writer.

The tech stock analysts who predicted a limitless future for e-books have tried to explain their misjudgment in terms of the current state of technology: all that is lacking for their bright forecasts to be fufilled is a better tool for downloading and reading. Something small, light, and easily perused while the reader is riding on a bus, eating a sandwich, or propped up against pillows. Something like . . . a paperback book? A much more likely explanation for the e-book fizzle is that reading for pleasure — as distinct from necessary, often work-related reading for information — is in certain respects antithetical to the whole experience of reading on computers and portable digital devices. The Internet is the perfect delivery medium for reference books and textbooks, which were never designed to be read from cover to cover. But a narrow, time-saving focus is inimical not only to reading for enjoyment but to reading that encourages the retention of knowledge. Memory, which depends on the capacity to absorb ideas and information through exposition and to connect new information to an established edifice of knowledge, is one of the first victims of video culture. Without memory, judgments are made on the unsound basis of the most recent bit of half-digested information. All mass entertainment media, and the expanding body of educational media based on the entertainment model, emphasize "stand alone" programming that does not require a prior body of knowledge. The media provide the yeast, which, when added to other American social forces and institutions, creates a fertile culture for the spread of invincible ignorance throughout the public square.

The second major spur to anti-intellectualism during the past forty years has been the resurgence of fundamentalist religion. Modern media, with their overt and covert appeal to emotion rather than reason, are ideally suited to assist in the propagation of a form of faith that stands opposed to most of the great rationalist insights that have transformed Western civilization since the beginning of the Enlightenment. Triumphalist Christian fundamentalism, mainly though not entirely Protestant, is based on the conviction that every word in the Bible is literally true and was handed down by God Himself. Public opinion polls conducted during the past four years have consistently found that more than one third of Americans believe in a literal interpretation of the Bible, while nearly six in ten believe that the bloody predictions in the Book of Revelation —

which involve the massacre of everyone who has not accepted Jesus as the Messiah — will come true.[11]

Beginning with the radio evangelist Billy Sunday in the twenties, American fundamentalists, with their black-and-white view of every issue, have made effective use of each new medium of mass communication. Liberal religion, with its many shades of gray and determination to make room for secular knowledge in the house of faith, does not lend itself as readily to media packaging and is at an even greater disadvantage in the visual media than it was on radio. From the rantings of Pat Robertson on the *700 Club* to Mel Gibson's movie *The Passion of the Christ,* religion comes across most powerfully on video when it is unmodified by secular thought and learning, makes no attempt to appeal to anything but emotion, and leaves no room for doubt. Gibson's *Passion,* for instance, is rooted in a Roman Catholic brand of fundamentalism, long rejected by the Vatican itself, that takes the Gospel of Matthew literally and blames Jews for the crucifixion of Jesus. The core audience for the immensely popular movie in the United States was drawn not from mainstream Catholics, whose faith does not rest on biblical literalism, but from right-wing Protestants.

Even when the entertainment media are not promoting a particular version of religion, they do promote and capitalize on widespread American credulity regarding the supernatural. In recent years, television has commissioned an unceasing stream of programs designed to appeal to a vast market of viewers who believe in ghosts, angels, and demons. More than half of American adults believe in ghosts, one third believe in astrology, three quarters believe in angels, and four fifths believe in miracles.[12] The American marketing of the Apocalypse is a multi-media production, capitalizing on fundamentalism and paranoid superstition. Mainstream denominations have long downplayed the predictions in Revelation, which modern biblical scholars say was written at least sixty years after the death of the historical Jesus and has only the most tenuous relationship to the Gospels. One of the many rational developments rejected by fundamentalism, however, is biblical scholarship since the mid-nineteenth century. Who cares what some pointy-headed intellectual has to say about when various parts of the Bible were actually written and what, if any, relationship the text has to real history? Americans' enthusiasm for apocalyptic fantasy probably owes more to movies like *The Exorcist* and *The Omen* than to the Bible itself.

During the past fifteen years, and especially since the terrorist attacks on the World Trade Center and the Pentagon gave substance to every sort of paranoia, the driving force behind the "end times" — meaning the end of the world — scenario has been a series of books marketed through right-wing Christian bookstores and fundamentalist Web sites. Also known as the *Left Behind* series — meaning those left behind to be slaughtered for their unbelief after Jesus returns to earth for the Last Judgment — the religious horror stories for adults are accompanied by a series of children's books (*Left Behind: The Kids*); audiotapes; and last but not least, *Left Behind: The Movie*. The books are written by Jerry B. Jenkins, whose previous works consisted mainly of ghost-writing for sports celebrities, and are based on the scriptural interpretations of Tim La-Haye, a fundamentalist minister and founding member of the Moral Majority. More than 100 million copies have been sold in the United States. The saga is also known to aficionados as the Rapture with a capital "R."

Rapture is also a verb; "to rapture" means

to frolic in heaven after God has dispatched every skeptic on earth, thereby fulfilling the biblical prophecy that "Eye hath not seen, nor ear heard, neither have entered into the heart of man, the things which God hath prepared for them that love him" (1 Corinthians 2:9). As for those who doubted Him, the sadistic Armageddon script spells out their unenviable fate: "And there came out of the smoke locusts upon the earth: and unto them was given power, as the scorpions of the earth have power. And it was commanded them that they should not hurt the grass of the earth, neither any green thing, neither any tree; but only those men which have not the seal of God in their foreheads. . . . And in those days shall men seek death, and shall not find it; and shall desire to die, and death shall flee from them." (Revelation 9:3–4; 6). Another popular fundamentalist Web site, run by an Air Force mechanic in Bellevue, Nebraska, publishes a daily "Rapture Index," which its founder describes as a "Dow Jones Industrial Average of End Time Activity." The index at raptureready.com hit a high on September 24, 2001, as Armageddon enthusiasts concluded that the terrorist attacks signified the imminent end of the world.

What is most disturbing, apart from the

fact that millions of Americans already believe in the imminent end of days, is that the mainstream media confer respectability on such bizarre fantasies by taking them seriously. In a 2002 *Time* cover story on the Bible and the Apocalypse, the magazine soberly declared that "since September 11, people from the cooler corners of Christianity have begun asking questions about what the Bible has to say about how the world ends, and preachers have answered their questions with sermons they could not have imagined giving a year ago."[13] Notably absent from the *Time* story was any secular or rationalist analysis. The article quoted liberal Christians who said that *their* God would never behave as cruelly as a God who would obliterate millions of innocents at the Last Judgment, but it gave no space to those who dismiss the end-times scenario as a collective delusion based on pure superstition and who understand the civic danger inherent in the normalization of ideas that ought to be dismissed as the province of a lunatic fringe. Discussing Armageddon as if it were as real as the earth itself, the *Time* story was, on one level, an effort to capitalize on public fear and sell magazines. On a deeper level, though, the article exemplifies the journalistic conviction that anything "controversial" is worth covering and that both sides of an issue must always be given equal space — even if one side belongs in an abnormal psychology textbook. If enough money is involved, and enough people believe that two plus two equals five, the media will report the story with a straight face, always adding a qualifying paragraph noting that "mathematicians, however, say that two plus two still equals four." With a perverted objectivity that gives credence to nonsense, mainstream news outlets have done more to undermine logic and reason than raptureready.com could ever do.

Misguided objectivity, particularly with regard to religion, ignores the willed ignorance that is one of the defining characteristics of fundamentalism. One of the most powerful taboos in American life concerns speaking ill of anyone else's faith — an injunction rooted in confusion over the difference between freedom of religion and granting religion immunity from the critical scrutiny applied to other social institutions. Both the Constitution and the pragmatic realities of living in a pluralistic society enjoin us to respect our fellow citizens' right to believe whatever they want — as long as their belief, in Thomas Jefferson's phrase, "neither picks my pocket nor breaks my leg." But many Americans have misinterpreted this sensible laissez-faire principle to mean that respect must be accorded the beliefs themselves. This mindless tolerance, which places observable scientific facts, subject to proof, on the same level as unprovable supernatural fantasy, has played a major role in the resurgence of both anti-intellectualism and anti-rationalism. Millions of Americans are perfectly free, under the Constitution, to believe that the Lord of Hosts is coming one day to murder millions of others who do not consider him the Messiah, but the rest of the public ought to exercise its freedom to identify such beliefs as dangerous fallacies that really *do* pick pockets and break legs.

Modern American fundamentalism (the term was not widely used until the twenties) emerged as an identifiable religious and cultural movement after the First World War, and its defining issue was opposition to the teaching in public schools of Darwin's theory of evolution by means of natural selection. Intellectuals of that era, including nonfundamentalist religious believers as well as secularists, mistakenly concluded that the anti-evolutionists and fundamentalists had been dealt a decisive blow by the 1925 Scopes "monkey trial" in

Dayton, Tennessee. Clarence Darrow, the nation's leading trial lawyer and a crusading agnostic, took on the case of John T. Scopes, a high school teacher charged with violating Tennessee's law banning the teaching of evolution in public schools. His opponent was William Jennings Bryan, the three-time Democratic presidential candidate and hero of fundamentalists, who famously declared that he was "more interested in the Rock of Ages than in the ages of rocks." Bryan made the mistake of taking the stand as an expert witness on the Bible, and Darrow, whose skills at cross-examination were legendary, forced his onetime friend to admit that many biblical stories, such as the sun standing still for Joshua's armies, could not be taken literally in light of contemporary scientific knowledge.

Although Scopes's conviction by a fundamentalist jury was a foregone conclusion, northern journalists, scientists, and intellectuals believed that Bryan's humiliation on the stand had discredited fundamentalism once and for all. In 1931, the cultural historian Frederick Lewis Allen observed that "legislators might go on passing anti-evolution laws and in the hinterlands the pious might still keep their religion locked in a science-proof compartment of their minds; but civilized opinion everywhere had regarded the . . . trial with amazement and amusement, and the slow drift away from Fundamentalist certainty continued."[14] Intellectuals like Allen, who came of age in the early decades of the twentieth century, would surely have been incredulous if anyone had predicted that evolution would be just as controversial a subject in America at the dawn of the twenty-first century as it had been at the end of the nineteenth.

The perfect storm over evolution is a perfect example of the new anti-intellectualism in action, because it owes its existence not only to a renewed religious fundamentalism but to the widespread failings of American public education and the scientific illiteracy of much of the media. Usually portrayed solely as a conflict between faith and science, the evolution battle is really a microcosm of all of the cultural forces responsible for the prevalence of unreason in American society today. The persistence of anti-evolutionism, and its revival as a movement during the past twenty years, sets the United States apart from every other developed country in the world. On August 30, 2005, the Pew Forum on Religion and Public Life released the results of a public opinion poll that received almost no attention in the press because Hurricane Katrina had slammed into the Gulf Coast the day before. But the Pew findings, for those who bothered to read them, revealed an intellectual disaster as grave as the human and natural disaster unfolding in New Orleans. Nearly two thirds of Americans want both creationism, generally understood as the hard-core fundamentalist doctrine based on the story of Genesis, to be taught along with evolution in public schools. Fewer than half of Americans — 48 percent — accept any form of evolution (even guided by God), and just 26 percent accept Darwin's theory of evolution by means of natural selection. Fully 42 percent say that all living beings, including humans, have existed in their present form since the beginning of time.[15]

This level of scientific ignorance cannot be blamed solely on religious fundamentalism, because the proportion of Americans who reject evolution in any form is higher — by 15 percentage points — than the proportion who believe in a literal interpretation of the Bible. Something else must be at work, and that something else is the low level of science education in American elementary and secondary schools, as well as in many community colleges. The poor quality of public science education at anything below the university level is easily inferred from the educational disparities in responses to the Pew Poll on evolution. Only 27 percent of college graduates believe that living beings have always existed in their present form — although that in itself is an astonishingly high figure — but 42 percent of Americans with only a partial college education and half of high school graduates adhere to the creationist viewpoint that organic life has remained unchanged throughout the ages. A third of Americans mistakenly believe that there is substantial disagreement about evolution among scientists — a conviction reinforcing and reflecting the right-wing religious mantra that evolution is "just a theory," with no more scientific validity than any other cockamamie idea. Since evolution is just a theory, the anti-evolutionists contend, it must not and should not be viewed as scientific truth.

There are of course many scientific disagreements about the particulars of evolution, but the general theory of evolution by means of natural selection is a settled issue for the mainstream scientific community. The popular "just a theory" argument rests not only on religious faith but on our national indifference to the specific meanings of words in specific contexts. Many Americans simply do not understand the distinction between the definitions of theory in everyday life and in science. For scientists, a theory is a set of principles designed to explain natural phenomena, supported by observation, and subject to proofs and peer review; scientific theory is not static but is modified as new tools of measurement and research findings become available. In its everyday meaning, however, a theory is nothing more than a guess based on limited information or misinformation — and that is exactly how many Americans view scientific theory. To those who equate theory with uninformed guessing, Einstein's theory of relativity and Darwin's theory of evolution have no more validity than the convictions of a *Left Behind* enthusiast who declares, "My theory is that the end of the world will come after one more terrorist attack." Predictions about the end of the world are perfect examples of nonscientific theories: each time they fail to come true, the prognosticators simply set a new date for fulfillment of the prophecy. A specific set of calculations may be wrong, but the prophecy retains its status as an eternal and unverifiable supernatural truth. Who, after all, can prove that the end of the world is *not* just one more disaster away? In science, new information either unmasks a falsehood, as Copernicus's and Galileo's observations undermined the long-held belief that the sun revolves around the earth, or supports an earlier theory based on less complete information.

One of the most important contributors to the evolution tempest is local control of elementary and secondary schooling, an American tradition responsible for vast and persistent regional disparities in the quality of education throughout the land. In Europe, national curriculum standards prevail: Sicilians may have different cultural values from Piedmontese, but a high school graduate in either Italian region will have been taught the same facts about science. In the United States, the geographical dimension of the culture wars, with the powerful fundamentalist presence in the South and parts of the Middle West, means that teachers in those areas, even if they believe in evolution themselves, are wary of incorporating the subject into their biology classes. A turn-of-the-millennium report by the Thomas B. Fordham Foundation, an education research institute, concluded that schools in more than a third of American states, most in the South and the Midwest, are failing to acquaint students not only with the basic facts of evolution but with the importance of Darwin's theory to all modern scientific thinking.[16]

One of the most common strategies of schools kowtowing to anti-evolutionists is avoidance of the "E-word" and the substitution of bland, meaningless phrases like "change over time." Biological evolution is frequently ignored in favor of the geological history of the solar system, a phenomenon less disturbing to fundamentalists than the descent of man. Ron Bier, a biology teacher in Oberlin, Ohio — one of the states receiving a poor grade in the Fordham Report — summed up his teaching strategy for *The New York Times*. He believes in teaching evolution but tries to avoid challenges from fundamentalist parents by teaching the subject not as a "unit" but by putting out "my little bits and pieces wherever I can." Bier added, "I don't force things. I don't argue with students about it."[17] One might ask what the point of teaching is, if not to replace ignorance with knowledge — a process that generally does involve a fair amount of argument. But passivity and teacher avoidance of controversy are not the worst-case scenarios. Many teachers —

products of the same inadequate public schools — do not understand evolution themselves. A 1998 survey by researchers from the University of Texas found that one out of four public school biology teachers believes that humans and dinosaurs inhabited the earth simultaneously.[18] These misconceptions do not tell us anything about the teachers' religious beliefs, but they do reveal a great deal about how poorly educated the teachers are. Any teacher who does not know that dinosaurs were extinct long before *Homo sapiens* put in an appearance is unfit to provide instruction in late nineteenth-century biology, much less modern biology.

To add to the muddle, it seems that Americans are as ignorant and poorly educated about the particulars of religion as they are about science. A majority of adults, in what is supposedly the most religious nation in the developed world, cannot name the four Gospels or identify Genesis as the first book of the Bible.[19] How can citizens understand what creationism means, or make an informed decision about whether it belongs in classrooms, if they cannot even locate the source of the creation story? And how can they be expected to understand any definition of evolution if they were once among millions of children attending classes in which the word "evolution" was taboo and in which teachers suggested that dinosaurs and humans roamed the earth together?

On evolution, as in so many other vital areas of knowledge, popular infotainment culture reinforces public ignorance about both science and religion. The news media tend to cover evolution with the same bogus objectivity that they apply to other "controversies" like the Armageddon scenario. Even in nature documentaries, it is difficult to find any mention of evolution. The surprise hit movie of 2005, *March of the Penguins,* chronicled the bizarre reproductive cycle of the emperor penguin and managed, in a cinematic tour de force filmed in Antarctica, to avoid any mention of evolution. As it happens, the emperor penguin is literally a textbook example, cited in college-level biology courses, of evolution by means of natural selection and random mutation. The penguins march seventy miles from their usual ocean feeding grounds in order to mate in a spot that offers some shelter from the fierce Antarctic winter. By the time the birds pair off, the female is starving and must transfer her egg to be sheltered under the male's fur. Then she waddles back to water to stoke up on fish so that she may return, making another seventy-mile trek, in time to feed her new offspring and trade places with the male, who by then is starving himself and must return to the sea.

A scientist looks at emperor penguins and sees a classic example of random mutation, natural selection, and adaptation to the harshest climate on earth. A believer in creationism or intelligent design, however, looks at the same facts and sees not the inefficiency but the "miracle" of the survival of the species. Exactly why an "intelligent designer" would place the breeding grounds seventy miles from the feeding grounds or, for that matter, would install any species in such an inhospitable climate, are questions never addressed by those who see God's hand at the helm. The film has been endorsed by religious conservatives not only as a demonstration of God's presence in nature but as an affirmation of "traditional norms like monogamy, sacrifice, and child-rearing."[20] These penguin family values, however, mandate monogamy for only one reproductive cycle: mama and papa penguin, once their chick is old enough to survive on its own, flop back into the ocean and never see each other or their offspring again. In the next mating cycle, they choose new partners. But why quibble? Serial monogamy, if ordained by a supreme being, is apparently good enough.

The financial wisdom of avoiding any mention of evolution was borne out at the box office: a year after its release, the movie was the second highest grossing documentary of all time, exceeded at the time only by Michael Moore's *Fahrenheit 911.* There is no need to speculate about what would have happened to box office receipts in the United States if the filmmaker (National Geographic) and the distributor (Warner Independent) had used the E-word. In 2001, the Public Broadcasting Service produced an eight-part documentary, accompanied by materials designed for use in schools, boldly titled *Evolution.* The Christian right went beserk, labeling the series anti-religious, unscientific propaganda, and succeeded in keeping the supplementary educational materials out of most American schools. Furthermore, the evolution series prompted the Bush administration to begin monitoring all PBS productions for "liberal bias" and provided justification for further budget cuts in a government program already on the religious right's hit list.

In the evolution wars, the campaign on behalf of intelligent design deserves special mention because it achieved success in many communities by brilliantly employing an intellectual and scientific vocabulary to attack "elitist" scientists who reject religious attacks on Darwin's theory. The intelligent design movement is spearheaded by the Discovery Institute, a think tank based in Seattle and bankrolled by far right conservatives. The slick, media-savvy right-wingers who run the Discovery Institute prefer to downplay religion and highlight the anti-Darwinist views of a handful of scientific contrarians, many with ties to the religious right. That their views are almost universally rejected by respected mainstream scientists is seen by the intelligent design crowd as evidence of a liberal establishment conspiracy to protect its Darwinist turf. Institute spokesmen constantly compare their contrarian faith-based researchers with once scorned geniuses like Copernicus and Galileo — a contention conveniently ignoring the fact that the Catholic Church, not other seekers of scientific truth, was the source of opposition to the heliocentric theory of the solar system. Intelligent design does not insist on the seven days of creation but it does rest on the nonscientific hypothesis that the complexity of life *proves* the existence of a designer. "If you want to call the designer God, that's entirely up to you" is the intelligent design pitch — along with "teach the controversy." The lethal inefficiencies of penguins marching across a frozen wasteland in order to reproduce, or of blood requiring the presence of numerous proteins in order to clot and prevent humans from bleeding to death, are viewed not as accidents of nature but as marvels of intention. The obvious question of why a guiding intelligence would want to make things so difficult for his or her creations is never asked because it cannot be answered.

The proponents of intelligent design were dealt a major blow at the end of 2005, when Federal District Court Judge John E. Jones III handed down a decision prohibiting the teaching of intelligent design as an alternative to evolution in the public schools of Dover, Pennsylvania. Jones was forthright in his opinion, which states unequivocally that intelligent design is a religious, not a scientific, theory and that its teaching in schools therefore violates the establishment clause of the First Amendment. "To be sure, Darwin's theory of evolution is imperfect," Jones concluded. "However, the fact that a scientific theory cannot yet render an explanation on every point should not be used as a pretext to thrust an untestable alternative hypothesis grounded in religion into the science classroom or to misrepresent well-established scientific propositions."[21] Jones's opinion, grounded in science, will not of course be the last political word on the subject. President Bush — who must have failed to do his homework about his nominee's views of both the Constitution and science when he appointed Jones to the federal bench — has followed the anti-evolution script by vigorously advocating the teaching of both evolution and intelligent design.

When Bush endorsed the teaching of intelligent design, he was predictably cheered by the religious right and denounced by the secular and religious left, but no one pointed out how truly extraordinary it was that any American president would place himself in direct opposition to contemporary scientific thinking. Even when they have been unsympathetic to new currents in philosophical, historical, and political thought, American presidents have always wanted to be on the right side of science, and those who understood nothing about science were smart enough to keep their mouths shut. One cannot imagine Calvin Coolidge making pronouncements about the desirability of teaching alternatives to Einstein's theory of relativity or about the theory of evolution — even though Coolidge was in the White House when the Scopes trial became the subject of major national publicity and controversy.

Unlike its predecessor in the twenties, the current anti-rationalist movement has been politicized from the bottom up and the top down, from school boards in small towns to the corridors of power in Washington. Bill Moyers, who has long been under attack from the religious and political right for the pro-science, pro-rationalist, and anti-fundamentalist content of his programs on public television, described the process in a scathing speech about the end-times scenario. "One of the biggest changes in politics in my lifetime," Moyers said, "is that the delusional is no longer marginal. It has come in from the fringe, to sit in the seats of power in the Oval Office and in Congress. For the first time in our history, ideology and theology hold a monopoly of power in Washington. Theology asserts propositions that cannot be proven true; ideologues hold stoutly to a worldview despite being contradicted by what is generally accepted as reality. The offspring of ideology and theology are not always bad but they are always blind. And that is the danger: voters and politicians alike, oblivious to the facts."[22] In the land of politicized anti-rationalism, facts are whatever folks choose to believe.

The question is why now. It is much easier to understand the resurgent religious fundamentalism of the 1920s than it is to understand the politicization of anti-rationalism over the past twenty-five years. Both the fundamentalism of the early twentieth century and the anti-rationalism of the late twentieth century tapped into a broader fear of modernism and hatred of secularism that extend beyond the religious right and have always been an important component of American anti-intellectualism. But the reactionary fundamentalism of the twenties was deeply rooted in nostalgia — of which traditional religion was only one component — for a simpler time. Bryan, the leading populist and fundamentalist politician of his era, was the product of prelapsarian, late nineteenth-century small-town America, which had considered itself singularly blessed by God and in need of no further enlightenment from outside experts. It is understandable that fundamentalism and anti-rationalism would have appealed to many who longed for a return to the less exciting but also less pressured, less commercial, less confusing, and less dangerous world before the Great War. What Edenic past is calling out today to those who rail against experts, scientists, and intellectual "elites"? Most Americans would certainly like to return to the safety — or the perceived safety — of the world before September 11, 2001, but the rise of ideological anti-rationalism in American life antedates the terrorist attacks by several decades. Are we still arguing about evolution because we really long to return to the pre–digital revolution idyll of the seventies and early eighties? Or are we looking back on a more distant paradise, the decade in which American schoolchildren were trained to cower under their desks in order to protect themselves against atomic attack by the Soviet Union?

An equally puzzling question is why *us.* People throughout the world must cope with social, economic, and technological changes that call traditional verities into question, and the empire of mind-numbing infotainment knows no national boundaries. Yet the United States has proved much more susceptible than other economically advanced nations to the toxic combination of forces that are the enemies of intellect, learning, and reason, from retrograde fundamentalist faith to dumbed-down media. What accounts for the powerful American attraction to values that seem so at odds not only with intellectual modernism and science but also with the old Enlightenment rationalism that made such a vital contribution to the founding of our nation? Any attempt to answer these questions must begin with the paradoxical cultural and political forces that shaped the idea of American exceptionalism even before there was an American nation and became an integral part of the American experiment during the formative decades of the young republic. Many of these forces combine a deep reverence for learning with a profound suspicion of too much learning, and they have persisted and mutated, through economic and population changes that the first generation of Americans could never have envisaged, into our current age of unreason.

CHAPTER TWO:
THE WAY WE LIVED
THEN: INTELLECT
AND IGNORANCE IN A
YOUNG NATION

At noon on August 31, 1837, a procession of students, faculty, and newly minted graduates of Harvard College filed into a small hall to hear Ralph Waldo Emerson, the iconoclastic former pastor of the Old North Church and a writer still largely unknown to his countrymen beyond Boston, deliver the college's annual Phi Beta Kappa Day address. Fifty years after the signing of the Constitution, the American nation already possessed the nucleus of an intellectual elite, and some of its most impressive contemporary and future members were present on that day in Harvard Square. The academic community had assembled in Cambridge's First Parish Meetinghouse, which stood on the very site where Anne Hutchinson had been tried in 1637 and sentenced to exile from the Massachusetts Bay Colony for "traducing the ministers." The traduced theocrats were Puritans who had left England for the New World in order to obtain religious liberty for themselves but who did not wish to extend the same privilege to others. Two hundred years later, the thirty-five-year-old Emerson was about to offer, if not a traduction, a powerful shock to the establishment of his day. His speech on the topic of the American scholar was nothing less than a declaration of intellectual independence — not from European culture itself, but from a sense of inferiority to continental European and British culture. That Emerson himself was an admirer and friend of such British luminaries as William Wordsworth, Thomas Carlyle, and Samuel Taylor Coleridge only added to the impact of his oration.

Lengthy graduation exercises had occupied most of the preceding day: August, not June, marked the transition from one academic year to another. A general somnolence must have prevailed at the outset of the ceremony, because many of the new graduates had been celebrating the night before, in a manner that would not necessarily have met with the approval of their Puritan forebears. But the audience included more than a few young men — the gathering of Harvard students and professors was of course entirely male — who were ready to receive Emerson's message and put it to use in their own intellectual endeavors. Richard Henry Dana, the possessor of a newly minted diploma, had entered Harvard as a freshman in 1831, dropped out in 1833, and then spent two years as an ordinary seaman, sailing from the East Coast to California via Cape Horn. After returning to Harvard in 1835, Dana began chronicling his journey in an exposé of the virtual serfdom that was the lot of American sailors at the time: *Two Years Before the Mast* would be published in 1840 and would remain a classic of American literary muckraking. Another representative of the Class of 1837 was Henry David Thoreau, who already considered Emerson a mentor and was among the small group of readers acquainted with his early writing. (Emerson's first essay, "Nature," had been published anonymously in 1836 and had not sold well.) Also in attendance were James Russell Lowell (Class of '38) and Oliver Wendell Holmes (Class of '29). Yet another member of the audience, the already distinguished educational reformer Horace Mann, had not been particularly impressed by Emerson in the past but changed his mind as the speaker issued a call for nothing less than a revolution in

America's attitude toward learning — a sentiment very much in line with the improvements Mann hoped to effect as secretary of the newly established Massachusetts Board of Education.[1]

With the bold assertion that "we have listened too long to the courtly muses of Europe," Emerson threw down an intellectual gauntlet to the first generation of Americans — born after the conclusion of the War of 1812 — raised in an atmosphere in which the political independence of the United States was taken for granted. But the future sage of Concord, as he launched into a scathing description of the low aspirations of contemporary American culture, was addressing himself not only to the privileged scholars who stood before him but also to a broader public. "The mind of this country," he declared, "taught to aim at low objects, eats upon itself.

There is no work for any but the decorous and the complaisant. Young men of the fairest promise, who begin life upon our shores, inflated by the mountain winds, shined upon by all the stars of God, find the earth below not in unison with these, but are hindered from action by the disgust which the principles on which business is managed inspire. . . . What is the remedy? They did not yet see, and thousands of young men as hopeful now crowding to the barriers for the career do not yet see, that if the single man plant himself indomitably upon his instincts, and there abide, the huge world will come round to him. . . . Is it not the chief disgrace in the world, not to be a unit; — not to be reckoned one character; — not to yield that peculiar fruit which each man was created to bear, but to be reckoned in the gross, in the hundred, or the thousand, of the party, the section, to which we belong; and our opinion predicted geographically, as the north, or the south? Not so, brothers and friends — please God, ours shall not be so. We will walk on our own feet; we will work with our own hands; we will speak our own minds. The study of letters shall be no longer a name for pity, for doubt, and for sensual indulgence. The dread of man and the love of man shall be a wall of defense and a wreath of joy around all. A nation of men will for the first time exist, because each believes himself inspired by the Divine Soul which also inspires all men.[2]

At first glance, Emerson seems to be

contradicting his own assertion that it is time for Americans to stand on their own culturally. If the mind of a country has been "taught to aim at low objects," how can the national culture exist without the tutelage of its betters? But Emerson provides an answer that has given the speech its resonance for subsequent generations: change yourself, ground yourself in your own instincts, and the "huge world will come round." Then, and only then, will the life of the mind no longer be attacked in America as an impractical luxury composed of religious unorthodoxy, laziness, and effete European manners — "a name for pity, for doubt, and for sensual indulgence."

The young men in the audience would remember their excitement at Emerson's words until the end of their days. "No man young enough to have felt it can forget, or cease to be grateful for, the mental and moral *nudge* which he received . . . from his high-minded and brave-spirited countryman," recalled Lowell in 1868. "What crowded and breathless aisles, what windows clustering with eager heads, what enthusiasm of approval, what grim silence of foregone dissent! . . . It was our Yankee version of a lecture by Abélard. . . ."[3] Emerson's audience was well aware that the very phrase "American culture" was considered an oxymoron by many educated Europeans. Alexis de Tocqueville, one of the most sympathetic European observers of the young nation, concluded after his celebrated visit in 1831–32 that "in few of the civilized nations of our time have the higher sciences made less progress than in the United States; and in few have great artists, distinguished poets, or celebrated writers been more rare."[4] But Tocqueville dissented from the opinion, held by many of his aristocratic European contemporaries, that democracy itself was responsible for America's cultural deficiencies. Instead, he argued that the nation's close connection with England had enabled Americans to concentrate on developing the continent while drawing on the mother country's "distinguished men of science, able artists, writers of eminence." This unique circumstance had enabled the former colonists to "enjoy the treasures of the intellect without laboring to amass them" and to neglect intellectual pursuits "without relapsing into barbarism."[5] This was precisely the quasi-colonial dependency that Emerson was assailing in a speech that marked the end of the beginning of the American intellectual journey.

■ ■ ■ ■

For the men who made the Revolution, cultural and intellectual issues were inseparable from the political union they had succeeded in forging against considerable odds. Henry Adams, looking back from the last decade of the nineteenth century on America in its infancy, began his account with the first peaceful transfer of political power from one party to another — the replacement of his great-grandfather, John Adams, by Thomas Jefferson in 1800. Jefferson had been elected president of "a nation as yet in swaddling-clothes, which had neither literature, arts, sciences, nor history; nor even enough nationality to be sure that it was a nation." Adams succinctly summed up the formidable intellectual, cultural, and educational questions that lay before the new republic:

> Could it transmute its social power into the higher forms of thought? Could it provide for the moral and intellectual needs of mankind? . . . Could it give new life to religion and art? Could it create and maintain in the mass of mankind those habits of mind which had hitherto belonged

to men of science alone? Could it produce, or was it compatible with, the differentiation of a higher variety of the human race? Nothing less than this was necessary for its complete success.[6]

Adams was describing the sweeping Enlightenment vision that had given birth to the American Revolution and the Constitution — a vision tinged with a grandeur and grandiosity that, although it inspired deep reverence, was as poorly understood by most Americans in the 1890s as it is today. By "men of science," Enlightenment thinkers meant the tiny minority who had been exposed to learning; to create the habits of mind that had previously belonged only to an elite minority, it would obviously be necessary to extend learning to ordinary citizens on a scale undreamed of in societies based on the principle of aristocracy of birth rather than aristocracy of intellect. This vision was anything but anti-intellectual; in the late eighteenth and early nineteenth centuries, the best educated Americans — those steeped in Enlightenment concepts — were most likely to favor the support of schools by general taxation as well as the creation of a national, publicly supported university for outstanding scholars from every state. Yet there was immense disagreement about what the role of government ought to be in promoting the education of both common and uncommon men; and the victory of those in the revolutionary generation who wished the federal government to do nothing would cast a long shadow over American intellectual life, and contribute to the regional disparities in education that still exert a formidable anti-intellectual influence on American culture.

The founders of the American nation were, of course, anything but common men. More than half of the fifty-five members of the Constitutional Convention had been educated at colleges in America or Europe, mainly England.[7] Others, most notably Benjamin Franklin, were self-educated scholars of international renown. James Madison, wishing to enlighten his fellow delegates about previous experiments in federal unions, presented extensive material from his own studies of confederations in cities and states in both ancient and more recent times. The research drew on many books recently sent by Thomas Jefferson, at Madison's request, from France. As Madison explained, he was impelled to take detailed notes at every meeting of the convention precisely because there were only the sketchiest records of "the process, the principles, the reasons, and the anticipations" that had motivated politicians in ancient times. The absence of such historical documents, Madison said, "determined me to preserve as far as I could an exact account of what might pass in the Convention whilst executing its trust, the magnitude of which I was duly impressed, as I was with the gratification promised to future curiosity by an authentic exhibition of the objects, the opinions, and the reasonings from which the new System of Government was to receive its peculiar structure and organization."[8]

Only an intellectual would have described the need for accurate note-taking at what was, after all, a political assembly with a specific political purpose, in quite this way. The most influential and admired men of the era — Madison, Franklin, Jefferson, John Adams, Alexander Hamilton, and Benjamin Rush, to name only a few — were also polymaths at a time when it was still considered possible and necessary to comprehend every area of human knowledge and experience. Washington, whose education was sketchier than that of many of the other framers of the Constitution, held higher learning in such esteem that he left a bequest of several thousand dollars' worth of securities in his will in an effort to persuade Congress to appropriate money for a national university. His legacy went unclaimed in a political dispute that set the tone for many future controversies over the federal government's involvement in education. Congress, fearful that the use of Washington's bequest to found a national university would be seen as an assault on colleges founded by religious institutions, wanted nothing to do with the project.[9]

However they have been judged by history, the thoughtful public men of the American Enlightenment embodied the ideal Emerson would describe in his most famous speech as *"Man Thinking"* — as opposed to what he considered the degraded idea of a scholar as a "mere thinker" — a truncated specialist in no way superior to a "mere" mechanic, farmer, businessman, lawyer, or doctor. It is hard to overstate the prescience of Emerson's warning about the impact of specialization on human dignity in general and intellectual life in particular. In a society where the Enlightenment ideal of unity between thought and action was already fading, no one, in Emerson's view, could be fully human or fully thoughtful.

The planter, who is Man sent out into the field to gather food, is seldom cheered by any idea of the true dignity of his ministry. He sees his bushel and his cart, and nothing beyond, and sinks into the farmer, instead of Man on the farm. The tradesman scarcely ever gives an ideal worth to his work, but is ridden by the routine of his craft, and the soul is subject to dollars. The priest becomes a form; the attorney a statute-book; the mechanic a machine; the sailor a rope of the ship.

In this distribution of functions the scholar is the delegated intellect. In right state he is *Man Thinking.* In the degenerate state, where the victim of society, he tends to become a mere thinker, or still worse, the parrot of other men's thinking.[10]

Emerson, as men thinking with great passion are apt to do, exaggerated the prevalence of the phenomenon he was describing. He had, however, identified one of the important intellectual and social tendencies already laying the groundwork for a permanent schizophrenia in the nation's attitudes toward learning and intellect. The tendency toward specialization — to be sure, a cloud no bigger than a man's hand in the early nineteenth century — was closely related to the American insistence that education be tailored to provide direct practical benefits. The health of democracy, as so many of the founders had proclaimed, depended on an educated citizenry, but many Americans also believed that too much learning might set one citizen above another and violate the very democratic ideals that education was supposed to foster. The sort of education most valued by ordinary Americans was meant to train a man for whatever practical tasks lay at hand, not to turn him into *Man Thinking.* "I like a man that kin *jist* read," was the tart and telling comment of an Indiana farmer on the work of Bayard Rush Hall, a Princeton-educated minister who, in 1823, had traveled to the new territory to help found a public college that would eventually become Indiana University. When local residents rode by Hall's house in Bloomington, he was treated to remarks like, " 'Well, thar's whar the grammur man lives that larns 'em Latin and grand-like things — allow we'll oust him yet.' "[11] Such attitudes already separated much of the American public, especially on the frontier, from the well-schooled men who gathered to hear Emerson in Harvard Square.

Of all the anti-intellectual forces manifesting themselves in the early 1800s, the most important was the rise of fundamentalist religion during the period known as the Second Great Awakening.* The struggle had already been joined between a liberal religion that accommodated itself to new secular knowledge and a rigid faith that looked backward to biblically grounded certainties. Whatever the denomination or religion, fundamentalism has always been defined by its refusal to adapt to any secular knowledge that conflicts with its version of revealed religious truth; that refusal, in science and the humanities, has been the most enduring and powerful strand in American anti-intellectualism. Sidney Mead, one of the most distinguished historians of American Protestantism, argued in 1963 that an "ever-widening chasm between 'religion' and 'intelligence' " has been apparent since the rise of evangelical fundamentalism at the end of the revolutionary era. In Mead's view, the course of U.S. religious history

* Although the word "fundamentalism" did not enter the American language until the twentieth century, I have taken the liberty throughout this book of using the term to describe American religions and denominations whose faith is based on literal interpretations of a sacred text.

since 1800 has confronted Americans with a "hard choice between being intelligent according to the standards prevailing in their intellectual centers, and being religious according to the standards prevailing in their denominations."[12] That argument cries out for qualification; the "hard choice" was experienced not by all but by *many* Americans affiliated with *certain* religious denominations. A Unitarian in the early decades of the nineteenth century, for instance, would not have been unduly disturbed by new geological discoveries challenging the biblical notion of a four-thousand-year-old earth. But followers of countless semiliterate fundamentalist evangelists, competing for souls throughout the young nation, would indeed have been shaken by the news that rocks and fossils predated the biblical timeline.* Mead is surely right in his conten-

* In 1795, the Scottish geologist and naturalist James Hutton published *The Theory of the Earth,* which asserted that sedimentary rocks along the Scottish coast had been created not in a single flood but formed over time by a series of floods. The conclusion posed an implicit challenge to the notion that all of earth's geological formations were produced by the flood described in Genesis. Hutton's theory — that the earth was still being

tion that the more liberal, accommodation-ist forms of American Protestantism lost a great deal of ground to militant fundamentalism in the early republican era. That lost ground would never be regained.

The Second Great Awakening, one of many cycles of religious revivalism marked by a resurgence of anti-rational fundamentalist faith, was a response not only to the secular Enlightenment values represented by many of the founders but also to the unsettled, and unsettling, social conditions associated with the Revolutionary War. The American religious landscape at the conclusion of the Revolution was pluralistic and somewhat chaotic: it bore little resemblance to the portrait of a devout, churchgoing America that the religious right loves to paint today. Like all wars, the war for independence had disrupted established

---

shaped by geological forces that had existed in ancient times — was known as uniformitarianism. In the early 1830s, the British geologist Sir Charles Lyell, in his *Principles of Geology,* expanded on and popularized Hutton's theory. These geological theories did not cause as much controversy as Charles Darwin would in 1859, but they would strongly influence Darwin's research and thinking.

customs and institutions, including religious institutions. An official nineteenth-century history of Windham, Connecticut, offers a precise depiction of what was seen as post-revolutionary moral chaos by the forces of religious orthodoxy:

> Her [the town's] secular affairs were most flourishing, but religion had sadly declined. It was a transition period — a day of upheaval, overturning, uprootal. Infidelity and Universalism had come in with the Revolution and drawn multitudes from the religious faith of their fathers. Free-thinking and free-drinking were alike in vogue. Great looseness of manners and morals had replaced the ancient Puritanic strictness. . . . Now, sons of those honored fathers . . . were sceptics and scoffers, and men were placed in office who never entered the House of God except for town meetings and secular occasions.[13]

By most estimates, only 10 percent of Americans in 1790 were members of recognized denominations.[14] The highest church membership was in New England towns, the lowest in rural areas of the South and on the frontier. But, as the Windham history suggests, even church members were not necessarily regular churchgoers. In 1780, Samuel Mather, a member of the family that, in earlier generations, had produced the famous Puritan ministers Increase and Cotton Mather, lamented that only one in six of his fellow Bostonians could be counted on to attend church services regularly. These complaints about American irreligiousness were undoubtedly exaggerated; God was no more dead in post-revolutionary America than he would be two centuries later, when the "death of God" would become a fashionable prediction. Formal church membership in the eighteenth century involved a great many more practical obligations than church membership, except in strict fundamentalist denominations, does today; it would be anachronistic to equate an unwillingness to pay for a family pew with an absence of faith. Nevertheless, the influence of freethought and deism — called "Infidelity" by religious conservatives — was certainly one factor in the defection of a fair number of Enlightenment-era Americans from the faith of their fathers.

American freethought, though never a majority movement, enjoyed substantial public influence in the last quarters of both the eighteenth and nineteenth centuries; the first surge of freethought directly influenced the writing of the Constitution. Often incorrectly defined as a total absence of belief in God, freethought can better be understood as an outlook broad enough to encompass the truly anti-religious as well as those who adhered to a personal, unconventional faith revering some form of God or Providence — the term preferred by eighteenth-century freethinkers — but at odds with orthodox religious authority. Deism, a belief in a "watchmaker God" who set the universe in motion but then took no active role in the affairs of humans, was a form of freethought particularly prevalent among the founders. Outright atheists were probably nonexistent, although religious conservatives never stopped applying the atheist label to freethinkers like Thomas Jefferson and Thomas Paine.

Translated into politics, freethought demanded a government based on the rights of man and human reason rather than divine authority — in other words, a secular government. The Constitution, with its pointed and conscious omission of any mention of God, as well as its prohibition of all religious tests for public office, formalized and legalized the freethought ideal of a government free of religious interference.

The subsequent First Amendment, with its familiar declaration that "Congress shall make no law respecting an establishment of religion, or prohibiting the free exercise thereof," embodied the equally important freethought principle that religion must be protected from government interference. The Constitution's secular provisions came into being with support from a coalition of freethinkers and devout evangelicals, who believed that any state involvement with religion was an insult to God as well as a threat to religious liberty.[15] (It must be pointed out here that the word "evangelical" has often been misused, particularly by the press in recent years, as a synonym for fundamentalist. American evangelicals have always been proselytizers, and believers in an unmediated relationship between God and man, but they have not necessarily been adherents of a fundamentalist literal interpretation of the Bible. All Christian fundamentalists today are evangelicals, but not all evangelicals are fundamentalists.)

The religious controversies of the early republican period established a permanent American fault line over faith. The fissure, often masked by a civic ideology of religious tolerance, nevertheless opens up periodically — as it has most recently in the culture wars dating from the mid-1970s — to reveal raw and irreconcilable religious passions. Eighteenth-century American freethought appealed most strongly to the best educated members of society, including not only the minuscule number of college graduates but much larger numbers of the self-educated, while emotional evangelical revivalism had a much stronger appeal to the uneducated and the poor. The strongest impact of secularizing forces in late eighteenth-century America was felt at institutions of higher education originally founded for the purpose of producing an educated clergy. In 1650, the fourteenth year of Harvard's existence, fully 70 percent of Harvard graduates entered the ministry; a century later, only 45 percent of new graduates did so. By the 1790s, two thirds of Harvard graduates followed secular vocations such as law, medicine, teaching, or business.[16]

Lyman Beecher, destined to become one of the most influential and conservative American clergymen in pre–Civil War America, entered Yale in 1793, found the college in what he called "a most ungodly state," and blamed his fellow students' personal vices on the influence of free-thought. "That was the day of the infidelity of the Tom Paine school," he would recall.

"Boys that dressed flax in the barn, as I used to, read Tom Paine and believed him . . . most of the class before me were infidels, and called each other Voltaire, Rousseau, D'Alembert, etc., etc."[17] The association between freethought and alien, un-American philosophies, then emanating from revolutionary France, also became a part of the permanent template that shapes American thinking about religion.

Caught in the middle, between secularizing eighteenth-century freethought and emotional fundamentalist revivalism, were the old-line Protestant denominations, including the Congregationalist heirs of the Puritans and the Episcopal aristocracy that had considered itself part of the Church of England before the Revolution. Between 1790 and 1830, roughly half of the Puritan-descended Congregationalist churches in Massachusetts were transformed into much more liberal Unitarian congregations, characterized by a looser hierarchy and a flexible interpretation of the Bible.[18] One of these was Boston's historic Old North Church, where Emerson served as pastor from 1829 to 1832. However, even Unitarianism proved too confining for Emerson, who resigned his pastorate after a number of theological disputes with his parishioners,

the most significant of them apparently aris-
ing from Emerson's contention that Jesus
never intended the Eucharist, shared with
his apostles at the Last Supper, to become a
permanent sacrament.

A year after his American scholar oration,
Emerson severed his last ties to organized
religion when he addressed the faculty of
the Harvard Divinity School and told the
assembled clerics that a man could find
salvation only through his individual soul's
search for truth and not through the teachings of any church. After that speech, viewed
as a repudiation of Christianity, Emerson
was finished at Harvard: he would not be
invited to speak there again until 1866.
Although cultural historians have generally
and understandably emphasized the differences between Enlightenment rationalism
and Emerson's transcendentalism, his attitude toward religion was virtually indistinguishable from that of Thomas Paine, who
famously declared, "My own mind is my
own church."

Paine, the preeminent and once beloved
revolutionary propagandist, was already being reviled by the mid-1790s for his attack
on orthodox religion in *The Age of Reason*
(1794), which ridiculed biblical literalism
and set forth the astounding premise that

all religions were creations of man rather than God. Most twentieth-century historians have underestimated the influence of *The Age of Reason,* claiming that it was denounced more frequently by angry ministers than it was read by ordinary people. However, Paine's magnum opus was reprinted eighteen times in five American cities between 1794 and 1796, for a total of 25,000 copies — and the number of readers must surely have been many times greater than the number of copies printed and sold. Considering that the population of the United States in 1790 was under 4 million and that the nation's largest city, New York, had just over 33,000 residents, Paine's controversial book was a huge best seller — the equivalent of a hardback book selling 1.5 million copies in a two-year period today.

Both the evangelicals and the traditionalist Protestants hated everything Paine stood for. The few ministers who regarded Paine with any approval were intellectuals and Unitarians. When Paine died in 1809, the Reverend William Bentley, a brilliant Unitarian pastor from Salem, Massachusetts, praised the reviled freethinker for having been "the first to see in what part every System was most vulnerable. Even in his at-

tacks on Christianity he felt without knowing it, the greatest difficulties which rational
Christians have felt. Without their prejudices
he found what was simple, powerful &
direct, & what might be renounced without
injury to morality, to the reverence of God
& the peace of mind."[19]

But the "rational Christians" shaped by
the Enlightenment — whether they abandoned organized religion altogether or
found a home in the more liberal Protestant
denominations — did not prevail in the
American religious marketplace. As American Protestants split into an unprecedented
number of denominations in the early
nineteenth century, the proliferation of
paths to God produced a fork in the young
nation's intellectual road. The rational
Christian path, in whatever portions it chose
to mix rationalism with Christianity, encompassed and embraced intellect and higher
learning. The fundamentalist path turned
away from any form of learning that contradicted the Bible and therefore might serve
as an obstacle to personal salvation. That so
many Americans set out on the emotional
and anti-rational fundamentalist path at
such an early stage in the nation's history
ensured that a signficant portion of believing American Christians would harbor a

deep suspicion of any learning, and institutions of learning, not subject to church supervision.

By describing the fundamentalist path as anti-rational as well as anti-intellectual, I do not mean to suggest that intellectualism and rationality are synonymous: the demonstrably irrational and anti-rational ideas of many intellectuals of different generations, and of widely varying political and social convictions, would render any such suggestion ludicrous. It is also true that intellectuals may use the tools of logic and rationality to provide proofs of anti-rational convictions: both Thomas Aquinas and Freud come to mind. But while not all intellectuals are rationalists, nearly all anti-intellectuals are anti-rationalists. Supernaturalist fundamentalism is by definition anti-rational, because it cannot be challenged by any countervailing evidence in the natural world. To those who rejected attempts to inject rationality into religion, the very irrationality of their faith is seen as proof of emotional and spiritual superiority: *Blessed are they that have not seen, and yet believed.* Morever, rational Christianity was seen not only as emotionally unsatisfying but also as a threat to traditional morality.

Because the American separation of

church and state left every denomination free to compete for the souls of American citizens, there was a church and a preacher to fulfill every emotional and social need; if some needs remained unmet, entirely new religions sprang up to satisfy consumers. Mormonism, founded in 1830 on the conviction that its adherents were "latter-day saints," is one early example, and however much it differed doctrinally from earlier American creeds, it fell squarely on the proselytizing fundamentalist side of the fork staked out during the Second Great Awakening.* Historians have argued endlessly about the reasons why emotional evangeli-

* That Mormonism belongs to the evangelical fundamentalist tradition is no less true because early Mormons were hated and considered non-Christians by many of their fellow evangelicals. Mormons are no less fundamentalist than other fundamentalists because they have two sacred books — the nineteenth-century Book of Mormon, supposedly conveyed on golden tablets to Joseph Smith in upstate New York, as well as the Bible. Indeed, the Mormons' practice of polygamy, definitely sanctioned by the Old Testament, might be said to have made them more fundamentalist than other Christian fundamentalists. The church had to abandon its official

cal religion appealed more strongly to Americans than either the more conservative Protestant denominations such as the Episcopalians or Congregationalists or the secularized Protestantism of the Unitarians. Tocqueville, declaring that "nothing is more repugnant to the human mind in an age of equality than the idea of subjection to forms," suggested that many Americans might prefer religions emphasizing a direct emotional relationship with God because elaborate religious rituals were particularly unsuited to American democracy.[20] "Men living at such times are impatient of figures"; he observed, "to their eyes, symbols that appear to be puerile artifices used to conceal or to set off truths that should more naturally be bared to the light of day; they are unmoved by ceremonial observances and are disposed to attach only a secondary importance to the details of public worship."[21]

That may be so, but it does not explain why Americans preferred the Baptists and Methodists to Quakers and Unitarians, given that the latter religions were characterized by even simpler forms of worship. It

---

upholding of polygamy in return for Utah's admission to the Union in 1896.

seems more likely that poorly educated settlers on the frontier were drawn to religious creeds and preachers who provided emotional comfort without making the intellectual demands of older, more intellectually rigorous Protestant denominations — whether liberal Quakerism and Unitarianism or conservative Episcopalianism and Congregationalism. The more harsh the circumstances of daily life, the more potent are the simple and universal emotional themes of struggle, sin, repentance, forgiveness, and redemption that form the core of evangelical fundamentalist religion. The need for emotional solace does much to explain the appeal of fundamentalism not only to settlers on the frontier but to enslaved blacks in the South. When the storm is raging on the prairie, what comfort can be found in a debate over the nature of the Eucharist or the Holy Trinity? When the master is about to sell your children downriver, why would you want to listen to a preacher who told you that Jesus might be nothing more than a good and prophetic man instead of the all-merciful Savior who will wipe away every tear from your eyes?

In any event, the reasons why fundamentalism triumphed over "rational" religion in the American spiritual bazaar are less important than the fact that fundamentalism did succeed in capturing the hearts of large numbers of Americans during the very period when intellectuals like Emerson were finding even Unitarianism too rigid. If a combination of freethought and Enlightenment-influenced liberal Protestantism had been able to meet the emotional needs of the turbulent young nation, the course of American intellectual and religious history would have been radically altered.

It is the greatest irony, and a stellar illustration of the law of unintended consequences, that the American experiment in complete religious liberty led large numbers of Americans to embrace anti-rational, anti-intellectual forms of faith. In Europe, the prevailing unions between church and state made some form of rationalism — not another religion — the most common response of those who had lost faith in either their religion or their government. Early nineteenth-century Europeans who opposed church power over the state did not seek solace in revival meetings on the banks of the Tiber, the Arno, and the Seine. Instead, they sought their intellectual underpinnings in a continuation of the secular spirit of the Enlightenment and the struggle for democratization and political reform throughout much of the Continent. In America, the absence of a coercive state-established church meant that American citizens had no need to uproot existing religious institutions in order to change political institutions, and vice versa. Americans dissatisfied with their church simply founded another one and moved on, sometimes running for their lives as the Mormons did, if their neighbors objected to their beliefs.

In the North and on the frontier, the restless American tendency to found new churches with the manifestation of any new vision in the woods created both liberal and conservative sects. Religious restlessness also produced cultlike, unclassifiable denominations like early Mormonism and, decades later, Christian Science and the Jehovah's Witnesses. In the South, however, religious feeling was channeled almost exclusively into fundamentalism. During the early nineteenth century, as the church became a pillar of slavery and vice versa, devotion to freedom of conscience, exemplified by Madison and Jefferson, was replaced by adherence to ultra-conservative religion dedicated to upholding the social order. As W. J. Cash notes in *The Mind of the South* (1941), the South traded places with New England in its stance on religious freedom.

The combination of fundamentalism with slavery "involved the establishment of the Puritan ideal," thereby leading the "official moral philosophy of the South . . . steadily toward the [former] position of the Massachusetts Bay Colony."[22]

In both the North and the South, the violence that followed the early phase of the French Revolution only reinforced the general American respect for religion — as long as that religion was not dictated by government. American Protestants, many of whom were strongly anti-Catholic, were not bothered at first by the French revolutionary government's confiscation of church lands: the French were, after all, attacking the "popery" despised by so many in the New World. But the Jacobin Terror and the execution of Louis XVI changed many American minds and did a good deal to bolster the position of conservative clerics in the late 1790s and early 1800s. This was especially true in the South, where fear of slave uprisings was omnipresent. (Revolutionary France's loss of nearby Haiti as a colony, with slaves and former slaves playing a major role in violent rebellion, reinforced the southern conservatives' view of irreligion as a threat to the slavery supposedly ordained by God.) As despised as "papists" were by many Americans, any religion was seen as better than no religion at all.

Like the simultaneous and often paradoxical expansion of both religious and secular influences in the young republic, the development of American education was characterized by contradictory impulses. A deep belief in the importance of an educated citizenry was entwined with the equally potent conviction that education was too important a matter to be left in the hands of the educated. The Constitution, written by highly educated men, says nothing about education. The minority of intellectuals who favored a national school system — a group that included Benjamin Rush, Noah Webster, and James Madison — were influenced by the idealistic proposals for public schooling put forth during the early phase of the French Revolution by liberal intellectuals such as the mathematician Marie-Jean-Antoine-Nicholas Caritat, marquis de Condorcet. In a report to the French Legislative Assembly in late 1791 — a document widely circulated among American political leaders with similar views — Condorcet offered a ringing affirmation of the connection between public education and political equality.

> To afford all members of the human race the means of providing for their needs, of securing their welfare, of recognising and fulfilling their duties; to assure for everyone opportunities of perfecting their skill and rendering themselves capable of the social duties to which they have a right to be called; to develop to the utmost the talents with which nature has endowed them and, in so doing, to establish among all citizens a true equality and thus make real the political equality realised by law — this should be the primary aim of a national system of education, and from this point of view its establishment is for the public authority an obligation of justice.[23]

Those ideals, and the practical proposals to implement them, were subsumed in the Jacobin bloodbath; Condorcet himself was condemned for his opposition to the violence and died in prison. For many Americans, the Jacobin period blurred the distinction between liberal intellectuals like Condorcet and agents of revolutionary violence like Robespierre: early revolutionary ideals, among them the notion that government has a moral obligation to educate its citizenry, were conflated with Terror itself.

The distaste for ideas and intellectual proposals that seemed alien and unsuited to American social conditions was only one element in the triumph of local school control in the United States. Given the vastness of the continent, the Constitution's deference to states' rights, and the jealous maintenance of local prerogatives within states, it is almost impossible to imagine the emergence of any real political support for the views of the Enlightenment intellectuals who favored a national system of public education. Most politicians in the founding generation were opposed to all general taxation for education, including at the state and local levels. Not until the 1830s did the principle of taxation for government-supported schools truly take root — and then largely north of the Mason-Dixon line. In the 1790s, Madison and Jefferson had stood nearly alone in their advocacy of general taxation for schools, then thought to be the responsibility of parents who wanted education for their children and were willing and able to pay for it.

In a 1786 letter from Paris to his friend and tutor George Wythe, Jefferson expressed his conviction that the most important bill under consideration by the Virginia Assembly was his proposal "for the diffusion of knowledge among the people" — and that ignorance was the greatest enemy of the common good. Jefferson's interest in the diffusion of learning at public expense did not of course extend to slaves or women. He did, however, believe in a white male aristocracy of intellect that did not depend on aristocracy of birth. One of the distinctive features of his proposed law, which combined limited democratic and elitist ideals, was its provision that the most promising sons of poor parents be selected to continue their education through college at public expense. As the educational historian Adolphe Meyer notes, "if Jefferson inclined toward an elite of brains, something which in current America is sometimes suspect, then at least he did not assume, as did nearly all others of his era, that the common people had no business within that cultivated circle."[24] Jefferson's proposed law was never enacted; Virginia planters were uninterested in paying taxes for the education of anyone else's children.

Religion was also an important player in the battle over funding for education. In the early federal period, any movement toward

general taxation for common schools —
what are called public schools today — was
hindered by the plethora of state laws that
permitted public funding for the teaching
of religion. At the time the Constitution was
written, Virginia was the only state to
prohibit public funding for the support of
religious teaching in schools. In 1786, after
an intense political debate in which Madison led the opposition to taxation for
religious education, the Virginia Act for
Establishing Religious Freedom was passed
by the state's General Assembly. To the
dismay of religious conservatives, the Virginia law would serve as the template for
the secular provisions of the 1787 Constitution and its subsequent Bill of Rights. But
since the Constitution asserted no federal
power over education, the states were perfectly free to spend their own tax revenues
on sectarian textbooks for public schools,
and that is exactly what many of them did
during the early 1800s.

At the same time, however, the tide of
northern public opinion was turning against
sectarian teaching in community schools
that already existed, even though many of
them had originally been established under
church auspices. Ironically, the heightening
of religious fervor and the proliferation of

religious sects during the Second Great Awakening would strike the decisive blow against subsidies for religious teaching. With Baptists and Congregationalists and Unitarians sending their children to the same schools, it began to seem imprudently divisive to favor any one religion. Massachusetts stopped using tax money to buy sectarian texts for grammar schools in 1827. Ten years later, over the fierce opposition of many, though by no means all, churches, Massachusetts established a state board of education, with the reform-minded Horace Mann as its first superintendent. Those who favor tax vouchers for religious schools today frequently suggest that religion in public schools was taken for granted in the early decades of the republic, when the population was overwhelmingly Protestant. In fact, the secularization of common schools was initially a response to growing religious pluralism among Protestants and predated the arrival of the first large group of non-Protestant immigrants — Irish Catholics fleeing famine in the 1840s.

Mann was viewed as the Antichrist by many orthodox church leaders, but he was in no way opposed to moral education in public schools, including general Bible readings. But he did oppose and eventually prohibited any commentary on the Bible by public school teachers, and it was certainly true that under his stewardship, the secular content of the school curriculum in once Puritan Massachusetts expanded and the religious content shrank. All of this came to a head in 1838 — more than a decade after Massachusetts had banned the use of state funds for sectarian textbooks — when the Reverend Frederick A. Packard, recording secretary of the American Sunday School Union, attempted to persuade Mann to authorize the purchase of a book titled *Child at Home.* (The Sunday School Union, founded in 1824 in Philadelphia, was a major publisher of books for children, marketing its publications to the growing number of common schools as well as libraries and individuals. Throughout the nineteenth century, the Union successfully worked to create a body of American children's literature with a moralistic and moralizing tone.)

Alas for the Reverend Packard's ambitions in Massachusetts, *Child at Home* came close to preaching the Calvinist doctrine of predestination by asserting that children might be damned forever if they committed such small offenses as talking back to a parent or failing to carry out an assigned chore.

Mann promptly informed Packard that such a book "would not be tolerated in Massachusetts" because Unitarians and Universalists would not send their children to schools that indoctrinated them with Calvinist theology.[25]

Packard did not give up easily; he turned up in Mann's office, personally confronted him, and vehemently defended his belief that the schools had an obligation to teach about a God who punishes every evil deed, whether great or small. Mann shot back in another letter, "Is it possible, my dear Sir, you can mean to say that no person who does not adopt such views can be *pious*. Is no Universalist *pious*?"[*26] It should be

---

* This debate between religious conservatives and religious liberals over the relative gravity of sins was no abstract matter; it was being played out at exactly the same time between orthodox ministers and radical abolitionists over the evil of slavery. In 1836, the Reverend Lyman Beecher made a major speech in which he described the Sabbath as the "sun of the moral world" and lax Sabbath observance as the major moral issue in American society. The abolitionist editor William Lloyd Garrison, in the July 1836 and August 1836 editions of *The Liberator,* mocked Beecher for dwelling on Sabbath observance while at the same time "giv-

noted that neither Mann nor the more orthodox Packard questioned the advisability of mentioning God at all in school; however, there is no question that the dilution of a deity in order not to offend any religious denomination led inevitably, if not immediately, to a secular public school curriculum. The orthodox Calvinists, followed by American Catholic bishops, were right to see tax-supported education as an essentially secular enterprise, even though homogenized religious content survived in many schools throughout the nineteenth century and in some instances — especially in the South and rural areas — well into the twentieth century.

Although the battle for general taxation for common schools was won, at least in principle, in the more educated, prosperous sections of the country by the late 1830s, any proposal for either national taxation or national academic standards was even more unthinkable than it had been in the immedi-

---

ing his protecting influence to a system of slavery, which, at a single blow, annihilates not only the fourth commandment but The Whole DECALOGUE! and which effectively excludes from the benefits of the Sabbath, two millions and a half of his fellow-countrymen!!"

ate post-revolutionary era. In spite of the fact that some American states and towns did much to expand grammar school education, local autonomy and the reliance on local property taxes for the support of schools ensured the continuation of the grave inequities in public education that have never ceased to adversely affect learning in America. By the 1830s, it was already clear that urban areas would have better schools than rural areas, that wealthy communities and states would have better schools than poor ones, and that the most literate, best educated citizens would finance better schools for their children than their less literate and educated fellow citizens. Above all, it was clear that the North would have better schools than the South. Within the North, New England — especially Massachusetts — led the way. One of the most telling sets of statistics in the 1840 census is the comparative percentage of children in school in different regions of the country: in New England, the proportion of children enrolled in school in 1840 was twice that of the mid-Atlantic states and six times greater than that in the South. Although the mid-Atlantic States, the Middle West, and Pacific regions caught up with New England by the end of the nineteenth century, the severe disparity between the South and the rest of the nation persisted until after the Second World War — and the gap has not been fully closed even today.[27]

It is impossible to overestimate the importance of such regional and local disparities in the formation of American attitudes toward intellect and learning. The educational backwardness of the South, rooted first in slavery and then in segregation, deserves special mention in view of the current cultural division between so-called red and blue states. Even Virginia, which had led the way in providing a nonsectarian model that eventually did so much to foster the diffusion of learning in northern states, sank into the same intellectual torpor, dictated by a slavery-based class system and indifferent to the education of all but the rich, as the rest of the South. Part of the South's post-Reconstruction mythology maintains that everything wrong with southern education in the nineteenth and early twentieth centuries can be blamed on the destruction wrought by the Civil War and the vengeful postwar treatment of white southerners by the North. In fact, on the eve of the war, only North Carolina had established a public school system comparable to those in Massachusetts and other

New England states — or even the more laggard mid-Atlantic states. (North Carolina's exceptionalism was largely due to the efforts of one man, Calvin Henderson Wiley, who was known as the southern Horace Mann.)[28]

It is beyond the scope of this book to explore the full history of the discrepancy between public education in the South and the rest of the country; suffice to say that in a society based for so long on the supremacy of a planter aristocracy and belief in the innate inferiority of blacks, there was little reason to provide decent public education for poor whites, much less blacks. Why bother, when just being white — even an illiterate white — made an inhabitant of the South superior to any black? As for blacks, the public school systems of the South rarely provided any education beyond eighth grade until well into the twentieth century. The only thing that might have saved the South from falling further and further behind the rest of the nation in education in the late nineteenth century was massive federal aid — which the South would surely have suspected as a plot against its way of life even if the federal government had been willing to break with precedent and provide aid for the schooling of destitute former slaves and white sharecroppers. In the 1870s and 1880s, various legislators from New England introduced bills to provide federal aid to education for the poorest states and to hold them to some minimum, nationally determined standards. The proposals got no further in Congress than George Washington's effort to establish a national university had in the 1790s.

Local control of schools meant not only that children in the poorest areas of the country would have the worst school facilities and teachers with the worst training but also that the content of education in the most backward areas of the country would be determined by backward people. In Europe, the subject matter of science and history lessons taught to children in all publicly supported schools has always been determined by highly educated employees of central education ministries. In America, the image of an educated elite laying down national guidelines for schools was and is a bête noire for those who consider local control of education a right almost as sacred as any of the rights enumerated in the Constitution. For generations, the science and history taught in small towns in Alabama, Mississippi, and Louisiana was vetted by adults who believed in the innate inferiority of blacks and who also subscribed to fundamentalist creeds at odds with the growing body of secular scientific knowledge. The best educated regions of the country became better educated, and the most intellectually backward regions became more backward.

Localism and sectarian fundamentalism also had a major adverse impact on higher education, especially in the South, in the decade before Emerson's oration on the American scholar. Like Jefferson's University of Virginia, other state universities in the South had been founded by Enlightenment rationalists, even though their enlightenment did not encompass opposition to slavery. In the 1820s, South Carolina College at Columbia (now the University of South Carolina) was, along with Harvard, Yale, Dartmouth, Princeton, and Virginia, among the top ten institutions of higher education in terms of student enrollment, the size and quality of its faculty, and the number of library volumes. Its president was the Oxford-educated, English-born Thomas Cooper, one of the most distinguished men of letters in the young nation. Cooper had emigrated from England in 1794 because, like Paine, he was repelled by both the violence of the French Revolution and the right-wing British reaction, which had, among its other manifestations, resulted in Paine's trial and conviction in absentia for his anti-monarchist views expressed in *The Rights of Man.*

Cooper was a strongly anti-clerical deist, an outspoken anti-Calvinist, and a firm opponent, as a result of recent geological discoveries, of any literal interpretation of Genesis — all of which made him a controversial figure in South Carolina. Responding to one attack by the state legislature, Cooper asserted that he had come to the United States because the new American Constitution was the first attempt in history to attempt to dismantle a church-state coalition that inevitably stifled free inquiry in other nations. The state college, Cooper reminded the legislature, had not been founded as a seminary for the training of ministers of the Gospel. "Students are sent here to inquire useful knowledge, not sectarian theology," he said bluntly.[29] In 1832, Cooper was forced to resign along with the rest of the faculty members he had hired and was expelled from the faculty for religious heresy.

During the same period in the North, especially in New England, secularizing educational forces were extending new opportunities for learning to adults as well as school-age children. One cultural development in harmony not only with Emerson's call for a new respect for learning on native grounds but also with the expanding democracy of the late 1820s and 1830s — the Jacksonian era — was the American lyceum movement. The first community-based lyceum, established in 1826 in Millbury, Massachusetts, was intended as a vehicle for expanding the knowledge, especially scientific knowledge, of young men already employed in mills and the other new industrial enterprises springing up throughout New England. Through a series of lectures to be held in the evenings, after the end of the work day, employed adults might improve on the cursory education of their youth: it was never too late to learn. The Millbury lyceum was modeled on a British lyceum established in 1824, but the American lyceum movement quickly took on a character of its own and began to reach out to all segments of the community, including women. By 1831, there were between eight hundred and a thousand town lyceums.[30] Regardless of how few lectures were delivered in the smaller towns, that is an impressive figure for a country with a population of under 13 million at the start of the decade.

The father of the American lyceum was Josiah Holbrook, born in 1788 on a prosperous Connecticut farm and educated at Yale College. Holbrook entered Yale in 1806 and spent his last two years in New Haven as a laboratory assistant to Benjamin Silliman, Yale's distinguished professor of chemistry and minerology and the most important popularizer of science in America since Franklin. Although Holbrook envisioned the community lyceum as an institution focused on expanding the scientific and technical knowledge of young workmen, typical lecture programs from the 1830s demonstrate the rapidity with which lyceums broadened their concerns to reach a cross section of what would, a century later, be called the middlebrow public. A program from the 1838–39 lecture series in Salem, Massachusetts — by then a cosmopolitan town that no longer bore any resemblance to the seventeenth-century community notorious for its witchcraft trial — reveals the catholicity of subjects covered by lyceum lecturers. The Salem series opened with a talk titled "The Character, Customes, Costumes, etc., of the North American Indians," delivered by George Catlin, a portraitist and pioneering anthropologist. The subsequent lyceum agenda featured lectures on topics that included the causes of the American Revolution; the sun; the honeybee; geology; the legal rights of women; the life of Muhammad; Oliver Cromwell; the discovery of America by the Vikings; and the education of children (delivered by the ubiquitous Horace Mann).[31]

In New England, there was scarcely a distinguished scholar or public official who did *not* take the platform in a lyceum lecture: among the most popular speakers were Daniel Webster, Emerson, Thoreau, the Swiss-born naturalist and Harvard faculty member Louis Agassiz, the pioneering women's educator Emma Willard, and Nathaniel Hawthorne, who eventually served as corresponding secretary of Salem's lyceum. The absence of female lecturers attested to the social taboo against women speaking in public. Women did not begin to appear on public platforms until the abolitionist movement gained strength in the late 1830s, and the powerful abolitionist crusaders Lucretia Mott, Sarah Grimké, and Angelina Grimké were frequently castigated for conduct unbecoming the modesty of their sex.[32] Yet in every community where lyceums flourished, they garnered broad support from both men and women and from many segments of the community. Professors and writers donated their services as lecturers, and the cost for a series of weekly lectures that ran from early autumn through spring was low enough to be affordable for many workers. In Boston, the price was $2 for adults and $1 for minors; so many people signed up for the first series, in 1828–29, that the speakers agreed to repeat their lectures on two successive nights each week in order to satisfy public demand.

The lyceum movement, like the growing movement in favor of publicly supported education, was largely a northern phenomenon, appealing primarily to the middle class — both the upper middle class and the lower-middle-class workers who saw continuing education as a way to move up the economic ladder. The South simply did not have a large enough middle class to support regular lectures; New Orleans, Richmond, and Charleston were exceptions that proved the rule. And while wealthy New Englanders provided both financial and moral support for community lyceums, most southern planters had no interest in such activities. Many actively opposed the establishment of lyceums, which they associated, in view of the movement's New England origins, with the detested abolitionists. Their concern was largely unfounded, because most lyceum programs avoided controversial political and religious issues. However, it is easy to see why lectures on geology or the legal rights of women might threaten southern views on both religion and caste.

Finally, the Enlightenment culture that had produced Jefferson, Madison, and Washington no longer existed in the South: men of learning and science like Thomas Cooper were being exiled instead of recruited to build regional educational institutions. All of this converged in a culture in which the richest and most influential members, the planters, were noted for and proud of their lack of interest in intellectual pursuits. "The men who might in Boston have read books at the Athenaeum," observes Carl Bode, "in the South rode and hunted. Still interested, to all appearances, in physical activities rather than thoughts, they felt for the lyceum an indifference amounting almost to contempt."[33]

Thus, a half century into the political experiment intended to form a more perfect union, the intellectual life of the new nation was profoundly fragmented. In the older urban centers of the Northeast, there were visible signs not only of a diffusion of knowledge but of the unmistakable emergence of an intellectual aristocracy. In the South, what can only be described as an intellectual blockade was imposed in an effort to keep out any ideas that might threaten the social order. On the frontier, as settlers moved westward, the intellectual picture was mixed: in such raw social conditions, learning could not be a top priority, yet there were those whose hunger for civilization was such that their passion for books and learning might have shamed the heirs to privilege in Emerson's audience.

One of those passionate book lovers on the frontier was Abraham Lincoln, whose formal schooling, as he would later write, "did not amount to one year."[34] Lincoln would become the last self-educated American to be elected president, and his self-education was, as he made clear, a matter of necessity rather than choice. Even as Emerson, born in 1803, just six years before Lincoln, was embarking on his career as an essayist and philosopher in a world of books, Lincoln was struggling to master the principles of English grammar while earning his living as a clerk in a general store in New Salem, Illinois, a town of just twenty-five families in 1831. Carrying his own well-worn copy of Shakespeare's plays everywhere, studying a copy of Blackstone's *Commentaries* borrowed from the one educated man in town, Lincoln prepared himself to become a lawyer even as he became a figure of amusement to his neighbors because of his bookishness. A recurrent theme in Lincoln's accounts of his early life is his struggle to obtain books, usually by borrowing. What schoolchild has not heard tales of young Lincoln, after a day of honest toil, reading those books by the flickering light of a fire in a log cabin, of Ben Franklin exploring the secrets of electricity by flying his kite in a thunderstorm in the great American outdoors?

Reverential images of self-education have been deeply embedded in the American psyche from the colonial period and persist today, in an era characterized by a mania for specialized educational credentials that Emerson could not have imagined. Yet these images have cut two ways in shaping American attitudes toward intellect and education: they combine respect for learning itself with the message that there is something especially virtuous about learning acquired in the absence of a formal structure provided by society. After all, Ben Franklin invented the lightning rod and bifocals without government support for his research, and Abe Lincoln grew up to become president without ever attending a university. That Franklin was a genius and that Lincoln bitterly regretted his lack of systematic formal schooling is left out of the self-congratulatory story of American self-education. Tinged with a moralistic romanticism, the American exaltation of the self-educated man is linked to the iconic notion of rugged individualism and has often been used to refute any idea that education is, for government, an obligation of justice. In this version of American history, Lincoln was a better man, a better American, for having struggled to learn against the grain of his immediate environment. The triumph of the extraordinary self-educated man is transformed into a moral and social lesson: If you want to learn badly enough, no one can stop you, and the community has no special obligation to create conditions that provide support for the intellectual development of its members. Intellectuals themselves were conflicted about the relationship between formal, systematic learning and self-education. Emerson, who would become (after Franklin)

America's second intellectual celebrity, gave voice in his American scholar oration to what would become a permanent American argument over the most desirable way of learning and the value placed on knowledge by society. He warned against the meekness of young men who

> grow up in libraries, believing it is their duty to accept the views which Cicero, which Locke, which Bacon, have given; forgetful that Cicero, Locke, and Bacon were only young men in libraries when they wrote these books.
>
> Hence, instead of Man Thinking, we have the bookworm. Hence the book-learned class, who values books, as such; not related as to nature and the human constitution, but as making a sort of Third Estate with the world and the soul. Hence the restorers of readings, the emendators, the bibliomaniacs of all degrees. . . .
>
> Undoubtedly there is a right way of reading, so it be sternly subordinated. Man Thinking must not be subdued by his instruments. Books are for the scholar's idle times. When he can read God directly, the hour is too precious to be wasted in other men's transcripts of their readings. But when the intervals of darkness come,

as come they must, — when the sun is hid and the stars withdraw their shining, — we repair to the lamps which were kindled by their ray, to guide our steps to the East again, where the dawn is. We hear, that we may speak. The Arabian proverb says, "A fig tree, looking on a fig tree, becometh fruitful."[35]

Emerson, a supremely bookish man, has often been quoted out of context, in both the late nineteenth and twentieth centuries, by anti-rationalists who wish to claim him as one of their own. But Emerson was as much a product of the Enlightenment rationalism of his parents' generation as of early nineteenth-century Romanticism, and his transcendentalist philosophy partook of both. The American scholar speech was not only a declaration of American intellectual independence but also a response to many of the native anti-intellectual forces in American life — that portion of the American mind "taught to aim at low objects." Emerson's message to Americans was not that they had nothing to learn from the past but that they must be prepared to make their own contributions to the sum of cultural knowledge. Those contributions would be fed by the particular social and political circumstances of American life and would be rooted in a broader concept of democratic individuality under which each person had the right and the responsibility to develop his capabilities to the fullest.

Americans did not have long to wait for the first manifestations of a distinctive national literature and philosophy. Emerson's first collection of essays was published in 1841; Thoreau's *A Week on the Concord and Merrimack Rivers* (part of his Walden journals) and his famous essay "Civil Disobedience" in 1849; Hawthorne's *The Scarlet Letter* in 1850, Melville's *Moby-Dick* in 1851; and the first edition of Whitman's *Leaves of Grass* in 1855. That the public did not greet all of these works with enthusiasm in no way changes what they were — the foundation of a truly American literature that stood as a powerful rebuttal to the many European intellectuals who had blamed the low state of American culture in the early republic on democracy itself.

But the emergence of a richer cultural life, accessible to many more citizens, would not subsume the anti-intellectual forces rooted in religious and educational fissures as old as the nation itself. As Emerson spoke on the eve of the first flowering of a truly national literature, America stood with its intellectual house already divided.

CHAPTER THREE: SOCIAL PSEUDOSCIENCE IN THE MORNING OF AMERICA'S CULTURE WARS

The intellectual fissures that opened during the first half of the nineteenth century acquired an important new dimension in the decades after the Civil War, when many Americans embraced a form of ideologically driven pseudoscience intended to rationalize the Gilded Age's excesses of wealth and poverty. The new pseudoscience of social Darwinism, like the ancient pseudosciences of astrology and alchemy, used scientific language to mask an essentially unscientific essence.[*] While the old pseudosciences defied the laws of nature, the new social pseu-

[*] I use the term "social Darwinism" even though no one employed it in nineteenth-century America or England. The phrase was known in rarefied intellectual circles in nineteenth-century France and Germany, but it was not in common usage in America, even among academics, until the publi-

dosciences — of which social Darwinism turned out to be only the first example — appropriated laws of nature to justify or attack institutions in civilization. In America, social Darwinism was purveyed not by ignorant bumpkins but by some of the nation's leading business tycoons and intellectuals, including Andrew Carnegie, John D. Rockefeller, and William Graham Sumner, a Yale University political scientist and prototypical public intellectual. Social Darwinism constituted the first mass-marketed wave of pseudoscience, or what would today be called junk science, in American history. The ideological fixations of otherwise intelligent men in America's Gilded Age offer a recognizable precursor of the imperviousness to evidence that permeates many ideologies in our current age of unreason.

Sumner's writings are virtually unknown outside academia today, but he was considered the most influential social Darwinist in America at the turn of the nineteenth

---

cation in 1944 of Richard Hofstadter's *Social Darwinism in American Thought*. Hofstadter's book, originally written as his doctoral thesis at Columbia, went on to sell more than 200,000 copies in subsequent editions.

century. He was an intellectual mentor to thousands of the nation's future leaders at Yale between 1872 and 1910 and also possessed the knack of translating his ideas into readable articles for mass-circulation magazines.[1] The transformative scientific insight of the age, Darwin's theory of evolution by means of natural selection, was twisted by Sumner and his followers into a social philosophy — always described as "scientific" — that enshrined competition and validated the worthiness of whoever and whatever came out on top. Millionaires were explicitly compared to the superior biological species that had emerged from eons of evolution in nature: J. P. Morgan and Henry Clay Frick were, presumably, descendants of the first hominids to stand on two legs, while the poor were more closely related to creatures who lacked opposable thumbs and continued to grope on all fours. Sumner declared emphatically that the business titans of the Gilded Age were "a product of natural selection . . . just like the great statesmen, or scientific men, or military men." Because millionaires emerged from fair competition, governed by the supposedly scientific laws of the market, "all who are competent for this function will be employed in it . . ."[2]

Academics like Sumner would have done enough damage had their theories been confined to classrooms in which elite young men were indoctrinated in the worship of untrammeled capitalism, but they were able to extend their influence on a previously unimaginable scale by writing for national magazines like *Collier's,* aimed at a vast middle-class audience. Then as now, the public was overwhelmed by information and misinformation filtered through new technologies. Many Americans possessed just enough education to be fascinated by late nineteenth-century advances in both science and technology, but they had too little education to distinguish between real scientists and those who peddled social theories in the guise of science.

The cultural battle over evolution in post-Darwinian, late nineteenth-century America, like its descendant today, is generally viewed solely as a struggle between science and religion. But there were really two culture wars over evolution — the first centering on the challenge to traditional religion posed by Darwin's real science and the second rooted in a pseudoscientific social theory that attempted to transpose Darwin's observations about man in a state of nature into a prescription for the way human beings ought to treat one another in a state of civilization. In the first culture war, nearly all intellectuals were on the side of science; in the second, many (though not all) succumbed to the pseudoscience articulated by Sumner. The attraction of upperclass intellectuals to a theory maintaining that "tooth and claw" laws of survival in nature were appropriate and inevitable in society did much to exacerbate a religiously based anti-intellectualism already aroused by evolution's challenge to biblical literalism.

William Jennings Bryan, the three-time presidential candidate, economic populist, and hero of fundamentalists from the 1890s until his death in 1925, conflated the two culture wars. Bryan was fighting both the scientific theory of evolution and the pseudoscience of social Darwinism; the former threatened his religion, while the latter ran counter to his vision of social justice on earth. One of the great ironies of this phase of American intellectual history is that the intellectual social Darwinists and their fundamentalist opponents shared an inability to distinguish between science and social pseudoscience, and they passed on their confusion to a public that worshipped the fruits of science but was fundamentally ignorant of the scientific method.

In the half century between the end of the Civil War and the beginning of the First World War, American society was transformed by powerful economic and demographic forces that could never have been envisaged by the privileged men who had gathered in Cambridge in 1837 to hear Ralph Waldo Emerson's declaration of American intellectual independence. Between 1860 and 1910, in spite of the deaths of more than six hundred thousand men in the Civil War, the American population nearly tripled — from some 31 million to more than 92 million — as a result of immigration from Southern and Eastern Europe. It is a familiar yet still awe-inspiring demographic statistic, a raw number that would seem to rule out any possibility of successful assimilation or absorption — if we did not know that the task was indeed accomplished. During the 1880s and 1890s, a network of public elementary and secondary schools, colleges, and libraries emerged to meet the challenge of absorbing millions of non-English-speaking immigrants and raising the educational level of the entire American population.

Cities, home to the vast majority of the

new immigrants, were responsible for the most significant expansion of public education at both the elementary and secondary school levels. Public schools were viewed as vital instruments of assimilation, by the WASP establishment that still controlled most American cities and by the immigrants themselves — especially the East European Jews, whose pent-up desire for education finally found an outlet in a society with no legal anti-Semitic restrictions. In 1878, there were fewer than eight hundred public high schools in the United States; by the eve of the First World War, the number had increased to more than eleven thousand. Between the 1880 and the 1900 censuses, the official illiteracy rate declined from 17 percent to 11 percent — a remarkable accomplishment, even allowing for those missed by the census takers, in an era when almost none of the new immigrants had any knowledge of English before they set foot on American soil.[3] The passage of compulsory school attendance laws in many states raised the duration of the average American's schooling from four to six years between 1880 and 1914 — again, a notable accomplishment in view of the influx of immigrants with no schooling at all.[4]

The expansion of secondary education

was paralleled by the growth of adult education programs and the creation of a public library system, spurred across the nation by the money and leadership of the self-made Carnegie (who believed in private philanthropy as strongly as he detested the idea of government handouts), which offered broad access to ordinary citizens. In large cities, not only neighborhood libraries but central research libraries — the nucleus of what would become some of the greatest research collections in the world — were open to anyone with a library card. When the grand Forty-second Street headquarters of the New York Public Library opened its doors to the public for the first time on May 24, 1911, some fifty thousand New Yorkers passed through the Fifth Avenue entrance — guarded by the stone lions that would soon become famous civic landmarks — to view the marvels within.[5] The first book delivered to a reader was a Russian-language volume of philosophy, attesting to the evolution of a civic culture in which ordinary citizens were gaining access to cultural and intellectual resources previously locked away from all but the wealthiest, most privileged members of society.[*]

[*] The book was N. Y. Grot's *Nravstvenniye Ideali*

The Gilded Age was also the golden age of the lecture as a source of both entertainment and instruction. The old community-based lyceums were replaced by national lecture bureaus that offered high fees to well-known speakers but were able to keep ticket prices low because of huge popular demand. When a lecture bureau presented such famous personages as Emerson; Henry Ward Beecher, the leading clerical orator of the era; Thomas Huxley, the British naturalist and defender of evolutionism; Elizabeth Cady Stanton, the founding mother of the women's rights movement; and Robert Ingersoll, a tireless antagonist of orthodox religion, the size of the audience was limited only by the size of the hall. As an editorial in Horace Greeley's *New York Tribune* noted in 1869, "When the historian of a later day comes to search out the intellectual antecedents of modern society, he will devote an interesting chapter to the rise and progress of ideas as illustrated in the institution of the public lecture. He will record that at one time Emerson, [Bronson] Alcott, [Wendell] Phillips, Beecher, [William Lloyd]

Nashevo Vremeni (Moral Ideas of Our Time: Friedrich Nietzsche and Leo Tolstoy), and it was delivered in just six minutes.

Garrison, and a great many other awakeners of American intelligence were lecturers; that philosophers and scientists were persuaded out of their studies and laboratories to take a stand on the platform; in short, that Plato's Academe and Archimedes' workshop were turned into the lecture room."[6] The failure of the *Tribune* to mention any female speakers reflects the contemporary male opinion about who did, and did not, count in intellectual matters. In fact, controversial feminists like Stanton, Susan B. Anthony, and Lucy Stone drew huge audiences, as did female evangelists, leaders in the temperance movement, and Henry Ward Beecher's even more famous sister, Harriet Beecher Stowe, the author of *Uncle Tom's Cabin*.

The rising literacy rate, and the proliferation of adult education programs, libraries, museums, and lecture series, intensified the public's appetite for intellectual amusements and information of every kind. Book publishers churned out cheap editions of everything from adventure stories and housekeeping manuals to the classics of nineteenth-century literature from all nations. Publishers shamelessly pirated some of the greatest works of literature from Europe and England for "reprint libraries," because the United States had refused to sign the Berne International Convention of 1886, which provided the first copyright protection for authors published in more than one country. Even works originally published in English were not protected by copyright in the United States unless the books had actually been assembled and printed here. Between 1880 and 1900, American publishers tripled the number of book titles issued each year. Periodicals, which ran the gamut from mass-circulation magazines specializing in pulp fiction to highbrow literary publications and specialized scientific journals, offered something for every literate person. Between 1885 and 1905, approximately eleven thousand periodicals were published, although many had life spans as brief as those of unsuccessful Internet blogs today.[7] One literary historian has estimated that the circulation of monthly magazines in relation to the total American population increased by 700 percent between 1865 and 1905.[8]

The proliferation of information sources affected American cultural life in many ways, and the growth of the publishing industry and the lecture circuit — then, as now, kissing cousins in the book business — played a vital role in publicizing Darwin's theory of evolution. Both religion and science were hot topics, and evolution combined the two. Edward Livingston Youmans, who founded the pro-evolution *Popular Science Monthly* in 1872, was one of the most popular and indefatigable American lecturers. He was, alas, a committed social Darwinist as well as a popularizer of Darwin's theory of evolution. Youmans was responsible for the then famous International Scientific Series, published by the distinguished New York firm D. Appleton & Company, that brought the works of the world's most eminent scientists (including Darwin himself) to the American public.

When Thomas Huxley made his first visit to the United States to deliver a series of lectures in 1876, he received the kind of coverage that the American press would eventually accord only two of his compatriots — Winston Churchill and Princess Diana. *The New York Times* published front-page stories about Huxley's sold-out lectures in Manhattan's Chickering Hall, while the *Tribune* reprinted the lectures in full. The news coverage was glowing, prompting the more conservative *Times* editorial page to pronounce that "for Mr. Huxley to speak of the evidence for evolution as being on a par with Copernican theory, only shows how far [astray] theory will lead a clear brain."[9] Whether the publicity was favorable or unfavorable, it ensured that a broad swath of the late nineteenth-century public had at least heard about evolution — a general awareness that far exceeded the knowledge of the early nineteenth-century public regarding geological discoveries that also challenged the biblical creation story. Indeed, the size of the reading and lecture-going public ensured that the culture wars over evolution would not be confined to an elite, highly educated segment of society.

The debate over biological evolution and its relationship to religion was, for the most part, an extended family quarrel among different kinds of American Protestants. The Roman Catholic Church, like fundamentalist Protestant denominations, opposed evolution as a part of its general hostility toward all forms of secularism; the Catholic hierarchy's desire to shield immigrant children from secular science and history was largely responsible for the establishment of the nation's first organized parochial school system. At the time, there was no American Catholic equivalent of the sizable faction of theologically liberal Protestants determined to make room in their faith for the new secular knowledge. With insular church leaders and a laity composed largely of uneducated immigrants, American Catholicism stood apart from the most sophisticated intellectual discourse of the nineteenth century.

The real debate was also largely confined to the North — another result of the intellectual isolation originally encouraged by the battle to preserve slavery and maintained after the Civil War by the South's aggrieved mythologizing of the antebellum status quo. The negative impact of adamant southern fundamentalism on higher education, especially scientific education, had been apparent since Thomas Cooper's heretical views on the ages of rocks led to his dismissal from the presidency of the University of South Carolina in 1832. After Darwin, the gap between contemporary scientific knowledge and southern religion grew much wider. In 1873, the shipping and railroad magnate Cornelius Vanderbilt donated one million dollars to turn what was then Central University in Nashville, Tennessee — an institution founded for the training of Methodist ministers — into a real university. The hitch: the Methodist Church would retain control of the board of trustees, thanks to a close personal relationship between Vanderbilt and a Methodist bishop, who was named president for life of the trustees at the time of Vanderbilt's gift.

Nevertheless, even the most religious trustees were eager to use Vanderbilt's money to raise the institution's prestige, and they took the step of hiring Alexander Winchell, an evolutionist, as president. Winchell should have been the perfect choice for a southern university aspiring to greatness, given his belief that Darwin's theory of natural selection actually proved the inferiority of the Negro race. Why? Because, as Winchell argued in an 1878 screed titled *Adamites and Preadamites,* Negroes were too biologically inferior to have been descended from Adam — who, as everyone knew, was white. Therefore, the human race must be older than the biblical Adam, and blacks represented an earlier evolutionary stage. Even though Winchell was using evolution to bolster white supremacy — a theme that would resurface at many other points in white America's rationalization of racial segregation and discrimination — the southern Methodists were still upset by his position that any human life, in however inferior a form, existed before Adam. So they fired the president they had hired to bring their institution into the late nineteenth century. Winchell headed north to a distinguished career — unhampered at the time by his crackpot theory melding evolution, eugenics, and the Bible — as professor of paleontology and geology at the University of Michigan. His departure was replicated throughout the South, as scientists who did not hew to a literal interpretation of the Bible were forced to seek employment elsewhere.

Winchell's academic success as a eugenicist evolutionist, and the respect in which he was held by most of the scientific community, illustrates the utility of social Darwinism in blurring the distinction between real science and pseudoscience. The combination of eugenics with social Darwinism enabled proponents to validate the worthiness not only of individuals but of groups — beginning with American-born Caucasians of Anglo-Saxon heritage — who came out on top in society. Interest in eugenics was certainly not limited to America; but biological justifications for racial discrimination had a particular appeal, covert and overt, in a nation that had long enslaved a large population of a different race and had done little since the end of slavery to ameliorate the damage inflicted on that minority. Eugenics also tapped into the fears of a society that, unlike any nation in Europe, was being flooded by immigrants — including Jews, Slavs, and Italians — with cultural backgrounds that differed markedly from that of the existing population.

The leading American social Darwinists of the late nineteenth century were, almost without exception, upper-class, white Anglo-Saxon Protestants (some of whom had crossed the divide between liberal Protestantism and agnosticism). The class-based bias of leading social Darwinists against any evidence that contradicted their philosophical views is startling, because they were all men who, on an intellectual level, revered rationality. And yet, many described their intellectual awakening in the language of religious conversion. "I remember that the light came as in a flood and all was clear," Carnegie would later explain in his autobiography. "Not only had I got rid of theology and the supernatural, but I had found the truth of evolution. 'All is well since all grows better,' became my motto." Incredibly, considering that the posthumously published autobiography was written amid the pointless carnage of the First World War, Carnegie went on to assert that man "is an organism, inherently rejecting all that is deleterious, that is, wrong, and absorbing after trial what is beneficial, that is, right."[10]

The phrase "social Darwinism," even if it had been known in America, would have been unpopular precisely because late nineteenth-century academics like Sumner belonged to the first generation of American intellectuals and educators to insist that their social theories were a branch of objective science. Joining the captains of industry who proclaimed that biological evolution and social progress were one (a view that Darwin never entertained), the social Darwinists in academia claimed that anyone who opposed their views was actually opposing science itself. The new idea that social science was as firmly grounded in principles of objective observation and experimentation as the natural sciences did much to endow eugenics and social Darwinism with intellectual respectability. Intellectuals who fully accepted Darwin's theory of evolution by means of natural selection but rejected its extension into the social realm were in a distinct minority, and they were frequently ridiculed and accused of retrograde anti-scientific attitudes. This small but elite group included Ralph Waldo Emerson and William James, and it is significant that both men belonged not to the new world of social science but to the older American tradition of broad education in the humanities and natural sciences.

The influence of social Darwinism on America, and on American intellectuals in particular, is largely attributable to the writings of Herbert Spencer, a British-born philosopher little read today but of enormous stature in the nineteenth century. "The survival of the fittest" was a phrase coined not by Darwin but by Spencer. Pithily described by Hofstadter as "the metaphysician of the homemade intellectual and the prophet of the cracker-barrel agnostic," Spencer also appealed to nonfundamentalist religious believers because he asserted that whatever science might reveal about the natural world, scientists could never comprehend "the Unknowable" — in other words, God.[11] This was the perfect escape hatch for millions of theologically liberal believers, who wanted to have their God and Darwin too, but it did not suffice for fundamentalists, who could never be persuaded to accept the Bible as a mere metaphor. The publication of Spencer's multivolume, 6,000-page *System of Synthetic Philosophy* was made possible by the support of Americans; Carnegie, Rockefeller, and Thomas Edison provided direct financial backing, and dozens of prominent New England intellectuals subscribed in advance to each new volume of Spencer's tome, a marketing practice equivalent to today's publishing blurbs. The best known early subscribers included the historian George Bancroft, the botanist Asa Gray, the former Harvard University president Jared Sparks, and the poet James Russell Lowell — as elite a group of intellectual backers as any publisher could hope to find.

Spencer preached the gospel of laissez-faire economics as the only way to ensure that the fittest would triumph in society through a process of "social selection" equivalent to Darwin's natural selection, and the Spencerian gospel found a far more receptive audience in America than in England. Spencer's first pedestrian musings about the universal laws of social selection were published in 1858, a year before Darwin's *On the Origin of Species* — a timeline Spencer never tired of emphasizing. Nevertheless, the metaphysician of the homemade intellectual immediately seized on Darwin's scientific research to support his philosophical rationalization for unrestrained industrial capitalism. The British philosopher was unequivocally and fanatically opposed to all government programs that he viewed as obstacles to social selection — including public education, health regulations, tariffs, and even postal service. In this he was more consistent than the American tycoons who revered him, given that the great industrialists were only too happy to benefit from tariffs that protected their products from foreign competition. Men like Carnegie, whose grants for libraries created a model partnership between government and private philanthropy, clearly did not take Spencer any more literally than they did the Bible. Academic social scientists, however, tended to be fundamentalist Spencerians.

William Sumner, an ordained Episcopal minister, had evolved into an agnostic under the influence of both Spencer's theories and the new biblical criticism, which emphasized the human authorship of the Scriptures. As Charles and Mary Beard note, Sumner trained thousands of Yale undergraduates in "individualism as if it was an exact science, trying to convince even young Republicans that a protective tariff was no permissible departure from its [social Darwinist individualism's] extractions."[12] Because Sumner was able to invest his pseudoscientific theories with scientific authority and an aura of rationality, in popular publications as well as scholarly journals, he must be ranked not only as one of the most influential academics of his day but as the philosophical forefather of the right-wing public intellectuals who have exercised similar influence in American society since the early 1980s. Sumner's ideas would fit perfectly today in the position papers of the Heritage Foundation and the American Enterprise Institute. In his repeated arguments against taxing the rich — "no man can acquire a million without helping a million men to increase their little fortune" — Sumner advocated what would now be called trickle-down economics. Socialism, as well as Progressive Era reform proposals, were not matters for political debate but nothing more than attempts to undo the natural order of existence as revealed by science.

Sumner elaborated on this philosophy, throwing brickbats over his shoulder at the Enlightenment, in his "Reply to a Socialist," published in 1904 in *Collier's* in response to a call by the muckraking novelist Upton Sinclair for laws to regulate labor practices in garment factories.

The notion that everybody ought to be happy, and equally happy with all the rest, is the fine flower of the philosophy which has been winning popularity for two hundred years. All the petty demands of natural rights, liberty, equality, etc., are only stepping-stones toward this philosophy, which is really what is wanted. All through human history some have had good fortune and some ill fortune. For some the ills of life have taken all the joy and strength out of existence, while the fortunate have always been there to show how glorious life might be and to furnish dreams of bliss to tantalize those who have failed and suffered. So men have constructed in philosophy theories of universal felicity. They tell us that everyone has a natural right to be happy, to be comfortable, to have health, to succeed, to have knowledge, family, political power, and all the best of the things which anybody can have. . . . Then they say that we all ought to be equal. That proposition abolishes luck. . . . The unlucky will pull down the lucky. That is all that equality ever can mean.[13]

(Take that, you misguided authors of the Declaration of Independence!)

Because Spencer allowed for belief in "the Unknowable," he was embraced as enthusiastically by theologically liberal but economically conservative Protestant intellectuals as by agnostics. Beecher, pastor of the influential Plymouth Congregational Church in Brooklyn and the most famous minister in the nation, argued that the gross economic inequalities of the Gilded Age were mandated not only by natural selection but by the Bible — an odd twist for a theologian who also argued that the Bible must be viewed metaphorically when it came to the creation story itself. The poor were poor because God had ordained their state in life, and Darwin's findings about the competition for survival within nature offered scientific "proof" of God's intent that men compete for survival in society. It is simply stunning to read Beecher's sermons on the fecklessness of the poor and the un-Americanness of trade unions, socialism, and communism, conflated as European-bred evils. In 1877, in a sermon quoted in *The New York Times,* Beecher intoned that "God has intended the great to be great and the little to be little. . . . I do not say that a dollar a day is enough to support a working man. But it is enough to support a man!" European notions "that the Government should be paternal and take care of the welfare of its subjects and provide them with labor, are un-American." In a final peroration, Beecher declared that men "who have been cast down from affluence to poverty should not grunt and grumble, but bear matters unflinchingly. They should never forget that they are men, even though they die of hunger. An Indian, uncivilized though he was, never flinched when fire was applied to his body. The manly way to meet misfortune is to go down boldly to poverty."[14]

Poverty was a misfortune that Beecher was never required to address, boldly or otherwise. In 1875, his former friend and parishioner, Theodore Tilton, had sued the pastor for alleged adultery with Tilton's wife. After the adultery trial ended in a hung jury, Beecher retained his Brooklyn pulpit, and the scandal and its attendant fame enabled him to command even higher fees on the lecture circuit. Over the next decade, Beecher did more than any other clergyman to convince theologically liberal Protestants that belief in God as First Cause could be reconciled with the particulars of evolution, and he argued forcefully that just as the survival of certain species in nature proved their fitness, the accumulation of wealth proved the greater "fitness" of the rich in society — and the greater fitness of rich societies in the world order.

Darwin never said any such thing. He stated explicitly in *The Descent of Man* that environmental factors and moral concerns take precedence over natural selection as soon as man moves from a state of nature into a state of civilization. "The aid which we feel impelled to give to the helpless is mainly an incidental result of the instinct of sympathy," he observed, "which was originally acquired as part of the social instincts, but subsequently rendered . . . more tender and widely diffused. Nor could we check our sympathy, even at the urging of hard reason, without deterioration in the noblest part of our nature. . . . [I]f we were intentionally to neglect the weak and the helpless, it could only be for a contingent benefit, with an overwhelming present evil."[15]

There was also a close relationship between the rise of social Darwinist pseudoscience and the replacement of Emerson's ideal of democratic individuality with an exaltation of "rugged individualism" — another mantra that has endured into the twenty-first century. For Emerson, as for America's founding generation, there was no conflict between political equality and individuality: men were equal as human beings and as citizens "because each had his unique place as a representative man, and his natural right was the right to opportunity for the full development of his particular potentialities . . . the equality of all men meant not that all are alike or have the same interests and capacities but that all are equally important in the Universe."[16] The Gilded Age concept of American individualism, so often accompanied by the adjective "rugged," meant something entirely different: it suggested not just that individuals have different natural capacities but that those different capacities proved some human beings to be much worthier than others in the social universe.

For the most part, the equation of natural selection with social selection was not effectively challenged by prominent intellectuals until the Progressive Era began around the turn of the century. The most notable exception was William James, who, unlike most of his scholarly contemporaries, saw through the junk science at the heart of Spencerian social Darwinism. A trained physician and naturalist as well as a philosopher, James addressed the confusion between natural selection and social selection from both a scientific and a metaphysical perspective. Born in 1842, he was a member of the first generation to come of age after the publication of *On the Origin of Species,* and was at the height of his intellectual influence when the American enthusiasm for Spencer was also at its zenith. It was James who made the case that while social Darwinism was perfectly suited to the contemporary worship of rugged individualism, the philosophy had little regard for *individuals.* Even more important, James defined social Darwinism not as bad science but as a nonscience.

In an 1880 lecture before the Harvard Natural History Society, James argued that Spencer, by appropriating Darwin's brilliant insights about change in nature as an overarching explanation for all change in society, was in fact as illogical as a soothsayer. "If we proceeded on this method," James contended, "we might say with perfect legitimacy that a friend of ours, who had slipped on the ice upon his door-step and cracked his skull, some months after dining with thirteen at the table, died because of that ominous feast." Indeed, James continued, he knew of such a fatal accident and might, "with perfect logical propriety," contend that the slip on the ice was predetermined.

"There are no accidents," I might say, "for science. The whole history of the world converged to produce that slip. If anything had been left out, the slip would not have occurred there and then. To say it would is to deny the relations of cause and effect throughout the universe. The real cause of the death was not the slip, *but the conditions which engendered the slip,* — and among them his having sat at a table, six months previous, one among thirteen. *That* is truly the reason he died within the year."

No one, before or since, has presented a more cogent case against the misappropriation of genuine evidence-based science in the service of unverifiable, monistic, metaphysical, and social theories. In a brilliant conclusion to his lecture, James drew a clear distinction between social theory and scientific theory:

The plain truth is that the "philosophy of evolution" (as distinguished from our special information about particular cases of change) is a metaphysical creed and nothing else. It is a mood of contemplation, an emotional attitude, rather than a system of thought — a mood which is as old as the world, and which no refutation of any one incarnation of it (such as the Spencerian philosophy) will ever dispel; the mood of fatalistic pantheism, with its intuition of the One and All, which was and is, and ever shall be, and from whose womb each single thing proceeds. Far be it from us to speak slightingly here of so hoary and mighty a style of looking at the world as this. What we at present call scientific discoveries had nothing to do with bringing it to birth, nor can one easily conceive that they should ever give it its *quietus*. . . . A critic, however, who cannot disprove the truth of the metaphysic creed, can at least raise his voice in protest against its disguising itself in "scientific" plumes . . . the Spencerian "philosophy" of social and intellectual progress is an obsolete anachronism, reverting to a pre-Darwinian type of thought just as the Spencerian philosophy of "Force," effacing all previous distinctions between actual and potential energy, momentum, work, force, mass, etc., which physicists have with so much agony achieved, carries us back to a pre-Galilean age.[17]

Perhaps only someone trained as both a natural scientist and a philosopher could have spotted, at such an early stage in the culture wars over evolution, the bloviating arrogance of metaphysical theories that ignore inconvenient facts, as distinct from scientific theories subject to modification by the discovery of new facts. Because James's brief against social Darwinism was based on its illogic rather than on its implications for contemporary social policy (though the latter were bad enough), his argument has a timeless quality. It would have been equally relevant to early twentieth-century illusions about "scientific Communism" or to the quasi-religious belief, at its height in America in the 1950s, in the scientific basis of Freudian psychoanalysis.* It could be applied today to intelligent design or to the repackaged social Darwinism that exalts modern post-industrial capitalism — as the old social Darwinists exalted industrial capitalism — as an edifice governed by immutable laws of nature.

* James, who was extremely interested in Freud's work at a time when it was virtually unknown in America, was on hand in 1909 at Clark University to welcome Freud and Carl Jung to the United States. However, James commented at the time on the ideological rigidity of both men, which he described as a tendency to be "obsessed with a fixed idea."

Just as James had laid bare the unscientific psychological and emotional underpinnings of Spencerian thought, Thorstein Veblen — who had studied under Sumner at Yale but had reached very different conclusions from those preached by his teacher — eviscerated the economic basis of the claim that social Darwinism was a science. *The Theory of the Leisure Class* (1899) bequeathed to future generations not only the trenchant phrase "conspicuous consumption" but a devastating critique of the notion that vast disparities in wealth and income are the result of forces similar to those in nature. To Veblen, the most advantaged members of society — those affluent enough to constitute a leisure class whose conspicuous consumption functions as a continuous advertisement of their success — are in fact the enemies of natural selection, acting "to retard that adjustment to the environment which is called social advance or social development." The leisure class assumed, as Carnegie proclaimed, that "whatever is, is right," but Veblen argued that the law of natural selection proved precisely the opposite — "Whatever is, is wrong." In Veblen's view, governing institutions always lag behind the social exigencies of any era; and in periods of rapid change, like the late nineteenth century, the gap widens between society's needs and the institutional capacity to meet those needs.

> They [social institutions] are the result of a more or less inadequate adjustment of the methods of living to a situation which prevailed at some point in the past . . . and they are therefore wrong by something more than the interval which separated the present situation from the past. . . . The institution of a leisure class, by force of class interest and instinct, and by precept and prescriptive example, makes for the perpetuation of the existing maladjustment of institutions, and even favours a reversion to a somewhat more archaic scheme of life; a scheme which would be still farther out of adjustment with the exigencies of life under the existing situation even than the accredited, obsolescent scheme that has come down from the immediate past.[18]

Unlike Sumner, Veblen was not invited to write for *Collier's*.

In the years between the turn of the century and America's entry into the First World War, some intellectuals also turned to real social science — based on direct observation and large-scale statistical studies — to challenge social pseudoscience. One of these was William English Walling, an unjustly forgotten figure and an innovative socialist thinker who, after his education at the University of Chicago and Harvard, worked at Jane Addams's Hull House in Chicago and as a factory inspector for the state of Illinois. In *The Larger Aspects of Socialism* (1913), Walling placed special emphasis on new anthropological evidence challenging the premises of eugenics. Citing a contemporary study by the pioneering Columbia University anthropologist Franz Boas, Walling noted that all recent immigrants to the United States — whether East European Jews, Sicilians, Bohemians, Hungarians, or Scots — had grown taller and heavier, as a result of a better diet, within a single generation. "This epoch-making report of Boas," Walling noted, "shows that even children born within a few years after the arrival of their parents in this country differ essentially from their progenitors."

Then Walling homed in on a point that, had anyone but other left-wing intellectuals paid attention, might have persuaded at least some anti-intellectual fundamentalists to moderate their view of evolution. "The duty of man is not to study how evolution creates," Walling argued, "but to create evolution." Natural selection, far from being the efficient mechanism exalted by Spencer, was portrayed by Walling (as it is by evolutionary scientists today) as highly inefficient. "According to Darwin himself," Walling reminded his readers, "nature does all possible experiments as long as possible, that is, until that species is extinct. . . . Instead of being governed by the laws of chance, like Darwin's fortuitous variations, scientific experiments reduce the element of chance to the minimum. Men may make in a single year ten thousand times as many crucial tests as Nature blunders upon in ten thousand years."[19]

There is no evidence that such intellectual critiques of social Darwinism ever reached middle-class Americans around the turn of the century. For Americans on the anti-evolution side of the early culture wars, Darwin's theory of evolution was indistinguishable from its distortion by conservative social scientists, and religion — a combination of fundamentalism and the Social Gospel — was their weapon in the war against godless science and godless pseudoscience. Bryan, the champion of both anti-evolutionism and economic populism, seems not to have read Spencer or any of

Spencer's intellectual critics. For that matter, there is no evidence that he ever read Darwin. At the Scopes trial in 1925, Bryan quoted not from Darwin but from a crude 1914 high school biology textbook (*A Civic Biology*, by George Hunter) that presented an "evolutionary tree" attempting to estimate the number of creatures in each species. And although the text was filled with social Darwinist eugenics, Bryan did not mention that at all — even though the author had described the mentally ill as "true parasites," adding that "if such people were lower animals, we would probably kill them off to prevent them from spreading." That idea really should have been banned from classrooms, but the "monkey trial," as its popular nickname suggests, revolved solely around the clash between biblical literalism and the idea that man was descended from lower forms of life.

Perhaps, as the historian Michael Kazin suggests, Bryan simply had not read the provocative pages offering suggestions for what society might do to prevent the unfit from reproducing. Another likely explanation is that Bryan had so conflated social Darwinism and Darwin's own theory of evolution that he made no distinction between the two and took for granted that the jury, and his courtroom audience, would share his assumptions.[20] Conservative intellectuals like Sumner had distorted Darwin's ideas into an argument against all social reforms: if a brutal struggle for survival must characterize human existence in a state of civilization as well as in a state of nature, any attempt at reform instigated by the same human protagonists in that brutal struggle must be doomed. To that argument, a Christian populist like Bryan could only respond with an unequivocal no. He described survival of the fittest — a phrase he probably never realized had nothing to do with Darwin's views about what ought to be the behavior of civilized humans — as "the merciless law by which the strong crowd out and kill off the weak."[21]

It is not surprising that someone with as parochial an education as Bryan would confuse Darwin's theory of natural selection with Spencer's ideas about social selection, because the influence of Spencerian pseudoscience was such that even highly educated Americans (including some who rejected social Darwinism) made the same mistake. Theodore Roosevelt, who was completely familiar with the writings of Darwin, Huxley, and Spencer, spoke with regret in a 1912 speech to the American

Historical Association about the conflation in the public mind between the "doctrine of evolution" and the "doctrine of natural selection."[22] What Roosevelt really meant was that the public had confused Darwin's theory with Spencerian *social* selection. As a strong advocate of government action and Progressive reforms, Roosevelt accepted evolution in nature while rejecting the application of "survival of the fittest" to society. That a celebrated naturalist and historian could speak so imprecisely before a group of professional historians attests to the pervasiveness of Spencerian concepts even among opponents of social Darwinism.

The importance of social Darwinism in the history of American pseudoscience, anti-rationalism, and anti-intellectualism has been underestimated for a number of reasons, not least the fact that the pervasive upper-class intellectual ideology of social Darwinism was never called by that name at the height of its popularity in the United States. Unlike, say, communism, which had both a name and, after the Bolshevik Revolution, a home address in Moscow, social Darwinism was, as William James suggested (though he too never used the term), a metaphysical creed disguised in scientific plumes. Nameless philosophies surrounded by an amorphous scientific aura lend themselves more easily than well-defined ideologies to repackaging for new audiences in different eras.

Forgotten in their original form but not gone, the worst pseudoscientific ideas emanating from the late nineteenth century are constantly being marketed under new brand names in the United States. Social Darwinism has never died: it manifested itself as a bulwark of eugenics until the Second World War; in the tedious midcentury "objectivist" philosophy of Ayn Rand; and, most recently, in the form of market economy worship that presents itself not as political opinion but as a *summa* of objective facts. All of the theories included in the general category of social Darwinism may be summed up in the immortal line uttered by the hero of Rand's *The Fountainhead* (1943): "The only good which men can do to one another and the only statement of their proper relationship is — 'Hands off!' " Rand was an atheist, but Americans have managed to translate her social Darwinism into the language of faith: according to a recent poll, a majority mistakenly believe that "God helps those who help themselves" is a line from the Bible.[23]

It is useful to recall that intellectualism was not always synonymous with liberalism, especially economic liberalism, in the American mind. The irreconcilable conflict between evolutionism and biblical literalism would probably have been sufficient to engender a permanent fundamentalist antagonism toward all intellectuals and scientists who disputed any part of the creation story in Genesis. But the fact that so many prominent intellectuals once used Darwinian evolution as an argument against all social reform provided yet another reason for populist fundamentalists to dismiss not only the theory of evolution but the rich intellectuals who seemed to be its most ardent proponents. Bryan would no doubt have been astonished had anyone told him in 1896, when he made his "Cross of Gold" speech, that by the end of the twentieth century, many Americans who shared his religious beliefs would ally themselves with the political party favoring the interests of the rich — and that the Social Gospel, enjoining Christians to help their fellow man, would be replaced by the conviction that the Lord helps those who help themselves (and that the Bible tells us so).

Regardless of political reversals of position, two critical ingredients of American anti-intellectualism and anti-rationalism have remained largely unchanged since the 1890s. The first is the belief of a significant minority of Americans that intellectualism and secular higher learning are implacable enemies of their faith. The second is the toxin of pseudoscience, which Americans on both the left and the right continue to imbibe as a means of rendering their social theories impervious to evidence-based challenges.

CHAPTER FOUR:
REDS, PINKOS,
FELLOW TRAVELERS

Just as the pseudoscience of social Darwinism captivated many nineteenth-century
American intellectuals, the social pseudoscience of communism exerted a powerful
pull on twentieth-century American intellectuals between the world wars.* Unlike

---

* Like Herbert Spencer, Karl Marx appropriated
Darwin's theory of evolution by means of natural
selection in service to a social and economic ideology. For Marx, the struggle for survival in nature
paralleled the struggle between classes for survival
in society. It took Soviet power, with its endless
litany of failed economic and agricultural experiments, to reveal the social pseudoscience at the
heart of the most dogmatic interpretation of
Marxism (which, by then, had little to do with
what Marx actually thought). Under Stalin's
anointed biologist, Trofim D. Lysenko, Soviet
Party hacks maintained that the genetic makeup
of species could be altered by changes in the

social Darwinism, communism came to be seen as an anti-American philosophy by a majority of ordinary citizens, in large measure because the world's first ostensibly Communist state, the Soviet Union, became a superpower and America's chief international rival. But the suspicion of intellectuals originally engendered by the Old Left's attraction to Marxist ideology has outlasted communism itself. It is bizarre that even today, the *idea* of Communism with a capital "C" — seventeen years after the legal dissolution of its Soviet homeland and more than a half century since Marxism possessed any proselytizing appeal in the West — continues to be used in the United States as

---

political system — a theory, if you will, of political eugenics. With the ringing declaration that "the zygote is no fool," Lysenko launched a series of disastrous agricultural programs based on this premise, which also ignored Mendelian genetics. Soviet scientists who spoke out against Lysenkoist pseudoscience were dismissed from their jobs, and many died in the Gulag. The Lysenkoists, of course, always maintained that their own theories were pure, objective science — even when proved wrong by experiment after experiment, not in the laboratory but on real farms, with real animals and crops.

a bludgeon against various kinds of liberalism and liberal intellectualism. A week before the 1994 midterm elections, Newt Gingrich, architect of the historic Republican takeover of both houses of Congress, advised Republican lobbyists that the way to win was to portray Democrats as proponents of "Stalinist" policies and as opponents of "normal" American values.[1] Stalin had been dead for more than forty years and the Soviet Union itself had ceased to exist three years before Gingrich's comments. Yet the concept of a "Party line" without a Party — an idea that resurfaces repeatedly in the right-wing universe — still serves as a handy phantasm for impugning the patriotism of liberals and obscuring the distinctions among the many left-of-center American political movements since the Progressive Era.

Much of the groundwork for the American public's suspicion of the patriotism of intellectuals was laid during the xenophobic Red Scare after the First World War, when some of the nation's best known political radicals were of foreign birth. On November 11, 1918, the armistice ending combat was signed in a railway car in the French forest of Compiègne. A week later, the mayor of

New York prohibited public displays of red flags, the symbol of the year-old Bolshevik government in Russia. The same month, a peaceful Madison Square Garden rally of American Socialists, who detested the Bolsheviks, turned into a rout when hundreds of demobilized soldiers and sailors — indifferent to and ignorant of political distinctions on the left — stormed the doors of the Garden and had to be subdued by mounted police. The hunt for Reds was under way.

It is a long psychological reach from the isolationism that followed the First World War — when much of the public still yearned for a return to a more innocent era in which the nation was responsible neither for nor to the rest of the world — to the triumphalist acceptance of empire that followed victory over the Axis in the Second World War and saw Americans turn against those citizens thought to be overly sympathetic to our recent ally and chief international rival, Stalin's Soviet Union. Nevertheless, the first Red Scare, uniting isolationist and nativist tendencies with fear of the foreign ideology of Bolshevism, prepared the way for a more lasting public mind-set in which the politics of liberal intellectuals were regarded most charitably as expressions of naïveté about enemies of the American way of life — one more manifestation of the general gullibility of eggheads — and most harshly as a form of treason. The proportion of Americans who subscribe to this suspicion of liberal intellectuals (a.k.a. "the elites") and the depth of the suspicion vary considerably according to the political climate; but the negative image of the intellectual as pinko is always available for political exploitation during periods of social stress.

During the First World War, the government had prosecuted more than two thousand cases under a sedition law prohibiting "any disloyal, . . . scurrilous, or abusive language about the form of the government of the United States." In 1919, using lists compiled by a diligent and ambitious young employee named J. Edgar Hoover, the Department of Justice began targeting foreign-born radical intellectuals and political activists. On December 20, 249 immigrants involved in various forms of leftist politics — many had lived in the United States for decades and professed anti-Marxist anarchism rather than communism — were deported to the Soviet Union on a ship dubbed the "Red Ark" by the mass-circulation press. Most of the deportees were Jews born in territories of the former Tsarist empire. The best known passenger on the Red Ark was the fiery anarchist and feminist Emma Goldman — dubbed "Red Emma" by the press — who was sixteen when she immigrated to the United States from Russia in 1885 and was schooled not only on European social theorists but on Thomas Paine, Walt Whitman, Emerson, and Thoreau. She read the American writers for the first time in a New York City prison library in 1893, after being jailed for making a speech urging workers to take bread if they could not find jobs. Like Paine in Paris during the Jacobin Terror, Goldman knew betrayal of revolutionary ideals when she saw it. Her deportation to the Soviet Union would produce *My Disillusionment in Russia* (1923), one of the earliest, most powerful left-wing indictments of the budding Soviet totalitarian state under Lenin. Although Goldman, an international celebrity in leftist circles, was greeted warmly by Soviet officials in 1919, she soon discovered that the rest of her fellow deportees had been placed under military guard, "driven out of America for their political opinions, now in Revolutionary Russia again prisoners."[2]

Back in America, more than six thousand

Communists and Communist sympathizers had been rounded up and arrested in their homes and workplaces by the end of 1920. In a festive touch, Attorney General A. Mitchell Palmer, who called himself "the fighting Quaker," launched a series of coordinated raids on Party offices on New Year's Day, when the faithful comrades traditionally gathered to celebrate the holiday. Clarence Darrow, the nation's best known defense lawyer, would later describe the period as "an era of tyranny, brutality, and despotism, that, for the time at least, undermined the foundations upon which our republic was laid."[3] The American Civil Liberties Union, officially established on January 20, 1920, came into being as a direct result of the Palmer raids.

The first Red Scare lost steam fairly rapidly, as the nation moved into a decade of unprecedented prosperity and the public lost interest in the hunt for radicals — foreign or American-born. The crusade against Reds really ended in 1924, with the passage of a new immigration quota system designed to shut the Golden Door on immigrants from Southern and Eastern Europe — the fulfillment of a nativist dream dating from the 1880s. If radical labor agitation and alien intellectual philosophies were the work of foreigners, keeping foreigners out would surely remedy the problem. Ethnic prejudice and anti-Bolshevism worked in tandem to provide support for the limitations on immigration, aimed primarily at East European and Russian Jews and Italians, that would have such tragic consequences in the thirties for Jews trying to flee the Nazis.

Restrictive immigration policy was a direct and obvious consequence of the Red Scare; a more subtle but equally important result was the insertion of anti-communism into American cultural conflicts that had previously been viewed as homegrown battles between traditional religion and secularization. In the battle over evolution, Bolshevism took the place of Spencerian social Darwinism as the enemy of old-time religion. Even William Jennings Bryan, whose economic populism had always been as mighty a pillar of his political career as his defense of literal biblical faith, began to link Darwinian evolution with Bolshevism instead of with unconstrained capitalism. In 1924, just a year before the Scopes trial, Bryan used the revealing phrase "scientific soviet" to describe a cabal "attempting to dictate what shall be taught in our schools, and, in doing so, to mold the religion of the nation."[4]

Three enduring elements of twentieth-century American anti-intellectualism may be inferred from Bryan's rhetorical melding of fundamentalist faith with opposition to the world's first Communist state and its offical atheism. First and foremost is the portrayal of experts — not just a "soviet" but a "scientific soviet" — as an alien organism within the American body politic. Bryan then expresses resentment toward an educated minority seen as a separate class, determined to impose its views on the majority. Finally, this separate class is identified as an enemy of religion. Darwin's theory of evolution, which has always been seen by its opponents as ideological and metaphysical rather than scientific, tapped into the vague resentment most people feel toward experts on whom they depend but whose work they do not understand. (Consider the public's ambivalent attitude toward the medical profession today.) But the anti-evolutionists also drew on a deeper, more focused anger toward ideological intellectuals who presumed, by virtue of having read more books than the average person, to know what is best for society. The increasing importance of intellectuals as experts in the early twentieth century —

especially in the physical sciences and technology — did not, as far as most Americans were concerned, translate into intellectual authority on political, social, or religious questions.

The attraction of twentieth-century intellectuals to communism, although that attraction was, for most, only a brief flirtation, elicited a resentment resembling the fundamentalist response to intellectuals who promoted evolutionism. If evolutionism challenged the foundations of religious faith, Soviet Communism challenged the broader economic and political foundations of America's faith in itself. The challenge had little potency during the prosperous twenties but seemed much more real and potentially threatening after the 1929 stock market crash and the onset of the Depression — events that many Americans, not only Marxist intellectuals, saw as the beginning of the end of capitalism as they had known it.

For intellectuals who came of age between the First and Second World Wars and gravitated toward the political left, the possibilities ranged from New Deal liberalism — which was not, in fact, located on the left but at the very center of the American political spectrum in the 1930s — through various varieties of socialism with native as well as European roots, to, for a small minority, the Moscow-financed American Communist Party. But for every intellectual who actually joined the Party, there were unquestionably many more who sympathized with communism in general and with Stalin's Soviet Union in particular. They were known as "fellow travelers," a term not widely used in the United States until the Cold War and originally used in Russia to describe writers who actively engaged in literary propaganda on behalf of the Bolsheviks but did not join the Party.[*]

The 1930s vitiated the hopes of those who believed that restricting immigration would immunize Americans against the virus of radical philosophies. Throughout the thirties, American left-wing intellectualism and political radicalism, although greatly augmented by the presence of brilliant German Jewish refugees who got out in time, would

[*] "Fellow traveler" (*poputchik*) was not a pejorative in Russian during the early Soviet era but was always used as a pejorative in the United States after the Second World War. The Bolsheviks needed *poputchiki* during the twenties but dispensed with most of these less than wholehearted fellow travelers during the purges of the thirties.

become increasingly homegrown. The children of earlier generations of working-class immigrants, especially Jews, prepared to step onto the American intellectual stage (although their presence would not be fully felt in the larger culture until after the war). The most prominent intellectuals who came of age between the wars were American-born and should have had "Made in the U.S.A." stamped on the covers of their books. "I am an American, Chicago-born," the famous opening line of Saul Bellow's *The Adventures of Augie March* (1953), might have been the epigraph for the works of his entire Jewish American intellectual generation — regardless of politics.

A considerable imaginative leap backward is required to understand why so many American intellectuals of the thirties generation were deluded for so long not only about the real nature of Stalin's Soviet Union but about the likelihood of some sort of Marxist revolution taking hold and sweeping away capitalism in the United States. It is certainly easy to understand the attraction of communism in light of the panic and economic desperation of the early thirties, before the New Deal infused Americans with the hope that capitalism might reform itself. It is difficult, however, to comprehend the reasons why any intelligent citizen — intellectual or nonintellectual — could have continued to imagine after the 1936 election that Americans might actually be receptive to a radical change in their form of government. With the nation still in dark economic straits in 1936, Americans overwhelmingly reelected Franklin D. Roosevelt; the tiny Communist Party vote dropped from .3 percent to .2 percent of the electorate, while the American Socialist Party, always much stronger at the ballot box than the Communists, dropped from 2.2 percent to .4 percent. It would seem obvious that most citizens, even if on the far left of the political spectrum and still enduring personal economic hardship, had taken heart and hope from the New Deal.

Intellectuals, by contrast, were even more attracted to communism in the mid-thirties than in the early years of the Depression — partly, though not entirely, because they were more concerned than other Americans about the rise of fascism in Europe. Membership in the American Communist Party rose steadily between 1935 and 1939, to around seventy-five thousand, during the period known as the Popular Front. Throughout those years, the Soviets ostensibly dropped their objections to non-Communist leftist movements in order to make common cause against fascism, and the Party drew in not only intellectuals but Communist sympathizers in certain unions. At a time when many Americans underestimated the threat of Nazism and most were committed isolationists, the ideals of the Popular Front had enormous appeal to leftist intellectuals who saw Hitler (but not Stalin) for the evil creature that he was. The vast majority never joined the Party, and participation in organizations or literary endeavors sympathetic to Soviet-backed causes — the most urgent and appealing being opposition to Nazism — was the most common form of fellow traveling for intellectuals.

This was also the period when a sharp split began to emerge between Communists and anti-Communist liberals, the latter group including such disparate men as the progressive educator John Dewey and the philosopher Sidney Hook, who had been a Marxist and a supporter of the Communist candidate for president in 1932. In spite of their history of Communist sympathies, intellectuals like Dewey and Hook were not deceived when Stalin branded one old Bolshevik after another as traitors and disposed of both real and imaginary opponents in the purge trials of 1937 and 1938. There were also younger leftists who never flirted with Stalin's version of communism; the best descriptions of what it was like to be a fledgling soldier in the irregular army of the anti-Stalinist left are to be found in Irving Howe's and Irving Kristol's memoirs of their sentimental political education at the City College of New York from 1936 to 1940.[5] Howe and Kristol were on the same side back then, although Kristol would become the hardest of hard-line neoconservatives in the 1970s, while Howe would, to a considerable extent, remain true to the democratic socialist ideals of his youth instead of rejecting them as guileless unrealism.

The anti-Stalinists held forth in Alcove 1 of the City College lunchroom, and the Stalinists made their pronouncements from Alcove 2, whose denizens included Julius Rosenberg, destined to be executed for atomic spying. Howe's description, perhaps befitting a democratic socialist, makes Alcove 1 sound like a fairly jolly forum.

> You could walk into the thick brown darkness of Alcove 1 at almost any time of day or evening and find a convenient argument

about the Popular Front in France, the New Deal in America, the civil war in Spain, the Five-Year Plan in Russia, the theory of permanent revolution, and "what Marx really meant." . . . One friend, Izzy Kugler, had a large body of knowledge and near knowledge. In a clash with a Stalinist boy whom we had lured across the border into Alcove 1, Izzy bombarded him with figures about British imperialism, and when the poor fellow expressed disbelief, Izzy sternly directed him to the library where he could "look it up." A fact was a fact. But had Izzy really been hammering him with facts? I asked about those statistics and he answered with a charming smile that, well, he had exaggerated a little (which is to say, a lot), since you had to do *something* to get those Stalinist sluggards to read a book![6]

But for many intellectuals — even if they were not actually Party members — it took the 1939 Nazi-Soviet Pact, which allowed Hitler to gobble up Poland and thereby ushered in the Second World War, to reveal Stalin's absolute cynicism. Even so, after Hitler attacked Russia and the United States entered the war on the side of the Soviets and Great Britain, Soviet-led Communism regained the loyalty of many. Although the Party had lost nearly half of its American members after the Nazi-Soviet Pact, it doubled in size from 1941 to 1944, reaching a high point of about eighty thousand members.[7] It is easy to sympathize with the exasperation of the character played by Robert Redford in the 1973 movie *The Way We Were,* which chronicles the doomed postwar marriage of an apolitical WASP and a Jewish ex-Communist, played by Barbra Streisand. "Should we get in the war, should we not get in the war?" the WASP character asks his pinko lover. "Stalin's for Hitler, Stalin's against Hitler. It's all a lot of political double-talk, but you hold on. I don't know how you do it. . . ."

It takes another imaginative leap to understand the complicated relationship between the internecine intellectual battles over Soviet Communism in the thirties and the largely ineffectual, sometimes craven response of the liberal intellectual community to the anti-Communist inquisitions of the late forties and fifties. Many, arguably most, features of American anti-intellectualism — including religious fundamentalism and suspicion of too much education — have little or no connection to the real deeds of intellectuals. But the public's view of the relationship between intellectuals and communism is an exception to this rule, and that is the main reason why the intellectual wars over Stalinism in the thirties cannot be dismissed as an arcane chapter in American intellectual history. The Old Left intellectuals who had been savaging one another in the thirties over Stalinism were still doing it in the fifties — this time not only in "little" intellectual magazines but in the mass-circulation press and before congressional committees. The public became accustomed to the unedifying spectacle of fellow travelers and former Party members, including those who passed through the Party in revolving-door fashion, informing on one another before congressional and state legislative bodies.* The same intellectuals would have another go at one another in

* Irving Howe and Lewis Coser, whose anti-Communist liberal credentials are impeccable, make an airtight case, based on the American Communist Party's own documents, that the Party succeeded in repelling a majority of Americans who took the step of joining during the thirties. From July 1931 to December 1933, 70 percent of newly recruited members turned into Party dropouts. See *The American Communist Party: A Critical History,* pp. 528–29.

the late sixties and seventies, as some of the old anti-Communist liberals, like Kristol, metamorphosed into hard-line conservatives and inevitably discovered some Red Diaper babies — children of ex-Communists — in the ranks of the New Left.

The continuing fascination with the ancient relationship between some intellectuals and Soviet Communism — the right-wing and left-wing cottage industry of picking scabs off the wounds of the Alger Hiss case is a prime example — cannot be attributed solely to the activities of the handful of American Communists who actually spied for the Soviet Union or even to the broader phenomenon of fellow traveling. Another crucial factor in the postwar conflation of anti-communism and anti-intellectualism was the retrospective exaggeration by intellectuals themselves of their own importance and the importance of their twenty-year-old political and personal feuds.

Throughout the thirties, the Old Left intellectuals were a marginal group of highbrows addressing themselves and their ideas primarily to one another, in publications like *Partisan Review,* a bastion of anti-Communist liberalism by the late thirties, and *The Nation,* with an editorial policy much more sympathetic to Communism and the Soviet Union. Only in the late forties and fifties, when elements of highbrow culture began to manifest themselves in cultural institutions that reached a broader portion of the educated public, did many of the Old Left writers, artists, and scholars — Edmund Wilson, Mary McCarthy, Nathan Glazer, David Riesman, Daniel Bell, Lionel Trilling, and Sidney Hook, to name only a few — develop the larger careers, reaching educated, middle-class readers of popular fiction, literary criticism, and sociology, for which they are now known. These people were located at very different points on the political spectrum, but what they had in common was the memory of communism as the defining political issue of their young adulthood. Many remained as obsessed with their youthful political ideas — even if they had long since modified or abandoned them — as their congressional inquisitors.

I do not mean to suggest that communism was unimportant but that the significance of communism — specifically, Soviet Communism — as a cultural force in the United States was exaggerated not only by McCarthyite politicians but by intellectuals themselves. The exaggeration was promulgated by those who repented of their early communist sympathies as well as those who did not; by those who resisted the pressure to inform during the fifties and those who did not; by those who remained anti-Communist liberals with the emphasis on "liberal" and by those who abandoned liberalism altogether.

A typical overstatement appears in a 1993 memoir by Diana Trilling, an anti-Communist liberal who did not renounce her liberalism along with her fellow-traveling past. She argues that few Americans are capable of understanding "the extent to which Stalinism dominated American culture in the years before the Second World War: in art, journalism, editing and publishing, in the theater and entertainment industries, in the legal profession, in the schools and universities, among church and civic leaders, everywhere in our cultural life the Soviet Union exercised a control which was all but absolute."[8] The very use of the word "Stalinism" by an American intellectual is an artifact of the thirties, when not only the small minority of Party members but everyone with communist sympathies and Marxist beliefs was presumed to approve of Stalin and the Soviet Union. That these people *should* have taken a closer look at the realities of a system existing for them primarily as an intellectual abstraction is indisputable, but it is an entirely different issue from the scope of so-called Stalinist cultural influence.

If it is true that Americans today would not accept Trilling's notion of an "all but absolute" control of thirties culture by Stalinism, the rejection of such a one-dimensional analysis is rooted in a better understanding of reality than that displayed by many of the Old Left intellectuals. "Stalinism" did not, in fact, dominate the culture of most Americans, who had better things to do during the Depression and the Second World War than to contemplate the latest twists in the Party line. That a writer with the centrist liberal loyalties of Diana Trilling should describe the cultural influence of Stalinism in such absolutist terms reveals more about the inbred nature of the New York intellectual world of both her youth and old age than it does about the reach of Soviet ideology at any point in American cultural history. Intellectuals and artists with strong left-wing sympathies, which included communism, certainly were well represented in most of the industries and enterprises cited by Trilling; but that hardly translated into a cultural world in which the Soviet Union exercised a control that was "all but absolute." The offices of

New York magazines, the stages of Broadway theaters, and the sets of Hollywood movies were packed with fellow travelers as well as a few "card-carrying" Communists; but how did that translate into Soviet domination?

It is a fact that many international policies espoused by the Soviet government were also supported by American leftists and, after America's entry into the war, by rightists who stopped being isolationists on the day Pearl Harbor was attacked. Anti-Nazism belongs in this category, and it is true — especially in the late thirties — that a growing number of movies, plays, and novels reflected anti-fascist and not anti-Communist sentiments. The general public, unlike intellectuals, wanted to ignore both Hitler and Stalin throughout most of the thirties. Even after Great Britain entered the war and parts of London were being reduced to rubble on a daily basis by the blitz, it took all of President Roosevelt's political guile to sell the Lend-Lease program to the American public and push it through Congress. In August 1941, Congress passed the administration's bill to extend the Selective Service Act by just one vote — a measure of the strength of isolationism even after the Nazi armies had gobbled up most of continental Europe.

So if some anti-Nazi movies and novels written by fellow travelers helped to erode powerful isolationist sentiment, and to prepare public opinion for America's eventual entry into the war, was that a bad thing? Was the reading public a dupe of Stalin because it responded enthusiastically to John Steinbeck's *The Grapes of Wrath* in 1939? Steinbeck certainly had Communist friends, and he and his first wife, like many writers, visited the Soviet Union and allowed the wool to be pulled over their eyes. One can only assume that Stalin continues to dominate American culture from beyond his now inconspicuous grave, given that *The Grapes of Wrath* remains one of the most popular American novels of all time. Or perhaps it was another victory for Stalinism when Yip Harburg, a lifelong socialist, wrote the lyrics for "Over the Rainbow"? Not only Dorothy but the Tin Man, the Scarecrow, and the Cowardly Lion must have been Stalinist dupes. No matter that Harburg, who also wrote the lyrics for the 1932 Depression classic, "Brother, Can You Spare a Dime?", exemplified the kind of humanistic socialist for whom hard-core Communists had only contempt. He was blacklisted during the fifties anyway — a pinko mistaken for a Red.

One important lesson that the Old Left of the thirties failed to learn from the Red Scare generation was the indifference of nonintellectual Americans to distinctions among shades of pink and red. As far as ordinary Americans were concerned, anarchists, Trotskyists, Stalinists, and socialists, whether homegrown or imported, all belonged in the same boat — preferably a boat bound for Russia. The crucial importance of sectarian distinctions to leftist intellectuals, and the passion with which they attacked one another over their disagreements, would leave the entire intellectual community vulnerable to political attack when, once again after the Second World War, the public began to care about Reds.

More than a half century after the McCarthy era, the polarization of American politics has ruled out any consensus on either the justifications for, or the long-term cultural impact of, the hunt for domestic Communists that began shortly after the Second World War. Right-wing pundits and politicians frequently make astonishing claims linking those who oppose the war in Iraq today with those whose pro-Stalinist "treason" was unmasked during the McCarthy era. (Do a Google search combining the names "Stalin" and "Saddam Hussein," and see how many hits turn up in the right-wing blogosphere.) On the left, some journalists and historians use loaded words like "purges" to describe the firings of college teachers and blacklisting of entertainers and screenwriters during the late forties and fifties. I find this metaphor as offensive and inaccurate as the promiscuous use of the term "Holocaust" to describe all kinds of multiple murders. A purge is, by definition, something permanent: the Stalinist purges of 1937–38 condemned millions to death, either by immediate execution or starvation and hard labor in the Gulag. Somehow, the Hollywood blacklist, which lasted from 1948 until the early 1960s, does not exactly qualify as a purge; writers sent to the Gulag did not continue to make comfortable livings by producing screenplays under pseudonyms.

The period known in American shorthand as the McCarthy era (although McCarthy himself was not an important player at the beginning) extended roughly from 1946, when Winston Churchill memorably declared that "an iron curtain" had descended across the continent of Europe, to an indeterminate point in the second half of the fifties, when both politicians and voters seemed to lose interest in the spectacle of middle-aged men and women being called to account for ideas and associations that appeared as drab and played-out as many of the people sitting in the witness chairs. The facts are beyond dispute, regardless of how one views the goals and methods of the Communist hunters: several thousand people lost their jobs; several hundred went to jail; and two — Julius and Ethel Rosenberg — were convicted of atomic spying and put to death in the electric chair. In a book that expresses the conventional opinion of the left about the postwar anti-Communist crusades, the historian Ellen Schwecker asserts that "McCarthyism was amazingly effective" and "produced one of the most severe episodes of political repression the United States has ever experienced." The government investigations and congressional hearings represented "a peculiarly American style of repression — nonviolent and consensual. Only two people were killed; only a few hundred went to jail. Its mildness may well have contributed to its efficacy."[9]

Although mindful that general fear can be spread by relatively few arrests, I am not at all certain about the overall effectiveness of McCarthyism. Longevity is surely a critical measure of the success of any effort to stifle thought and intimidate dissenters, and by that measure, in spite of the unmeasurable toll in derailed careers and private fears, the crusade against Communists was a miserable failure. The rapidity with which new social protests emerged — the civil rights movement is the first and most obvious example — as anti-Red fever receded is the most powerful argument against overstating the overall cultural impact of the postwar hunt for Communists. The height of the McCarthy era is separated by less than a decade from the greatest triumphs of the civil rights movement; the no longer young but still immensely powerful J. Edgar Hoover did his best to persuade the American public that Communists were behind the battle for racial justice, but he did not succeed. If McCarthyite political intimidation had been truly effective in an enduring sense, the charge of Communist influence would have been enough to stop the civil rights movement before it ever had a chance to make its case to the American public at large.

The impact of the McCarthy era on both the individual fortunes and the general reputation of intellectuals in American society is also open to some historical dispute. At the time, the reputation of intellectuals was blackened in two ways. First, intellectuals — or people who looked and sounded like what intellectuals were thought to look and sound like — were indeed disproportionately represented among those called to testify before state and national investigating bodies, including the House Committee on Un-American Activities (HUAC) and McCarthy's Senate subcommittee on investigations.[*] It could hardly have been otherwise in view of the fact that, apart from certain unions in which the Party had gained a foothold, intellectuals had been the class most influenced not only by communism but by other, more democratic leftist movements. After the war, intellectuals with communist or, much more frequently, fellow-traveling pasts naturally tended to be employed in the teaching profession at all levels, in the arts, and in those offices of government requiring the services of statisticians, historians, political analysts, and publicists.

At the state as well as the national level,

[*] Academic scholars generally use the acronym HCUA, but I have used HUAC, the pronounceable acronym employed by the press and in conversation for more than sixty years.

the frequent presence of "eggheads" in the witness chair at loyalty hearings could not have failed to reinforce the general impression that intellectuals were, if not actual communists, sympathetic to a nation that was now an enemy of America. Many loyalty oaths, modeled after the Truman oath instituted for federal employees in 1948, were aimed at what were thought to be intellectual professions of particular importance — such as teaching — and reinforced the old American suspicion that knowledge itself could be a dangerous thing. Madison Avenue account executives, surely as strategically placed as teachers to influence the minds of America's youth, might also have been suspected by the public of harboring chronic un-American sentiments had they been required to take loyalty oaths in the forties and fifties by their professional associations.

Another powerful element in the suspicion of intellectuals fostered by the McCarthy era was an emotional melding of religion with anti-Communist patriotism, prefigured by but even more strenuously promoted than the same linkage had been during the Red Scare after the First World War. Bryan's depiction of evolutionary theory as the plot of a "scientific soviet" was mild in comparison with Billy Graham's declaration in 1954 that "Communism must die, or Christianity must die." As for Communists, "the devil is their God; Marx, their prophet; Lenin, their saint" — and Marx "spewed this filthy, ungodly, unholy doctrine of world socialism over the gullible people of a degenerate Europe." Like all fierce postwar anti-Communist crusaders, Graham was having none of the distinctions, so prized by intellectuals, between socialism and communism.[10] The influence of the strongly anti-Communist Roman Catholic Church was also much greater in the America of the fifties than the America of the twenties, and clerical anti-Communism was particularly strong in New York, the bastion of the Old Left intellectuals. During the 1950s, as a result of his television show *Life Is Worth Living,* Bishop Fulton J. Sheen (who was particularly proud of his success at converting former party members to Catholicism) would become the best known Catholic cleric in the United States. By then, the coupling of atheism with Communism had become a staple in the rhetoric of anti-Communist crusaders throughout the nation.

Intellectuals as a group were highly vulnerable on this score because many were, if not unabashed atheists, secular humanists with little regard for traditional religion. If communism could not be proved, atheism was a handy fallback, as it was in 1949 in the case of Luella Raab Mundel, ousted as head of the Fairmont State College art department in the small town of Fairmont, West Virginia. Mundel's case, like so many firings involving teachers at small, little-known institutions, would never have received wider attention had it not been described in detail in a national publication by a well-known author, William Manchester, who followed the case from start to finish in a 1952 article in *Harper's.* It seems that Mundel, by standing up at a seminar sponsored by the American Legion and challenging the view that liberals and communists were identical, aroused the ire of a powerful member of the West Virginia State Board of Education.

The board member demanded that the college president inspect Mundel's FBI file, and when it turned out that Mundel had no FBI record at all, she was fired anyway on grounds that she was an "atheist." When she sued for slander, Mundel was treated to courtroom speeches in which the opposing counsel described "atheists, Communists, horse thieves and murderers" in the same breath and demanded that academic institutions hire only teachers "without any high-falutin ideas about not being able to prove there is a God."[11] The slander suit was dismissed, and the state board of education went on to fire the president of the college, who had been Mundel's chief character witness. Because irreligion has been associated with foreign influences and too much learning from the earliest years of the republic, the popular American image of intellectuals as irreverent atheists has proved even more enduring then the image of intellectuals as pinkos. And although American intellectuals, like other Americans, are more likely to believe in some form of God than their European counterparts, it is perfectly true that intellectuals as a group tend to be secularists — especially when it comes to the conduct of government.

Finally, the image of intellectuals in the fifties was undermined by their own conduct as informers before state legislative and congressional investigating committees. No one likes informers, even when informers are providing what legislators and the public believe they have a right to know. To say this is not to engage in the retrospective moral judgment that comes all too easily to those of us who, thanks primarily to the fortunate timing of our births, have never been called on to risk middle-class liveli-hoods, much less anything more important, in the service of our moral or political convictions. The ex-Communists or onetime fellow travelers who named names of those they had known in leftist circles in the thir-ties and forties were able to continue to earn a living in their respective professions, but they were not liked, admired, or even toler-ated by their peers who had taken a differ-ent position. Furthermore, they were not even respected by many hard-line anti-Communists. Although some of the wit-nesses named names out of a genuine conviction that anyone who had flirted with Communism posed a threat to the United States and deserved to be outed, it was perfectly obvious — even to committed Communist hunters — that most of those testifying as friendly witnesses were acting out of principles no more exalted than those of any Mafia informer. Intellectuals and art-ists who named names, unless they had long been open and committed anti-Communists, looked weak and weaselly even to the congressional inquisitors de-manding their compliance. But a natural contempt for informers does not fully explain the gut-level anti-intellectualism that is one of the most destructive legacies of the relatively brief era when witnesses were called on not only to apologize for their own pasts but to wreck the lives of others.

With the exception of the small minority who had never abandoned their illusions about the Soviet Union, intellectuals in the forties and fifties were denouncing themselves for having once held opinions that were, though not praiseworthy, inseparable from and understandable within the social and international context of the thirties and the wartime alliance. To have been wrong about Soviet Communism was seen, by the public and also by many intellectuals themselves, not merely as a mistake but as something more like a sin — not only against their own government but before the bar of history. This condition is eloquently described by Arthur Miller, who was subpoenaed by HUAC in 1956, seven years after the overwhelming success of his play *Death of a Salesman* and four years after the Broadway production of *The Crucible,* with its implicit comparison of the Salem witch trials to the hunt for Communists.

Miller, who was never a Party member but who, like other writers of his generation, surely counted many former Communists among his friends, agreed to answer questions about his own political past and opinions but refused to name the names of others. Unlike many writers who made self-aggrandizing statements of principle against informing (the sanctimonious Lillian Hellman comes to mind) and then shielded themselves from going to jail by taking the Fifth Amendment, Miller did not take the Fifth and was convicted of contempt of Congress in 1957. His conviction, coming as it did in the twilight of anti-Communist fervor, was overturned on appeal. The parallel between the Salem witch trials and anti-Communist hysteria, Miller writes in his autobiography *Timebends,* was the guilt

of holding illicit, suppressed feelings of alienation and hostility toward standard, daylight society as defined by its most orthodox proponents.

Without guilt the 1950s Red-hunt could never have generated such power. Once it was conceded that absolutely any idea remotely similar to a Marxist position was not only politically but morally illicit, the liberal, with his customary adaptations of Marxist theory and attitudes, was effectively paralyzed. The former Communist was guilty because he had in fact believed the Soviets were developing the system of the future, without human exploitation and irrational waste. Even his naïveté in seeing Russia not as an earthly empire but rather as a kind of spiritual condition was now a source of guilt and shame.

. . . as in Salem, a point arrived, in the late forties, when the rules of social intercourse quite suddenly changed, or were changed, and attitudes that had been merely anticapitalist-antiestablishment were now made unholy, morally repulsive, if not actually treasonous then implicitly so. America has always been a religious country.[12]

The nonideological sector of the broad nonintellectual public — that is to say, the majority of Americans — did not exact lasting penalties from intellectuals and artists who responded as Miller did, by talking about themselves without informing on others. Furthermore, the turn of the historical wheel was relatively swift. By the early sixties, *The Crucible* was already considered enough of a classic to be included in many high school as well as college English classes. In my high school in Okemos, Michigan — hardly a center of left-wing politics — we studied *The Crucible* in my sophomore English class in 1961 even though the teacher avoided discussing the contemporary American political context.

Of course, many of those who did name names also went on to achieve fame and success, or further success, in their chosen professions. The director Elia Kazan's *On the Waterfront,* probably his best known movie and a commercial and critical success, was released in 1954, two years after he testified about his own brief Communist past and named names of friends in the theater who were also Party members in the thirties. When the eighty-nine-year-old Kazan was presented with a Lifetime Achievement Award at the 1999 Oscar ceremonies, there were bitter protests from those who could never forgive him for his testimony before HUAC. "I hope somebody shoots him," said Abraham Polonsky, a screenwriter blacklisted during the fifties. "It will be an interesting moment in what otherwise promises to be a dull evening."[13] Miller, to the surprise and displeasure of many, defended the award to Kazan. The two had once been close friends, before Kazan bowed to the HUAC demand to inform on former Communists. Although Miller's negative view of Kazan's role as an informer had not changed, he took the position that Kazan's achievements in the theater and film merited the award and that to deprive him of recognition for political reasons amounted to a rewriting of history. Of course, both Miller and Kazan were already famous at the time they were forced to decide how to respond to their congressional inquisitors, and fame affords protection as well as vulnerability.

For unknown college professors and teachers, like Luella Mundel, faced with the same choice — with their $5,000- to $10,000-a-year salaries on the line — there was only vulnerability. It will never be possible to assess the toll that government investigations exacted from men and women of modest means and modest ambitions when they were faced with the same choice as those with considerable resources, outsize talent, and first-rate lawyers. Even as the memory of who admitted to exactly what before whom was relegated to the dust-bin of American history, what remained was the suspicion that un-American ideas might be held and promulgated not only by a famous movie director, playwright, or Harvard professor, but by a local high school history teacher or a professor at a nearby state college attended not by the children of wealth and privilege but by everyone's children.

It is, however, one of the great cultural ironies of the postwar era that the fortunes of intellectuals improved in undreamed-of fashion during the very period when intellectuals as a class were being targeted by the anti-Communist crusaders in government. The expansion of higher education, fueled by the GI Bill, created an ever-increasing demand for teachers at the university level, and faculty members who had once earned salaries close to the poverty line were bringing home middle-class paychecks by the end of the fifties. Even as HUAC and its state equivalents focused on leftist influence in higher education, colleges were scrambling to hire intellectuals who, in the thirties, never dreamed that their knowledge would bring in a living wage. "By the early fifties word began to reach New York that it might be possible to find a job — no one I knew thought of it as a career — teaching in a university," recalls Irving Howe. Even though he was a member of a socialist group on the Attorney General's list of subversive organizations, Howe was hired in 1953 to teach in the English department at Brandeis University.

Founded in 1948, with a faculty and

student body almost entirely Jewish, Brandeis was more receptive to the many different kinds of Jewish leftists than many other universities — but that very receptiveness could have left the institution especially vulnerable to an anti-Communist inquisition. In any case, Howe's experience was far from unusual: even at the height of postwar American anti-Communism, the need for teachers was so great that it trumped any desire for political purity. The new professors, then in their thirties and forties, who formed the core of the expanding university faculties throughout the fifties had been shaped by the politics of the thirties. To eliminate every teacher who was once attracted to communism would have meant slamming the classroom door in the face of the growing numbers of Americans who wanted to and were financially able to send their children to college. Prosperity and demography were not on the side of those who wished to expunge leftists from cultural and academic institutions.

Thus the fifties, which generated the last serious Red Scare of the twentieth century, were also a turning point in America's need for services and products that only intellectuals — or, at the very least, people with educational credentials associated, whether rightly or wrongly, with intellectualism — could provide. For nonintellectuals, the combination of suspicion and need led to a conundrum, sometimes subliminal but often explicit, that has never been resolved. If intellectuals were politically untrustworthy, how could they be trusted with something as important as the education of American youth? But who else was qualified, by temperament and training, to assume the practical burden of instilling knowledge in the next generation and fulfilling the aspiration, so integral to old and new American dreams, of raising children who would exceed the achievements of their parents? At midcentury, the most profound hopes of adults who subscribed to what was then called middlebrow culture were vested in the higher education of their children. The parents of baby boomers dreamed of educating a son who would work with his head instead of with his hands and a daughter who would marry a man capable of earning a living with his head and not his hands. And that, too, posed a problem for Americans who needed intellectuals to help fulfill their hopes. Just as many Americans continued to suspect intellectuals of being pinkos, they also suspected — and the latter suspicion was better founded — that snobbish intellectuals looked down on many of the middlebrow aspirations of the people who were willing to pay for their services.

CHAPTER FIVE: MIDDLEBROW CULTURE FROM NOON TO TWILIGHT

Middlebrow culture, which began in organized fashion with the early nineteenth-century lyceum movement — when no one thought of culture in terms of "brows" — and extended through the fat years of the Book-of-the-Month Club in the 1950s and early 1960s, was at heart a culture of aspiration. Its aim was not so much to vanquish the culture of the gutter, although that was part of the idea, as to offer a portal to something more elevated. I grew up in a family permeated by and devoted to middlebrow values; that I never heard the term "middlebrow" until I took a college course in American intellectual history is the surest sign of how middle our brows were. Had I read Virginia Woolf's description of middlebrow (circa 1942) as "this mixture of geniality and sentiment stuck together with a sticky slime of calf's-foot jelly," I would not have recognized the mean-spirited caricature of my own home.[1] But then, I never heard the name of the highbrow Virginia Woolf until I saw the 1966 movie, starring Elizabeth Taylor and Richard Burton, of Edward Albee's play *Who's Afraid of Virginia Woolf?*[*] Some details of Woolf's portrait of English middlebrow gentility certainly applied to the Jacoby household in Okemos, Michigan, in the late fifties. We did indeed, as Woolf observed disgustedly, have "pictures, or reproductions from pictures, by dead painters" on our walls; my mother's taste ran to Van Gogh, Renoir, and Degas. I can still see the Degas ballerinas who adorned my bedroom walls, and it would not surprise me if that early exposure to middlebrow reproductions had something to do with a passion for art that did not emerge until my mid-twenties.

It is not that Americans with middlebrow ambitions were aiming for the highbrow — a term already in wide and often pejorative use, in the same sense that "egghead" would

* It is a pity that Woolf did not live to comment on the taking of her highbrow image and name in vain, not only by Albee but in *The Hours* (2002), in which the role of Woolf is played by the movie goddess Nicole Kidman, her beauty disguised by a large false nose.

231

be used in the 1950s — at the beginning of the twentieth century. In 1915, the literary critic Van Wyck Brooks observed that until the beginning of the twentieth century, it was assumed that "the only hope for American society lay in somehow lifting the 'Lowbrow' elements in it to the level of the 'Highbrow' elements." Brooks suggested, by contrast, that it was necessary for Americans to express themselves "on a middle plane between vaporous idealism and self-interested practicality."[2] The association of highbrow culture with "vaporous idealism" and lowbrow culture with "self-interested practicality" exemplified the widespread acceptance, by intellectuals as well as nonintellectuals, of the idea that devotion to the life of the mind must somehow be opposed to a decent regard for the exigencies of everyday life.

The distinctive feature of American middlebrow culture was its embodiment of the old civic credo that anyone willing to invest time and energy in self-education might better himself. Many uneducated lowbrows, particularly immigrants, cherished middlebrow values: the millions of sets of encyclopedias sold door to door from the twenties through the fifties were often purchased on the installment plan by parents who had never owned a book but were willing to sacrifice to provide their children with information about the world that had been absent from their own upbringing. Remnants of earnest middlebrow striving survive today among various immigrant groups, but the larger edifice of middlebrow culture, which once encompassed Americans of many social classes as well as ethnic and racial backgrounds, has collapsed. The disintegration and denigration of the middlebrow are closely linked to the political and class polarization that distinguishes the current wave of anti-intellectualism from the popular suspicion of highbrows and eggheads that has always, to a greater or lesser degree, been a part of the American psyche. What has been lost is an alternative to mass popular culture, imbibed unconsciously and effortlessly through the audio and video portals that surround us all. What has been lost is the culture of effort.

The fifteen-year period after the end of the Second World War has frequently, and mistakenly, been portrayed as a cultural wasteland by those whose memories of the fifties seem limited to Norman Rockwell's *Saturday Evening Post* covers and Richard Nixon's Checkers speech. Statistics tell a different story. In 1960, there were twice as many American symphony orchestras — 1,100 — as there had been in 1949. The number of community art museums had quadrupled since 1930. Recordings of classical music accounted for 25 percent of all record sales by the end of the fifties, compared with under 4 percent today. (The figure compares record sales in 1960 with CD sales in the early 2000s and does not take iTunes downloads into account. There is little reason, however, to think that classical music will be more popular among downloaders than it is among CD buyers.) "Art" movie houses also proliferated in the fifties; there were more than six hundred in 1962, compared with just a dozen in 1945.[3] What sophisticate-manqué of my generation can forget the thrill of seeing a foreign movie for the first time in an art moviehouse in a small midwestern college town? Finally, these were the years of the paperback book revolution, a development of fundamental importance to middlebrows because middlebrowism was, above all, a *reading* culture.

To be raised in a middlebrow family in the fifties meant that there were books, magazines, and newspapers in the house and that everyone old enough to read had a library card. If much of the reading material was scorned by highbrow intellectuals, the books certainly provided ample food for growth. It simply staggers me to recall the variety of popular contemporary or near-contemporary novels, some of which came to us through the Book-of-the-Month Club but primarily from the public library, scattered throughout the house during my childhood. A potpourri of favorite fiction read to tatters by age fifteen would include James Michener's *Sayonara, Tales of the South Pacific,* and *Hawaii;* Howard Fast's *Spartacus;* Lloyd C. Douglas's *The Robe* (as long as a book had something to do with ancient Rome, I did not care whether it was written from the perspective of a Christian, an atheist, or a lion); Irving Stone's *The Agony and the Ecstasy;* John Hersey's *The Wall;* James Jones's *From Here to Eternity;* Edwin O'Connor's *The Last Hurrah;* J. D. Salinger's *The Catcher in the Rye;* Nevil Shute's *On the Beach;* Herman Wouk's *Marjorie Morningstar;* and — a harbinger of things to come — Philip Roth's *Goodbye, Columbus.*

One of Roth's short stories, "Defender of the Faith," was printed in 1959 in *The New Yorker,* a magazine that bridged the gap between middlebrow and highbrow and was revered in our home as a weekly emissary from the capital of sophistication and excitement. My hodgepodge of contemporary fiction was only dessert reading, on top of the classics — the meat and potatoes my parents never pushed but somehow assumed I was ingesting. And they were right: I had read a good deal of Shakespeare, Twain, and Dickens (my favorite "old" novelist), as well as a fair amount of first-rate eighteenth- and nineteenth-century poetry, by the time I began high school. A true middlebrow by Woolf's definition, I had read almost no poetry or fiction written in the early decades of the twentieth century.

In addition to reading and displaying reproductions of works by dead painters, middlebrow parents promoted an interest in history and current affairs. When you took summer vacations, they always included places of historic significance: Lexington and Concord, Gettysburg, Hyde Park, Appomattox. (Yes, the *BOMC News* had alerted us to Bruce Catton's *A Stillness at Appomattox* in 1954.) As soon as Edward R. Murrow's *I Can Hear It Now* broadcasts were released on the new long-playing 33 rpm records, my parents bought them so that we could hear the famous speeches of Winston Churchill, Franklin Roosevelt, and

Adolf Hitler — as well as Murrow's broadcasts from London during the Second World War. When William Shirer's *The Rise and Fall of the Third Reich* (another BOMC selection) was published in 1960, I could hardly wait to read it because I had already heard the voices of some of the monumental historical figures of the era. My parents were also great believers in the educational value of television; when CBS's high-minded *Playhouse 90,* featuring live productions of plays, appeared in the television listings, we were allowed to stay up even if it was a school night.

There were of course many individual, ethnic, and regional variations in middlebrow culture. My father had no use for the weighty outlines of history and philosophy, such as Will Durant's *The Story of Civilization,* considered *de rigueur* in so many middlebrow homes and much mocked by intellectuals. His view, and it probably would have surprised him had he known that it was shared by the people he called eggheads, was that the story of civilization was already available on library shelves, in books by novelists and poets whose words were open — without the necessity of writing a check to some commercial enterprise — to anyone who cared to read them. Classical music was another middlebrow enthusiasm that never entered our home. Many of my contemporaries, brought up in Jewish and Italian-American households, recall the strains of the Metropolitan Opera broadcasts that permeated their houses every Saturday afternoon. I never heard an opera or, for that matter, any piece of classical music other than Tchaikovsky ballet scores until my first post-college boyfriend, whose middlebrow upbringing *had* included children's symphony concerts, introduced me to what I had been missing.

I make no claims about the greatness of the middlebrow mosaic of my childhood; the certification of pieces of cultural experience as "great" in order to market them to middle- and lower-middle-class Americans in search of guidance was a justifiable source of amusement — and not only, as my father's distrust of cultural arbiters indicated, on the part of highbrow intellectuals. I look back on the middlebrow with affection, gratitude, and regret rather than condescension not because the Book-of-the-Month Club brought works of genius into my life but because the monthly pronouncements of its reviewers were one of the many sources that encouraged me to seek a wider world. In our current infotainment culture, in which every consumer's opinion is supposed to be as good as any critic's, it is absurd to imagine that a large commercial entity would attempt to use an objective concept of greatness as a selling point for anything. That people should aspire to read and think about great books, or even aspire to being thought of as the sort of person who reads great books, is not a bad thing for a society.

Moreover, highbrow and middlebrow culture in America were always more closely and fruitfully intertwined than members of each group — especially the highbrows — were willing to admit. Although it was possible, in the first three decades of the twentieth century, for American intellectuals to emerge from intellectually and educationally improverished lowbrow backgrounds, cultural leaps of such magnitude were the exception rather than the rule. The increasing specialization of knowledge, as well as a growing demand for formal academic credentials, had closed off self-education as a route to various professions and also to less measurable but even more important cultural enthusiasms. There would be little or no room in the new American century for the self-taught marvels of the nineteenth century — an honor roll including, among many others, Clarence Darrow, Frederick Douglass, Thomas Edison, Robert Ingersoll, Abraham Lincoln, Mark Twain, and Walt Whitman.

Most of the prominent American-born intellectuals who came of age in the early decades of the twentieth century, before the First World War and in the twenties and thirties, were the offspring of solidly middlebrow families that placed a high value on formal education — regardless of the parents' economic status, ethnic background, or the far more powerful factor of race. To read the memoir of the great African-American historian John Hope Franklin, born in 1915, about growing up in a poor but proud and cultured family in Oklahoma, or an account by Diana Trilling (1905–1996) of a prosperous childhood as the daughter of assimilated Jewish immigrants in Brooklyn and the suburbs of New York City, is to be struck by the broad reach of middlebrow aspirations that transcended geography, class, and race. Young Diana took violin and voice lessons and dreamed, in an unfocused way, of becoming a singer; sixteen-year-old John wanted to hear a live performance of an opera so much that, over the objections of his parents, he acquiesced to segregated seating in Tulsa so that he could attend the visiting Chicago Civic Opera Company's performances of *La Traviata* and *La Bohème*. Franklin's parents believed that Negroes should pass up "optional" public activities, such as opera, rather than give in to segregation. "I chose to attend, and to this day I continue to reproach myself," Franklin writes. "Whenever I hear *La Traviata* or *La Bohème*, I still, more than seventy years later, recall the humiliating conditions under which I learned to appreciate those great musical masterpieces."[4] But Franklin did learn to appreciate those masterpieces; his middlebrow parents and middlebrow teachers, in segregated schools, had made sure that white America could not segregate his mind.

Even when there was no trace of middlebrow culture in a future intellectual's family tree, there was generally an outside middlebrow mentor to light the way. Former *Commentary* editor in chief Norman Podhoretz, in *Making It* (1967), describes the process by which his emergence from the tough, lower-class Brownsville section of Brooklyn in the 1940s was facilitated by a high school English teacher:

In those days it was very unusual, and possibly even against the rules, for teachers in public high schools to associate with their students after hours. Nevertheless, Mrs. K. sometimes invited me to her home, a beautiful old brownstone located in what was perhaps the only section of Brooklyn fashionable enough to be intimidating. I would read her my poems and she would tell me about her family, about the schools she had gone to, about Vassar, about writers she had met, while her husband, of whom I was frightened to death and who to my utter astonishment turned out to be Jewish (but not, as Mrs. K. quite unnecessarily hastened to inform me, *my* kind of Jewish), sat stiffly and silently in an armchair across the room, squinting at his newspaper through the first *pince-nez* I had ever seen outside the movies. But Mrs. K. not only had me to her house; she also — what was even more unusual — took me out a few times, to the Frick Gallery and the Metropolitan Museum, and once to the theater, where we saw a dramatization of *The Late George Apley,* a play I imagine she deliberately chose with the not wholly mistaken idea that it would impress me with the glories of aristocratic Boston.[5]

If middlebrow culture was transmitted by

families and individual mentors, the transmission always occurred within the broader context of mass marketing. Beginning in the 1820s, with the invention of the Napier Steam Press, capable of turning out an unheard-of total of 2,000 copies per hour, middlebrow culture was always closely linked to technological changes in book publishing. In the twentieth century, especially during the prosperous decades following both the First and Second World Wars, the power of advertising greatly expanded the audience for the products of middlebrow publishing. As Joan Shelley Rubin notes in her lively and evenhanded *The Making of Middlebrow Culture* (1992), the publishing industry, long a WASP gentleman's club, was considerably altered in the 1920s by an influx of young Jewish executives who believed that the potential book market was much larger than had traditionally been imagined and who were determined to reach that market through more aggressive advertising tactics.[6]

The first manifestation of the enormous public demand for books that would make sense of proliferating and specialized knowledge was the success in 1920 of H. G. Wells's *The Outline of History,* the archetype of the many outlines, including Durant's blockbuster series, that would continue to sell strongly until the sixties. Wells was already famous as the author of *The Time Machine, The Island of Dr. Moreau,* and *The War of the Worlds* (although he would become much more famous after Orson Welles's panic-inspiring 1938 radio version of the fictional invasion of planet Earth by Martians). But Wells's recognizable name was only one factor in the success of his outline. The First World War provided the critical stimulus to the public's desire for a greater understanding of both the origins of civilization and the potential threats to what humans had built: the horror at the ability and willingness of supposedly civilized nations to tear one another and themselves apart was fresh in the minds of Americans and Europeans.

In his introduction to the second edition of the *Outline,* published in 1926, Wells provided a moving description of the emotions that had impelled him to begin the original project in 1918. "It was the last, the weariest, the most disillusioned year of the great war," Wells wrote. "Everywhere there were unwonted privations; everywhere there was mourning. The tale of the dead and mutilated had mounted to many millions. Men felt they had come to a crisis in the world's affairs. They were not sure whether they were facing a disaster to civilization or the inauguration of a new phase of human association . . . there was a widespread realization that everywhere the essentials of the huge problems that had been thrust so suddenly and tragically upon the democracies of the world were insufficiently understood. . . ." When people tried to recall the "narrow history teaching of their brief schooldays," Wells observed, they found nothing but "an uninspiring and partially forgotten list of national kings and presidents." The public had been taught history in "nationalist blinkers, ignoring every country but their own."

The answer to the old-fashioned, parochial view of history was, of course, Wells's very own book, with its broad attempt to encompass the biological origins of human life along with European, Middle Eastern, and Asian cultures. Why should a generalist not try to take on the entire history of the universe at a time when "all the intelligent people in the world, indeed — who were not already specially instructed — were seeking more or less consciously to 'get the hang of' world affairs as a whole. They were, in fact, improvising 'Outlines of History' in their minds for their own use"?[7] The first edition, a runaway best seller that topped nonfiction lists for two years, went through twenty-two printings.

Eighty years later, Wells's *Outline* holds up well, and it seems likely that the books, packed with engaging illustrations, were not just bought for show but were actually read. One of the most striking aspects of this mass-marketed project is the author's un-abashed acceptance of and proselytizing for Darwinian evolution. Wells had been one of Thomas Huxley's students. The 1926 edi-tion, published just a year after the Scopes "monkey trial," begins with a cheerfully colored full-page frontispiece of three dinosaurs titled "Animals That Lived before the Coming of Man." One can only wish that book would be made available today to the 25 percent of American high school biology teachers who told University of Texas researchers that dinosaurs and hu-mans inhabited the earth simultaneously.

The first nine chapters of the *Outline,* which deal with the origins of the universe and of all animal, including human, life, make up a naturalistic and scientific coun-terpart to Genesis. George Bernard Shaw made the tongue-in-cheek suggestion that the early chapters of Wells's *Outline* be substituted for Genesis altogether. That such books were often purchased by libraries, and by parents hoping to expose their school-age children to the best of contemporary thought, says a good deal about the secular character of middlebrow culture at the time. "And first, before we begin the history of life," Wells opens,

> let us tell something of the stage upon which our drama is put and of the background against which it is played. . . .
>
> In the last few hundred years there has been an extraordinary enlargement of men's ideas about the visible universe in which they live. At the same time there has been perhaps a certain diminution in their individual self-importance. They have learnt that they are items in a whole far vaster, more enduring and more wonderful than their ancestors ever dreamed or suspected. . . .
>
> The curtain that hid the unfathomable abyss of stellar distances has been drawn back only in the last three centuries. Still more recent is our realization of the immense duration of our universe in time. Among ancient peoples the Indian philosophers alone seem to have had any perception of the vast ages through which existence had passed. In the European world,

until little more than a century and a half ago, men's ideas of the time things had lasted were astonishingly brief. In the *Universal History,* published by a syndicate of booksellers in London in 1779, it is stated that the world was created in 4,004 B.C. and (with a pleasant exactitude) at the autumnal equinox, and that the making of man crowned the work of creation at Eden, upon the Euphrates, exactly two days' journey above Basra. The confidence of those statements arose from a too literal interpretation of the Bible narrative. Very few even of the sincerest believers in the inspiration of the Bible now accept them as matter-of-fact statements.[8]

The secularizing influence of middlebrow culture has generally been overlooked, in part because it bore little resemblance to the atheism and agnosticism that permeated highbrow intellectual circles. Like liberal Protestantism and Reform Judaism since the last quarter of the nineteenth century, middlebrow thought took an accommodationist stance toward the relationship between science and religion. With their emphasis on information and facts, middlebrow authors tended to adopt the argument implicit in Wells's *Outline,* which suggests that science and religion need not conflict unless one insisted on a literal interpretation, inappropriate in light of contemporary knowledge, of holy books.

This is precisely the position taken by many scientists today in the battle against the religious right's attempts to incorporate creationism and intelligent design into high school biology classes, but the current attempt to reconcile evolution and religion is essentially reactive and defensive in nature. The old middlebrow outlines, by contrast, were unabashed in their proselytizing for the scientific and the rational; while Wells did not tell people they had to abandon religion in order to accept evolution, he did tell them that they had to abandon the idea that the Bible was a factual historical record. Because middlebrow culture placed a high value on scientific discoveries and progress, its degeneration has played an important role in the melding of anti-intellectualism with the fundamentalist war on science during the past three decades.

Will Durant, whose outlines of civilization would eventually outsell Wells's pioneering work, was also a thoroughgoing secularist, an atheist who had once intended to become a Roman Catholic priest. Before his name became the household word that so annoyed my father, Durant worked on another enormously successful commercial venture, the Little Blue Books published by the eccentric Emmanuel Haldeman-Julius. The son of a Russian immigrant bookbinder, Haldeman-Julius was a publishing genius who combined the pamphleteering of the Enlightenment, the ideas of cooperative economic effort that characterized the Progressive Era, and the new mass-marketing techniques of the 1920s. His project was a "university in print," which would sell for 25 cents apiece in a standard three-and-a-half by five-inch, 15,000-word format with blue covers. He launched his venture in 1919 in a fashion that was simplicity itself: a direct mail appeal asking for $5 each from 175,000 onetime subscribers to a defunct socialist weekly paper. In return, Haldeman-Julius promised the subscribers fifty pamphlets containing some of the world's great literature and ideas, to be delivered over time as each publication came off the presses.

The first two Blue Books were *The Rubáiyát of Omar Khayyám* and Oscar Wilde's *The Ballad of Reading Gaol.* By the early twenties, Haldeman-Julius's press was turning out 240,000 Blue Books a day, including portions of the Bible, the Greek classics, Goethe, Shakespeare, Voltaire, Zola, H. G. Wells, and the lectures of Robert Ingersoll. In 1922, Haldeman-Julius commissioned Durant to summarize the writings of major philosophers, including Plato, Aristotle, Spinoza, and John Dewey; the pamphlets were advertised as aids to "Self-Education and Self-Improvement." But Durant's expertise was also emphasized: he was listed as Will Durant, Ph.D. (at a time when doctorates were rare) or as Dr. Will Durant (a usage already considered pretentious by highbrows and false advertising by medical doctors).[9] In 1925, Haldeman-Julius proposed that all of Durant's Blue Book essays on philosophy be marketed in a single volume by a large publisher — which turned out to be the newly established firm of Simon & Schuster. Durant's *The Story of Philosophy,* a 600-page tome, consisted almost entirely of word-for-word reprintings of the Blue Book texts. By the end of 1925, *The Story of Philosophy* headed the best-seller list, establishing the prototype for the *Story of Civilization* series that would make Durant a millionaire many times over. Haldeman-Julius, having commissioned the original essays, also became a wealthy man.

The Little Blue Books, with their strong

debt to and component of nineteenth-century freethought as well as twentieth-century psychology, philosophy, and sociology, represented the traditional American ideal of self-education, as distinct from the dawning era of self-help, which would place far more emphasis on improving personality and public image than on improving one's mind. More than 300 million Blue Books were published from 1919 to 1949, just before commercial publishers began entering the paperback marketplace in a big way. During the Depression, fifty secondhand Blue Books could be bought for a dollar apiece and resold after reading, ensuring a huge circulation among the vast majority of readers who could not afford hardcover books. "There is no way of estimating how many millions read these books," notes Harry Golden. "Other thousands upon thousands of 'little blue books' floated around hospitals, penal institutions, CCC [Civilian Conservation Corps] camps, and military barracks."[10]

No discussion of middlebrow commerce would be complete without mentioning two enterprises most mocked by intellectuals: the Book-of-the-Month Club (BOMC), founded in 1926, and the "Great Books of the Western World" collection, introduced with immense fanfare in 1952. The latter was a 100-pound, 32,000-page, 54-volume, 25-million-word behemoth, consisting of 440 works by 76 authors, published by the *Encyclopaedia Britannica* for only $10 down, with the total price of $249.95 to be paid on the installment plan. All of these facts were reported by the highbrow critic Dwight Macdonald in a scathingly funny attack published in *The New Yorker*.[11] Given the well-known scrupulousness of the magazine's fact checking, it must be assumed that scales and yardsticks were applied to the actual books in the publication's former offices on West Forty-third Street in Manhattan and that the word count was as precise a figure as could be attained in the pre-computer era. Macdonald's byline in *The New Yorker* was one of the many signs of the convergence of middlebrow and highbrow cultures after the Second World War.

The Great Books were vetted and chosen by a board headed by Robert Hutchins, the legendary former chancellor of the University of Chicago (which, as a leading player in the academic-cultural-industrial complex, was part owner of the *Britannica*), and Mortimer J. Adler, a former philosophy professor at Columbia University in the twenties and later at the University of Chicago under Hutchins. As might be expected, philosophers and theologians were heavily represented — Plato, Aristotle, Augustine, Thomas Aquinas, Descartes, Spinoza, Hegel, Kant, but (mystifyingly) no Nietzsche, Marx, or Freud. The series naturally included most of the big literary names before the beginning of the twentieth century — Homer, Aeschylus, Sophocles, Euripides, Chaucer, Dante, Shakespeare, Cervantes, Milton, Tolstoy, Dostoyevsky. Twentieth-century fiction was largely ignored, and the omission was logical because the arbiters of middlebrow taste were, as Woolf observed, unremittingly hostile to modernism in literature as well as the visual and performing arts. A posh and financially and culturally incestuous banquet was held for "founding subscribers" at New York's Waldorf-Astoria Hotel, and an ingratiating after-dinner speech was made by the Book-of-the-Month Club judge Clifton Fadiman, also host of the popular radio quiz show *Information Please.* Fadiman, who had been a student of Adler's at Columbia, told the assembled customers that they were the equivalent of the "monks of early Christendom" because they had taken on the task of preserving, through another Dark Age, "the visions, the ideas, the deep cries of anguish, the great eurekas of revelation that make up our patent to the title of civilized man."[12] "Civilized" meant civilization as defined by the gatekeepers of greatness on the installment plan.

The eurekas of this particular civilization originated in a seminar organized by Adler in 1943 for Chicago business executives. Dubbed the "Fat Man's" class — for the size of the pocketbooks, and perhaps the girth, of the participants — the Chicago seminar led to the formation of similar groups across the nation, enrolling some 20,000 Americans by 1946. Contemporary observers attributed much of the enthusiasm for the seminars to a renewed realization of the fragility of civilization, comparable to the reaction that produced the demand for outlines of history after the First World War.[13] There was also a strong element of conspicuous consumption in both the seminars and the Great Books series. One advertising executive who participated in Adler's seminar summed up the commercial pitch by devising slogans for each of the Great Books under discussion. Aristotle's *Ethics* was encompassed with the line: "The rich don't know how to live, but they sure know where."[14]

The Great Books, unlike the outlines of the twenties, were launched at what would prove to be a commercially inauspicious time for such an expensive hardback venture — the very point when the marketing of books was about to be transformed by paperback publishing. Macdonald noted that all of the authors in the series were still in print and that their works could be purchased separately at a price much lower than $249.95; what he did not know, in 1952, was how much cheaper every great book would be in paperback within a few short years. But as Macdonald and my father said in their nearly identical rants on the subject, the Great Books were intended not so much to be read as to prove to the world that one was the sort of person who did read and who could afford the price of a conspicuous display of printed volumes. One of Macdonald's most telling points was that the selection of books made little allowance for the fact that in some fields, especially science, later knowledge contradicts earlier received truths, thereby rendering the authors of outdated versions of the truth (like Hippocrates) relevant only to the history of their particular disciplines.

Macdonald places Aquinas, who basically

repackaged Aristotle for Roman Catholic theology, in the same category. It is easy to sympathize with a reviewer stupefied by Aquinas's musings on such questions as "Whether We Should Distinguish Irascible and Concupiscible Parts in the Superior Appetite?" or "Whether an Inferior Angel Speaks to a Superior Angel?" Still, one never knows what any reader might learn when he or she happens to open a Great Book. When I was around age eleven, and a student at St. Thomas Aquinas School in East Lansing, Michigan, I had a friend whose family owned the entire set of books, which fascinated me chiefly because of the amount of space they took up in the crowded living room of a good Catholic household with ten children. On one overnight visit, I opened a volume of Aquinas — its stiff binding suggesting that it had never been opened before — and read more of the *Summa Theologiae* than was good for anyone who was supposed to grow up to be an orthodox Catholic. I was actually looking for explanations of some of the nuns' teachings that had begun to strike me as utter nonsense. Why were there three persons in God, not four or five? Who made God? Why would God arrange things so that babies would be born with a stain of sin?

Aquinas had answers, all right, and they seemed even more absurd to me than the simpler formulations of the Baltimore Catechism. The "infection" of sin was automatically passed on through "procreation" — I had been specifically searching for anything about procreation — and therefore the means of procreation themselves were particularly infected. I am sure that I would have gotten around to doubt and atheism eventually, but reading a handy chunk of the *Summa* hastened the day. That there is virtue in making knowledge readily available, even in a dreary, pretentious, highly selective format, is a truth that many satirists of middlebrow culture failed to grasp.

The Book-of-the-Month Club fell into a different category from the Great Books project, in that the former was designed primarily to entertain rather than to enlist Americans in the legions of "the monks of early Christendom." At the same time, the BOMC judges always displayed a strong predilection, in their fiction as well as nonfiction selections, for books that were, in a literal sense, heavy with informational content. From its founding in the twenties until the mid-sixties, when hardback book clubs began to lose much of their raison d'être as a result of competition from paperbacks, BOMC epitomized middlebrow and middle-class American taste. Like the Great Books project, BOMC was based on the idea that ordinary people needed to be shepherded through the thickets of culture by better-educated and more sophisticated guides. A 1927 advertising brochure summed up the club's pitch by appealing to the desire for convenience and simultaneously playing on the customer's intellectual insecurity. Employing a nannyish tone, the brochure cited the prototypical American "booklover" who hears about an interesting-sounding book, says to himself, "I must read that," but then fails, through indolence and memory lapses, to follow through on his good intentions. The BOMC went on to paint a pathetic picture of the remorseful slackard: "Perhaps afterward, in a group of bookish people, again he hears the book recommended. He confesses sadly that he had 'never got round to reading it.' "[15]

The values of those in charge of BOMC selections in the twenties and thirties were embodied by the judging board's first chairman, Henry Seidel Canby, a onetime Yale English professor, founding editor of the *Saturday Review of Literature,* and representative of the genteel tradition in American letters. Canby was an antagonist of literary realism and modernism, although his anti-modernist views would soften somewhat over the decades. Born in 1878, he had serious reservations about such disparate contemporary writers as William Faulkner, Ezra Pound, T. S. Eliot, Ernest Hemingway, Thomas Wolfe, F. Scott Fitzgerald, James Joyce, and D. H. Lawrence — none of whose works were picked as a main selection in the twenties and thirties. (In 1940, Hemingway would finally make it with *For Whom the Bell Tolls*.) Those omissions alone could certainly constitute an indictment of middlebrow taste before the Second World War. But centrist literary taste was not static: Hemingway, Wolfe, and Fitzgerald, and to a lesser extent Faulkner, would become middlebrow literary icons after the Second World War. Nor can it be argued that the BOMC fiction and nonfiction selections of the twenties and thirties were without literary merit. Main selections during the period included Erich Maria Remarque's *All Quiet on the Western Front*, Sigrid Undset's *Kristin Lavransdatter*, Willa Cather's *Shadows on the Rock*, Frederick Lewis Allen's *Only Yesterday*, Richard Wright's *Native Son*, and Ignazio Silone's

Bread and Wine.

After the war, BOMC selections, as well as the many other books reviewed in the subscribers' newsletters, began to reflect a wider range of tastes, although the judges' belated homage to Faulkner and Heming- way resulted in the selection of books vastly inferior to the authors' earlier works. The book club, like middlebrow culture itself, was at the height of its influence from the late forties through the early sixties. The list of books reviewed in the BOMC news from 1947 to 1965 includes many works of fic- tion and nonfiction that not only had a major impact at the time but have stood the test of time: Norman Mailer's *The Naked and the Dead;* Truman Capote's *Other Voices, Other Rooms;* Arthur Miller's *Death of a Salesman* (in 1949, the first play ever chosen as the club's main selection); George Orwell's *1984;* J. D. Salinger's *The Catcher in the Rye;* Ralph Ellison's *Invisible Man;* Shirer's *The Rise and Fall of the Third Reich;* James Baldwin's *Nobody Knows My Name* and *The Fire Next Time;* Joseph Heller's *Catch-22;* Rachel Carson's *Silent Spring* (reviewed in 1962 by Supreme Court Justice William O. Douglas, a passionate environmentalist); Mary McCarthy's *The*

Group; Harper Lee's *To Kill a Mockingbird;* and *The Autobiography of Malcolm X.*[16]

Many of these books would probably have been best sellers of a lesser order of magnitude without any notice from BOMC, whereas others — most notably *Catch-22* — did not immediately attract favorable notice from critics and surely benefited from being brought to the attention of BOMC subscribers. What must be said of this list is that it contains many books that, though they were all "good reads," also made intellectual demands on their audience and challenged much of the received opinion of the period. That the BOMC also endorsed many books that have not stood the test of time and are of interest today only because of what they reveal about contemporary conventional wisdom is equally true. One of my youthful favorites — Wouk's *Marjorie Morningstar* — whose 565 pages explore the earth-shaking importance of a Jewish princess's loss of her virginity — belongs in the latter class.

Middlebrow historical novels, perennial best sellers throughout the fifties and early sixties, fell into another category altogether. Highbrow critics looked down on the fiction of authors like James Michener and Irving Stone, but the sheer amount of meticulous historical research that went into the making of these novels is an important measure of the gap between popular culture then and now. Only recently have serious critics begun to appreciate the virtues of the heavily researched historical novels of the middlebrow era. In an article in *The New York Review of Books* in 2006, the art critic Ingrid Rowland makes a telling comparison between *The Agony and the Ecstasy,* Irving Stone's best-selling 1961 historical novel based on the life of Michelangelo, and Dan Brown's 2003 blockbuster *The Da Vinci Code.* Stone's 703-page novel is faithful to what is known about Michelangelo and is suffused with real art history. *The Da Vinci Code,* by contrast, distorts art history in the service of a supernatural thriller that has nothing to do with the real Leonardo, even though many gullible readers eagerly seeking out the *Code* sites in Europe — and providing a new source of income for neglected cathedrals — are unaware of the spurious nature of the evidence. Commenting on a major exhibition of Michelangelo's drawings, Rowland observes that the biographical notes in the catalogue bear a strong resemblance to the novel because "Stone's careful research used the same sources to tell the same tale. . . . In these days of *The Da Vinci Code,* with its slapdash analysis of Leonardo and its yarns about the Holy Grail, Stone's novel looks especially impressive, not least because he managed to present Michelangelo's attraction for men sympathetically in days when that was not so easy."[17]

The historical accuracy of Stone's novel was not replicated in the 1965 movie, in which Michelangelo, woodenly played by Charlton Heston, was given a female love interest. The final scene features Heston "sweating amid the marble quarries of Cararra, [while he] conjures up the celestial vision of a dirty brown Sistine Chapel as the heavens resound with the (as yet unwritten) *Hallelujah Chorus.*" Both the novel and the movie of the *Code* are equally unburdened by the facts of art history. One of Brown's most comically anachronistic claims is that the somewhat effeminate image of the "beloved disciple" John in Leonardo's *Last Supper* was really intended to represent Mary Magdalene. Ergo, the "Code." In fact, John was always represented in Renaissance art as a youth with flowing locks because he was thought to have been the youngest of the twelve apostles. The notion that the John in Leonardo's fresco was really Mary Magdalene was necessary to Brown's thesis that Jesus did not die on the cross and that he eventually married Mary, who was pregnant with his baby at the time of the crucifixion.[18]

I read *The Agony and the Ecstasy* when I was fifteen and was so fascinated by Stone's descriptions of the Sistine Chapel ceiling and Michelangelo's sculptures that I sought out reproductions in an art book in a library for the first time. That kind of connection between popular middlebrow culture and high culture is so obvious that it is almost impossible to understand why the idea of a reader's actually learning something important from such works was dismissed so contemptuously by highbrow critics of the thirties, forties, and fifties. How did Virginia Woolf think a girl in museumless Okemos, Michigan, was supposed to acquire an inkling of what great sculpture might look like? I could not, after all, take the Tube to the British Museum to see the frieze that Lord Elgin swiped from the Parthenon.

The sheer length of many best-selling novels attested to the middlebrow reader's desire for as much information as possible. Book buyers were interested in long reads, not quick reads. Allen Drury's *Advise and Consent* (1961), a political novel of more than 700 pages, did not confine itself to political skulduggery and sex in Washington but provided a carefully researched portrait of the procedures of the House and Senate. (This novel also offered one of the first sympathetic portraits of homosexuality, in the person of a tortured, closeted gay Mormon senator from Utah, in popular American fiction. I suspect that I was not the only teenager who learned about the existence of homosexuals — and the pain they endured while concealing their sexuality — from reading *Advise and Consent.*) Michener's *Hawaii,* which ran to more than 900 pages, covered everything from Presbyterian missionary history to the geological origins and characteristics of tsunamis.[*] If these hefty novels often lacked literary grace, their length also attests to the diminution of literate America's attention span during the past forty years.

America's postwar affluence and the expan-

[*] I immediately thought of *Hawaii* when I read about the number of lives lost in the December 2004 Indian Ocean tsunami because many people, watching the tide suddenly recede, had walked out to see the creatures and coral formations revealed on the ocean floor, only to have the tsunami wave return with deadly force. Michener describes a similar scene in his novel.

sion of higher education were the driving forces in the rising demand for all of the products of middlebrow culture, from books to those cheap reproductions of great paintings. And money also drove the cultural shift that saw an unprecedented mingling, at least on the printed page, of intellectual highbrows and middlebrows. This shift was a source of considerable anxiety and embarrassment to the very highbrows who profited from publishing their work in middlebrow magazines, but the eagerness of middlebrow editors to provide a forum for — or co-opt, depending on one's point of view — genuine intellectuals was surely a tribute to the vitality of American culture at the time. A pinko past, even if one might be called on to explain it publicly at any time, did not prevent left-wing intellectuals from obtaining book contracts, reporting for newspapers, writing for or editing popular magazines, or generally benefiting from the rising demand for all types of cultural commentary.

By the 1950s, some of the most prominent New York intellectuals who had come of age in the thirties — known (to themselves) as "the family" and predominantly but by no means wholly Jewish — had broken out of their small, highly politicized intellectual magazines. In the forties and fifties, the bylines of highbrow writers began appearing in the decidely upper-middle-class *New Yorker* and even in mass-circulation magazines like the *Saturday Evening Post*. Heading the list of those who published regularly in the *The New Yorker* was Dwight Macdonald, one of the leading figures in the entangled bunch of New York intellectuals whose brilliance was exceeded only by their propensity for savaging one another over everything from serious matters like Stalinism to quibbles about whether it was possible to like lowbrow and middlebrow Hollywood movies and retain any claim to intellectual stature. Macdonald, who had attacked *The New Yorker* in the thirties (in *Partisan Review*) for its middlebrow commercialism, began writing for the enemy in the forties. With his impeccable contrarian credentials, he apparently had no qualms about feeding at the hand he had once bitten. Not so the young Norman Podhoretz, who, when asked to write book reviews for the magazine in the early fifties, fell into a dither of anxiety about what selling out would do to his intellectual status in New York. How could a true intellectual sully himself by writing for a publication whose pages were filled with ads for fashionable

Fifth Avenue department stores, diamond jewelry, vintage champagne, and expensive WASP resorts? Podhoretz's tortuous answer: it was all right to appear in *The New Yorker* because it "was never exactly a middlebrow magazine, for it has its roots in, and was perhaps the only remaining literary exemplar of, the cultural traditions of the premodernist period — the period, that is, before the highbrow-middlebrow split occurred."[19] Oh, never mind!

Edmund Wilson, Mary McCarthy, Lionel Trilling, and Alfred Kazin, among others, either lacked Podhoretz's delicate sensibilities or were sensible enough to realize how ridiculous such intellectual snobbery really was. In the late forties, Irving Howe, one of many men of his generation who faced the rude shock of trying to make ends meet after their GI Bill benefits ran out, had taken a part-time job reviewing books for *Time* before he eventually landed his job as an English professor at Brandeis. The conservative Luce publishing empire had, ironically, kept numerous radical New York intellectuals financially afloat over the years; Macdonald was once a staff writer for the business magazine *Fortune.* Some female members of "the family" even wrote for women's magazines. When Diana Trilling began contributing to *Partisan Review* in the late forties, she had already published in *Glamour* — undoubtedly a first for both magazines. In her memoir, Trilling looks back on the cultural moment of intermingling between middlebrow and highbrow with a shrewd sense of what the presence of genuine intellectuals in large-circulation magazines meant for postwar American society. She recalls that

> the editor of one of the popular women's magazines would tell me that there had been a recent moment in which the editors of all the large-circulation journals . . . had had to decide whether to seek a more general public or, as she put it, to "raid *Partisan Review.*" The magazines which chose the latter course increased their readership; those which strove to become more popular lost circulation. What she was describing was the moment in the cultural life of this country in which what had previously been a virtually unnavigable distance between the world of high seriousness and our more popular culture began suddenly to narrow.[20]

I suspect that the editor's talk about a connection between highbrow bylines and increased circulation was a prevarication designed to flatter Trilling, but the fact that anyone in charge of a popular magazine would bother to tell such a fib only reinforces Trilling's point about the narrowing of cultural distance. The gap would narrow even further during the early sixties, as the Kennedy administration made astute use of intellectuals to highlight the difference between the New Frontier and the staid Eisenhower administration. By that time, the writings of intellectuals were widely reviewed in newspapers and magazines intended for a much broader educated public. Four examples from the first half of the sixties were Paul Goodman's *Growing Up Absurd,* originally published in *Commentary* (before Podhoretz abandoned liberalism and turned the American Jewish Committee's flagship publication into the voice of neoconservatism); Hannah Arendt's *Eichmann in Jersualem;* Baldwin's *The Fire Next Time;* and, perhaps most striking, Michael Harrington's *The Other America,* all published in *The New Yorker.* Harrington's book was closely read by intellectuals in the Kennedy and Johnson administrations and helped give birth to Lyndon Johnson's war on poverty.

271

Yet even as middlebrow culture, bolstered by highbrow contributions, seemed at its most robust, it was entering a period of gradual enfeeblement fostered by social forces that first manifested themselves in the mid-fifties and became more dominant in the sixties. The most important of these was of course television, a luxury that, in the course of just one decade, came to be considered a necessity. The new medium could not corrupt highbrow culture, because there basically was no highbrow culture on the air, but it could and did help to corrupt middlebrow culture.

Many of the men who shaped the early television era had decidedly middlebrow aspirations; they saw "quality" programming, from the dramas broadcast on *Playhouse 90* to Edward R. Murrow's documentaries, as a complement to rather than a competitor with middlebrow institutions like the BOMC. Not every component of a television and radio network was expected to make a large profit. Popular programs with mass appeal would subsidize more serious programs with a narrower audience — a philosophy that also ruled book publishing at the time. The classic example on television was the relationship between Edward R. Murrow's hugely popular *Person to Person,* on which he conducted celebrity house tours and interviewed stars like Liberace and Humphrey Bogart, and *See It Now,* which featured serious, hard-hitting, and controversial documentaries. *Person to Person,* which made Murrow's face as familiar in households with television as his voice had been during the radio era, premiered in the autumn of 1953, just three weeks before one of Murrow's most memorable *See It Now* programs on the human fallout of the congressional hunt for Communists. The *See It Now* documentary chronicled the travails of Milo Radulovich, an Air Force Reserve officer forced to choose between his military commission and his parents, who allegedly had Communist associations. Murrow's biographer reports that "when a friend ragged Murrow once in afteryears about 'hamming it up on *Person to Person* — don't say you don't enjoy it,' he [Murrow] turned to the man in sudden anger: 'Listen, do you know what I can get *away* with because *Person to Person* is such a big hit?' "[21] Yet the serious side of television, and the more serious people in its first generation, were rapidly losing out to the unstoppable entertainment side of the new medium.

The corruption of middlebrow aspirations by mass entertainment values was embodied most dramatically in the fifties by the rigged quiz shows — a "sticky slime of calf's-foot jelly" if ever there was one. The quiz show phenomenon, which began with *The $64,000 Question* in 1955 and ended abruptly in 1958 with a New York grand jury investigation revealing that many contestants were given answers in advance, combined the middlebrow reverence for facts with the mass appeal of any get-rich-quick scheme. My family was among the millions who tuned in to watch brainiacs like Dr. Joyce Brothers dominate *The $64,000 Question* (in her case, everything was on the level) on the strength of, among other specialized areas of knowledge, her vast store of facts about boxing. And we were watching the show *Twenty One* when Charles Van Doren, a lecturer in the English department at Columbia University and the son of the legendary English scholar Mark Van Doren, vanquished his opponent, Herbert Stempel, according to a script in which both had been fed the answers and told exactly what to do to keep the show's suspense going. Van Doren, an intellectual prince, carried himself with the air of the dreamy Ashley Wilkes as played by Leslie Howard in *Gone With the Wind*. Poor Stempel, who looked like what he was — a classic nerd and a Jew in an America where Jewish intellectuals had not yet become fashionable — never had a chance in the popularity contest. Popularity with the audience determined who would be told by the network to give the right answer and who would be required to take a dive.

Some of the questions on *Twenty One* really were difficult, in the sense that anyone without a broad reading background would be unlikely to come up with the answers. On the night of the fixed match between Stempel and Van Doren, however, the questions were ridiculously easy. Van Doren was asked to name the actress (Eva Marie Saint) who played Marlon Brando's girlfriend in *On the Waterfront*. Stempel, who was, as it happened, a movie buff, was asked the simple question of which film won the 1955 Oscar for best picture. The answer was *Marty,* starring Ernest Borgnine, but Stempel went along with the script and pretended not to know.

I was eleven years old, and what I remember is that everyone in my family, except my eight-year-old brother, knew the answers to both questions. My father, an accountant and reformed gambler, snickered and said, "Do you know what the odds are against a lonely guy from Brooklyn *not* knowing that *Marty* won the Oscar last year?" My mother replied in a shocked voice, "Bob, I don't think the television networks would dare to do something like that. Stempel probably just got nervous and forgot." Dad snickered again and said, "Just wait and see."

Nearly three years later, Van Doren admitted before a congressional committee that he had perjured himself when he denied involvement in the rigging of the show before the New York grand jury. In 1959, Van Doren, still weaseling in his testimony, admitted that he had been the "principal symbol" of the quiz show deception but claimed that he had also been a victim because he did not know, at the beginning, how thoroughly rigged the proceedings would be. Coming as they did at the end of the Eisenhower era, the quiz show scandals have often been cited as the miner's canary for what would become a general loss of faith in American cultural and political institutions during the following decade. That may be true — I certainly think the revelations had a considerable impact on those who were my age at the time — but the disillusionment centered more on individual cheaters like Van Doren than on television or any other American institution. Van Doren's life was wrecked, in part because he came from an intellectual milieu where this type of cheating was seen as traitorous not only to the public, not only to oneself, but to the sacred vocation of scholarship.

The network executives who presided over the fiasco quickly found a commercial solution to what they perceived as a purely commercial problem: they substituted multiple sponsors for the single sponsors who had pressured the shows to retain some contestants and dispose of others. What the shows had been selling was a combination of fact-based knowledge, celebrity, and money; the possession of certain kinds of knowledge, and the ability to recall facts before an audience of millions, could provide both fame and fortune. In the fallout from the quiz show scandals, network executives dispensed with the middlebrow facts and kept the celebrity and the money, proceeding from shows with difficult questions to shows in which fourth-graders could come up with most of the answers. However disappointed Americans may have been in Van Doren, television itself emerged largely unscathed, free to continue the expansion of its influence at the expense of the print culture.

At first, the process was all but imperceptible. The precipitous decline of reading and writing skills, now attested to by every objective measure — from tests of both children and adults to the shrinking number of Americans who read for pleasure — was more than two decades away. Books still mattered enormously, not only at the beginning of the sixties but also throughout the social convulsions of the late sixties. Yet there were visible signs and portents for those able to read them. Afternoon newspapers were beginning to lose readers throughout the country, in metropolises and small towns, by the early sixties, and evening papers would be well on their way to becoming an extinct species by the end of the decade. Venerable old middlebrow magazines like the *Saturday Review* were also hemorrhaging subscribers, as new editors and owners tried desperately, with little success, to put a more trendy gloss on their hopelessly earnest middlebrow format and contents. Even the mass-circulation titans of the Luce empire had begun to lose ground by the mid-sixties.

Again, the main reason was television, which came into its own as the chief source of breaking news during the days following President Kennedy's assassination. Although few cultural observers saw it coming, all print media were already struggling to survive in the lengthening shadow of television. In this precursor of twilight, middlebrow culture — so long an instrument of self-education for those who aspired to something above the lowest common denominator — had nowhere to go but down.

During the past decade, middlebrow culture has once again attracted the attention of various social commentators, most with a right-wing political ax to grind. Cultural conservatives today like to place blame for the decline of the middlebrow not on the profit-driven infotainment industry but squarely on lefties and pinkos — both the New Left of the sixties and the highbrow Old Left of the thirties. David Brooks, a columnist for *The New York Times* and a ubiquitous stuffy pundit on television, assigns a heavy share of the blame to highbrow radical intellectuals, such as Macdonald, Wilson, Mary McCarthy, and the art critic Clement Greenberg, who were shaped by the thirties and became even more culturally influential in the fifties and sixties. "The intellectuals launched assaults on what they took to be middlebrow institutions," Brooks writes darkly, "attacks that are so vicious that they take your breath away."[22]

What Brooks must have had in mind was Macdonald's blast against everything middlebrow in his essay "Masscult and Midcult," published in *Partisan Review* in 1960 and read at the time mainly by that journal's small readership. Macdonald did have some very nasty things to say about both mass culture and middlebrow culture.

> *Life* is a typical homogenized magazine, appearing on the mahogany library tables of the rich, the glass cocktail tables of the middle class, and the oilcloth kitchen tables of the poor. Its contents are as thoroughly homogenized as its circulation. The same issue will present . . . an editorial hailing Bertrand Russell's eightieth birthday (A GREAT MIND IS STILL ANNOYING AND ADORNING OUR AGE) across from a full-page photo of a matron arguing with a baseball umpire (MOM GETS THUMB); nine color pages of Renoir paintings followed by a picture of a roller skating horse. . . . Somehow these scramblings together seem to work all one way, degrading the serious rather than elevat-

ing the frivolous . . . that roller skating horse comes along, and the final impression is that both Renoir and the horse were talented.[23]

It should be noted that Macdonald considered *Life* a Masscult, not a Midcult, magazine. One skating horse seems a fair bargain for nine full pages of Renoir paintings. But Macdonald could not have imagined a mass-circulation magazine world, just around the corner, in which no editor would dream of devoting nine pages to any form of real art. At that point, Henry Luce was still crying all the way to the bank.

But Brooks's notion that the *Partisan Review* crowd was in some way responsible for the collapse of middlebrow culture is ludicrous. First, intellectuals did not have that kind of influence on the general public, in spite of their visible presence in middlebrow cultural venues. The forays of intellectuals into middlebrow publications — in the case of *The New Yorker,* upper-middlebrow publications — did nothing to undermine and everything to improve the quality of those magazines. If Americans stopped buying *Life* and *Look* at some point in the sixties, it was not because they had paid attention to writers like Macdonald but because still pictures, even by some of the nation's best photographers, could not provide the excitement of film footage on television. When intellectuals attacked institutions like New York's Metropolitan Museum and the Museum of Modern Art for pandering to popular taste, no one outside the intellectual community — and not too many intellectuals outside New York City — paid the slightest attention. The sixties saw the beginning of a sharp rise in museum attendance; museums, probably because they did not depend on the printed word, were among the few middlebrow institutions to emerge from the sixties and seventies in a stronger financial and cultural position.

Macdonald saw Midcult as a greater threat than Masscult because the former represented "a corruption of High Culture" that was "able to pass itself off as the real thing." Examples of Midcult passing itself off as the real thing included Thornton Wilder's *The Skin of Our Teeth* (indebted to Joyce's *Finnegans Wake* but nevertheless "pretentious and embarrassing"); the Museum of Modern Art; Vance Packard's bestselling books *The Hidden Persuaders* (1957) and *The Status Seekers* (1959); the infiltration of design features adapted from Bauhaus modernism into pop-up toasters, supermarkets, and cafeterias; and the American Civil Liberties Union, described as "once avant-garde and tiny . . . now flourishing and respectable." The inclusion of the ACLU on the list is especially bewildering, given that the ACLU's battles against censorship were more frequently fought on behalf of High Culture than Midcult. The main question as Macdonald saw it in 1960 was whether all of what he labeled Midcult atrocities merely represented "growing pains" on the road to High Culture.

Don't rising social classes always go through a *nouveau riche* phase in which they imitate the forms of culture without understanding its essence? And won't those classes in time be assimilated into High Culture? It is true that this has usually happened in the past. . . . Before the last century, the standards were generally agreed on and the rising new classes tried to conform to them. By now, however, because of the disintegrative effects of Masscult . . . the standards are by no means generally accepted. The danger is that the values of Midcult, instead of being transitional — "the price of progress" — may now themselves become a debased, permanent standard.[24]

Macdonald almost had it right. Americans would move toward a debased culture as generally accepted standards were defined downward; but it was Masscult, not Midcult, that triumphed. And the dyspeptic jeremiads of highbrows looking down on the bourgeois middle class had nothing to do with what happened. Middlebrow's salient features — an affinity for books; the desire to understand science; a strong dose of rationalism; above all, a regard for facts — had been taken for granted since the beginning of the twentieth century by large numbers of Americans who wanted a better life for themselves and their children. However one regarded middlebrow culture at the beginning of the 1960s, the erosion of its values was neither predicted nor hastened by aging highbrow intellectuals who assumed that Midcult would emerge triumphant from the long era of postwar prosperity. Middlebrow values would soon face a sustained challenge not only from the New Left — a much more plausible villain than the graying Old Left for conservatives — but from an anti-intellectual right that would establish the framework for a counter-counterculture beneath the sixties' media radar. Middle-class America would no longer leaf through magazines that featured reproductions of Renoirs along with photographs of equine skaters, because both the Renoirs and the horses' legs emerging from roller skates would soon be displaced by a cavalcade of vulgar images inviting comparisons to a very different portion of the horse's anatomy.

CHAPTER SIX:
BLAMING IT ON THE
SIXTIES

The Sixties, with a capital "S," are unquestionably the favorite whipping post for those
who apparently believe that American anti-
intellectualism and anti-rationalism first
manifested themselves somewhere between
the Beatles' 1964 debut on *The Ed Sullivan
Show* and the 1969 Woodstock festival
embodying the slogan: "We Are the People
Our Parents Warned Us Against." When
both conservatives and liberals talk about
what Philip Roth once described as the
"demythologizing decade," they are generally referring to political and social rebellion from the left, including the civil rights,
antiwar, and early feminist movements, as
well as everything that came to be known as
"the counterculture" — the sexual revolution, experimentation with mind-altering
drugs, disruptions of university life, and,
last but not least, the reign of rock music
over the young. Moreover, most debates

about the sixties are based on the premise that the social protests of the decade were largely the doing of the baby boom generation.

The conflation of these movements and cultural forces is a serious historical error, as is the premise that people in their late teens and early twenties were the most influential instigators of demands for social change. Irving Kristol could not have been more wrong when he asserted in 1977 in *The New York Times Magazine* that "the radicalism of the 60s was a generational movement, bereft of adult models and adult guidance."[1] Kristol was recalling the days of his radical youth in the thirties, before he turned his back on Trostskyism and socialism and began his journey toward right-wing Republican adulthood. Nevertheless, he viewed the left-wing activists of the thirties as superior to the radicals of the sixties, because the Old Left, however philosophically misguided, was "decidedly an adult movement, in which young people were permitted to participate," rather than the "bewildering and self-destructive tantrum" of the puerile New Left. Of course, most of the people providing the "adult guidance" for radical intellectuals of Kristol's generation were either Stalinists or Trotskyites.

Notwithstanding the famous admonition against trusting anyone over thirty, many leaders of the various protest movements of the sixties were long removed from their bright college years.[2] Martin Luther King, Jr., was thirty-four when he delivered his "I Have a Dream" speech from the top step of the Lincoln Memorial in 1963. The same year, when *The Feminine Mystique* was published, Betty Friedan was forty-two. Daniel Ellsberg was forty when he leaked the Pentagon Papers to *The New York Times* in 1971. Gloria Steinem was thirty-seven when she helped found *Ms.* magazine the following year. As for the antiwar movement, some of its most respected and indomitable figures were men and women whose children and, in some instances, grandchildren had already reached draft age. Dr. Benjamin Spock, the Reverend William Sloan Coffin, and Bella Abzug, to name just three, were heroes to younger antiwar demonstrators. What the conservatives really meant — what they still mean today — by their dismissal of all social protests of the sixties as a giant temper tantrum was that regardless of age, anyone who thought there was something very wrong with American society was acting like a baby. To characterize opponents as children — or, as the sixties bashers contend, demon seed — obviates any necessity to engage their arguments in serious fashion.

The first half of the sixties, despite the shock of the Kennedy assassination and the social unrest associated with the civil rights movement, was a basically stable period that continued the more hopeful cultural trends — including the battle for racial justice and the movement to control nuclear arms — of the late fifties. One reason for the burgeoning fortunes of liberal intellectuals in the early sixties was the developing public consensus that nuclear war, however deeply Americans might dislike Communists, was no longer an acceptable option — something that left-wing intellectuals had been saying for years and that Kennedy articulated as government policy in his famous 1963 American University speech calling for negotiations with the Soviets on a nuclear test-ban treaty. Not even a decade separated the days of my childhood, when schoolchildren were drilled in hiding under their desks to protect themselves from atomic attack, from the years when Americans began to pack movie theaters to see films, including *On the Beach* (which led the way in 1959), and *Dr. Strangelove* and *Fail Safe,* both released in 1964. There was also a sea-change in attitudes toward nuclear scientists who, backed up by expertise as well as civic passion, had spoken out against the arms race in the heated anti-Communist climate of the early fifties. The physicist J. Robert Oppenheimer, known as "the father of the atomic bomb," had been deprived of his security clearance in 1954 after speaking out strongly against the arms race with the Soviet Union and in favor of international control of atomic energy. In 1963, a more mature Kennedy, chastened by his experience of nuclear brinkmanship with Nikita Khrushchev during the Cuban missile crisis, conferred the Enrico Fermi Award for lifetime achievement in science on Oppenheimer. The shift in public opinion had come about so naturally and peacefully — middlebrow magazines and books helped educate the public about what would happen to the United States even if it emerged on the "victorious" side of a nuclear conflict — that the change did not seem radical to a majority of Americans. Presidents of corporations, as well as the president of the United States, were saying things that might have brought them a subpoena from HUAC or Joe McCarthy's subcommittee in the early fifties. Even the trauma of Kennedy's assassination did not truly shake the sense of optimism that permeated those years before America's involvement in Vietnam changed everything.

The radically rebellious half of the sixties, whether one regards the period in a positive or a negative light, truly began with the escalation of the war in Vietnam in 1965 and 1966. Those sixties — what people usually mean when they excoriate or celebrate the decade — really lasted until the mid-seventies, when Saigon fell, the last American soldiers came home from Vietnam, and exhausted participants in the various protest movements started having babies, climbing the corporate ladder, or discovering forms of self-help and spirituality suited to the "Me Decade." During the rebellious sixties, it often seemed (and not only to those over thirty) that someone was saying the unsayable on a daily basis. Joseph Heller's *Catch-22,* set near the end of the Second World War and originally published in 1961 to mixed notices by bewildered reviewers, became a best seller many times over in the late sixties, as the public began to contemplate the irrationality of the Vietnam War. Novels did not have to be overtly political to derive energy from an environment in which both external censorship and self-censorship had lost much of their force.

Roth's best-selling *Portnoy's Complaint,* published in 1969, is a case in point. The connection between the novel's scandalous success and contemporary social upheavals has been best described by the author himself:

Without the disasters and upheavals of the year 1968, coming as they did at the end of a decade that had been marked by blasphemous defiance of authority and loss of faith in the public order, I doubt that a book like mine would have achieved much renown in 1969. Even three or four years earlier, a realistic novel that treated family authority with comical impiety and depicted sex as the farcical side of a seemingly respectable citizen's life would probably have been a good deal less tolerable — and comprehensible — to the middle-class Americans who bought the book, and would have been treated much more marginally (and, I suspect, more hostilely) by the media that publicized it. But by the final year of the sixties, the national education in the irrational and the extreme had been so brilliantly conducted by our Dr. Johnson, with help from both enemies and friends, that, for all its taste-less revelations about everyday sexual obsession and the unromantic side of the family romance, even something like *Portnoy's Complaint* was suddenly within the range of the tolerable. Finding that they *could* tolerate it may even have been a source of the book's appeal to a good number of its readers.[3]

Unlike Roth, many Americans who lived through the sixties have forgotten that the nation's education in the irrational, which often included attacks on rationality itself, was being conducted from both the right and the left. Some of these assaults, certainly the most widely publicized ones, came from the New Left and were experienced with particular force on university campuses. Others, however, came from the religious and political right and were either overlooked or dismissed as curiosities out of joint with the times by the national media. After the overwhelming defeat of Barry Goldwater in the 1964 presidential election, the mainstream press paid little attention to conservatives for the next ten years. Yet the foundation for a new brand of religion-infused conservatism was laid in the late sixties and early seventies. The old-fashioned libertarian conservatism of Goldwater was on the wane, but a new, religiously based conservatism was on the rise. During the sixties, Protestant fundamentalists built a kindergarten-through-college network of Christian schools whose graduates would become warriors in the army of the religious right in the 1980s. Even as students attacked the authority of secular universities, fundamentalist proselytizers were bringing millions of other young people into their fold. Yet nearly all evaluations of the legacies of the sixties, by liberals as well as conservatives, regard the presumably radical counterculture as the sine qua non of the entire era — certainly of those who were young.[*]

Moreover, the decade is customarily examined through a peculiar anthropomorphic lens, as if "the Sixties" had been an independent actor instead of a stage on which many comedic and tragic social dramas were played. One of the most embit-

[*] Notable exceptions include *The Conquest of Cool: Business Culture, Counterculture, and the Rise of Hip Consumerism* (1997), by Thomas Frank, and *America Divided: The Civil War of the 1960s* (2004), by Maurice Isserman and Michael Kazin. See also Todd Gitlin's afterword to *Reassessing the Sixties: Debating the Political and Cultural Legacy* (1996).

tered right-wing critics of the sixties, Robert Bork, takes the anthropomorphism a step further and calls the decade a cancer, incapable of cure and always ready to invade the body politic one more time. "As the rioting and riotousness died down in the early 1970s and seemingly disappeared altogether in the last half of that decade," Bork writes, ". . . it seemed, at last, that the Sixties were over. They were not. It was a malignant decade that, after a fifteen-year remission, returned in the 1980s to metastasize more devastatingly throughout our culture than it had in the Sixties, not with tumult but quietly, in the moral and political assumptions of those who now control and guide our major cultural institutions."[4] Bork's rejection by the Senate when Ronald Reagan nominated him for the Supreme Court in 1987 might account for his conviction that the eighties marked the second coming of the cancer first diagnosed in the sixties.

The right-wing take on the sixties is essentially a political indictment masquerading as a defense of Western culture. One infallible marker is the capitalization of the word "Movement" by right-wing intellectuals, who lump the serious with the absurd, the righteous with the cynical, the altruistic with the opportunistic whenever they refer to any of the social protest movements of the era. *Commentary* magazine, under the editorship of Norman Podhoretz in the early seventies, may have started this trend of referring to "the Movement" as if it were a disciplined organization like the American Communist Party of the thirties. Protesters against the immorality and futility of America's war in Vietnam? The Movement. Protesters who cherished a fantasy of Ho Chi Minh as a democratic socialist? The Movement. Nonviolent young demonstrators? The Movement. Bomb-planting Weathermen? The Movement. Feminists who wanted to legalize abortion? The Movement. Feminists who insisted that heterosexual women must stop "sleeping with the enemy"? The Movement. Students who wanted universities to hire more black and female faculty members? The Movement. Students who wanted to do away with grading, exams, and assigned reading lists? The Movement. Environmentalists? The Movement.

According to this logic, the first Earth Day, held in 1970, might as well have been May Day in Moscow's Red Square. And if members of "the Movement" were as unified in their views as the old Communists, then they must have been aided by — who else? — "fellow travelers." In his self-congratulatory memoir *Breaking Ranks* (1979), Podhoretz includes Ramsey Clark, the op-ed page of *The New York Times,* and the American Civil Liberties Union in his designated category of fellow travelers. (The ACLU may be the only organization with the distinction of having been stigmatized as a bourgeois dupe by Dwight Macdonald and as a fellow-traveling dupe by Podhoretz.) "On questions ranging from crime to the nature of art, from drugs to economic growth, from ecology to the new egalitarianism," Podhoretz asserts, "the dogmas of the Movement — both in their unexpurgated state and in the sanitized versions that had by now become the conventional wisdom of the fellow-traveling culture laying claim to the epithet [*sic*] 'liberal' — *Commentary* became perhaps the single most visible scourge of the Movement within the intellectual community."[5] For conservatives like Kristol and Podhoretz, the Movement could only be anti-intellectual because no real intellectual could possibly disagree with *them.* The existence of anti-intellectualism on the right was never acknowledged in the conservative perorations of the early seventies, because the concept of an all-powerful left was as essential to their demonization of radicalism and liberalism then as it is now.

For different reasons, many liberals have also downplayed the significance of the conservative sixties — the Other Sixties that formed a counter-counterculture. In liberal mythology, especially the mythology of those who participated actively in various dissident movements, the sixties were supposed to have been "our" time. It is still difficult for liberals of my generation to stomach the historical fact that the children of the sixties included not only those who helped bring down Lyndon Johnson's presidency but those who voted for Richard Nixon in 1968 and worked to create the "Reagan revolution" a scant six years after Nixon was driven from office by Watergate. One component of this emotional denial may be the guilt of many graying radicals at having helped elect Nixon by staying away from the polls in 1968. After the nomination of Hubert H. Humphrey and the police rampage against antiwar demonstrators at the Democratic National Convention in Chicago, the bitterness of many who opposed the war ran so deep that they would not even consider voting for Humphrey. Cold War Democratic Party liberals were seen as the enemy. University presidents who ruled their campuses with a firm hand were seen as the enemy. The real enemies of liberalism and intellectualism — the religious fundamentalists and far right political operators serving as mentors to young Tom DeLays and Newt Gingriches — were conducting *their* education in the irrational, far from the media spotlight, and young radicals therefore knew as little as most of the neoconservative New York intellectuals did about the Other Sixties. The cultural realities of the decade, and their long-term effect on intellectual life in America, do not fit neatly into either a conservative or a liberal political script.

College campuses were of course the setting for some of the major cultural battles of the era, and although the conflicts often began with an issue related to the Vietnam War, they eventually extended to virtually every aspect of university life, from rules governing students' social behavior to the curriculum. At the beginning of the decade all universities, both public and private, maintained an *in loco parentis* relationship to their undergraduate students. It should be recalled that twenty-one, not eighteen, was then the age of legal majority, and most college students were in fact minors in the eyes of the law. When I entered Michigan State University in 1963, a girl — applying the word "woman" to female students of that era is an anachronism — could be expelled simply for setting foot in an off-campus apartment occupied by a member of the opposite sex. Universities generally maintained a core curriculum that was the academic equivalent of Great Books. By the early seventies, most public and private universities had abandoned *in loco parentis* and diluted their core academic requirements. That these changes occurred is indisputable, but the reasons why they occurred are not. The conventional attack on the sixties from the right, issuing from professors who have somehow managed to flourish within academia in spite of their claim that the academy was destroyed by the upheavals of the demonic decade, portrays campuses overrun and paralyzed first by antiwar crazies, then by gun-toting black militants, and finally by bra-burning feminists — all sworn enemies of everything good in Western civilization. The script goes something like this:

Once upon a time (in the glorious fifties, to be precise), there was both order and freedom in American cultural life, especially in the universities that served as citadels of learning and beacons to the rest of society. Yes, a few left-leaning professors had problems during what liberals call the McCarthy era, but, really, McCarthy was too unimportant to attach his name to an "era." For the most part, students and professors pursued truth with little interference from the worlds of gross commercialism and gross politics. Think Periclean Athens, the University of Heidelberg in the nineteenth century, Oxford and Cambridge before the Great War, and that is the higher learning Americans enjoyed — except in much larger numbers than had ever been the case in human history. Then the barbarians stormed the gates — no, the barbarians were already inside the gates. Instead of studying for their exams and listening to their teachers, students began to fancy themselves liberators of Americans of a different color. Then they started demonstrating against a distant war — even though they themselves were safe on the campuses. Nice girls who never used to speak in graduate seminars unless they were spoken to started talking — and what did they have to say that was worth listening to, anyway? An embattled professor could not hope to do anything about this sad state of affairs, apart from pursuing tenure, continuing to collect his paycheck, and letting the kids do what they wanted. Oh, woe! Or, as Alexander Pope (someone none of those rotten little ignoramuses would ever bother to read) wrote: *"Lo! thy dread empire, Chaos! is restored; / Light dies before thy uncreating word; / Thy hand, great Anarch! lets the curtain fall, / And universal darkness buries all."*

The most influential academic conservative evisceration of the sixties was Allan Bloom's *The Closing of the American Mind* (1987), in which the University of Chicago philosophy professor, who died in 1992, asserted that in the fifties, "no universities were better than the best American universities in the things that have to do with a liberal education and arousing in students the awareness of their intellectual needs." Bloom accurately noted that since the mid-1930s, American universities had benefited greatly from the influx of émigré intellectuals fleeing Nazi Germany — producing an invigorated American academia that served as an intellectual refuge from tyranny and a storehouse of knowledge for the nation and the world. "If in 1930 American universities had simply disappeared," Bloom wrote, "the general store of learning of general signifi-

---

* Alexander Pope, *The Dunciad* (1743).

cance would not have been seriously damaged, although it would surely not have been a good thing for us. But in 1960, inasmuch as most of intellectual life had long ago settled in universities and the American ones were the best, their decay or collapse was a catastrophe. Much of the great tradition was here, an alien and weak transplant, perched precariously in enclaves, vulnerable to native populism and vulgarity. In the mid-sixties the natives, in the guise of students, attacked."[6]

That the "natives" were on the warpath against all forms of authority, including the educational authority of universities and the pieties of middlebrow culture, is beyond question. That the typical American university was a glorious center of higher learning at the beginning of the sixties is a sentimental falsehood, even though both public and private institutions did maintain a more rigorous core curriculum than they would by the mid-seventies. By the mid-sixties, Thorstein Veblen's 1904 description of university presidents as "captains of erudition" — a variation on the widely used turn-of-the-century phrase "captains of industry" — would or should have been considered a description entirely lacking in irony by anyone engaged in the business of higher education. The erosion of traditional liberal education got under way in earnest after the Second World War, when the GI Bill made it possible for millions of working-class veterans to become the first members of their families to attend college. Things may not have changed much in the Ivy League and Seven Sisters schools between 1945 and 1965, but they certainly had in most public institutions, which unabashedly embraced the unintellectual mission of providing vocational training for ever-expanding numbers of students. If institutions like Michigan State maintained certain core requirements, these were offered more in service to the fifties pop psychology ideal of "well-roundedness" than in the spirit of a traditional and demanding liberal arts education. Liberal arts were thought to be particularly important for girls, still presumed to be in pursuit of a "Mrs." Degree along with a bachelor's degree, because educated, well-rounded mothers — as my high school counselor had also emphasized — would be better equipped to educate their children.

The campus uprisings of the late sixties, which began at the most elite public and private institutions and quickly spread to less selective colleges across the land, were on one level a consequence of a conflict between two generations that had benefited from the postwar expansion of higher education. The veterans who took advantage of the GI Bill were profoundly grateful for the chance to go to college because a diploma was their passport to a white-collar job, but their children regarded higher education as a birthright and assumed that jobs would be there when they were ready to take on adult responsibilities. The generation gap was a special irritant at universities because, by the time the campuses began exploding in the late sixties, a considerable proportion of tenured faculty members and mid-level administrators were members of the grateful generation — in which I include not only the veterans but the small cohort born during the Depression.

Members of the grateful generation at universities had extra reasons to be grateful because an academic career, which seemed a sure route to genteel poverty in the early fifties, had turned out to be a comfortable upper-middle-class sinecure as university budgets and faculty expanded along with student enrollment. There was also an element of fear: middle-aged academics who had only recently attained financial security saw the student uprisings as a threat not only to the academic character but to the financial existence of universities — especially those dependent on public support. This mixture of gratitude and insecurity fostered inconsistent responses, alternating laxity and rigidity, when the boomers — yes, the ungrateful generation — rose up to say that there was something wrong with the education their parents had felt so lucky to receive. On the one hand, the grateful generation overestimated the power of the rebels and failed to understand and use every institution's biggest bargaining chip — the emotional and financial dependency of most of the young on the continuation of their status as college students in good standing. On the other hand, those in charge of universities also underestimated the degree to which the impersonal nature of undergraduate education at large institutions had alienated a critical minority of their students — often the best and the brightest. Most administrators had little idea of how and when to use either the carrot of talking seriously to the students or the stick of expulsion.

According to the right, traditional liberal arts requirements were abandoned in the second half of the sixties and the first half of the seventies because New Left faculty members, in cahoots with New Left students drunk on their power to disrupt campuses, were determined to shatter academic hierarchy and, in the process, replace Western Civilization with courses favored by the invading hordes of neo-Marxists, militant blacks, and angry feminists. The problem with that argument is that radical New Left activists never came close to attaining a majority among students, much less faculty, on most campuses — including the elite institutions that were centers of student protest and garnered the most extensive national publicity. At Columbia University, where the administration closed the school in response to a student strike in April 1968, only about 1,000 of the 4,400 undergraduates were actually on strike, and many fewer took part in the occupation of buildings. That was, as one historian notes, a large minority — but still a minority.[7]

At the time, the unremitting incidence of turmoil on college campuses made student protesters look much more dominant than they actually were. No one who lived through the period, whether as an outsider or a member of an academic community, will forget the birth of the Free Speech movement on the Berkeley campus of the

University of California in 1964 and the mass arrests at Sproul Hall; the student occupation of Low Library at Columbia in 1968; the menacing posture of black students wielding guns at Cornell University in 1969; or the shooting of antiwar demonstrators by National Guardsmen at Kent State University and by police at Jackson State College in 1970. The images are equally indelible for those who cherish, despise, or have a mixed view of the cultural legacy of the sixties. Conservatives, however, always focus on the acts of lèse-majesté committed by students and rarely mention either the shootings at Kent and Jackson State, or police actions authorized by other universities — except to maintain that *any* action taken to suppress the student protests was justified. And regardless of how student rebellions were handled at various universities, the disruptive protests were over by the mid-seventies. The rebels were replaced by devoted careerists, among students and faculty alike, with little time or inclination to challenge the existing order of things. Why, then, did campus upheavals that proved to be finite phenomena have such a far-reaching impact on American universities?

All of the campus protesters of the sixties,

including faculty as well as students, were enraged at academic hierarchies that had produced some of the leading strategists of the Vietnam War. Their anger was directed not at academic programs per se — especially not liberal arts — but at the quasi-corporate structure of universities and the close connections between some of the nation's most respected higher education institutions and research funded by the military. The covert institutional association between Columbia and the Institute for Defense Analysis (IDA), a weapons research think tank financed by the U.S. Department of Defense, typified the kind of affiliation that touched off antiwar demonstrations on campuses throughout the nation. At Columbia, the weapons research connection produced the mass protests that disrupted normal academic life on the Morningside Heights campus throughout the spring of 1968. (The university eventually severed its association with IDA.)

Staughton Lynd, an assistant professor of history at Yale and one of the most prominent New Left faculty members involved in the antiwar movement, had given voice to the anger directed at the "military-academic complex" at one of the first widely publicized teach-ins, on the Berkeley campus in

1965. Replying to accusations from other faculty members that there was nothing scholarly about his opposition to the war, Lynd declared, "I am employed by Yale University, the institution which produced the architect of the Bay of Pigs, Richard Bissell; the author of Plan Six for Vietnam, W. W. Rostow [special assistant to presidents Kennedy and Johnson]; and that unagonized reappraiser, McGeorge Bundy [also a hawkish aide to both Kennedy and Johnson]. . . . I think I know something about the Ivy League training which these unelected experts receive: a training in snobbishness, in provincial ethnocentrism, in a cynical and manipulative attitude toward human beings."[8] Lynd, who did not have tenure at the time, was fired by Yale and eventually became a labor lawyer.

Many of the best known leaders of the New Left initially sounded as disillusioned as conservatives would in later years about what they considered the academy's betrayal of traditional scholarly ideals. Mark Rudd, the most visible protest leader at Columbia, said that he had entered the university "expecting the Ivy Tower on the Hill — a place where committed scholars would search for truth in a world that desperately needed help. Instead, I found a huge corporation that made money from real estate, government research contracts, and student fees; teachers who cared only for advancement in their narrow areas of study; worst of all, an institution hopelessly mired in the society's racism and militarism."[9] One can charge dissidents like Rudd with naïveté or with a disingenuous concern for scholarship only insofar as it supported their own social views; but it is unfair — and unscholarly by any standard of disinterested scholarship — to call them anti-intellectual barbarians or, in Bloom's imperial argot, "natives." Yet there is no question that the anger in the air over the war, and over the connections between the defense industry and the university departments engaged in scientific research, metamorphosed into a general rage — sometimes focused and sometimes not — directed at all academic hierarchy.

If antiwar demonstrations did not always focus on the general curriculum, blacks and women did. And although many blacks and feminists were calling not for the exclusion of the classics but for the inclusion of minority and women's studies, some of the most vocal, vulgar, and stupid representatives of both groups — usually self-appointed and always skillful at gaining media attention — did want to jettison those portions of the curriculum dominated by what were scornfully called DWEMs (Dead White European Males). I was an education reporter covering many campus disputes for *The Washington Post* during those years, and I was the same age as many of the student protesters. It was never clear to me why anyone, among the students or the faculty, thought there was some inherent incompatibility between teaching the traditional Great Books and teaching works by the women and African Americans who never appeared on any of the old middlebrow or highbrow lists of essential reading. After years of reflection, I have concluded that the abandonment of many traditional academic requirements did not come about because radicals had more real power than academic traditionalists but because the majority of faculty and administrators, regardless of their academic and political views, reacted with a combination of spinelessness and animus — directed as much toward one another as toward the students — that precluded fruitful negotiation. More often than not, those who tried to mediate were attacked from all sides.

The right wing's view of student demands for changes in universities was conditioned by its hostility toward all social protest.

Neoconservatives in academia even blurred the distinction between the civil rights movement of the early sixties and Black Power militancy of the late sixties. Bloom, for instance, heaped scorn on white students from the North who participated in the civil rights movement in the South.

It [the civil rights activism of northern college students] consisted mostly in going off to marches and demonstrations that were vacationlike, usually during school term, with the confident expectation that they would not be penalized by their professors for missing assignments while they were off doing important deeds, in places where they had never been and to which they would never return, and where, therefore, they did not have to pay any price for their stand, as did those who had to stay and live there. . . . The last significant student participation in the civil rights movement was in the march on Washington in 1964. After that, Black Power came to the fore, the system of segregation in the South was dismantled, and white students had nothing more to contribute other than to egg on Black Power excesses, the instigators of which did not want their help. The students were unaware that the teachings of equality, the promise of the Declaration of Independence, the study of the Constitution, the knowledge of our history and many more things were the painstakingly earned and stored-up capital that supported them.[10]

I know of no other passage — certainly none in as influential a book — that so clearly exemplifies the reasons why the word of the right cannot be taken at face value in discussions of either the openings or closings of the American mind. Bloom's description of civil rights demonstrations in the South as "vacationlike" suggests not only that he lacked personal experience of the drawn-out and dangerous struggle for racial justice but that he never bothered to read the news of the day. Even his dates are wrong; by "the march on Washington," he presumably means the march led by King, which took place not in 1964 but in 1963. As for the statement that the march marked the end of significant student participation in the civil rights movement, Bloom apparently forgot the "freedom summer" of 1964 and the voter registration drive for which Andrew Goodman and Michael Schwerner, two white students from New York City, and James Chaney, a black Mississippian, gave their lives. Some vacation.

Bloom is certainly to be believed when he recalls that during the sixties, he sat on various committees at Cornell University and "continuously and futilely voted against dropping one requirement after the next."[11] But it must have been difficult for liberals to entertain seriously the academic arguments of a professor whose disdain for all social protesters was so pervasive. If I had been a young professor of classics at Cornell (hardly likely given the scant representation of women on university faculties at the time), I would have stood foursquare behind my favorite DWEMs until I heard men like Bloom handing down their opinions about "natives" — a group that surely included any woman who had the temerity to challenge male professors about anything. Then my innate cultural conservationism would probably have been overcome by the sort of rage that makes reasonable discourse impossible. I do not say that with pride, because any professor who would allow political anger to overwhelm academic judgment has no business on a university faculty. Yet that is exactly what happened — on both sides — in the sixties and early seventies.

Most of the fury was confined to departments in the liberal arts and social sciences; the "hard" sciences, apart from the termination of some defense-related research projects, were largely unaffected. There is no excuse for tenured professors — meeting with bloody-minded colleagues is, after all, part of their job description — who failed to give Bloom's academic arguments a fair hearing because they hated his politics. Neither is there an excuse for right-wing professors who failed to distinguish between their academic standards and their conservative social views. What is clear, however, is that liberals and conservatives were no more interested in talking to one another on campuses during the sixties than they are today: if one wishes to play the "blame game," there is plenty of blame to go around.

One of the most reprehensible results of this abdication of responsibility was the ghettoization of African-American, women's, and ethnic studies. With a combination of backbone and sensitivity, university faculty members — whatever their politics — might have dealt with student demands for curriculum change in a very different way. Who or what was to stop them from including black studies and women's studies in the core curriculum instead of assigning the new courses to an academic ghetto? Were professors of the sixties quaking behind their lecterns because they feared that the students would stop applying to universities and take their places in the workforce as janitors and waiters?

The liberals, and many conservatives as well, caved not because they were intimidated by student protests but because shunting ethnic and women's studies into a minority ghetto was the easiest thing to do. The creation of intellectual ghettos expanded the number of faculty jobs and left the still overwhelmingly white male faculties free to teach history or American literature or sociology as they had always taught it — from a white male viewpoint. One of the dirty little secrets of many white liberals on college campuses for the past thirty years has been that they share Bloom's contempt for multiculturalism but do not openly voice their disdain. Saul Bellow's famous remark, "Who is the Tolstoy of the Zulus? The Proust of the Papuans?", resonates throughout academia today. In the early nineties, there was grumbling in academia when Toni Morrison's novel *Beloved* (1987) began to make its way into college English syllabuses with what was considered unseemly speed. "The conservative canard heard in those days was that left-wing professors were casting aside Shakespeare in favor of Morrison," writes A. O. Scott in *The New York Times Book Review*.[12] In fact, some white liberals were spreading the same canard: a fair number of liberals as well as conservatives were quite willing to throw the multiculturalists a bone by including Morrison on their reading lists while continuing to make little room for the work of Langston Hughes or Ralph Ellison (to cite just two examples) outside of specialized courses in African-American literature. Too many white professors today could not care less whether most white students are exposed to black American writers, and some of the multicultural empire builders are equally willing to sign off on a curriculum for African-American studies majors that does not expose them to Henry James and Edith Wharton.

The same willingness to ghettoize is also evident in the teaching of history. A few years ago, I was delivering a lecture at a state university in Southern California and happened to mention John Hope Franklin's *Mirror to America.* Franklin's autobiography is unique because it applies the powers of observation of a great historian, born in 1915, to all of the important issues involving race in America in the twentieth century. It is a work of American history, not only African-American history, and belongs in every History 101 syllabus in every American college. After my lecture, a white student approached me and said she had read Franklin's book in her elective African-American history course. I asked her if there were any other white students in the class, and she said there was one Vietnamese-born student, but everyone else, including the professor, was black. The de facto segregation of minority studies that prevails at many institutions, in classes attended almost entirely by minority students and taught by professors from the same minority, is as bad for blacks, Hispanics, and Asians as it is for the white majority at universities, because putting such courses in a special category devalues them for anyone not planning a career in the multicultural studies ghetto.

"I sit with Shakespeare and he winces not," W. E. B. DuBois wrote in 1903 in *The Souls of Black Folk.* "Across the color line I move arm in arm with Balzac and Dumas, where smiling men and welcoming women glide in gilded halls. From out the caves of evening that swing between the strong-limbed earth and the tracery of stars, I summon Aristotle and Aurelius and what soul I will, and they come all graciously with no scorn nor condescension. So, wed with Truth, I dwell above the Veil. Is this the life you grudge us, O knightly America?"[13] It is nothing less than a tragedy that large numbers of twenty-first-century college graduates of all races are as ignorant of those words as I was on the day I received my diploma from Michigan State, more than forty years ago, without ever having been required to read a single word written by a black American.

Both the grateful and the ungrateful generations got their share of the spoils in the settlement that was reached on most university campuses in the mid-seventies. In many instances, university administrators not only signed off on but instigated such arrangements. Even at universities thought to be citadels of the counterculture, faculties were content to accommodate student demands within a traditional hierarchical structure, as long as there were enough jobs to go around. Sheldon S. Wolin, a political science professor who was one of the leading faculty supporters of protest movements at Berkeley in the 1960s, notes that by 1969, "the vast majority of the faculty drew back from the heavy civic commitment involved, not only in rethinking the nature of the university but in reorganizing it as well. Such an involvement seemed incompatible with the idea of a 'research university' that had attracted a distinguished faculty in the first place." The main desire of the faculty at Berkeley, as on many other campuses, was to return to the "real work" of research and publication.[14] As the historian Maurice Isserman notes, "The transformation of the intellectual class from a marginal, adversarial role to a securely institutionalized one went on apace in the 1960s regardless of the momentary radical ascendancy on campuses."[15]

Of course it is still possible to get a first-rate liberal education in any number of American colleges. Some institutions have more rigorous requirements than others, and, in any event, it is always possible for self-selected lovers of learning to learn. High culture can never be obliterated as long as the species continues to produce extraordinary individuals with the inclination and fortitude to pursue their interests and talents against the grain of the mass culture surrounding them. The real loser, throughout thirty years of steadily expanding enrollment in institutions of higher education, has been the large middle group of students — those who, in an era of more rigorous academic requirements, had a good chance of emerging from their studies with at least a liberal middlebrow education. Thanks to the erosion of core studies, it is now possible at many institutions of so-called higher learning for a student to receive a degree in psychology without having taken a mid-level biology course; for an African-American studies major to graduate without reading the basic texts of the "white" Enlightenment; for a business major to graduate without having studied any literature after her freshman year. And all of these college graduates, should they choose to become teachers at any level of the educational system, will pass on their narrowness and ignorance to the next generation.

During the past ten years, many institutions have moved to restore a stronger core curriculum (as they also did in the late seventies), but this grudging, formulaic trend is higher education's equivalent of the frantic emphasis on standardized testing in elementary and secondary schools: it has everything to do with politics — both academic politics and, in the case of public universities, the politics of getting financial support from state legislatures. When university officials start talking about a return to "the basics," it is a sure bet that some prominent state legislator or governor has zeroed in on the academic shortcomings of State U. and that no one is referring to the unquantifiable and more genuine learning whose importance within a society cannot be measured by test scores and can only be mourned in its absence.

At the height of the antiwar movement and the various rebellions playing out on college campuses and city streets, the Other Sixties were also unfolding, out of sight of the television cameras that brought social protest — or rather, television's version of social protest — into American living rooms on the nightly news. The press was out in force, however, for the Other America's largest demonstration of the decade: the inauguration of Richard Nixon on January 22, 1969. *The Washington Post* had assigned me, along with most of the younger reporters on the city staff, to the miserable task of standing outdoors on a raw day in order to follow the progress of Nixon's inaugural parade along Pennsylvania Avenue. Taking notes with numb fingers, I watched as a float filled with robotically cheerful young men and women passed by, to the strains of an infernal ditty titled "Up With People." The paean to ordinary people assured the shivering inaugural crowd that "you meet 'em wherever you go."

Here on parade was what Nixon had dubbed the silent majority, a collection of neatly groomed young people who were not long-haired weirdos but the sixties equivalent of our current president's beloved "folks." Like Nixon's own daughters, Julie and Tricia, the young Republicans converging on Washington looked as if they had never marched in a peace demonstration, failed to get regular haircuts, gone barelegged instead of wearing pantyhose with their skirts, or lived with a member of the opposite sex without being married. "The sixties are over," I moaned that night, as my colleagues and I drowned our inaugural sorrows in the scotch that, in spite of the popularity of marijuana among our contemporaries on college campuses, all young reporters of my generation still consumed in copious quantities in order to prove that we were one of the boys — especially if we were in the still tiny minority of girls.

The year 1968 had been filled with such terrible events that even an action-junkie journalist could not mourn its passing. At the *Post,* we had watched with horror as smoke and flames rose over our city during the days of rioting that followed King's assassination. Then came Robert Kennedy's murder, the Soviet Union's invasion of Czechoslovakia, and the Democratic National Convention in Chicago — the latter two events unfolding almost simultaneously on television in the third week of August. Blood flowed in the streets of both Prague, where Soviet soldiers killed more than seventy and wounded more than seven hundred, and Chicago, where Mayor Richard J. Daley's police clubbed demonstrators and television cameras recorded, in real time, the sight of bloodied young men and women fleeing for their lives and seeking refuge in the lobby of the Hilton Hotel. Hundreds were injured in Chicago but, "miraculously," no one died from the clubbings.[16] The demonstrators had waved signs proclaiming: "The Whole World Is Watching," and that was true. But the world — at least the part of the world composed of Americans who would vote for Nixon — would not interpret the events in Chicago as the demonstrators interpreted and experienced them. Instead of seeing out-of-control police attacking unarmed kids, much of the public saw defenders of law and order, pushed beyond endurance by unwashed hippies chanting obscenities and scorning every traditional notion of propriety and decency. To some degree, a vote for Nixon represented a vote for the silent majority's concept of desirable family values and manners — for Pat Nixon's good Republican cloth coat, for two dutiful daughters who dressed, looked, and spoke like the elder daughter in *Father Knows Best.*

It is impossible to single out one determining factor in Nixon's improbable comeback during that year of blood and rage. Many disillusioned supporters of Senator Eugene McCarthy, in their early twenties and eligible to vote for the first time, did sit out the election. Some Americans mistakenly thought that Nixon, simply because the Democrats had presided over the escalation of the war, was more likely than Humphrey to end it. But Nixon's support was always strongest among voters who hated antiwar protesters. Humphrey carried only one southern state, Texas, in 1968. Alabama governor George Wallace, running on a third-party ticket, carried Alabama, Arkansas, Georgia, Mississippi, and Louisiana, and Nixon carried all the other southern and border states. Had Wallace not been running, Nixon would certainly have won the entire South (as he did in 1972). Democrats were, after all, responsible for passing the Civil Rights Act of 1964, which mandated desegregation of public accommodations, and the Voting Rights Act of 1965: southerners had good reason to think that such challenges to their way of life would never have become law if a Republican had been in the White House.

Even absent the dying issue of legal segregation, Nixon was the perfect candidate for those who resented all of the cultural changes of the sixties. One of the persistent motifs of his career had been a barely disguised envy of those who benefited from educational and economic advantages that he had never enjoyed as a young man. At a time when college campuses were seen as the incubators of left-wing antiwar protests, Nixon's long association with anti-intellectualism and anti-Communism were campaign assets. Dick Nixon, the perfect representative of the Other Sixties, stood for everything and everyone opposed to draft-dodging eggheads who had never worked a day in their lives.

In 1969, a Gallup Poll conducted for *Newsweek* revealed the breadth and depth of the silent majority's disapproval of student demonstrators. (Significantly, the *Newsweek* poll was limited to white adults.

Blacks were not considered "middle Americans," the group targeted by the pollsters.) More than 84 percent felt that protesters on college campuses had been treated "too leniently" by university and law enforcement authorities. More than 85 percent also thought that black militants had been dealt with too leniently.[17] "It is almost impossible to overstate the resentment in middle America against the recent turbulence on the nation's college campuses," observed one analyst, adding that the resentment "has a special spice for those in the lower economic brackets" because they see the protests as a manifestation of "ingratitude and irresponsibility on the part of those who have a chance that they never got." Abraham Kaplan, a professor of philosophy at the University of Michigan — another major center of student protest and the birthplace of Students for a Democratic Society — commented that the young demonstrators had violated their parents' image "of what college is — a place where there are trees, where the kids drink cocoa, eat marshmallows, read Shakespeare, and once in the spring the boys can look at the girls' underthings."[18]

This image of ungrateful, privileged youth spilled over onto the intellectuals who were presumed to be running the colleges — and running them badly, in the opinion of parents who were not happy about writing tuition checks to institutions that had allowed classes to be canceled as a result of student disruptions. S. I. Hayakawa, president of San Francisco State College, became a hero to conservatives when he took strong action to suppress protest demonstrations on his campus, and his actions resonated throughout the country because they took place against the backdrop of a city regarded as the headquarters of the counterculture. It was not lost on Hayakawa's supporters that San Francisco State was then a commuter school with a large enrollment of students who represented the first generation in their families to attend college, while Berkeley, across San Francisco Bay, was one of the schools of choice for affluent Californians. College-educated parents were much more likely than others to feel that there was some justification for student protests; they were also less antagonistic toward the "sexual revolution" and less concerned about a decline in traditional religious values. As the sixties ended, the press generally treated the silent majority or middle America — presumed to be identical — as a group defined mainly by blue-collar job status and a relatively low level of education.

Two other elements — regional and religious identification — were largely ignored by the media except when civil rights issues were being discusssed. Yet religious and regional loyalties played crucial roles throughout the Other Sixties, as they have in the renewed culture wars of the past twenty years. The old combination of fundamentalism with anti-intellectualism, coupled with a new disdain for scientific as well as scholarly "elites," was one of the most undercovered stories of the demythologizing decade. George Wallace summed up the mixture of class, regional, and anti-intellectual resentment that animated his campaign when he declared, "The great pointy heads who knew best how to run everybody's life have had their day."

Of all the cultural phenomena slighted by the contemporary media and academic community, the rejuvenation of fundamentalist religion was unquestionably the most important. Not that fundamentalism had ever really gone away, but it received a jolt of adrenaline from both the civil rights laws of the early sixties and the cultural rebellions of the late sixties. The fundamentalist resurgence was profoundly anti-intellectual, in part because the pointy heads were seen as the source of school desegregation plans cooked up by rich liberal intellectuals at the expense of ordinary people who could not afford segregated private schools, or public schools in affluent lily-white neighborhoods, for their children. But an equally powerful element in the new fundamentalist anti-intellectualism was hatred of liberal intellectual trends within churches themselves. There is no question that the anti-liberal white Christian fundamentalists of the sixties — including those who were young at the time and those who were already important church leaders — have garnered more souls for their flock during the past forty years than socially liberal Christian religious figures, like the Reverend William Sloan Coffin and Father Robert Drinan, who were known for their crusading against the Vietnam War and on behalf of other progressive social causes. The fundamentalists concentrated on converting people to their particular religious beliefs, while clerics like Coffin and Drinan wanted to persuade people of many religious beliefs to support their vision of a more just America.

During the sixties, fundamentalist churches, from conservative Southern Baptists to sects like the Pentecostals, grew at the expense of mainstream, generally more liberal Protestant denominations ranging from the Lutherans and Presbyterians on the right to Unitarians on the left. The trend has continued to this day. A key figure in the fundamentalist movement of the sixties was the charismatic Dallas preacher W. A. Criswell, who, on October 13, 1968, delivered a rousing sermon titled "Why I Preach That the Bible Is Literally True" from the pulpit of his huge, 26,000-member First Baptist Church of Dallas. Criswell, who died in 2002 at age ninety-two, was described in an obituary in *Christianity Today* as "a holy roller with a Ph.D. . . . who preached with the bombast of Billy Sunday and the urgency of Savonarola." An important player in the post-1960 rightward movement of the Southern Baptist Convention — the largest denominational group in the nation — Criswell once excoriated political and religious liberals as "skunks."[19] A graduate of Baylor University, a Baptist institution since it was chartered in 1845, Criswell considered his alma mater far too liberal for the training of orthodox ministers and in 1971 founded his own fundamentalist seminary, the Criswell Center for Biblical Studies.*

Even more important for the future of what would come to be known as the Christian right, Dallas's First Baptist Church organized an entire system of private schools, originally designed to avoid desegregation but ultimately serving the much larger purpose of educating Christian children without secular influences like the teaching of evolution. Because Criswell was one of the most influential Baptist pastors in the South, his educational strategy was widely replicated by devout right-wing evangelicals throughout the region. The resulting private school system ensured that "the children of church members and like-minded people could move from kindergarten through graduate study in school environments that they considered theologically safe, unlike those found in the public schools and universities and in denominationally affiliated schools . . . considered wayward, such as Southern Methodist University and Baylor University."[20]

The resurgent fundamentalists were saying no to more than the counterculture of

* In 1991, a majority of the Baylor board of trustees voted to sever all legal ties with the Texas Baptist Convention.

the sixties; like William Jennings Bryan and his followers in the first three decades of the century, the new fundamentalist generation was also saying no to intellectualism and modernism. Outside the South, the strength and single-mindedness of the new fundamentalists were rarely noted. One exception occurred in June 1970, less than a month after the killings of the students at Kent State and Jackson State, when the Southern Baptist Convention held its 125th annual meeting. In this time of immense social turmoil, the main issue roiling the Southern Baptists was not the Vietnam War. What really angered the 13,355 delegates, called "messengers" and representing more than 35,000 Baptist churches, was the publication of a work of biblical criticism suggesting that the first five books of the Bible were drawn from many sources over a long period of time rather than dictated by God directly to Moses.

The view of the Bible as the work of many human hands and minds, albeit divinely inspired, has been held by mainstream biblical scholars, including many Jews and Catholics as well as Protestants, since the middle of the nineteenth century; the question of whether the Bible is the literal word of God has divided fundamentalists from more liberal Protestant denominations since the eighteenth century. Yet an overwhelming majority of the Southern Baptist delegates were outraged that their Sunday School Board had authorized publication of a work that cast doubt on the divine authorship of the Bible. In a front-page article — the prominent display was extremely rare at the time for any religion story unconnected to a racial dispute — *The New York Times* described the controversy as "a reflection of the growing tension between increasingly urban-oriented and academically qualified national leaders and traditional rural and anti-intellectual elements of the denomination." Defenders of the book were shouted down on the convention floor. One pastor rose to say that Southern Baptists were compromising their tradition of biblical literalism by "using psychology" and becoming involved in counterculture-inspired practices like "sensitivity training" for clergy. "I believe the Bible," said the Reverend Robert Scott. "Jesus believed the Bible. Southern Baptists believe the Bible. It's been said that we've got room for the most conservative and the most liberal in the Southern Baptist Convention. But brother, I say that's too much room."[21]

The author of the offending book, the

British Baptist scholar G. Henton Davis, also had the temerity to suggest that Abraham may have misunderstood God's command when he agreed to sacrifice Isaac. In fact, the Southern Baptists were right to identify creeping theological liberalism in this particular piece of biblical revisionism. Liberal religious believers have always had a problem with a capricious God who would be so cruel as to demand that a man sacrifice his only son, and placing the onus on Abraham certainly lets Jehovah off the hook. Moreover, if Abraham did misunderstand God, who is to say that Jesus did not misunderstand his Father's desires on that fateful day in Jerusalem? That would certainly be an unholy thought for any fundamentalist.

After the convention voted to bar its Sunday School Board from distributing the offending book, one prescient Baptist official linked the reaction to a broader political polarization and an "ultraconservative tide" sweeping the country. "Southern Baptists as a whole have always mirrored their culture, and this is a tragedy," said the Reverend Lee Porter, pastor of the First Baptist Church of Bellaire in Houston. "I wish this weren't so, but it is."[22] Over the next twenty years, what the *Times* referred to as "urban-oriented and academically qualified" Southern Baptists were overwhelmed by politically and culturally conservative anti-intellectuals. Baptists who believed that religion was compatible with science and modern scholarship (including biblical scholarship) wound up leaving and joining churches affiliated with the more liberal American Baptist Convention — a move reminiscent of the northward journey made by pro-evolution scientists in the nineteenth century. And many Southern Baptist Convention pastors and church members became Christian soldiers in the army of the New Right.

An equally important development was the rise of a powerful Christian right-wing youth movement, the Campus Crusade for Christ, whose members were dubbed "Jesus freaks" by their contemporaries on the left. The Campus Crusade was actually founded in 1951 by Bill Bright, a southern California businessman, but it did not gain any real traction at universities outside the Bible Belt until the late sixties, when the evangelists began appealing to young men and women, many disillusioned with drugs and the sexual revolution and looking for a way to remake their lives. In a move of great symbolic importance, the group held its national convention in 1967 at Berkeley, where a young evangelist named Jon Braun stood on the steps of Sproul Hall and praised Jesus as "the world's greatest revolutionary." As Isserman and Michael Kazin point out in their history of the divided sixties, the initial appeal of the Campus Crusade evangelists was greatly enhanced by their deliberate adoption and adaptation of counterculture dress and language, minus the obscenities, for the purpose of preaching old-time religion.

With long hair and tie-dyed clothes, the religious crusaders looked exactly like their radical left contemporaries. Some organizations adopted imitation-hip names like the Christian World Liberation Front and the Jesus Christ Light and Power Company and opened shelters for young people burned out by drugs.[23] The appeal of the Christian fundamentalists was similar to that of strict Hasidic sects in the Jewish community: they offered rules and certainty to some young men and women who had found only unhappiness where others had found personal freedom. The Campus Crusade, which had only 109 paid employees in 1960, grew into a national organization with 6,500 staffers and a budget of $42 million by the mid-seventies.[24] Today, the Crusade is a proselytizing international organization — its activities are especially controversial in Muslim countries — with more than 27,000 paid staff and 225,000 volunteers in 190 countries.*

During the sixties and early seventies, the resurgence of militant fundamentalism was largely ignored not only by the general press but the emerging new breed of pointy-headed conservative intellectuals. To fundamentalists, as to most of the American public, pointy heads were synonymous with liberals. The conservative pointy heads, many of them New York Jews, may have known as little about fundamentalists as fundamentalists did about them — or they

---

* At American colleges today, one of the Campus Crusade's more effective endeavors is counter-programming aimed at speakers presenting a liberal or secular point of view. When I delivered a lecture about my book *Freethinkers* at Eastern Kentucky University, the large and active Campus Crusade chapter sponsored a combination lecture/revival meeting featuring a speaker who claimed to have overcome his pedophile impulses by being born again in Christ. My speech attracted only about 150 students, and I was told that the recovering pedophile drew an audience of 500 on the same night.

may simply not have known what to say about the right-wing religious revival. In 1970, the year *Commentary* came out of the neoconservative closet and launched its attack on the counterculture, the editors had nothing to say about the fundamentalist counter-counterculture in the making.

Of course, *Commentary* was published by the American Jewish Committee and edited mainly by Jews, and conservative secular Jewish intellectuals have always had a problem facing and 'fessing up to the pivotal role of Christian fundamentalists in the overall conservative movement. Ten years before the Christian right flexed its muscles during the Reagan campaign, it probably never occurred to the Jewish defenders of the new conservative faith that they would have to deal seriously with political allies who strongly supported the state of Israel mainly because it is home to the plain of Armageddon — the place where Jesus is expected to return for the final battle of good against evil, which will put an end to Jews and everyone else who has not accepted Jesus as the Messiah. On that day, contributors to *Commentary* and *The Nation* — past and present — will finally be bound for the bottomless pit in the same boat.

Also destined for the pit are large numbers

of liberal Catholics. In viewing the American religious landscape of the sixties, American Catholicism must be regarded as a special case because the reform movement within the Catholic Church was led from the Vatican and began with the 1958 election of John XXIII as pope. The Catholicism in which I was baptized in 1945 and confirmed in 1956 represented, as one Catholic wit noted, "the only *the* Church." The Reverend Andrew M. Greeley writes, "the mantra that governed Catholic life in the 19th and early 20th centuries was that 'the church should not change, cannot change, and will not change' — a counterpart of the old Baltimore Catechism's contention that 'God always was, always will be, and always remains the same.' "[25] But the church did begin to change under Pope John, the octogenarian who was the most progressive pontiff in centuries. Everything one heard about the rotund pope, born Angelo Giuseppe Roncalli and known for the aid he had rendered imperiled Jews during the Second World War, was humane and endearing. One of his first actions was to abandon the old custom, adhered to by his gaunt predecessor, Pius XII, that the pope always eats alone. In 1962, John convened the Second Vatican Council in Rome in an effort to update rituals and doctrine and breathe new life into an institution that had long been dominated from the top by anti-modernism and an obsession with controlling the sexual practices of the faithful. When he greeted Jewish observers (another first) attending Vatican II, the pope, alluding to his middle name and the Bible story of Joseph and his brothers, welcomed the rabbis with the statement: "I am Joseph, your brother."

To those not raised on pre–Vatican II Catholicism, it is difficult to convey the aura of freedom and hopefulness that fueled debate within the church during the brief period of John's papacy. Many Catholics hoped that priests would be allowed to marry, that the church would ease its condemnation of divorce and allow remarried Catholics to receive the sacraments, and, above all, that the Vatican would rescind the ban on artificial birth control that tortured married Catholics with the prospect of eternal damnation for the mortal sin of having sex while using contraceptives. The work of Vatican II had barely begun when Pope John died, and, given the authoritarian nature of the church, no attempts at institutional liberalization could succeed without the support of a committed activist pope.

But the genie could not be returned to the bottle for Catholics in the United States and Europe. During the sixties, American-born Catholics became more like mainstream Protestants in their relationship to religious doctrine and ecclesiastical authority: they still wanted to be baptized, married, and buried in the church, but they were not about to let priests, bishops, or popes tell them what to think or how they should behave in the privacy of their bedrooms. "Cafeteria Catholics" was the contemptuous term invented by theological conservatives to describe their more liberal brethren.

However, there was also a very different breed of "cafeteria Catholics," deeply angered by changes in ritual, such as the abandonment of the Latin mass, and by the increasingly outspoken opposition of many priests, nuns, and even bishops to racial discrimination and the Vietnam War. Although many grassroots Catholic social conservatives were as anti-intellectual as southern fundamentalist Protestants, their anti-intellectualism was rooted not in biblical literalism but in a longing for the pre–Vatican II church of their youth. These disillusioned right-wing Catholics would, in the years after the 1973 Supreme Court decision legalizing abortion, form a previously unimaginable alliance with fundamentalist Protestants. Like the fundamentalists, who were suspicious of secularizing forces at Protestant institutions such as Baylor, the right-wing cafeteria Catholics disapproved of secularizing trends at the oldest, most venerated Catholic institutions of higher education. The best American Catholic universities, encouraged by John XXIII's ecumenicism, were turning themselves into first-rate centers of secular as well as religious learning during the late fifties and early sixties, and the influence of liberal Catholic intellectuals at those institutions remains a thorn in the side of Vatican conservatives to this day. American Catholic battles over the changes set in motion by John XXIII were also fought out at a high intellectual level, with the liberal Catholic intellectuals of *Commonweal* and the Jesuit weekly *America* on one side and the right-wing warriors of William F. Buckley's *National Review* on the other. Buckley himself, the voice of young conservatism since the publication in 1951 of *God and Man at Yale,* was anti-secular, not anti-intellectual. His defense of traditional Catholicism was only one part of a broader cultural, political, and economic conservatism that anticipated the neoconservative revolt of many Jewish intellectuals by fifteen years.

By 1968, Richard Nixon already understood that conservative religious believers, including fundamentalist Protestants and right-wing Catholics, could form a new base for the Republican Party. During the campaign, Dick and Pat Nixon did not bother to call on Reinhold Niebuhr, the most prominent liberal Protestant theologian in America; they did, however, make a well-publicized appearance in Pittsburgh at one of Graham's "crusades." At the inauguration, Graham returned the favor by offering thanks to a God who "hast permitted Richard Nixon to lead us at this momentous hour of history." And when Nixon opened the White House to religious services, Graham was the first speaker. He was often seen at gala events, including a White House dinner for Neil Armstrong.[26] Just six months into the Nixon administration, Niebuhr attacked what he called the "Nixon Graham doctrine" for its insistence that America's massive problems of race and poverty be remedied by individual spiritual solutions rather than social action in which government had a responsibility to participate.[27] His article, titled "The King's Chapel and the King's Court," was published in *Christianity and Crisis,* a major organ of liberal

Protestantism. The followers of evangelists like Graham formed a new pool of conservative voters who had already abandoned the old New Deal coalition, and they were ripe for the political alliance with conservative Catholics that would emerge after the 1973 Supreme Court decision legalizing abortion.

But whenever religious trends were analyzed in the sixties and early seventies, both the press and distinguished scholars concentrated almost exclusively on the secularizing and liberalizing religious impulses most evident among people like themselves. In his magisterial *A Religious History of the American People* (1972), the Yale University historian Sydney E. Ahlstrom describes "religious antitraditionalism" as the spiritual hallmark of the sixties. One of the strongest elements of this anti-traditionalism, he argues, was a "growing commitment to a naturalism or 'secularism' and corresponding creeping doubts about the supernatural or sacral." The secularist influence, he adds, had been reinforced by "increasing doubt as to the capacity of present-day ecclesiastical, politial, social, and educational institutions to rectify the country's deep-seated woes."[28] A footnote on the penultimate page of Ahlstrom's book offers a fascinating insight into the reasons why most intellectuals, whether liberal or conservative, failed to perceive the strength of the anti-secular and anti-intellectual fundamentalist revolt brewing between the coasts — and especially in the South.

In April–May 1970 the final two weeks of my course on American religious history were swallowed up in the turmoil of demonstrations and protest related to a widely publicized trial of several Black Panthers in New Haven, the American invasion of Cambodia, the National Guard's killing of four students at Kent State University, and the police slaying of two more at Jackson State College. The course, in other words, merged with the subject matter in this concluding chapter [on the sixties]. . . . Only with the passage of time, if ever, will it become clearer which elements of the situation had the most enduring effects and which ones, therefore, should have registered their impact on would-be historians. How much more impossible it is to account for a whole nation's turmoil during an entire decade![29]

There is no awareness in this passage of the existence of millions of devoutly religious Americans who thought that professors had no business teaching religious history in the first place if they allowed their courses to be "swallowed up" by worldly events. Far from being impressed by the naturalistic and secularistic logic that was supposedly sweeping the nation, the resurgent fundamentalists of the sixties reaffirmed their faith in the supernatural — including the God-blessed exceptionalism of the United States — and their contempt for an intellectualism based on either secularism or rationalism.

In politics, education, and above all religion, both the left- and the right-wing children of the sixties were leaving what would prove to be a lasting anti-intellectual imprint on the culture. But the most powerful legacy of the sixties would be the decade's youth culture, which crossed class, racial, and religious lines and, in doing so, unleashed more potent anti-intellectual and anti-rational forces than those engendered by any form of politics and social protest.

CHAPTER SEVEN: LEGACIES: YOUTH CULTURE AND CELEBRITY CULTURE

Of the many potent myths associated with the sixties, the most wrongheaded is a widespread tendency to equate and conflate the decade's youth culture with its left-wing counterculture. The youth culture derived its immense power precisely from its capacity to transcend social and ideological boundaries that Americans had long taken for granted, and that transcendence was made possible by the huge young demographic and a completely apolitical marketing machine eager to meet every desire of those under the magical mark of thirty. Youthful preferences in fashion, movies, television programs, poetry (remember Rod McKuen?), and, above all, music became indistinguishable from popular culture as a whole.

My reservations about the sixties youth culture, and my characterization of many of its attributes as anti-intellectual, have more to do with its ubiquitousness than with its particulars. A popular culture driven almost entirely by the preferences of the young — as opposed to one in which generational tastes form a distinctive but not necessarily dominant new strand — discourages the making of important intellectual and aesthetic distinctions and tends to discard the best expressions of popular culture from the past. My eyes may grow misty, along with the millions of my contemporaries who turn out for Paul McCartney's concerts, when I hear "Yesterday" or "When I'm 64," but that attests to nothing except my nostalgia for a time when the possibility of being sixty-four years old was as unreal as the possibility of celebrating my thousandth birthday. The decline of jazz in the sixties, even in the black community that gave birth to this distinctively American art form, is just one example — a particularly depressing one — of what can go wrong when youth culture and pop culture become synonymous. Both young liberals and young conservatives bought into the mass-marketed, cleverly packaged pop ethos of their generation, and the cleverness of the packaging was demonstrated by the conviction of millions of the young that their product choices, unlike those of an older generation brainwashed by "Madison Avenue," were expressions of free-spirited individuality.

It was a burst of sheer brilliance, if not divine inspiration, for the Christian Crusade's young evangelists to raise their profile by preaching from the steps of Sproul Hall and letting their hair grow. The unmistakable and powerful message was that you could love both Jesus and John Lennon — notwithstanding Lennon's 1966 comment that "the Beatles are more popular than Jesus," which set off protests throughout the Bible Belt and earned Lennon a personal rebuke from the Vatican. As more than one observer noted at the time, iconographic depictions of the Christian savior did bear a strong resemblance to the long-haired Lennon of the late sixties. The Christian Crusade message had so little intellectual content — *Jesus, the greatest revolutionary of all time* melded to *love, love, love* — that it could be spun to please anyone of almost any political persuasion, and to sell anything to almost anyone. Both the Christian right and the Christian left are still spinning it today, along with the Chase Manhattan Bank, which in 2006 launched a spectacularly successful television commercial that assured prospective customers, "All You Need Is Love," while displaying one image after another of sexy-looking men and women lovingly swiping their Chase-issued credit cards. The same apolitical marketing techniques, enhanced by the proliferation of portable devices for storing and listening to music, have been equally effective during the past twenty years in persuading rich white kids and poor black kids to embrace the misogynist, violent, often racist, and always vulgar lyrics of most rap and hip-hop.

In an ironic twist, the mass marketing of sixties pop music was intimately connected with the depoliticization of older songs long associated with the Old Left. Folk songs that had been considered faintly or forthrightly subversive during the McCarthy era served as an important link between the dissident bohemian culture of the fifties and the broader counterculture of the sixties, but they also became quite acceptable — albeit in sanitized versions omitting certain lyrics that could be considered critical of America — to those who hated everything else about the counterculture. Woody Guthrie's "This Land Is Your Land," written in 1940 and considered a left-wing anthem throughout the forties and into the fifties, exemplified the mainstreaming of the once subversive. In his novel *Going All the Way,* set in the early fifties in Indianapolis, Dan Wakefield describes his young, insecure protagonist's first encounter with the song: "It was a record of a guy singing and playing the guitar, but it wasn't hillbilly music exactly. It sounded to Sonny more like English folk songs but it was about America. Something about This land is your land, and it's my land. . . . The words seemed a little communistic."[1]

Not by 1968, when "This Land Is Your Land," with singers sounding more like the Mormon Tabernacle Choir than Guthrie, blared cheerfully from the "Up With People" float during the Nixon inaugural. Pete Seeger's "If I Had a Hammer," performed at Communist rallies in 1949 by Seeger and his group, the Weavers, was recorded in 1962 by Peter, Paul, and Mary, and led the Hit Parade. A year later, "If I Had a Hammer" was mainstream enough for the group to sing it from the steps of the Lincoln Memorial before Martin Luther King delivered his oration. By then, no one cared that the song had been written by a man cited ten times for contempt of Congress after testifying before the House Committee on Un-American Activities in 1955. Which side were you on during the sixties? There were many ways to tell, but taste in pop music was not among them. It is all the more remarkable that this depoliticization occurred at a time when opposing political passions seemed to be tearing the country apart.

Of course, every generation has its beloved music, rituals, drugs, and sentimental history. What set the children of the sixties apart from their predecessors was the disproportionate size of the baby boom bulge in relation to the overall population. Nearly 78 million children were born from 1946 through 1964 — the baby boom period as defined by demographers — and more than two thirds were born before 1960. They now make up nearly 28 percent of the American population, and in the year 2030, when the youngest boomers will turn sixty-six and the oldest will be eighty-four, they will *still* account for 20 percent of Americans.[2] The younger boomers were not old enough actually to participate in the protests of the sixties, but they were old enough to absorb the commercial youth culture created by their near contemporaries. A child born in 1957, which marked the high point of the baby boom, grew up with the sights and sounds of the sixties youth culture — the television, the music, the cultural reference points highlighted by the media.

Moreoever, the boomers helped shape and change the tastes of their parents as well as their younger siblings. A glance at family snapshots from the fifties, for instance, shows a society in which teenagers dressed very differently from adults, but by the early seventies, the family album shows the different generations wearing the same unisex clothes — especially at casual events. The Gap was established in 1969, supposedly to supply the casual clothing demands of those on the younger side of the generational divide, but the retail chain and its many imitators actually obliterated the generation gap in clothing. In the thirties and forties, teenage girls had looked to movie stars like Katharine Hepburn, Bette Davis, and Joan Crawford for style cues: the goal for the young was to look like sophisticated grown-ups. In the early sixties, Jacqueline Kennedy and Audrey Hepburn — still grown-ups — were style icons. By the end of the decade, however, the grown-ups were taking their cues from the young. Even Jacqueline Kennedy Onassis, albeit at the highest level of fashion, was dressing younger by the end of the sixties; her long hair, casual-seeming, artfully and expensively tailored pants, and silk T-shirts made her look younger at forty than she had as the carefully coiffed, white-gloved First Lady of Camelot in her early thirties.

The point is not that these changes were bad (although some of the more monomaniacal neocons have linked casual dress — yet another plot of the Movement! — with sloppy thinking) but that those who were young forty years ago have exerted a disproportionate and lasting influence, for better and for worse, on every generation they have touched. Baby boomers — the oldest just sixty-two and the youngest just forty-four — are running just about everything today. They are in charge of media conglomerates, government agencies, universities, the computer software business, service industries, and retailing. Marketing decisions about how to appeal to what is always described as "the coveted 18-to-34 age group" are being made, in many instances, by people whose membership in that age group expired in the early years of the Reagan administration. Given their political and financial power, those who came of age in the sixties and early seventies — on the political right and left — can hardly avoid accepting their share of responsibility for what has happened to American popular culture over the past four decades.

My somewhat jaundiced view of the sixties youth culture was shaped by an accident of personal history that isolated me, for two crucial years in my mid-twenties, from the kaleidoscope of distractions that had filled my days and nights and to which, through my role as a reporter, I had made my own modest contribution. In 1969, at age twenty-four, I married the *Post*'s Moscow correspondent, took a leave of absence from my reporting job, accompanied my new husband to Russia, and began work on my first book. I had landed on the moon — the drab and repressive Soviet Union ruled by a gerontocracy in which Leonid Brezhnev, who got along very well with Richard Nixon, was first among equals. Without the distractions offered by a prosperous and relatively uncensored society, I found that writing, reading, thinking, and talking with friends offered the only means of occupying my mind and my time. Strict Soviet censorship meant that the classics of drama, ballet, and music were the only enjoyable sources of public entertainment, and commercial sources of private entertainment — including the Internet and small, portable devices for recording music — did not yet exist.

The Soviet Union did of course have television, but apart from sports, the programming included nothing that could remotely be classified as entertaining. There were many things to see and do in Moscow, but everything worth seeing and doing was, in some fashion, a serious matter. An evening at the theater usually meant a Chekhov play or an adaptation of a great Russian novel. Concerts meant classical music, because the authorities frowned on most Western popular music. The performers were generally musicians of the first rank, because government travel restrictions meant that artists were not free to control their own careers by performing abroad. One of the most exciting, meaningful nights of my life was a performance in February 1971 by the stellar Russian cellist Mstislav Rostropovich and his students from the Moscow Conservatory. He had just written an open letter defending his friend Aleksandr Solzhenitsyn, and the Soviet authorities had already begun to punish him by canceling his performances abroad. Everyone in the audience knew this, and everyone in the hall stood for ten minutes and applauded before he began to play with tears in his eyes.

As it turned out, this would be the last

time Rostropovich was allowed to perform in Moscow until his return in 1993, after the dissolution of the Soviet Union. "Music and art are a whole spiritual world in Russia," he told me in an interview, after he had been forced to leave his homeland by the authorities. "In Russia, when people go to a concert, they don't go to it as an attraction, as an entertainment, but to feel life. . . . For us art is bread. I would like to communicate that to people here."[3]

Rostropovich's observation was a precise description of every aspect of the private cultural life Russians shared with their friends. The value that my Russian friends placed on high culture opened a new world to me. An evening in a Russian home might easily include an impromptu jazz concert and a recitation of the verses of the great twentieth-century Russian poets — Anna Akhmatova, Boris Pasternak, and Osip Mandelstam, whose works had been suppressed throughout most of the Soviet era. (Mandelstam, who was arrested and died in the Gulag in 1938 after writing an irreverent verse about Stalin, was not published at all.) Russian friends also wanted to leaf through my art books and pore over reproductions of famous paintings from Western museums, in cities — New York, Boston,

Paris, Florence, London, Amsterdam — they were sure they would never be able to visit because no one with their political views would ever be allowed to travel outside the Soviet Union. I reconstructed a recent visit to Florence for an artist friend, and as I tried to describe specific streets and views in my less than perfect Russian, I felt a searing shame at having taken for granted my freedom to travel anywhere to gaze on the masterpieces of Western culture.

There was a dissident youth culture in the Soviet Union; but in contrast to the Western youth culture, the rebellious young in Russia were intimately and self-consciously tied to the Russian cultural past. The written word was all important. A cultural "happening" was not a performance by a rock band but the arrival at someone's apartment of a typewritten *samizdat* manuscript — perhaps some new poems by the young Leningrad poet Joseph Brodsky or a copy of *Vospominaniye,* the powerful memoir by Osip Mandelstam's widow, Nadezhda.[*] The Russians I knew were true intellectuals — men and women who lived for ideas and

[*] Madame Mandelstam's memoir was published in English in 1970 under the title *Hope Against Hope* (Atheneum).

beauty and cultivated both under great duress. For them, devotion to all that was best in Russian and world culture was a survival strategy in a society they would never have chosen. For a fortunate young American, free to come and go as she pleased, there was great value in living for a time in a world of scarcity, in which serious men and women, bound by external constraints unimaginable to most Westerners, sought and maintained inner freedom. My Russian years enabled me, in fact forced me, to view many aspects of American society — especially its smug self-congratulation about liberties that were an unearned birthright for most citizens — from a very different perspective. But my time in Moscow altered my responses to American popular culture to a much greater degree, because I had been granted the privilege, for two impressionable young years, of living among people whose tastes were impervious to mass marketing — whether the product was being pushed by government or business.

When I returned to the United States, with the poetry of Akhmatova and Brodsky in my mind and heart, I found myself ill at ease in a cultural milieu where Paul Simon and Bob Dylan were being lionized as true poets, with Dylan sometimes being compared to Milton, Byron, Donne, and Keats. There was nothing new about the tendency of young people in the sixties to evaluate the arts solely on the basis of their capacity to evoke strong emotions: every generation judges popular music, in particular, by its ability to elicit tears and sexual excitement — the more of both the better. One of the more droll right-wing diatribes against the sixties concerns rock music, which cultural conservatives like Bloom, Bork, and the Harvard government professor Harvey C. Mansfield criticize not only because they make a principle of hating everything about the era but on the specious ground that rock differs from all other popular music in its direct appeal to lust. "Rock is sex on parade," Mansfield soberly declares.[4] As opposed to forms of pop music in which sex is not on parade? Mansfield praises jazz and the blues; he apparently thinks that the "jelly" in "Jelly Roll Blues" refers to a substance eaten with peanut butter.

The most aggravating result of the reign of rock was that everyone took it too seriously. Undeterred by the censorious grumbling of the cultural right, the gaseous theologians of the cultural left have long attempted to enshrine the music of the sixties counterculture — as if this particular pop manifestation possesses a mystical and philosophical significance raising it above the level of mere entertainment. Songwriters of the sixties were hailed as great poets by a pretentious new class of academic critics — much longer in the tooth than the average music consumer — who hitched old techniques of literary criticism to the rising generation of pop stars. Christopher Ricks, a professor of humanities at Boston University and the Oxford Professor of Poetry, compared Dylan's "Lay, Lady, Lay," in which said lady is told to extend herself across a "big brass bed," to John Donne's elegy, "To His Mistress Going to Bed." (Ricks, who is a truly distinguished scholar of real English poetry, inexplicably ignores Dylan's role in confusing the distinction between "lie" and "lay" for boomers who came of age under the spell of this song.) The publication in 2003 of Ricks's *Dylan's Visions of Sin,* an unreadable 517-page tome that makes one long for a Dwight Macdonald to give it the skewering it deserves, was a landmark in the continuing hagiography of sixties pop culture.

Dylan and Simon, as it happens, were always quick to dismiss such nonsense. Simon spoke most forcefully on this point in a 1968 interview, in which he observed that "the lyrics of pop songs are so banal that if you show a spark of intelligence, they call you a poet. And if you say you're not a poet, then people think you're putting yourself down. But the people who call you a poet are people who never read poetry. Like poetry was something defined by Bob Dylan. They never read, say, Wallace Stevens. That's poetry."[5] Simon added that he did not consider himself, Dylan, or the Beatles real musicians, because real musicians must be virtuosos on their instruments. Dylan, asked what his songs were "about," famously replied, "Some of them are about three minutes and some are about five minutes."[6]

Of course most pop music enthusiasts never knew or cared what academics were saying about their favorite songs, but the combination of respectful criticism from certified intellectuals with increasingly sophisticated mechanisms for the marketing of mass entertainment offered a preview of a future in which the entire idea of critical authority, of any objective standards for assessing artistic quality, would be considered laughable. Resistance to the idea of aesthetic hierarchy is unquestionably one of the most powerful cultural legacies of the sixties, and it is now a leitmotif of much of the art, music, and literary criticism produced by baby boomers who write for mainstream media. A perfect specimen of the genre is an essay by Allan Kozinn, a classical music critic for *The New York Times* who also occasionally writes about pop music. Kozinn compares new versions recorded by new bands — known in the trade as covers — of legendary Beatles songs.

Lately I've been wondering why, as a more than casual Beatles fan, I'm not interested in note-perfect covers by Beatles tribute bands, even though, as a classical music critic, I happily spend my nights listening to re-creations — covers, in a way — of Beethoven symphonies and Haydn string quartets. What, when it comes down to it, is the difference?

Obviously, this is something of a comparison between apples and oranges: we first heard the Beatles' music on their own recordings, whose sounds are imprinted on our memories and are definitive. Our first encounters with, say, Beethoven's Ninth Symphony were through performances that, however spectacular, have no direct link to Beethoven himself. Yet Beethoven's score of the work is a detailed blueprint of how he expected it to sound, and any performance will be governed by that, allowing for interpretive leeway that may be subtle or dramatic. A cover band, hoping to reproduce the original recording, has less flexibility.[7]

What, when it comes down to it, is the difference? It is the difference between Beethoven's Ninth Symphony (or any Beethoven symphony) and any song or collection of songs by the Beatles. The difference is the infinitely greater emotional richness, technical complexity, and beauty of Beethoven. I too am a Beatles fan, but, let's face it, if you've heard one version of "Sgt. Pepper's Lonely Hearts Club Band," you've pretty much heard them all. (An exception was a doo-wop version recorded in the nineties, and about that, the less said the better.) In his heart, Kozinn must know this, or he would be a rock music critic and not a classical music critic. Of course it is possible — in fact, it is easy — to love both Beethoven and the Beatles, but any suggestion that they rise to the same level of musical genius is a generational delusion propelled by marketing and the sentimentality to which marketers cater so assiduously.

In 1956, Chuck Berry's hit single "Roll

Over Beethoven" heralded the rise of fifties rock-and-roll with the sassy line, "Roll over Beethoven and tell Tchaikovsky the news." The song, which can still make me jump off a couch and start gyrating, became even more popular in the sixties after being recorded and performed frequently in concert by the Beatles. However, many of the younger, second-generation "Roll Over Beethoven" fans of the sixties and seventies had never listened to Beethoven or Tchaikovsky. Just as "This Land Is Your Land" was removed from its historical context by the Nixon cheerleaders, the title "Roll Over Beethoven" lost its wit and its sting at a time when fewer and fewer young people had any interest in DWEM composers. In the long run, nothing dumbs down culture more effectively than the ripping of popular art — good, bad, or indifferent in quality — from its specific cultural antecedents.

The decline of once common cultural knowledge among the young was encouraged throughout the sixties not only by the ever-enlarging maw of the entertainment behemoth but by changes in the curriculum of public elementary and secondary schools. Until the mid-fifties, most public schools in cities and suburbs included music classes in a standard curriculum that forced children to learn something, if only cultural reference points like the first few bars of Beethoven's Fifth Symphony, about classical music. In a considerable number of these schools, children also learned how to read music. That began to change in the late fifties, with the panic over Sputnik, and the trend continued throughout the sixties, as public schools made haste to jettison music and art classes — called "frills" — in favor of beefed-up science and mathematics designed to ensure that the Russians would never again beat us in a space race.

Max Rafferty, a crochety right-winger who served as California's elected Superintendent of Public Instruction throughout most of the decade, providing another example of the counter-counterculture at work, decried art and music programs as "finger painting" and "folk dancing."[8] Although he was a tireless proponent of Latin, Rafferty was either uninterested in or unable to imagine an art or music curriculum that emphasized classics, and California voters approved of his combination of anti-intellectual rhetoric and opposition to progressive education.[*]

[*] In 1970, in a characteristic California about-face, Rafferty was defeated for reelection by Wilson C. Riles, a noted black educator, a liberal, and

Throughout the nation, the American tendency to value education only in terms of its practical results — a phenomenon as old as the republic — reasserted itself strongly in the "no frills" decisions of many local and state school boards. That the eliminated frills had once provided children with some exposure to a higher culture than pop was a matter of little concern to the public.

All of the driving social forces of the sixties — the counterculture, the counter-counterculture, and the popular youth culture — were stimulated by television. In a history devoted entirely to the events of 1968, Mark Kurlansky writes that "all of this [was] occurring at the moment that television was coming of age but was still new enough not to have yet become controlled, distilled, and packaged the way it is today." Yes and no. It is true, as Kurlansky argues, that in the late sixties, "the phenomenon of a same-day broadcast from another part of the world was in itself a gripping new technological wonder."[9] Yet in one critical respect, coverage of news and the people

a strong supporter of the federal aid to education programs established under the Johnson administration.

who made it — not only in the political arena but in the arts and in the vast realm of private experience that included sexual behavior and drug use — was already assuming its present packaged and distilled form.

The culture of celebrity, defined by the media's circular capacity to create stars who shine not because of specific deeds but mainly because they are the objects of media attention, was a true child of the sixties. No one summed up the process better than the Yippie-turned-entrepreneur Jerry Rubin, who, looking back on his sixties escapades in 1976 from the ripe old age of thirty-seven, boasted: "People respect famous people — they are automatically interested in what I have to say. Nobody knows exactly what I have done, but they know I'm *famous.*"[10] A decade later, Rubin would grasp the spirit of yet another age by organizing "networking" nightclub events for upscale Manhattanites and trying to drum up investors for a vague plan to establish a national chain of "networking restaurants."

Of course, there was nothing new about the importance of celebrities — some of them even intellectual celebrities — in American culture. Charles Lindbergh was a bigger celebrity in the twenties than Neil Armstrong was in the sixties; Ernest Hemingway, even without television and book tours, was more famous than Norman Mailer.[11] What distinguished the sixties from earlier stages of the American love affair with celebrities was not just the growing power of television but the proliferation of movements and causes, all requiring individuals — celebrities — for purposes of illustration. Had the sixties really given birth to the overarching Movement of right-wing myth, there would have been no need for the media to seek, find, and anoint so many demi-celebrities as leaders. There was no feminist or antiwar or black power central headquarters for a reporter to call, and there was no reliable way to ascertain who spoke for whom or how many.

King was arguably the last American leader of a social protest movement whose claims to leadership, while ultimately certified and publicized by the media, were grounded in years of grassroots work that made him a genuine rather than a media-appointed spokesman for millions of black Americans. For whom did Rubin, Mark Rudd, Abbie Hoffman, Eldridge Cleaver, or Timothy Leary speak? Who knew? As Rubin's 1976 comment suggests, it took Ameri-

371

cans less than a decade to forget exactly what his connection had been with the antiwar movement and with various events such as the San Francisco "Be-In" of 1967. At the "Be-In," tens of thousands of young and not so young people, decked out in love beads and smoking pot in full view of national television cameras, gathered in Golden Gate Park to hear speakers who included Rubin, Allen Ginsberg, and Timothy Leary, the ex-Harvard psychologist whose chief mission had become propagandizing for psychedelic drugs and delivering the message, "Turn on, tune in, drop out."

What Americans saw on their televisions was a spontaneous-appearing gathering — carefully orchestrated, in fact, by the media-savvy expressionist painter Michael Bowen — that conflated antiwar messages, hatred of government bureaucracy, drugs, gurus, and, as always, rock music. The highlighted speakers ranged from serious people to dangerous frauds like Leary, but the toxic fumes of celebrity culture were the strongest drugs being dispensed and consumed. The selling of Leary personified what the sociologist and media critic Todd Gitlin has aptly called "the marketing of transgression," a process that worked for the transgressions and transgressors of the sixties and continues to work, on a more sophisticated level and with an ever-expanding reach, for the most popular transgressive products of the twenty-first century.

Leary was a lunatic, as anyone not blinded by the celebrity machine knew forty years ago. He was nothing more, as one student observed at the time, than "a Harvard professor who dropped acid."[12] He had been hired by Harvard's psychology department in 1959 on the strength of his reputation as a specialist in personality assessment — an area of expertise apparently absent from the deliberations of his Harvard interviewing committee — but he was fired in 1963 as a result of the negative publicity surrounding his proselytizing for LSD. Yet he became famous largely on the strength of his ability to convince some members of the media that there might be something to his claim that psychedelics could unlock previously hidden creativity (perhaps even turn a newspaper or television reporter into a poet or a novelist). He also had a gift for hooking up with immensely rich people who financed his proselytizing and his drugs. In the mid-sixties in Millbrook, New York, where Leary threw lavish tripping parties on an estate provided by three heirs to the Mellon fortune, the former professor became the object of numerous prosecutions by the local assistant district attorney, G. Gordon Liddy, before Liddy acquired his own fame as one of the masterminds of the Watergate break-in at Democratic National Committee headquarters.

The tale of Leary's escapades, ending with his arrest in 1973 on federal drug charges and his decision to turn state's evidence in order to avoid a twenty-five-year prison sentence, unfolds in all of its sordid detail in Robert Greenfield's *Timothy Leary: A Biography* (2006), an exhaustive and exhausting 704-page tome. The book, which received an enormous amount of publicity, is a tribute to the lasting power of celebrity, including vintage celebrity, branding. Some worthless celebrities really do get more than fifteen minutes of fame.

Both the sentimentalizers and the bashers of the sixties have a stake in building up scarecrow celebrities who are held up as heroic or cautionary examples of the splendid or sordid developments of the decade. Leary's role in the drug culture of the sixties was a case of the times making the man rather than the reverse; he was born, after all, in 1920, and his "gateway drug" to psychedelics was not marijuana but the legal chemical substance, alcohol, favored by his generation. For a variety of reasons, the appeal of drugs — which had never really broken out of a bohemian "some get a kick from cocaine" subculture in the past — expanded in the sixties to a broader middle-class public. It is doubtful that Leary would have had any cultural influence at all, except on those students unlucky enough to cross his path personally, if the television cameras had never been tuned into and turned on for his performances.

One thing is certain: more American kids got hooked on marijuana, LSD, and heroin in Vietnam than they did listening to Leary in Harvard Yard or Golden Gate Park. Like rock music, the drug culture crossed racial, class, and political barriers. By focusing on a celebrity as the embodiment of a phenomenon that was reaching every level of American society, the media generated publicity that both demonized and glamorized drugs but eschewed any real analysis of why drug use was on the rise and what the change in behavior meant for the future. Watching reports about the "Be-In" on the evening news, Middle Americans might have been thinking about what a jerk Leary was or how shocked they were at the sight of a girl whose love beads did not quite hide the outline of her nipples. The younger members of the audience — for they were an audience, just as the event itself was a performance — might have been thinking about how much they would like to be in San Francisco themselves to take a firsthand look at the goings-on. At that point, it is unlikely that many audience members — whether adherents of the counterculture or the counter-counterculture — were thinking about American boys getting hooked on heroin in the back alleys and brothels of Saigon.

I have spoken mainly of television as the medium through which the culture of celebrity was propagated, but the print media — far more important then than now — also played an important role. I was proud of working for a newspaper that gave reporters the time and space to tell stories in greater depth than television was able to provide, and at the time I did not view print journalism as a competitor of television. There were still three newspapers in Washington, and the *Evening Star* was the main competitor of the *Post.* The job of television, as I saw it, was to provide same-day pictures of what was happening around the world; the job of the newspaper — *my* job — was to explain why these things were happening. But even forty years ago, as I walked around Washington with my reporter's notebook in hand, and phoned my stories in to the city desk if there was breaking news, the expansion of television news was subtlely changing the way newspaper reporters did their jobs.

My awareness that self-appointed spokesmen, always the quickest protesters to step up to the television microphones, would be appearing on the evening news before my story appeared in the morning paper created extra pressure to find my own spokesmen — in effect, to anoint my own local celebrities. In general, my approach to the problem was to look for representatives less flashy and more thoughtful than the ones who appeared on television. In the spring of 1968, Howard University, the nation's oldest and best known black institution of higher education, was wracked by the same kind of student protests that were disrupting predominantly white campuses across the nation. Some of the issues, including the war and the limits of free speech, were identical to those at white colleges, but others involved the increasingly abrasive debate between young blacks and their parents' and grandparents' generations about how far blacks should go to accommodate themselves to a white world.

Most of the Howard students featured on television were angry-looking young men, Stokely Carmichaels manqués sporting Afros and dark sunglasses. I chose to interview the editor of the student newspaper, Adrienne Manns, partly because she *was* the campus newspaper editor, partly because she seemed more thoughtful than some of the other student leaders, and partly because she was a woman — and, in what was still the pre-feminist era, I was getting tired of always seeing men identified as the only leaders whose opinions counted. Manns introduced me to the sardonic phrase "chitterling education," a philosophy rooted in the era of segregation, when Howard was the pinnacle of achievement for any outstanding black scholar because white universities did not hire Negroes (as they called themselves then). To lose one's job at Howard meant there was nowhere to go but down, and that made for a quiescent faculty.

Protesters at Howard believed that chitterling education accounted for the older faculty's expectation that students refrain from any criticism of the education they were getting because they should be grateful to be getting any education at all. If

378

white veterans were members of the grateful generation, the Negro elders at Howard were doubly grateful. The older generation also expected students to be deferential to whites, Manns said, citing as an example the administration's sharp curtailment of all speech on campus after Howard students had shouted down the Selective Service Administration's director general Lewis B. Hershey. I was impressed by Manns's argument: it was certainly true that Howard students had done no more than white students had done across the nation when military recruiters appeared on campus. "The administration is not sympathetic to the new mood of the black student," Manns told me. "Most of them don't understand; if they do understand, they view what we're saying as a challenge to what they've built up, to their own identity."

Later, when I interviewed the university's sixty-seven-year-old president, James M. Nabrit, Jr., he brought me up short by reminding me that it had only been twenty years since President Harry S. Truman desegregated the military by executive order. Twenty years was not enough time, he said, for members of his generation to approve of students drowning out the voice of a general who had come to their campus to speak. In the same vein, Nabrit mused about his days as the lone Negro in his law school classes at Northwestern University:

> When I was a student at Northwestern, my white classmates would all stamp their feet whenever I started to recite . . . the professors never called on me. One day I asked my question anyway. The professor just turned to the class and said, "As I was saying before we were interrupted. . . ." If I had been thin-skinned, I would have left but I stayed on to make the highest average in the class. Today's Negro students armor themselves in a different way . . . those of us who are older have difficulty breaking away from our own experiences so we can be receptive to new ways of thinking.[13]

Both Nabrit and Manns were right, but I left my interview with the conviction that the president of Howard understood the students much better than they realized — and that he certainly understood them much better than they understood him. The entire affair was infinitely more complicated than the action-filled story I had told in my daily articles for the *Post*. I do not think that I turned Manns, or any other student leaders at Howard, into celebrities, and much of the material from my interviews with both Manns and Nabrit did originally appear in the paper. Nevertheless, I could not do justice to the story — which was really a tale of the limits white America had long placed on the ambitions of black Americans and differing generational views of those limits — until *Saturday Review*, in the waning stage of its middlebrow life, gave me 4,000 words to write about Howard. The more limited the space, the greater had been the temptation to rely on a demi-celebrity and shortchange what was really a story about history. And if I had failed to fully convey the complicated historical roots and implications of the Howard controversy in the many articles I wrote for the *Post*, television had broadcast what amounted to a daily cartoon of angry young men in phony dashikis and embarrassed-looking old men in suits and ties.

The celebrity-making role of the media was even more evident in New York newspaper coverage of the student uprising at Columbia, which came to a head soon after the student rebellion at Howard. The New York television stations and newspapers fixated on Mark Rudd as the dominant campus leader. And because New York was the media capital of the nation, Rudd — who combined articulateness, a fair portion of wild-eyed charisma, and the story line of a nice Jewish boy taking on "the system" instead of working toward the goal of becoming "my son, the doctor" — was converted almost instantly from a local spokesman into a national celebrity. The influence of the celebrity culture on the print media was evinced by the decision of *The New York Times Magazine* to reject the idea of running an article on the entire student movement or on Columbia's military connections and instead to try to obtain a profile of Rudd.[14]

In *The Whole World Is Watching* (originally published in 1980, when former editors' memories were still relatively fresh), Todd Gitlin provides an insightful account of the magazine's editorial process. The process was circular: the pressure to "personalize" was directly proportional to the bigness of the story, and the story grew bigger the more it was personalized. That a major university's relationship with the defense establishment was a real story in itself — worthy of investigation with or without the campus turmoil, with or without the presence of television cameras — was beside the point. Without the student demonstrations, there was no story as far as either newspapers or television were concerned, and without a media-anointed leader, there was no focal point for news coverage. Newspapers could dig deeper than television, but they could not take a completely different tack. If a reporter failed to quote someone who appeared in a television news segment, her editor would ask why.

The insistence on celebrity personalization would become even more intense with the birth of the new feminist movement, because judging women on the basis of their appearance is as acceptable in the culture of journalism as it is throughout American culture. It was no accident that journalists who wished to advance the cause of feminism seized on the glamorous Gloria Steinem as the voice of the women's movement. With her mane of streaked hair and a svelte body that had once enabled her to pass as a Playboy bunny while doing research for a magazine article, Steinem was a living refutation of the negative stereotype of a feminist as an ugly woman who could not possibly hope to get a man. Steinem was in fact a real leader, but that is not why she got so much more coverage than other, equally real feminist leaders. Anti-feminist journalists, by contrast, loved to focus on writers like Andrea Dworkin, a fat, unkempt woman considered by some to be a brilliant and original thinker but utterly lacking in conventional feminine attractiveness. Feminists who were careless about their appearance, and who clearly did not care about making themselves attractive to men, supported all of the stereotypes about "women's libbers" as frustrated losers in the dating game. The image became the message.

In an astute essay on the ways in which contemporary preoccupations influence every historian's assessment of the past, Arthur Schlesinger, Jr., observes that it is impossible to "put a coin in a slot and have history come out. For the past is a chaos of events and personalities into which we cannot penetrate. It is beyond retrieval and it is beyond reconstruction. All historians know this in their souls." He adds that "conceptions of the past are far from stable," and that when "new urgencies arise in our own times and lives, the historian's spotlight shifts, probing now into the shadows, throwing into sharp relief things that were always there but that earlier historians had carelessly excised from the collective memory."[15] Schlesinger was speaking of history in general, but his observation is even more pertinent when the history in question is relatively recent and the "historians" were themselves actors in the drama.

Conceptions of the past known as "the Sixties" are not only unstable but, for the moment, irreconcilable. Current assessments of the sixties are in no way comparable to the many books written in the fifties, sixties, and seventies about America in the thirties, because there is no consensus today about the political legacy of the sixties. The legacy of the New Deal, by contrast, was assimilated during the postwar years by nearly every group within American society — something the Bush administration discovered only when it started pushing for the privatization of Social Security and most voters reacted with fear and anger. No politician understood the irreversibility of certain New Deal precepts better than Ronald Reagan, who was shrewd enough never to say a cross word about Social Security or its offspring, Medicare, and who always took great pains to emphasize that his political conservatism in no way detracted from his respect for Franklin Roosevelt.

The sixties, however, remain a source of bitter controversy in a nation whose presidents for the past sixteen years have been

Bill Clinton, an exemplar of the counterculture, followed by George W. Bush, a product of the conservative Other Sixties (although the reports of Bush's wild youth suggest that he too sampled the wares in the counterculture bazaar). Most "histories" of the sixties being written today are really memoirs by authors intent on justifying or repudiating their youthful selves and taking one more whack at their old adversaries. Debates about the cultural legacy of the sixties are generally conducted on the same politicized ground, in a fashion obscuring the fact that the most enduring and important anti-intellectual forces of the decade were apolitical: they could — and would — be used in the service of any and every form of politics.

The real importance of the sixties in American intellectual history is that they marked the beginning of the eclipse of the print culture by the culture of video: the political street theater of the late sixties was perfectly suited to video, and vice versa. It will never be possible to tell the tail from the dog, because video works well for nearly every actor on the political stage — whether a student celebrity shouting through a megaphone on the steps of a university library or a president bragging "Mission Accomplished" on the deck of an aircraft carrier. The only kind of politics that does not lend itself to video images is any political appeal to thoughtfulness, reason, and logic. The fusion of video, the culture of celebrity, and the marketing of youth is the real anti-intellectual legacy of the sixties. If — if only! — this trifecta had been narrowly political, it could never have gained the power it exercises in every area of American culture today.

CHAPTER EIGHT:
THE NEW OLD-TIME
RELIGION

In spite of various pronouncements concerning the "death of God" in the late sixties, there was never any likelihood that religion would wither away in American life. It did seem likely, though, that the religious landscape of the late twentieth century would acquire a less dogmatic character and that the prosperity and expanded educational opportunity of the postwar era would undermine the more ardent, literal, parochial, and anti-rational forms of faith that had long flourished in the uniquely free American religious marketplace. Growing up in the fifties and sixties in a small town in mid-Michigan, I breathed in the ethos of a community in which religion occupied a private, not a public, role. I attended both public and Roman Catholic parochial schools, and my parents' decisions on such matters were determined by their evaluation of the quality of the public schools in the neighborhoods where we lived — by secular rather than religious considerations. They took my brother out of a public school where he was having trouble learning to read, and they decided against Catholic high schools because the local public schools were thought to provide more rigorous preparation for college-bound students.

From a child's vantage point, the main difference between parochial and public schools was that mass, prayer, and catechism classes were not a part of the public school day. The absence of prayer and religious instruction in public schools was taken for granted: if you wanted your children to receive religious teaching or spiritual exhortations in class, you paid tuition to a parochial school for that purpose. Although nearly everyone in our Michigan suburb went to some church on Sunday, and a few — a very few — went to temple on Saturday, there probably would have been hell to pay if some teacher had decided to open her class with a prayer or if a prayer for the victory of Okemos High School had been offered up over the loudspeaker before a football game.

The 1962 Supreme Court decision *Engel v. Vitale,* which declared even nondenominational school prayer unconstitutional and aroused the ire of conservative Protestant and Roman Catholic clerics across the nation, caused scarcely a ripple in our school district. We did not pray in our schools anyway, so why should anyone have been upset about the decision? In its omission of public school prayers, Okemos, Michigan, was the rule rather than the exception. The day after the *Engel* decision was handed down, a survey of education officials found that prayer was a routine practice in only one third of the nation's school districts.[1] School prayer was generally confined to areas of the country and neighborhoods, usually in rural settings or small towns, with homogenous student bodies. There were no Christian clubs or Christian proselytizers in the Okemos public schools, because it was highly unusual for anyone, of any religion, to make a conspicuous public show of faith. Those who did so, like the Jehovah's Witness family across the street and the Christian Scientists down the block, were considered decidedly peculiar.

I now realize that many Okemos residents of my parents' generation were children or grandchildren of immigrants and had grown up in city neighorhoods where religion and ethnicity were assumed to be the most important predictors of the future. By becoming the first members of their families to attend college and moving to the expanding postwar suburbs, these second- and third-generation Americans had cast their lot with a different way of life. Both suburbanization and higher education were secularizing forces, in that they brought together people of different faiths and ethnic backgrounds on the same turf in a manner that could not help but erode certain traditional loyalties. The unprecedented incidence of interfaith marriage among baby boomers, even though such unions were strongly opposed by many religious leaders as recently as the sixties and seventies, offers what may be the most powerful evidence of the decreasing importance of sectarian religious loyalties in the private lives of families bringing up children in the two decades after the Second World War. Most baby boomers were not raised to fear that they would go to hell or, in the case of Jews, that their parents would sit *shiva,* if they married outside their faith.

As for public life, John Kennedy could never have been elected the nation's first Catholic president if religion had not been on the wane as a divisive force. An integral element of Kennedy's election strategy was his portrayal of religion as a private rather than a public affair. "I do not speak for my church on public matters — and the church does not speak for me" was the famous reassurance uttered by the candidate at a press conference before Protestant ministers in Houston. One did not have to be among George Wallace's "great pointy-heads" to have concluded, by the middle of the 1960s, that less traditional forms of religion, incorporating secular values, would become more influential in American culture and politics during the closing decades of the twentieth century. I cannot prove it, because public opinion pollsters were not asking many questions in the sixties about specific religious beliefs or their influence on public issues, but I think that most of the adults in my neighborhood would have scoffed at any suggestion that Genesis should receive equal time with Darwin in public school biology classes. I am quite certain that they would have been puzzled by the question, because the teaching of evolution was even less of an issue than school prayer.

That is not to say that my parents' friends and neighbors were irreligious or anti-religious but that they were perfectly comfortable with the idea that Caesar and God had separate domains. Like so many American academics and liberal clergy of that era, they would have seen fundamentalist biblical literalism as a primitive form of faith that belonged to a less educated past, in which religion had yet to come to terms with modern knowledge. The Other Sixties, and their stirrings of resurgent right-wing religious fundamentalism, were as invisible to residents of the middle-class suburb where I was raised, populated by families with middlebrow aspirations, as they were to the governing and academic elites.

As we now know, the conclusion that American fundamentalists were a dying breed was a misjudgment of historic (dare one call it biblical?) proportions. The growth of fundamentalist denominations at the expense of mainstream and liberal Protestantism, which began in the fifties, accelerated throughout the sixties, seventies, and eighties and gave birth to the Christian right. Only 46 percent of American Protestants in 2003, compared with 59 percent in 1960, identified themselves as members of "mainline denominations."[2] Episcopalians, Presbyterians, Methodists, and Unitarians, four of the oldest and most influential Protestant mainline denominations, lost ground steadily to churches affiliated with the Southern Baptist Convention, which had reasserted its fundamentalist identity so strongly during the turbulent sixties. In 1960, the Methodist Church alone had 2 million more members than Southern Baptist churches; by the beginning of the twenty-first century, Southern Baptists would outnumber Methodists, Presbyterians, Episcopalians, and members of the United Church of Christ combined.

Between 1979 and 1985, the hard-core fundamentalists within the Southern Baptist Convention — those who agreed with the Reverend W. A. Criswell's view of religious liberals as "skunks" — gained control of the denomination's elective and administrative offices.[3] Many church members allied with the libertarian side of Baptist tradition found a new spiritual home in the more liberal evangelical American Baptist Churches of the U.S.A., the current name for the northern denomination that emerged after Baptists originally split over the issue of slavery in 1845. Fundamentalist influence among the Southern Baptists solidified just in time for the 1980 presidential campaign, and Ronald Reagan became the first Republican candidate to openly court conservative Christian voters. The movement of Protestant fundamentalists into the Republican Party represented a political shift of historic proportions, and political analysts who had ignored the right-wing religious undercurrents during the Other Sixties were taken by surprise.

Many observers have argued that the current fundamentalist revival is simply one more cyclical manifestation, like the First Great Awakening in the mid-eighteenth century and the Second Great Awakening in the early nineteenth century, of the emotional, personal religion that always played an important role in American culture. In this view, the revival of fundamentalism in the last three decades has been a response to the social upheavals of the late sixties and early seventies, with the defining event being the 1973 Supreme Court decision, *Roe v. Wade,* legalizing abortion. Just as the Second Great Awakening arose from the social dislocation of the American Revolution, the late twentieth-century fundamentalist resurgence can be viewed as a "course correction" in an unsettled society. This explanation is certainly comforting to the nonreligious, who long to believe that there will be an end to a phenomenon that discomfits and baffles them; secularists would like to think that American fundamentalists, even though they are not likely to disappear before the "rapture," will nevertheless settle down for a good long rest and stop interfering with secular matters.

But this soothing analysis does not take into account the disjunction that exists today between fundamentalist faith and the sum of human knowledge: it is much easier to understand why an American would have sought the answer to life's problems in a passionate "born again" relationship with God in 1800 than in 2000. Furthermore, the potential for lethal practical consequences increases as the gap between evidence-based science and faith widens. It did relatively little harm in the early nineteenth century for preachers to proclaim that sickness and death must be accepted as God's punishment for sin, because science and medicine had almost nothing to offer as an alternative to acceptance of the divine will. It does great harm today, however, for Protestant fundamentalists and right-wing Catholics to insist, against all scientific evidence, that condoms do nothing to halt the spread of AIDS and that abstinence — the only method sanctioned by God and the course least likely to be followed by humans — is the single morally legitimate way to fight life-threatening disease. Nor did it really matter if vast numbers of

Americans believed, at the time of the Second Great Awakening, that the earth was exactly four thousand years old. It matters very much today because creationism, which denies the most critical scientific insights not only of the twentieth but of the nineteenth century, has adversely affected public education in many areas of the nation and is one important reason why American high school students know less about science than their contemporaries in Europe and Asia.

What does it mean to be an American fundamentalist in the first decade of the twenty-first century? The word "fundamentalism" is rarely used in surveys of Americans' religious self-identification, in large measure because the term is considered a pejorative even by many fundamentalists themselves. Pollsters usually ask whether Americans consider themselves "evangelicals," because evangelical is a broader, less loaded term that can encompass both theological liberals and theological conservatives. Former President Jimmy Carter and President George W. Bush are both evangelicals, but Bush's statements indicate that he is a fundamentalist while Carter, who strongly supports the teaching of evolution in schools, falls on the liberal side of the evangelical divide. The main difference between fundamentalists and evangelicals, although they share a faith that rests on an intimate, personal relationship between God and man, is that not all evangelicals regard the Bible as literally true but all fundamentalists do.

Yet inconsistencies abound even among the one third of Americans who say that they consider the Bible the literal word of God — not merely "inspired by God" but, from the serpent in the Garden of Eden to Jesus' resurrection from the grave, an explicit blueprint handed down by the deity, with Part I going directly to Moses and Part II through Jesus to the twelve apostles. Even more Americans — four in ten — believe that God made man in his present form, in one distinct act of creation, during the past 10,000 years. There is something mysterious about the finding that Americans are more likely to believe in the creation account set forth in Genesis than they are to credit the literal truth of the whole Bible. Apparently many people accept the story that God created Adam out of dust and Eve out of Adam's rib but balk at subsequent whims of the Supreme Being, say, sending a flood to destroy everyone on earth but one family or making a ninety-year-old woman pregnant by her hundred-year-old husband Abraham, the progenitor of the Jewish people, and then asking Abraham to kill his only son. A similar inconsistency is apparent in polls showing that nearly two thirds of Americans believe in heaven but fewer than half believe in hell.[4] It seems that the American tendency to choose from a cafeteria-style theological menu is not limited to Catholics.

Regardless of how fundamentalists fine-tune their beliefs, there is unquestionably a powerful correlation between religious fundamentalism and lack of education. Approximately 45 percent of those who have no education beyond high school believe in the literal truth of the Bible, while only 29 percent with some college — and just 19 percent of college graduates — share that old-time faith. Secularism, skepticism, and acceptance of mainstream science all rise with education; two thirds of college graduates, but only about one third of high school graduates, believe that living beings have evolved over time — with or without the guiding hand of a creator.[5]

Fundamentalists understandably resent any mention, especially when the subject is mentioned by secularists, of the correlation between poor education and biblical literalism. It is a fact, however, that the South remains the most educationally backward region of the nation, and southerners are far more likely than other Americans to profess fundamentalist faith. The education gap between northern and southern states has of course diminished since the time of the Scopes trial — most markedly after the Second World War — but the South still lags several percentage points behind the Northeast, Midwest, and West in its proportion of both college and high school graduates. Some states in the Deep South, including Louisiana, Mississippi, and Arkansas, lag at least 10 percentage points behind the West and Northeast in high school graduation rates.[6]

Since the end of legal segregation, boosterism about the "New South" has obscured the fact that the Old South still lives on in many public school systems that fail to serve either blacks or poor whites. The abysmal state of public education in New Orleans became apparent to the rest of the nation only when Hurricane Katrina cast a harsh light on the poverty of many of the city's residents. The causes of the South's education deficit are complex and inseparable from the region's heritage of segregation, but there is no question that religious fundamentalism — particularly since the sixties — encourages lack of commitment to public education or that poor education encourages biblical literalism. In politics, the nexus between fundamentalism and lack of education has enabled right-wing Christian candidates to tap into suspicion of educated "elites."

At the same time, the Christian right has placed increasing emphasis on the development of its own "elites" through of a network of ultra-conservative Christian colleges. Institutions like Bob Jones University in Greenville, South Carolina — now an obligatory stop for all Republican presidential candidates — and Patrick Henry College in Purcellville, Virginia, whose motto is "For Christ and for Liberty," were intended not only as an alternative to purely secular institutions but also to universities with religious roots, such as Baylor and Southern Methodist, which fundamentalists consider corrupted by secular values. Patrick Henry, located about fifty miles west of Washington, D.C., was established specifically to train conservative fundamentalists for jobs in government. Most of its students are the products of home schooling, a practice lauded by the most extreme elements of the Christian right, and campus life is carefully supervised in an effort to maintain the religious and ideological purity of the students' faith-based elementary and secondary education. For several days before the 2004 presidential election, classes were canceled because so many students were working in the campaign to reelect Bush.[7] By placing students in a college environment that reinforces rather than challenges the values they learned as children — a mission contrary to that of secular institutions — American fundamentalists are attempting to produce a new generation with a higher education good enough to dispel old backwoods stereotypes but limited enough to protect the young from the secular culture's assaults on biblically literal Christianity.

Another critical difference between the fundamentalist revivals of the past and the present is the political engagement of modern fundamentalists on the side of one party and their belief that it is both a right and a religious duty to institutionalize their moral values. As William Jennings Bryan's long career demonstrates most forcefully, fundamentalists were never completely disengaged from politics, but their civic involvement was rarely — Bryan's anti-evolution campaign being the exception —

focused on the propagation of their religious beliefs. Eighteenth- and nineteenth-century fundamentalists, as well as evangelicals who did not adhere to strict fundamentalism, were generally more concerned about being let alone by the government to practice their religion than about imposing their religious practices on others. Modern fundamentalists have forgotten, if they ever knew, that they owe their liberty of conscience to the demonized Enlightenment rationalism that gave birth to the secular Constitution.

In a 2006 survey by the Pew Forum, one question asked, "Which should be the more important influence on the laws of the United States? Should it be the Bible or should it be the will of the American people, even when it conflicts with the Bible?" An astounding 60 percent of white evangelical Christians replied that the Bible, not the will of the people, should shape U.S. law. That point of view was held by only 16 percent of white mainline Protestants, 23 percent of Catholics, and 7 percent of those identifying themselves as secularists. Black Protestants, by a margin of 53 to 44 percent, were the only other group that favored the Bible instead of the people's will. As has often been noted, African Americans are the one group for whom biblical literalism translates into support for liberal rather than conservative social policies — a mind-set directly descended from the days when slaves looked to the Bible, especially the story of Exodus, as a divine source of hope for liberation from slavery.[8]

These findings are particularly striking because they suggest that nonfundamentalists are losing ground within the evangelical movement itself. If six in ten white evangelicals believe that the Bible should provide the basis for American law, it stands to reason that the same proportion of evangelicals belong not to the tolerant side of evangelical Protestantism represented by Carter but to the authoritarian side embodied by such organizations as James Dobson's Focus on the Family and Pat Robertson's Christian Coalition. These people may prefer to call themselves and be called by the more socially acceptable name "evangelical," but they are in fact hard-core fundamentalists dedicated to the Christianizing of American public institutions.

Many scholars and journalists who might be considered members of "the elites" simply do not understand the depth and sincerity of literal biblical faith in America today. In the question-and-answer sessions following my lectures, I have often been asked by secular skeptics whether I think that openly religious political leaders like Bush really believe what they say about their faith or whether they are simply using religion, in cynical fashion, to satisfy their political base. My audiences often express surprise when I offer my opinion that Bush believes every word he says about religion and that a religious hypocrite might make a less dangerous president. When Bush famously told Bob Woodward of *The Washington Post* that he had consulted a "Higher Father" instead of his earthly father, President George H. W. Bush, about going to war in Iraq, he was offering a key to his thinking that should have been taken at face value by his opponents as well as his supporters. After encountering opposition from some members of his own party over the issue of the administration's treatment of imprisoned terrorist suspects, the president comforted himself with the notion that his foreign policy designs might yet be saved by Americans experiencing "a Third [Great] Awakening." He knew this, he told conservative columnists, because so many ordinary citizens had told him that they were praying for him.[9]

Bush's use of the term "Awakening" is

revealing because it shows that the president, however deficient he may be in his knowledge of world history, is steeped in the history of his religion. In the reality-based universe, Republicans like Senator John McCain, a former prisoner of war tortured by the North Vietnamese, were concerned not about the direction of American prayers but about the likelihood that if America unilaterally jettisoned the rules laid out in the Geneva Conventions, other countries would feel perfectly free to torture U.S. prisoners of war.

Serious misconceptions about the true nature of modern American fundamentalism can be found among members of the nation's genuine intellectual elite. In October 2006, *Foreign Affairs* published an article, "God's Country," by Walter Russell Mead, who bears the weighty title of Henry A. Kissinger Senior Fellow for U.S. Foreign Policy at the Council on Foreign Relations. The Council on Foreign Relations is just about as high in the establishment as one can go, and *Foreign Affairs* is its bible. In his discussion of evangelical influence on foreign policy, particularly in the Bush administration, Mead unintentionally shows himself to be a perfect example of his contention that "most students of foreign policy in the

United States and abroad are relatively unfamiliar with conservative U.S. Protestantism." He first draws a dubious distinction among fundamentalism, liberal Protestantism, and evangelicalism:

> The three contemporary streams of American Protestantism (fundamentalist, liberal, and evangelical) lead to very different ideas about what the country's role in the world should be. In this context, the most important differences have to do with the degree to which each promotes optimism about the possibilities for a stable, peaceful, and enlightened international order and the importance each places on the difference between believers and nonbelievers. In a nutshell, fundamentalists are deeply pessimistic about the prospects for world order and see an unbridgeable divide between believers and nonbelievers. Liberals are optimistic about the prospects for world order and see little difference between Christians and nonbelievers. And evangelicals stand somewhere between these extremes.[10]

Those distinctions had more validity a century ago — although many religious historians would regard Mead's description as a gross oversimplification of nineteenth- as well as twentieth-century evangelicalism — but they have little meaning today. Mead's basic error is his failure to recognize that a majority of conservative evangelicals today — the six in ten who want the Bible to determine U.S. law — *are* fundamentalists dedicated to remaking American society and the world in their biblical image. What is the war in Iraq, if not a foolishly optimistic effort to bring "enlightened" democracy to a nation in darkness? The unquestioning support for Israel that Mead describes as the most prominent example of "evangelical" influence on U.S. foreign policy is really an example of fundamentalist influence on foreign policy. Fundamentalists support Israel's occupation of all biblical lands, and strongly oppose the establishment of a Palestinian state, because they regard the Jewish presence in the Holy Land as part of God's plan for the second coming of Jesus. The reappearance of Jesus, which will mean the disappearance of Jews and other non-Christians who no longer have a divine purpose to serve, may not be an optimistic scenario for members of the Council on Foreign Relations, but it is certainly the height of optimism for far right Christians who support their self-interested form of

Zionism.

Representatives of the liberal evangelical tradition, including former presidents Carter and Bill Clinton, are committed to avoiding Armageddon (figuratively and literally) and have therefore tried to work out a negotiated settlement between Israelis and Arabs. Incredibly, Mead also insists that fundamentalists, "despite some increase in their numbers and political visibility, remain less influential [than evangelicals]." It is undoubtedly comforting for advocates of realpolitik to believe in the fantasy that important government decisions have been influenced by an amorphous but basically rational group called evangelicals rather than by rapture-anticipating fundamentalists, who are immeasurably less sophisticated about international realities than Bryan was when he served as Woodrow Wilson's secretary of state.

Apart from Israel, the willingness of fundamentalist evangelicals to sanction American military and diplomatic intervention abroad is generally limited to situations in which Christians, or the freedom of Christians to proselytize, are threatened. American fundamentalists have displayed little concern about violent clashes between Shiite and Sunni Muslims in the Middle

East — except in Iraq, where American forces are threatened — but they speak out forcefully, and advocate for American action, wherever Muslims threaten Jews or Christian Arabs. In 2006, when a Muslim convert to Christianity was threatened with execution under Islamic law in Afghanistan, the Bush administration quickly made it clear to the Afghan government that the United States would not tolerate such an action, and the convert was whisked away as a refugee to Rome. In its focus on the rights of Christians around the world, the fundamentalist evangelical posture on foreign policy today bears a strong resemblance to the old anti-Communist alliance between Protestant fundamentalists and American Catholics. The Soviets were equal opportunity suppressors of Christian, Jewish, and Muslim religious liberty within their sphere of influence, but American policy in the forties and fifties, to the extent that it was influenced by domestic religious forces, focused almost entirely on the Christian "captive nations."

As for Catholics, whom Mead simply ignores as an influence on foreign policy, another critical difference between American fundamentalism in the present and the past is the absence of anti-Catholicism from the current wave of biblically based religious revivalism. Protestant fundamentalist leaders have now allied themselves with the most conservative wing of American Catholicism in a fashion that would have been unthinkable fifty years ago. In order to be elected, Kennedy had to assure both liberal and conservative Protestants that he would not be taking his orders in the Oval Office from the Vatican. Back then, in spite of their shared opposition to "atheistic Communism," hard-core fundamentalists still called Catholics papists. Today, although fundamentalists are just as leary of liberal Catholics as of liberal Protestants, the Protestant right is closely allied to the minority of right-wing American Catholics whose defining characteristic is devotion to the dogma of papal infallibility and its attendant prohibitions against abortion, homosexuality, premarital sex, and birth control.

This group, although its adherence to dogma runs counter to the more liberal views of the majority of lay American Catholics, now includes nearly every bishop and cardinal in the United States. On issues such as homosexuality and abortion, the Catholic laity's position is closer to that of Americans who profess no religion, as well as to the stance of mainline Protestants and

Jews, than to the views of Protestant evangelical fundamentalists. More than two thirds of white Catholics and mainline Protestants reject the idea that school boards ought to have the right to fire homosexual teachers, but 60 percent of white evangelicals think that homosexual teachers ought to lose their jobs. Only 37 percent of Catholics, compared with 58 percent of Protestant evangelicals, want stricter abortion laws. Perhaps the most telling finding about the difference between mainstream Catholics and right-wing Protestants is that fewer than one in four Catholics regard the Bible as literally true.[11]

The alliance between the Protestant and Catholic right is really rooted in the sixties, even though it was solidified in 1973 by *Roe v. Wade.* When Pope John XXIII died, dissident Catholics who had hated the reforms of the Second Vatican Council hoped for a reaffirmation of traditional dogma and papal infallibility. John's successor was the much more cautious and conservative Pope Paul VI, who reigned from 1963 to 1978; and when Paul VI died, the College of Cardinals elected Karol Wojtyla, a Polish prelate of great personal charisma, as the next pontiff.* As Pope John Paul II, Wojtyla combined a command of the mass media with the most conservative theological posture since Pope Pius IX, who in the nineteenth century pushed the doctrine of papal infallibility through the First Vatican Council. As church leaders shaped by the modernizing impulses of the sixties began to die off during the twenty-six years of John Paul's papacy, he managed to undo much of the work of Vatican II by appointing bishops and cardinals who shared his theological conservatism.

The continuing rift within American Catholicism divides those who approved of the modernizing and democratizing trends envisioned during the Vatican II era from those who welcomed John Paul II's reassertion not only of papal infallibility but of traditional Catholic doctrine on sexual morality, in which artificial birth control, masturbation, homosexuality, and remarriage after divorce are all considered mortal sins. The political alliance between traditionalist American Catholics and fundamental-

* The elevation of Wojtyla was preceded by a one-month interregnum, in which the Italian cardinal Albino Luciani reigned as Pope John Paul I before dying unexpectedly.

ist Protestants is based not only on a shared view of sexual morality but on a shared piety and devotion to regular religious observance. Post-election studies showed that the most reliable predictor of support for President George W. Bush was not religious affiliation, for either Protestants or Catholics, but frequency of church attendance. Whatever their religion, those who attended church at least once a week voted overwhelmingly for Bush in 2004. Monthly churchgoers split their votes almost evenly, while those who attended only a few times a year voted overwhelmingly for the Democratic ticket. "The idea that there is a Catholic vote was simply not borne out in this election," observed John K. White, professor of political science at the Catholic University of America. "The gap seems to be between regular attendance at church and less regular attendance."[12] Among both Catholics and Protestants, the frequent churchgoers identified themselves as "traditionalist" and gave Bush more than three quarters of their votes.

Yet Mead claims, contrary to all available evidence, that combatting Catholic influence is still one of the major aims of American fundamentalism. What unites Protestant fundamentalists and right-wing Catholics today, in both the religious and political arenas, is a shared hatred of secularism and the influence of secular values on culture and public life. There are some significant differences between the Catholic hierarchy and Protestant fundamentalist leaders; despite their common ground on sexual issues with the Protestant right, the Catholic bishops do not embrace politically conservative values on matters of economic and social justice. Many Catholic bishops, for instance, have spoken out strongly against proposals to deal harshly with illegal immigrants. On other crucial cultural issues, however, the far right factions within Catholicism and Protestantism are in full agreement. Like neoconservative Jews as well as fundamentalist Protestants, right-wing Catholics explicitly link liberal trends within their church to the secular rebellions of the sixties.

The Reverend John McCloskey, a prominent priest in Washington and a member of the shadowy right-wing organization Opus Dei, calls the years after Vatican II (the late sixties) a "generally unfortunate period for our country and our Church." He inveighs against what he calls "nominal" Catholic universities such as Notre Dame and Georgetown because they have committed the ghastly offense of endorsing concepts like "openness, just society . . . diversity, and professional preparation."[13] McCloskey has supervised the conversions to Catholicism of such high-profile Washington figures as Senator Sam Brownback, a Republican from Kansas and a former Methodist, and the columnist Robert Novak, who was born a Jew. In his zeal for conversion of prominent personalities, McCloskey follows in the footsteps of Fulton J. Sheen, who specialized in repentant ex-Communists in the forties and fifties but also snagged such luminaries as Clare Boothe Luce and Henry Ford II.

The conservative Catholic opposition to secularism is based not on biblical literalism but on the belief that there can be no personal morality, and no legitimate political system, that does not acknowledge God as the ultimate authority. Presumably, representatives of the Catholic and Protestant right do not discuss their differing views about the Bible and papal authority when they sit down together at anti-abortion strategy meetings or "abstinence" conferences designed to discourage contraceptive use among teenagers and promote chastity as the only way to avoid pregnancy. At the highest levels of government, the alliance with the Catholic right has provided Protestant fundamentalists with cover against charges that the real goal of American fundamentalism is a right-wing Protestant theocracy. It is no accident that Bush chose extremely conservative Catholics, John G. Roberts and Samuel A. Alito, to fill the first two vacancies that opened up on the Supreme Court during his presidency.

One of the strangest spectacles in the political history of the past eight years was the Protestant right's uprising, in 2005, against Bush's nomination of his personal lawyer, Harriet Miers, to the Supreme Court. Bush's core constituency was up in arms about Miers's nomination because she was suspected of being insufficiently dedicated to overturning *Roe v. Wade* — even though Miers was not only a conservative Southern Baptist but a member of a church in Dallas where abortion is frequently denounced from the pulpit. She did make a 1993 speech suggesting that disputes over such issues as abortion might best be resolved at the state rather than at the federal level. Who knows? Perhaps Miers once confided, over barbecue and a few too many beers (or iced teas, if she is a teetotaling Southern Baptist), that she thought there ought to be an exception to allow abortion if it was needed to save the life of the mother. In any event, Miers, ever loyal to her boss, withdrew from the fray, and Bush promptly nominated Alito, a devout and conservative Roman Catholic whose wife is an anti-abortion activist. The Protestant right responded to the nomination of a papist with overwhelming approval, as it had to Roberts's selection to replace William H. Rehnquist as chief justice the previous fall.

Today, nominations of conservative Catholics to high office carry an extra dividend: it is difficult for anyone to raise questions about conflicts of loyalty between American law and church doctrine without being accused of anti-Catholicism. In fact, five out of the nine current members of the Supreme Court are Roman Catholics: Roberts, Alito, Antonin Scalia, Clarence Thomas, and Anthony Kennedy. Of these, only Kennedy, as evinced by his unpredictable votes on abortion cases, can be considered a mainstream Catholic in his attitudes toward church and state. Kennedy also voted to uphold Oregon's physician-assisted suicide law, while Roberts, Scalia, and Thomas (Alito was not yet on the high court) abandoned their usual conservative support for states' rights and voted to strike down a law ratified three times by Oregon voters. The church's position on assisted suicide and the "right to die," like its position on abortion, is a matter of dogma.

Scalia, a profoundly conservative Catholic as well as a profoundly conservative jurist, has said bluntly that Catholic officeholders should resign if asked to uphold any public policies that contradict church doctrine — a position antithetical to the stance that helped elect John Kennedy. It is certainly not "anti-Catholic" to raise the question of whether anyone who owes his highest allegiance not to American law but to Canon law belongs on the Supreme Court. This is not a question of a conflict between the law and personal belief, which judges must, however painfully, resolve in favor of the law, but an issue of allegiance to a church that, unlike most other church hierarchies, claims to be infallible in matters of faith and morals. Many Catholics do not take papal infallibility literally, but Scalia has said that he does. His comments were made in the context of his strong support for the death penalty, which contradicts the anti–death penalty position of Pope John Paul II and the U.S. Conference of Catholic Bishops. But, as Scalia correctly noted, opposition to the death penalty is not a matter of doctrine but merely the advisory opinion of the church hierarchy. Thus Scalia considers himself free as a Catholic to follow his own judicial and political inclinations — which have led him to the conclusion that the state has a right to execute even children and the mentally retarded.

Scalia's rationale for the death penalty merits close inspection because it comes directly from the Bible and is identical to the arguments used by Protestant fundamentalists against secular government and secular values. In Scalia's view, democracy itself is responsible for opposition to the death penalty, because secular democracy rests on the principle that governmental power comes not from the consent of the governed but from God. "Few doubted the morality of the death penalty in the age that believed in the divine right of kings," Scalia noted in a speech delivered at the University of Chicago Divinity School. Then he went on to observe that "the more Christian a country is the *less* likely it is to regard the death penalty as immoral. Abolition [of capital punishment] has taken its firmest hold in post–Christian Europe, and has least support in the church-going United States. I attribute that to the fact that, for the believing Christian, death is no big deal."[14] That death is no big deal for believing

Christians strikes me as a dubious proposition; but even if it were true, it would fall within the Jeffersonian category of something that gives no offense to those who are less sanguine about dying. It is, however, a big deal for a justice of the United States Supreme Court to base important legal decisions, affecting Americans of all faiths and no faith, on his religious belief in an afterlife.

Scalia's argument belongs properly to the realm of theology, not to the worlds of jurisprudence, domestic policy, or international affairs. It is more accurate to call such arguments anti-rational than anti-intellectual, because one of the strengths of the new right-wing Protestant-Catholic alliance in America is its use of intellectual tools, including logic, within a closed system — a system that begins by postulating the existence of an all-powerful God and the inferiority of human judgment. The cloaking of anti-rational premises in the language of either philosophy or science has proved useful to both Protestant and Catholic anti-rationalists and is one of the hallmarks of the new old-time religion.

Yet even as the size and influence of the right-wing religious minority has grown since 1970, the secular American minority has also expanded. The number of Americans with no formal ties to any religion more than doubled, from 14.3 million to 29.4 million, between 1990 and 2001. Sixteen percent of Americans describe their outlook on the world and public affairs as wholly or predominantly secular.[15] This committed secular minority is small in comparison with the nonreligious population in other developed nations, but its influence is greatest among scientists (especially top-level scientists), academics, journalists, and those with advanced degrees — thus providing another round of ammunition against the elites. Although the secular minority is fifteen to twenty times larger than any of the smaller American religious minorities, including both Jews and Muslims, secularists are routinely ignored on civic occasions thought to require an ecumenical presence.* A minister, priest, rabbi, and imam were all invited to participate in the quasi-religious ceremony following the terrorist attacks of September 11, 2001, in which the main ad-

* Religious Jews, as distinct from Jews as an ethnic group, make up just 1.3 percent of Americans. Muslims make up less than one half of 1 percent.

dress was delivered by Bush from the pulpit of the National Cathedral. No spokesperson for secular values was included — a particularly striking omission in view of the religious fanaticism critical to the motivation of the attackers. Of course, by then everyone was busy denying that "real" religion had anything to do with terrorism: the Islamists who turned planes into weapons did not, could not, represent the "true" Muslim faith but were renegades.

Between the fundamentalists and the secularists lies a much larger group of religious centrists or moderates, but it is not entirely clear what it means to be a religious moderate in the United States today. Forty-three percent of Americans take the centrist religious position that the Bible is divinely inspired but not to be taken literally. Add the centrists to the secularists, and 63 percent of Americans believe that the will of the people, not the Bible, should exert the greatest influence on American law and government. On the other hand, when the centrists are added to the fundamentalists, 75 percent of Americans believe in a supernatural supreme being who guides the destiny of individuals and nations — and most of these people also believe that liberal secularists have gone too far in trying to remove religion from public life. The centrist believers approve of religion in general, and of expressions of religion in public life, but they disapprove of extreme positions like Bush's imposition of a religious veto on embryonic stem cell research. Yet this group has generally been no political match for the True Believer mentality of the fundamentalists, and religious moderates have frequently followed the path of least resistance and let the fundamentalists and anti-modernists have their way on public issues.

The tendency of religious centrists to accept compromise solutions, with no regard for consistency, is one explanation for the seeming absurdity of public support, by a two-to-one majority, for the teaching of both creationism and evolution in public schools.[16] Fundamentalists are effective at getting their way because religion forms the absolute, immovable core of their lives. Unlike religious moderates who, like most human beings, want to have things both ways — God and science, belief in eternal life and the medical pursuit of every means to prolong earthly life — fundamentalists have no doubts. A middle-class fundamentalist cannot be swayed, as someone of more fluid religious convictions might be, by the argument that he ought to vote for secular liberal candidates because they are more likely than Republicans to institute tax policies that help families making less than $100,000 a year. For Catholics in the Scalia mold, the prospect that embryonic stem cell research might help cure them of Parkinson's disease or Alzheimer's means nothing next to the belief that God, through their church, has said no. Cultural and moral issues tied to religion, such as abortion and gay marriage, trump self-interest.

There are, however, a few encouraging signs that the moderate religious majority is finally losing patience with anti-rationalist fundamentalist politics. In the 2006 midterm elections, opponents of stem cell research, even in otherwise politically conservative congressional districts, took a drubbing from candidates who stood up and said that *their* faith required support for medical research aimed at alleviating human suffering. In Missouri, where Democratic candidate Claire McCaskill narrowly defeated the incumbent Republican senator Jim Talent, McCaskill's support for an initiative to overturn the state's ban on embryonic stem cell research was believed to be the decisive issue. Voters in many areas reacted with disgust when the right-wing radio talk show host Rush Limbaugh used crude gestures to mock the actor Michael J. Fox, who suffers from Parkinson's and is a leading supporter of stem cell research. Appearing in a television ad supporting stem cell initiatives around the country, Fox was unable to conceal the nervous gestures and twitches that are side effects of the medication he takes. On election day, Democrats defeated six conservative incumbent representatives who had made opposition to stem cell research a major issue in their campaigns.

Still, the hallmark of these campaigns was not overt opposition to religious antirationalism but emphasis on the candidate's own, more moderate, science-friendly form of faith. Here is where unapologetic secularists have a point when it comes to the peculiarly American form of religious tolerance that refuses to call religious fanaticism by its real name. In *The End of Faith: Religion, Terror, and the Future of Reason,* Sam Harris argues that Americans "cannot say that fundamentalists are crazy, because they are merely practicing their freedom of belief; we cannot even say that they are mistaken in *religious* terms, because their knowledge of scripture is generally unrivaled. All we can say, as religious moderates, is that we don't like the personal and social costs that full embrace of scripture imposes on us."[17]

That twenty-first-century Americans would remain so much more religious than people in the rest of the economically developed world — and that Bible-based fundamentalism would expand its influence at the expense of more moderate faiths — would have seemed implausible to American intellectuals and scientists even at the beginning of the twentieth century. In an essay on Galileo published in 1902, my great-uncle, Harold Jacoby, an astronomy professor at Columbia University, dismissed the idea that religion would ever again align itself against science as the Catholic Church had against Galileo's heliocentric theory. "When we consider events that occurred three centuries ago," Jacoby wrote, "it is easy to replace excited argument with cool judgment; to remember that those were days of violence and cruelty; that public ignorance was of a density difficult to imagine to-day; and that it was universally considered the duty of the Church to assume an authoritative attitude upon many questions with which she is not now required to concern herself in the least."[18] It is unlikely that my great-uncle, a well-known popularizer of science who was regularly interviewed by newspapers about new discoveries until his death in 1932, anticipated that American religious denominations in the twenty-first century would continue to concern themselves with the very questions he thought had been settled by the end of the nineteenth century.[*]

Scientists and intellectuals in the early 1900s certainly did not expect secularism to replace religion in mainstream America, but they did think that the more rationally inclined forms of religion would replace not only biblically literal creeds but the many strange sects, offshoots of Christianity but uniquely and eccentrically American (the most prominent being Mormonism, Christian Science, and the Jehovah's Witnesses), born in the nineteenth century. It was always unlikely that America would become as secular as what has been called "post–Christian Europe"; the absence of a state-established church from America's experi-

* Uncle Harold, whose full name was Levi Harold, was the son of a Jewish immigrant from Breslau. He dropped the name Levi when he became one of the first full-time Jewish faculty members at Columbia, and converted to Episcopalianism when he met his future wife, a gentile.

428

ence as a nation meant that Americans —
unlike the French or the Italians, for example — would almost never be obliged to
choose between faith and citizenship. Even
when there was strong social discrimination, and sometimes outright persecution,
of minority religions in the United States,
American law always came down eventually
on the side of freedom of conscience. On
only one occasion — when the Church of
Jesus Christ of Latter-Day Saints agreed in
1896 to renounce polygamy as the price of
statehood for heavily Mormon Utah — did
the government explicitly and permanently
require a religious denomination to compromise a central belief in deference to public
consensus. Even so, the Mormons' po-
lygamous past continues to surface unpre-
dictably and mar the image of middle-class
probity that the church elders have worked
unceasingly to foster. The feisty bands of
unrepentant polygamists are branded as —
what else? — extremists and renegades by
the official Mormon Church and the state
of Utah.

For the most part, Americans throughout
the nation's history have been content to
view themselves as a predominantly Christian people with a secular government — a
civic paradox and a delicate balance that

seemed entirely natural for most of the nation's history, as it did to my parents and neighbors in the fifties. The reasons why that balance has been upset by the resurgence of an intolerant fundamentalism during the past three decades are not altogether clear. The explanation cannot be found in the original American separation of church and state and the existence of a "free market" of faiths, because the distant past offers few answers to the question of why so many Americans today are attracted to forms of religion that educated men and women were beginning to reject a century ago.

The rise of feminism in the seventies, with its challenge to fundamental assumptions about the roles of women, men, and families, has often been seen as the major spur to the religious right. It is certainly true that the battle over abortion, which cannot be separated from late twentieth-century feminism, created a unifying cause for right-wing Protestants and right-wing Catholics. But it is often forgotten that a large majority of Americans in 1973 actually favored liberalization of state abortion laws — and that public opinion had changed dramatically in a relatively brief period of time. In 1968, a Gallup poll found that only 15 percent of Americans favored making abortion more accessible; by 1972, 64 percent did.[19]

Because the Christian right opposed all relaxation of strict anti-abortion rules, it set out to portray *Roe* as a radical break with contemporary standards. While the Supreme Court decision may have been ahead of public opinion in its broad scope, it was nevertheless in line with a general trend favoring greater choice and compassion for women coping with unwanted pregnancies. At the heart of Justice Harry A. Blackmun's majority opinion was the unequivocal assertion that "the word 'person,' as used in the Fourteenth Amendment, does not include the unborn.' "[20] That single sentence kindled a religious conflagration that is still burning. Although Blackmun's opinion was delivered more than two decades before any member of the general public had ever heard the phrase "embryonic stem cell research," the religious right's position has been consistent since that day: not only is the fetus entitled to full Fourteenth Amendment rights, but so too is a six-day-old collection of embryonic cells.

The intricate thirty-five-year history of the battle by the religious right to overturn *Roe* is beyond the scope of this book, but it is a mistake to view the issue of abortion as distinct from all other "values issues" involving the position of women, men, and families within society. The people who did and do want to recriminalize abortion are the same people who succeeded in defeating the Equal Rights Amendment to the Constitution, passed by Congress in 1971 but never ratified by enough states. The old arguments endlessly trotted out in opposition to the amendment, including unisex toilets and women in combat, seem quaint today in a nation that has become accustomed to seeing female soldiers come home in body bags — or rather, *not* seeing them under the administration policy of shielding the public from the ugly reality of military coffins and funerals. The end of the draft, and the attendant need to expand the pool of volunteers for the armed services, accomplished what proposals to amend the Constitution could not do: a de facto acceptance that women, too, could be called on to die for God and country.

But the undeniability of the vast changes in women's traditional social and economic roles, in spite of fierce resistance from religious conservatives, has inflamed rather than dampened the anti-rational passions in American culture. "Wedge issues" such as

abortion and gay marriage are often errone-
ously dismissed as "purely symbolic" because the majority of voters are much more
concerned about such matters as the war in
Iraq, terrorism, and the economy. Symbolic
issues are symbolic precisely because they
stand for something deeper than the everyday problems and concerns that preoccupy
most people most of the time. To speak
about finding "common ground" on the
abortion issue, as secularists and religious
moderates often do, is to speak about a
rational, pragmatic compromise that can
only be located in the natural world. But
Americans who want to force women to go
through with unwanted pregnancies are
adhering to a supernatural imperative: abortion is murder forbidden by the law of God
and must therefore be forbidden by the law
of man. The fundamental question is why
these supposedly symbolic religious issues
are so much more potent in the United
States than in the rest of the developed
world.

Like America, Europe has experienced
major social dislocations that began in the
1960s. Like Americans, Europeans have
been affected by recent biomedical research
that challenges, at a basic physiological and
psychological level, our assumptions about

what it means to be a human being and how much control humans can and should exert over their own destinies. But Europeans have responded by becoming more rather than less skeptical about traditional religious dogma: homosexuality, abortion, embryonic stem cell research, and the teaching of evolution are simply not divisive political issues in most of Europe today. On the Continent and in the United Kingdom, religious fundamentalism is almost entirely the province of Muslims — a social reality that attests powerfully to the refusal of many Muslim immigrants to identify with and assimilate themselves to Western values. For the most part, secular Europe is utterly baffled by the anti-rational sector of the American religious landscape. In 2003, a survey by *The Economist* concluded that "Europeans consider religion . . . the strangest and most disturbing feature of American exceptionalism. They worry that fundamentalists are hijacking the country. They find it extraordinary that three times as many Americans believe in the virgin birth as in evolution. They fear that America will go on a 'crusade' . . . in the Muslim world or cut aid to poor countries lest it be used for birth control."[21]

Some absolutist secular antagonists of

religion, most notably the British evolutionary biologist Richard Dawkins, have argued in recent years that moderate religions — forms of faith not based on literal interpretations of holy books — are every bit as anti-rational as fundamentalism. Dawkins sees the American predisposition to hold all religion in high esteem as dangerous in itself. "I think moderate religion makes the world safe for extremists," he says, "because children are trained from the cradle to think that faith itself is a good thing."[22] Dawkins's two-part anti-religious documentary, *The Root of All Evil?*, was shown on television in England but was considered too hot to handle by media executives in the United States — even those in charge of small cable networks. The reluctance of the media to give an airing to Dawkins's acidic brand of atheism is understandable in commercial terms: nearly two thirds of Americans, compared with only one in five Europeans, say that religion plays a very important role in their lives.

In the United States, Dawkins has been attacked not only for his general criticism of religion but for his uncompromising defense of Darwin's theory of evolution. One conservative American writer describes Dawkins as a "poor public intellectual" because, in articulating his views on the randomness of nature, he "appears to be utterly indifferent to the spiritual and emotional difficulties that his writings cause for many of his readers."[23] It is hard to imagine exactly how anyone might function as a public intellectual while taking care to avoid all issues that might trigger a spiritual, emotional, or intellectual crisis among his or her readers. It is not necessary, however, to be concerned about the emotional difficulties of Dawkins's audience to conclude that he is somewhat off the mark in his assessment of the compromise between faith and reason represented by what is generally called "moderate" religion. While Dawkins is clearly right in his contention that religion — any religion — should be fair game for critics, his brand of purist atheism is grounded more in philosophy than in a clear-eyed look at the real world or the way religion works in American society. The difference between moderate religion and fundamentalism, now as in the past, is that moderate faith attempts to accommodate itself to secular education and secular government: the American religious right rejects both. If there were only minuscule numbers of unreconstructed fundamentalists within the United States, American religious exceptionalism would not seem so peculiar or so threatening to so many Europeans.

The Economist survey quoted Peter Berger, head of the Institute of Religion and World Affairs at Boston University, to the effect that secular Europe, not religious America, is the real exception in the world. Berger, like many other prominent scholars of religion, has argued that the rise of militant Islam in the Middle East and the Far East, as well as the appeal of Catholicism and Protestant evangelical sects in Africa and South America, has refuted the old idea that countries inevitably become more secular as they modernize. However, the kind of "modernization" taking place in the Third World today has little in common with the modernization associated with secularizing forces in the United States and Europe in the nineteenth and early twentieth centuries. The development of modern industries in much of the Middle East and Africa, for example, has profited a tiny and greedy elite, leaving the bulk of the population in poverty, often subject to the whims of brutal dictatorships. In such circumstances, faith flourishes — as it always has — among those who have little or no hope of a better life in this world. It is the absence of broadly based economic and political modernization, not its presence, that has encouraged the most retrograde forms of religion and religious violence in many areas of the world. Even in nations like India, where modernization has reached a broader segment of the population than it has in Africa, fanatical Hindu nationalism has flourished among those who have been largely bypassed by the global, English-language-oriented sector of the economy.

In Africa, the Roman Catholic Church has made many new converts in spite of the fact that the church proposes to fight AIDS without distributing condoms; it is difficult to imagine equally successful proselytizing in areas of the world where most people have a basic understanding of how the disease is spread. It is also difficult to imagine that radical Islam's suppression of women could flourish in regions where women have equal educational opportunities and political rights. The United States is the only developed nation in which Pentecostals and Charismatic Christians — who practice religious rituals such as "speaking in tongues" and faith healing — are garnering new converts. It is astounding that the United States has almost as large a proportion of citizens who call themselves

Pentecostals or Charismatics (23 percent) as Nigeria (26 percent).[24] Based on the prevalence of anti-rational religion, a visitor from another planet would have to conclude that the United States must be a nation of poor, hungry, and warring people who can only look to the supernatural for a way out of their miserable earthly existence. Among countries that have experienced true modernization, characterized by broad educational opportunity and rising living standards for the entire population, America *is* the religious exception.

A general attraction to the supernatural, extending beyond narrowly defined fundamentalism, lies at the heart of the profound divide not only between religious America and secular Europe but also between devout religious believers and secularists within the United States. "People are reaching out in all directions in their attempt to escape from the *seen* world to the *unseen* world," George Gallup, Jr., told a correspondent for *U.S. News & World Report* in 2002. "There is a deep desire for spiritual moorings — a hunger for God."[25] The desire to escape from the seen to the unseen world is not confined to Americans who profess an ultra-conservative form of faith or, for that matter, any form of orthodox faith. "Escape" is the key word: the resurgence of fundamentalism in the United States has occurred within the context of a pervasive nonreligious anti-rationalism that reinforces more extreme forms of religion and also affects the broader public's views about science, education, and reality itself. At the dawn of the twentieth century, scientists like my great-uncle made the entirely reasonable assumption that the expansion of knowledge about every aspect of the natural world would produce a less credulous American public. They assumed that the growing availability of scientific, historical, and anthropological evidence would deter the spread of both religious and nonreligious beliefs that not only lacked a basis in reality but frequently contradicted reality. That assumption, reasonable as it seemed at the time, was wrong.

CHAPTER NINE:
JUNK THOUGHT

"Junk science," which has become a fashionable pejorative in recent years, does not always mean what a reasonable person would expect it to mean. To scientists themselves, the phrase is generally synonymous with pseudoscience, encompassing old and new systems of thought, that, whether they attempt to explain the physical or the social universe, can neither be proved nor disproved. Although cloaked in scientific language, as social Darwinism was in the nineteenth century and intelligent design is today, the leaden heart of pseudoscience is its imperviousness to evidentiary challenge. As the astronomer Carl Sagan notes, real science differs from pseudoscience in that the former "thrives on errors, cutting them away one by one," while the latter involves theories "often framed precisely so that they are invulnerable to any experiment that offers a prospect of disproof, so even in principle they cannot be invalidated." Then, when real scientists refuse to accept a pseudoscientific premise, "conspiracies to suppress it are deduced."[1]

But junk science also has a politicized meaning, diametrically opposed to what genuine scientists mean by the phrase. It has been appropriated by right-wing politicians and journalists to describe any scientific consensus that contradicts their political, economic, or cultural agenda. The Internet offers a boundless array of right-wing Web sites that pin the label "junk science" on everything from climatological research on global warming to studies indicating that condoms reduce the spread of sexually transmitted diseases. Even DNA testing has been dubbed junk science by the right, because it has led to the reversal of old convictions based on eyewitness identifications or circumstantial evidence — and anything that releases prisoners, even if they were wrongfully convicted in the first place, is tantamount to being soft on crime in the far right universe.

The right-wing distortion and politicization of junk science is nothing more than a branch of a more pervasive phenomenon best described as junk thought. The defining characteristics of junk thought, which manifests itself in the humanities and social sciences as well as the physical sciences, are anti-rationalism and contempt for counter-vailing facts and expert opinion. It cannot be stressed enough that junk thought ema-nates from both the left and the right, even though each group — in academia, politics, and cultural institutions — thrives on ac-cusing the other of being the sole source of irrationality.

The right loves to pin the label of political correctness (meaning just about anything opposed to right-wing values) on junk thought, while the left tends to concentrate on junk thought as a by-product of religious fundamentalism and superstition. More-over, the much lionized American centrists, sometimes known as moderates, are in no way immune to the overwhelming pull of belief systems that treat evidence as a tire-some stumbling block to deeper, instinctive "ways of knowing." We are talking not about psychotics drinking poisoned Kool-Aid at Jonestown or Scientologists who believe that babies will be traumatized for life if they hear anyone tell their mothers to "push" during labor. The real power of junk thought lies in its status as a centrist phenomenon, fueled by the American credo of tolerance that places all opinions on an equal footing and makes little effort to separate fact from opinion. In a stunning example of the mainstreaming of junk thought coupled with junk science, Supreme Court Associate Justice Anthony Kennedy, writing the 5-to-4 majority opinion that upheld a ban on "partial birth abortion" in 2007, cited the "severe depression and loss of esteem" that may follow an abortion as one rationale for the Court's decision. Kennedy even admitted that "we find no reliable data to measure the phenomenon," but said, nevertheless, that "it seems unexceptionable to conclude that some women come to regret their choice to abort the infant they have created and sustained."[2]

In fact, Kennedy was alluding to a junk science concept — "post-abortion syndrome" — invented by anti-choice organizations and based entirely on anecdotal accounts gathered by those groups. No randomized studies exist to prove the existence of a "post-abortion syndrome" comparable to post-traumatic stress disorder, but a major randomized study of more than five thousand women, conducted over an eight-year period by the American Psychological Association, found no significantly higher incidence of depression or stress-related illnesses in women who have had abortions.[3] Yet the Court majority chose to ignore real scientific studies and rely instead on anecdotal findings that are the essence of junk science. Of course "some women" come to regret the choice to have an abortion. "Some women" also suffer from severe postpartum suicidal depression (which, unlike "post-abortion syndrome," is a scientifically documented condition), but we do not pass laws preventing all women — or even those with a history of postpartum psychosis — from bearing children.

The difference between those who purvey junk thought from the margins of the ideological spectrum — the conspiracy theory bloggers — and those who reside near the center, even in the august halls of the nation's highest court, is that the latter pick their poison both from Column A and Column B. How could it be otherwise? For ordinary Americans, including those not naturally disposed toward the irrational, the national menu of junk thought is as broad and accessible as its offerings of junk food. Junk thought is a state of mind that is hard to avoid. Press the remote, point and click the mouse, open the newspaper, and worlds of anti-rationalism open up.

- In entirely straight-faced fashion,

445

Newsweek magazine began a 2005 cover story, titled "Boy Brains, Girl Brains," with the following paragraph:

"Three years ago, Jeff Gray, the principal at Foust Elementary School in Owensboro, Ky., realized that his school needed help — and fast. . . . So Gray took a controversial course for educators on brain development, then revamped the first- and second-grade curriculum. The biggest change: he divided the classes by gender. Because males have less serotonin in their brains, which Gray was taught may cause them to fidget more, desks were removed from the boys' classrooms and they got short exercise periods throughout the day. Because females may have more oxytocin, a hormone linked to bonding, girls were given a carpeted area where they sit and discuss their feelings. Because boys have higher levels of testosterone and are theoretically more competitive, they were given timed, multiple-choice tests. The girls were given multiple-choice tests, too, but got more time to complete them. . . ."[4]

- In February 2006, in a dutiful attempt to add some culture to its marathon coverage of the winter Olympics in Turin, Italy, NBC sent Katie Couric on a whirlwind tour of Rome, Florence, and Milan. Couric naturally made a visit to the chapel of Santa Maria della Grazie in Milan, where the newly restored Leonardo da Vinci fresco of the Last Supper was attracting even more tourists than usual because of the brouhaha surrounding the movie *The Da Vinci Code.* Couric asked a bemused art historian to explain why, if there was no truth to Dan Brown's yarn, Leonardo had created an image of the apostle John that looked so much like a girl. The art historian tried her best to explain that the depiction of John as a beardless youth with long hair was standard Renaissance iconography. No matter. Couric grinned and shook her head, with a skeptical "hmmm" suggesting to the *Today* audience that it should not allow any facts of art history, coming from a pointy-headed professor, to interfere with a cryptological tale cooked up by a best-selling author.

- A long-awaited study concerning the power of prayer to promote healing found that cardiac patients recovering from heart surgery derived absolutely no benefit from prayers offered by strangers — although the research did not cover prayers by friends and relatives.[5] The study, involving more than 1,800 patients over a ten-year period, cost $2.4 million, most of it donated by the John Templeton Foundation, which finances research on spirituality. The U.S. government, not to be outdone in diligent attempts to link science and religion, has also allotted $2.3 million to prayer research since 2000. The patients in the Templeton Foundation study were prayed for by communities of Roman Catholic monks and nuns as well as a Protestant evangelical prayer ministry, and the group prayers proved equally and ecumenically inefficacious — recalling the line in Christopher Durang's play, *Sister Mary Ignatius Explains It All for You,* "God always answers our prayers. Sometimes the answer is no." Undaunted by the results, proponents of the prayer study said that further study was needed and that regardless of what the research showed, they knew that prayer worked because they had personally experienced its power.

What these three seemingly unrelated examples of junk thought have in common is their tenuous or nonexistent relationship to evidence. *The Da Vinci Code* is of course pure fantasy. The prayer study was an unsuccessful attempt to find scientific evidence of what the devoutly religious have always believed — that prayer can heal the sick. If the findings had turned out otherwise, the headlines would have read, "Science Proves Power of Prayer." As it was, believers simply shrugged off the results. Bob Barth, spiritual director of Silent Unity, the evangelical ministry involved in the prayer study, pooh-poohed the results, declaring that "we've been praying a long time, we've seen prayer work, we know it works, and research on prayer and spirituality is just getting started."[6]

The "boy brain, girl brain" experiments are a more complicated case of junk thought, because they are based on theories of education that do have some relationship to facts, beginning with obvious hormonal and anatomical differences between the sexes. But the existence of certain culturally or biologically influenced differences in learning styles between boys and girls, to the extent that they do exist and can be substantiated, hardly justifies a transformation of public education designed to emphasize the differences rather than the much greater similarities between the sexes. The *Newsweek* article, for example, never addressed the question of what will happen to boys who have been allowed to run around classrooms when they are required to work in a normal office with desks and cubicles and what will happen to girls who have been allowed extra time to take tests when they have to take an exam with the same time limit as their male peers. Junk thought may proclaim that men are from Mars and women from Venus, but the truth is that men are from Earth and women are from Earth. (The credit for this observation goes to Cathy Young, a contributing editor to *Reason* magazine.) Give junk thought practitioners enough sex-segregated public school classes for experimental purposes, however, and they will undoubtedly be able to make a case for the benefits of catering to whatever might be seen as innate differences between boys and girls.

One of the most maddening aspects of junk thought is that it uses the language of science and rationality to promote irrationality. The magic words for the "boy brain, girl brain" school experiments are oxytocin and serotonin; if the principal had assigned girls to a separate pink classroom because studies demonstrate that girls prefer pink, he would have been laughed out of town. Oxytocin is a magic word that keeps popping up throughout the realms of junk thought. Dr. Eric Keroack, the Bush administration's choice to head the only federally subsidized birth control and reproductive health program aimed at low-income teenagers (although he resigned abruptly in April 2007 amid a brewing Medicaid scandal involving his former clinics in Massachusetts), was actually an opponent of contraceptives — at least for unmarried women.[7] Before moving on to Washington, Keroack aggressively proselytized on behalf of the pseudoscientific proposition that premarital sex damages any prospect of a long-lasting relationship because the participants "lose" oxytocin — the bonding hormone that promotes intimacy — each time they engage in intercourse. Keroack's oxytocin theory, ostensibly derived from research on a small rodent called the prairie vole, also recalls the fear of Communists gaining control of "precious bodily fluids" so memorably articulated by General Jack D. Ripper in *Dr. Strangelove*. It is a true sign of Keroack's membership in the junk thought community that he did not simply say, "Bad girls go to hell," but found a scientific-sounding rationale for his faith-based quackery.

It is impossible to determine whether nonreligious anti-rational systems of thought are more or less prevalent in the United States than they were fifty years ago. We know that the ranks of fundamentalist Christians have grown because public opinion pollsters have been asking the same questions about religious attitudes for decades and because churches keep membership records. We cannot, however, ascertain with any degree of accuracy how many Americans today, in comparison to the public at midcentury, believe in self-help movements whose results cannot be evaluated in any scientific way; physiological or psychological therapies of unknown effectiveness; or, for that matter, in traditional purveyors of junk thought such as astrologers and psychics. One reason why it is difficult to quantify such phenomena is that they are simultaneously amorphous and pervasive, crossing boundaries that used to place limits on the number of anti-rational philosophies people could encompass simultaneously. New Age spirituality, a player in the universe of junk thought since the eighties, is much more flexible than traditional religion and enables its adherents to hold logically incompatible beliefs with minimal psychological and intellectual discomfort.

The absence of rules and internally consistent theology constitutes a huge part of the appeal of New Age philosophy; a practicing Catholic and most Protestants must believe in redemption through Jesus Christ, but New Age creeds allow people to believe in any plan of salvation, or no plan at all, while still deriving comfort from the idea of a mystical, benevolent intelligence that somehow gives meaning to earthly existence. Amorphous spirituality does not require people to choose a specific organized church, with a defined set of ethical principles and practical obligations that include the obligation to put money into the collection plate. A third of Americans may believe that the Bible is literally true, but another third — the groups might even overlap — describe themselves as "spiritual but not religious."[8]

What can be said with a fair degree of certainty is that anti-rational junk thought has gained social respectability in the United States during the past half century, that it interacts toxically with the most credulous elements in both secular and religious ideologies, and that it has proved resistant to the vast expansion of scientific knowledge that has taken place during the same period. Since the late sixties, there has been a growing acceptance of social and psychological theories in which great weight is accorded the passionate emotional convictions of believers. In this realm of emotion, absolute value is placed on personal testimony based on personal experience. If a woman believes that breast implants caused her ill health, for example, it is difficult for an attorney to introduce contradictory scientific evidence without looking heartless. And Justice Kennedy can conclude that amicus briefs filed by individual women who regret having had abortions are as persuasive as studies of thousands of women conducted by disinterested researchers.

In a general sense, both the overtly anti-scientific and the emotionally based strains of junk thought received a boost from the more paranoid phenomena of the sixties — including the left's suspicion of all research associated with the military-industrial complex and the right's equally strong distrust of liberal intellectuals in the humanities and social sciences. However, the realm of junk thought greatly expanded its reach during the seventies, as onetime social protesters retreated into narcissistic New

Age and self-help movements. By the eighties, anti-rationalism had become a huge, multimedia, apolitical commodity, comparable to the youth culture of the sixties and marketed by baby boomers who had been on both sides of the barricades. It is easy to sell anti-rationalism, because junk thought always involves a shortcut — whether a diet requiring no reduction in calorie intake; a responsibility-evading bogus apology for bad behavior ("I'm sorry that you were hurt" instead of "I'm sorry that I hurt you"); or a cure that depends largely on whether a sick patient has a positive attitude.

Finally, the virulent outbreak of anti-rationalism in late twentieth-century America is also rooted in a much older, nonpolitical tendency in American thought — a chronic suspicion of experts that dovetails with the folk belief in the superior wisdom of ordinary people. Ironically but perhaps predictably, the upsurge in mistrust of expert authority followed several decades in which public deference to scientific and technological authority, a deference so great that it was sometimes exaggerated and misplaced, stood at an all-time high.

Throughout my childhood in the 1950s,

Americans regarded science and medicine with a respect bordering on reverence. American technology and science were given the lion's share of the credit for the Allied victory in the Second World War, and few ordinary Americans doubted either the wisdom or the morality of the atomic attacks on Hiroshima and Nagasaki that finally brought an end to the fighting in the Pacific. As far as the public was concerned, American preeminence in science was a given until the Soviet Union launched its Sputnik in 1957, but fear that the Russians might win the space race actually raised the prestige of science by providing a rationale for large increases in government spending on basic scientific research and science education. The moon landing in 1969 would probably never have happened without the blow to America's sense of superiority twelve years earlier. Neil Armstrong's walk on the moon, however, represented more than a national and nationalistic achievement: it was a unique moment in which not only technological prowess but the imaginative possibilities of science and exploration were illuminated for Americans and millions of others around the globe.

I happened to be in Florence on that July day, and I watched the moon landing, along with a crowd of fellow tourists and Florentines, in a television store. We all caught our breaths at Armstrong's famous line, "That's one small step for a man, one giant leap for mankind." An Italian aptly remarked that we were especially privileged to be watching this event on ground hallowed by "the footsteps of Galileo." It seems that many people misheard the line on Armstrong's scratchy audio transmission from the moon and thought he had delivered a less poetic sentence that made no sense: "That's one small step for man, one giant leap for mankind." The article "a" — underscoring the comparison between the individual and the human race — is of course what gave the astronaut's spontaneous exclamation its beauty and emotional power. Its omission is the equivalent of the maddeningly common declaration, "I could care less" — when what the speaker really means is "I couldn't care less."

All of us in the Florence television store heard Armstrong's line correctly, but only in 2006, when the original tape was digitally remastered, did the press finally get the quote right. (Armstrong commented that he had always known he said "a man.") In 1969, it did not bother me in the least that the military-industrial complex responsible for the Vietnam War was the same military-industrial complex sending men into space; this inconsistency was part of coming of age in the sixties, and anyone who says that he or she was unmoved by Armstrong's walk on the moon is either lying or was stoned at the time.

Weaponry and space exploration, integral as they had been to the national self-image, probably played a less important role than medicine in fostering the average American's respect for science. In the fifteen years following the end of the war, antibiotics and vaccines conquered the most common, serious diseases that had killed or crippled tens of thousands of children each year. Antibiotics also made it possible for children and adults to routinely survive conditions, such as pneumonia and complications from childbirth, that had frequently proved fatal in the past. In the mid-1930s, one out of every one hundred and fifty women died in childbirth; by the 1950s, that grim statistic had fallen to just one in two thousand — partly because penicillin was available to treat postpartum infection. (Today the rate of maternal death in childbirth is only one in ten thousand.[9]) And no one my age can possibly forget summers shadowed by fear of polio — a fear communicated to us not only by our parents but by the common sight of child polio victims wearing braces — before the Salk vaccine became available in 1954.

My mother, fearful of adverse side effects from a procedure that had never been tried before on large numbers of people, was undecided about whether my brother and I should be vaccinated. But like nearly everyone in those days she took the advice of our pediatrician, who told her that there was no question about whether we should be immunized. "This works," he advised her. "Your children are going to be part of the greatest medical miracle of our time." And so it was. The late forties and fifties were an age of medical miracles, all the more impressive because, unlike more recent medical miracles such as organ transplants, the advances of my childhood addressed themselves to diseases that threatened everyone — and not in the distant past, but within the recent memory of every living person above the age of reason. Had anyone told me, in 1969, that an anti-vaccination movement — embodying both junk science and junk thought — would emerge in the 1990s and be treated by the news media with respectful attention, I would have considered the prediction sheer lunacy.

The inseparability of junk science from junk thought is evinced by the telltale marks of endemic illogic coupled, in many instances, with deliberate manipulativeness. The first and most fundamental warning sign is an inability to distinguish between coincidence and causation — a basic requirement for scientific literacy. The anti-vaccination movement is rife with conspiracy theories tied both to the right wing's distrust of government and the left's distrust of traditional medicine — the latter a heritage of the extreme wings of the holistic health and New Age movements of the late sixties and seventies. During the past twenty-five years, there appears to have been a significant increase in the incidence of autism in children around the world. (I emphasize the word "appears," because many epidemiologists question whether there really has been an increase in autism cases and attribute the phenomenon to an expanded diagnosis that applies the autistic label to children with other neurological or behavior disorders.) Whatever the reason for the rise in reported cases of autism, it has coincided with an increase in the number of recommended child immunizations. Anti-vaccination groups have focused on a relatively new triple vaccine, introduced in

1987, that immunizes children against measles, mumps, and rubella (German measles). The first MMR immunizations are normally administered to toddlers between ages fifteen and seventeen months, around the age when observant parents sometimes begin to notice the early signs of autism, which include a lag in normal speech development and withdrawal from play activities. The anti-vaccine warriors have pounced on the MMR shot as a possible cause of autism — either by itself or in conjunction with other vaccines. That the early signs of autistic behavior have always presented themselves around the end of the second year of life has not dissuaded the immunization opponents from pursuing their attempts to broaden legal exemptions and eventually make all immunizations voluntary.

Rigorous scientific research also has no effect on the purveyors of junk thought. The most convincing study on the subject was released in 2002 in Denmark, which, like nearly every other country, has recorded a marked increase in autism in recent years. With a small population and a national health system, the Danes are able to keep meticulous medical records, and they found that the reported increase in autism cases

461

has occurred at an equal rate among immunized and nonimmunized children.[10] This important report is never cited in the growing number of heartrending television interviews with parents who first noticed the signs of autism in their children several days, weeks, or months after childhood vaccinations. The emotional convictions of the parents, who understandably want an explanation for the curse that has stricken their children, are given absolute weight.

What researchers have not yet been able to do is identify the real causes of autism, a failure that reinforces the confusion between causation and coincidence that drives the anti-vaccine movement. Anti-vaccine crusaders dismiss public health concerns based on the severity and frequency of measles outbreaks reported in communities, like the Amish, that receive religious exemptions from immunization. It is clear from these outbreaks that killer childhood diseases could easily make a comeback if enough people manage to evade state laws requiring immunization before children can enter public schools. Opponents of compulsory immunization believe, with a near-religious fervor, that no child should ever be subjected by government fiat to the slightest risk — and all drugs, as is well known, have some risk of negative side effects.

Furthermore, the anti-vaccine warriors know that their children will, in effect, get a free ride as long as the vast majority of their peers are immunized: ironically, unimmunized children would be in real danger only if the anti-vaccination movement succeeded in its campaign against compulsory laws designed to protect the population against ancient scourges. Junk science plays on the fears of parents who understand little about risk-benefit equations or about the history of the terrible diseases prevented by immunizations. A typical example, on the Web site "Acupuncture Today," notes that the risk of dying from pertussis (whooping cough) today is one in several million, while the risk of a serious adverse reaction to the vaccination that prevents whooping cough, diphtheria, and tetanus is 1 in 1,750 and "deaths attributed to the vaccine outnumber deaths due to the illness."[11] Of course the risk of dying of whooping cough in America today is negligible, because vaccinations now protect millions of children from getting the disease at all. The purveyors of junk thought are urging the public to abandon the very immunizations that are responsible for cutting the death rate from infectious diseases.

A second telltale sign of junk thought is the appropriation of scientific-*sounding* language without underlying scientific evidence or logic. Consider the following interview in *The New York Times Magazine* with Barbara Loe Fisher, president of the National Vaccine Information Center, an organization that actually opposes compulsory immunization.

Q: Many people consider vaccination one of the greatest medical successes of the 20th century. Do you disagree with that assessment?

[*Fisher's reply*]: Certainly with the implementation of mass vaccination policies in the last 40 years we've seen a decline in infectious diseases of childhood. However, we have at the same time seen a doubling of asthma and learning disabilities. A tripling of diabetes. Autism is affecting one in 500 children. We need to look at whether an intervention used with every child is perhaps contributing to the background rate of chronic disease and disability.[12]

Fisher's smooth segue from the admission that infectious diseases have declined to the observation that "at the same time" there has been "a doubling of asthma and learning disabilities" and a "tripling of diabetes" exemplifies the bogus reasoning that confuses coincidence and causation. The past forty years have also witnessed an increase in the divorce rate and in the age of childbearing, but no one infers that these phenomena are caused by immunizations. Of the four phenomena mentioned by Fisher — learning disabilities, asthma, diabetes, and autism — only autism remains a horrible medical mystery. In fact, there has been no rise in genetically determined Type I diabetes at all, but there has been a sharp increase in Type II diabetes, which used to develop only in adulthood but is now appearing in children and adolescents. That increase correlates almost exactly with a steady increase in obesity among Americans, and medical authorities now believe, on the basis of numerous clinical studies, that weight loss could prevent the development of more than half of all new diabetes cases each year. Learning disabilities are another matter altogether, because they were so rarely recognized or diagnosed forty years ago that it is impossible to determine whether they are more common today. Dyslexia, a well-established syndrome in which children of normal intelligence have great difficulty learning to read and write, was generally attributed to laziness, stupidity, or rebelliousness when I was a child.

A third important element in much of junk thought is innumeracy — a lack of understanding of basic mathematical and statistical concepts. Innumeracy is deeply implicated in the media's and the public's overreaction to many studies involving medical risks. News stories frequently report that a particular drug or consumption of a particular type of food increases or decreases the risk of one disease or another by a large percentage. The critical issue, though, is not the magnitude of the increase but the incidence of risk in the first place. Let us say, for the sake of argument, that a drug doubles the chance of contracting a fatal disease at age twenty. If there was only one chance in a million of developing the disease in the first place, an increase to two in a million is meaningless from a public health standpoint. But if two people in ten were already at risk for the hypothetical condition, an increase to four in ten would justify immediate removal of the drug from the market.

Numbers, and the ability to understand them, matter. When Barbara Fisher was interviewed by *The New York Times Maga-*

zine in 2001, she cited the then standard figure of 1 in 500 for the incidence of autism in children. In 2006, the standard changed, when the Centers for Disease Control and Prevention (CDC) released a report indicating that as many as 1 in 150 children might have autism "and related disorders." Most of the headlines and television stories asked no questions about whether the "related disorders" were in any way as severe as classical autism, which has generally been defined as a rare condition in which a child cannot speak intelligibly or relate emotionally to others. Instead, the standard headline was simply, "Autism Rate Higher Than Thought."[13]

In fact, the CDC's criteria include a whole range of developmental conditions that are now called "autism spectrum disorders," which involve everything from anger management problems to speech difficulties that fall far short of the profound pathology of children who display symptoms of classical autism. Two prominent epidemiologists, in an op-ed piece in *The New York Times,* challenged the junk thought orthodoxy portraying an "epidemic" of autism. They pointed out that while "older studies used narrow definitions of autism and were generally based on counting the number of patients in a clinic or hospital . . . modern methods use broader criteria and leave no stone unturned in the effort to find every autistic child in a defined geographic area, including those not previously given a diagnosis. This virtually guarantees that new estimates will be higher than previous ones, even if the underlying prevalence of the condition has not changed."[14] The piece drew an extraordinary number of outraged letters to the editor from representatives of groups for which the existence of an autism epidemic is as much a matter of dogma as transubstantiation is for the Roman Catholic Church. It in no way minimizes the seriousness of autism — or, for that matter, of less severe learning disabilities that share some of the characteristics of autism — to say the sudden discovery of a much higher incidence of a well-known disease must always be considered suspect. If 1.5 percent of all American children suffered from classical autism, as distinct from less serious developmental disorders that can be treated in a variety of ways, it would be a public health crisis of the first magnitude. And such dubious statistics, in a country where statistics are poorly understood by much of the population, will surely be used to define autism as a nationwide health crisis.

In more subtle ways, innumeracy is also involved in a variety of pop psychology theories and movements that rely on emotion and personal testimony. One example was the growing acceptance by psychotherapists in the 1980s and 1990s of "recovered memory" theory, based on the idea that most survivors of childhood sexual abuse have repressed their memory of the trauma but can be helped, in therapy, to remember what their conscious minds have forgotten. The promoters of recovered memory made unsupported, dubious claims about the number of women who had survived childhood sexual molestation. E. Sue Blume, a social worker and the author of *Secret Survivors: Uncovering Incest and Its Aftereffects in Women* (1990), claims that up to half of all American women have been sexually abused in their youth.[15] Half. In a country as large and diverse as the United States, an overpowering confluence of social forces is required before half of the population is affected by any phenomenon. Do more than half of all children eat fast food? They certainly do, because fast-food consumption is driven by multiple forces, among them the combined power of television advertising; the relative inexpensiveness of the food; the increase in the number of working mothers who have no time to prepare traditional meals; the loss of cooking skills among the young; and the growing number of single-parent households. Moreover, Americans' expenditure on fast food — unlike the prevalence of repressed memories — can be measured by objective criteria.

But what social forces could possibly account for half of all women having endured the horror of childhood sexual abuse and then forgotten the horror they endured? The claim makes sense only in the absence of any real idea of what the fraction "half" means. Of course, the recovered memory industry covers its back by offering a broad definition of sexual abuse that includes emotional as well as physical injury — and definitions so broad as to be meaningless are yet another telltale sign of junk thought. "The ordinary response to atrocities is to banish them from consciousness," declares the psychiatrist Judith Herman Lewis on the opening page of *Trauma and Recovery* (1992), which became the bible of therapists and patients who believe that many victims have repressed the memory of childhood incest.[16] Says who? Tell it to patients who have entered therapy precisely because they need help to deal with real and terrible events that they cannot forget.

Frederick Crews, a leading debunker of repressed memory theory, notes that one of the worst aspects of this type of junk thought is its capacity to cast a shadow on essential, honest, and ongoing efforts to combat still underreported sexual abuse of children. In the early seventies, the feminist movement did a great service to American society by forcing parents and public officials to confront the heretofore undiscussed and undiscussable reality of childhood sexual molestation. But it is one thing to say that sexual molestation of children — often perpetrated by parents, caretakers, teachers, and clergy who occupy what are supposed to be trust-inspiring positions in the lives of the young — is much more common than Americans ever realized or acknowledged before the 1970s, and quite another thing to claim that the crime is underreported because its victims have forgotten what happened to them. The pedophilia scandals that have shaken the American Catholic Church clearly demonstrate that the adult survivors of molestation by priests have *never* been able to forget the sexual assaults that stained their young lives. They had not unconsciously repressed their memories but deliberately suppressed them out of shame, the fear that they would not be believed, and a desire to shield their families and their faith.

Expert-bashing — a favorite tool of both the right and the left — is another distinguishing mark of junk thought, and the effectiveness of the technique depends on the public's inability to distinguish among good science, bad science, and pseudoscience. Scientific evidence, however overwhelming, is dismissed by the expert-bashers as politically biased. During the past decade, medical studies have detailed the grave public health consequences, most notably the Type II diabetes epidemic, of Americans' rising rate of obesity. At the same time, a new, nonscientific academic specialty called "fat studies" has emerged on a number of campuses. Professors who are beginning to make a living from fat studies — many of them already sociologists specializing in women's studies — dismiss the scientific data as the product of a larger social bias against overweight people. Says Abigail C. Saguy, professor of sociology at UCLA: "That raises really interesting sociological questions: Why has this [obesity] become such the concern [sic] that it is and why are we so worried about weight?"[17] Why? Could the concern have arisen because medical research has demonstrated conclusively that the nearly one third of Americans who meet the medical criteria for obesity — not merely ordinary overweight — are at a huge increased risk for diabetes, stroke, and a number of cancers? But the fat studies conspiracy theorists are unimpressed. Robert Buchholz, a history professor at Loyola University, presented a paper in 2005 at the annual meeting of the Popular Culture Association — a group that added fat studies to its list of topics deemed suitable for scholarly research — in which he claims that Queen Anne of England, who reigned from 1702 to 1714, has been neglected by historians solely because she was fat. The professor did not volunteer an explanation of why the same fat-phobic historians have paid ample attention to Catherine the Great of Russia, who was also well cushioned throughout much of her reign. Or, for that matter, to Queen Victoria, who, while not chubby by the standards of her day in her teens and twenties, managed to put on quite a few pounds before her Diamond Jubilee.

On the right, expert-bashers are no less active. Google the phrase "junk science," and what pops up is an endless succession of right-wing blogs devoted to the proposition that mainstream scientific consensus represents junk science and that brave dissidents, on issues ranging from vaccines to global warming, are being stifled by "the elites." Many of these blogs are financed by or have close ties to right-wing news organizations and corporations with an interest in debunking scientific findings that suggest a need for government regulation. Steven Milloy, who writes regularly for FOXNews .com, which has an extensive archive devoted to what it calls junk science, is also the publisher of his own JunkScience.com blog. Milloy, who was not impressed when a large chunk of the Arctic ice shelf broke free at the end of 2006, even savaged the anti-environmentalists' best friend, the Bush administration, for listing polar bears as a "threatened" species that might be imperiled by "the future loss of their sea-ice habitat."[18] Worry about polar bears, Milloy suggested, was just another conspiracy stirred up by the anti-business global warming lobby — and a potentially effective conspiracy, given that children (mistakenly) think of polar bears as cuddly friends.

The scientific consensus on global warming is a favorite target of right-wing purveyors of junk thought. In many instances, they compare current scientific views about global warming with the dire predictions of demographers in the late sixties about the consequences of unchecked population growth.[19] Junk thought always contains a nugget of truth, and prominent demographers did warn that both the United States and the world risked starvation if stern, compulsory birth control measures were not promoted by governments. Paul Ehrlich, author of *The Population Bomb* (1971), predicted that American cities would be convulsed by food riots in the 1980s. As we now know, the doomsday demographers were wrong about a great many things — most notably the capacity of the world to feed itself. There are still starving people today, but world hunger is a problem created by disastrous politics and an inequitable distribution of resources, not by the inability of agriculture to feed the planet's population. The demographers were wrong, in particular, in their assumption that voluntary birth control, even in developed societies, would never work. But they were certainly not wrong about everything: China's economic development, for example, could not have taken place had population growth not been checked by measures, including a mandatory limit of one child per family, that are draconian and anti-democratic from a Western point of view.

But the junk thought analogy between demography and climatology is either willfully or ignorantly misguided, because demography is not a science in the sense that climatology, physics, and biology are sciences. Demography belongs to the realm of social science — the general term for the study of human beings in all of their social relations. I use the term "science" here only because it is commonly accepted in academia, journalism, and public discourse; but the study of human reproductive choices is hardly as objective, or subject to objective verification, as, say, the study of the stars or the circulatory system. Social scientists, including demographers, use many of the tools of the physical sciences (including measurement and mathematics), but when they draw conclusions about the future behavior of the human species on the basis of past behavior, their reasoning is often highly unscientific. A psychologist studying women's reactions to abortion, like a demographer studying childbearing patterns, can only tell us how human beings have behaved in the past — not how they might behave under radically altered future conditions.

Ehrlich's predictions should have been made, and received, in the same spirit as the warning from the Ghost of Christmas Present, who told Scrooge that he foresaw the death of Tiny Tim if the shadows of the future remained unaltered. But the shadow of the future predicted by Ehrlich *was* altered — by the large-scale entry of women into the workforce, delays in childbearing age that reduced fertility, and the recognition that too many children were a burden rather than an asset in postindustrial economies. Today's climatologists, by contrast, do not assume that people are unable or unwilling to alter their behavior: what they have been careful to say is that the temperature of the earth's atmosphere will continue to rise, with adverse consequences for the planet, if we do not cut back our consumption of fossil fuels. It is also worth noting that because climatology is a physical rather than a social science, its assessment of the present situation is grounded in evidence rather than ideology. When demographers say that the United States is still overpopulated — and many, including Ehrlich, say just that — they are making subjective judgments about how many people, and which people, are too many. Their opinions may be influenced by heavy traffic on the freeway; the fierce competition for admission to prestigious colleges (a competition that, in states like California, third- and fourth-generation Americans are losing to first- and second-generation Asian Americans); or the conviction that the growing Latino population represents a major threat to the English-speaking, Anglo-Saxon heritage of the United States.

Whether one shares or dismisses such concerns, they are matters of opinion, not of fact. However, when climatologists talk about global warming in the present, they are referring to objectively measurable phenomena: the shrinking of the polar ice caps, the disappearance of snow from the upper regions of mountains, rising sea levels, threatened species that can no longer count on the frigid weather they need to survive, tropical plants suddenly blooming in temperate weather zones. Whether people are delighted or appalled by the thought of climbing Mount Kilimanjaro in bathing suits, it is a matter of observable fact that the snows are melting. The real matters of opinion revolve around the questions of whether we wish to modify our behavior today in an attempt to retard the forces of climate change and how long it will take for the worst consequences of global warming to manifest themselves if we do nothing.

Junk thought should not be confused with stupidity or sheer ignorance, because it is often employed by highly intelligent people to mislead and confuse a public deficient in its grasp of logic, the scientific method, and the basic arithmetic required to see through the pretensions of poorly designed studies. American schools, according to every international survey conducted during the past twenty years, are doing a poor job of inculcating basic mathematical and scientific principles in comparison to school systems in the rest of the developed world. The most recent assessment by the Organization of Economic Cooperation and Development (OECD), a Paris-based agency that conducts regular education evaluations in the world's most industrialized nations, found that American fifteen-year-olds ranked twenty-fourth out of twenty-nine countries in mathematical literacy. Only Portugal, Italy, Greece, Turkey, and Mexico ranked behind the United States in the 2005 assessment.

The OECD criteria focus on the ability of students to use math in real-world problem solving; the skills being tested are precisely those required to understand the meaning of fractions and percentages set forth in various claims by researchers.[20] In science, the United States is not among the worst-performing countries but is merely mediocre, fourteenth among twenty-five nations studied.[21] This is not to suggest that Americans are unique in their mathematical and scientific illiteracy but that there is a unique gap between America's image of itself as the world's leader in science and technology and the reality of a nation in which more students are spending more years in school while falling behind the most developed nations of Europe and Asia. In Turkey and Mexico, people are not constantly told that they are, or ought to be, "number one." Moreover, public ignorance in large and powerful countries is particularly dangerous to the rest of the world precisely because of the capacity of powerful states to inflict damage on the weak.

It ought to be unnecessary to have to state that scientific literacy and respect for the scientific method should not be equated with blind trust in experts and scientists and that antagonism toward evidence-based science should not be confused with an entirely healthy concern about the need for ethical oversight of scientific research. But junk thought has become so pervasive in the United States that as soon as someone criticizes, say, religion-based restrictions on stem cell research, the hucksters of illogic inevitably remind the public about Nazi doctors who performed cruel and scientifically useless experiments on human subjects; about Lysenkoist biology in the Soviet Union; and, last but not least, about the false and widely publicized claims of successful embryonic cloning by South Korean researchers. The last were of course exposed by other scientists, because all real scientific research must be and is subjected to rigorous scrutiny by peers. That is what separates science from pseudoscience and junk thought. Without a basic understanding of what constitutes good science, neither ordinary citizens nor the politicians who represent them can hope to make thoughtful judgments separating quacks, con men, and practitioners of bad science from thoughtful experts whose advice ought to be taken seriously.

Intellectual quackery extends throughout the landscape of academia; tenured professors in the humanities and social sciences, on the right and the left, are constantly purveying theories that are the philosophical, literary, and artistic equivalents of junk science. That many of the researchers consider themselves intellectuals is sad but unremarkable in the annals of quackery within academia: junk thought with an intellectual patina fosters anti-intellectualism as effectively as junk science with a scientific patina fosters public misunderstanding and suspicion of real science. This sort of junk thought knows no racial, political, or gender boundaries; among the most notable examples is a wacky but influential movement within academic feminism, mainly in the humanities and such fields as psychology and sociology, intent on attacking some of the most monumental fields of human endeavor as hopelessly tainted by the male lust for violence and domination. These tainted phallocentric pursuits include science and classical music. In a work published in 1986, Sandra Harding, professor of philosophy at the University of Delaware, compared the scientific method to "marital rape, the husband as scientist forcing nature to his wishes."[22] Harding also noted that feminist historians (I would describe them as a bad minority of feminist historians) had focused on the "rape and torture metaphors in the writings of Sir Francis Bacon and others . . . enthusiastic about the new scientific methods." She added:

A consistent analysis would lead to the conclusion that understanding nature as a woman indifferent to or even welcoming rape was equally fundamental to these new conceptions of nature and inquiry. Presumably these metaphors, too, had fruitful pragmatic, methodological, and metaphysical consequences for science. In that case, why is it not as illuminating and honest to refer to Newton's laws as "Newton's rape manual" as it is to call them "Newton's mechanics"?[23]

A kindred spirit in musicology is Susan McClary, who argues that the characteristic forms of classical music between the seventeenth and twentieth centuries constitute what is essentially a musical compendium of frustrated male desire, followed by violent release. The point of recapitulation in the first movement of Beethoven's Ninth Symphony "unleashes one of the most horrifyingly violent episodes in the history of music," and the entire symphony is "our most compelling articulation in music of the contradictory impulses that have organized patriarchal culture since the Enlightenment."[24] McClary's criticism has not been relegated to the lunatic fringe within academic feminism; instead, she received one of the coveted MacArthur Foundation grants, popularly known as "genius awards," in 1995.

Spread by news media also tainted by cultural and scientific illiteracy, the worst sorts of junk thought have displayed a tendency to migrate from one end of the political spectrum to the other; they mutate and are manipulated in a grotesque reversal of evolution by means of natural selection. Repackaged junk thought inevitably surfaces, far from its origins, in a seemingly new and controversial guise that impedes the ability of both intellectuals and nonintellectuals to recognize mutton dressed as lamb.

One of the most prominent recent demonstrations of the survival of the unfittest in intellectual life is the renewal of obsessive interest in supposedly innate differences between the sexes as an explanation for everything from the dearth of women at the top levels of science to the attention problems of boys in elementary school. Sometimes these differences are attributed to hormones, as in the marketing of school curricula designed to free testosterone-poisoned boys from the tyranny of desks and to allow oxytocin-rich girls to chatter away or text-message about their feelings without being scolded by the teacher for talking in class. Sometimes the putative differences are attributed to genetics — a trend that will no doubt become more marked as genetic research expands and the technical tools for brain imaging become even more sophisticated than they are today. The enthusiasm for new theories about the "boy brain, girl brain" dichotomy crosses political and cultural boundaries, extending from liberal academics to religious fundamentalists upholding the concept of divinely ordained separate spheres of responsibility for men and women.

Lawrence H. Summers, an economist who served as Bill Clinton's secretary of the Treasury before being appointed president of Harvard, set off an explosion that eventually cost him his Harvard job when he suggested that the low representation of women at the highest levels of science was more likely to be explained by innate gender differences in scientific and mathematical aptitude than by overt discrimination or subtle social discouragement. In a speech at a 2005 conference on women and minorities in science and engineering, Summers compared the relatively low female presence in science to the paucity of Catholics in investment banking, white men in the National Basketball Association, and Jews in farming and agriculture. These were unfortunate analogies as lead-ins to a discussion about innate talents because, with the exception of the genetically determined height of black basketball players, each of Summers's examples provides a spectacular illustration of the importance of culture and socialization in determining vocational choices and opportunities. Jews, needless to say, are very well represented in Israeli agriculture, and Catholics are in charge of the Vatican's financial operations. If the Catholic Church had established its headquarters in the Congo two thousand years ago, I have no doubt that the pope and his top financial advisers would be black African men.

Summers did not bolster his own credibility or reputation for objectivity when he added, "I guess my experience with my two-and-a-half-year-old twin daughters, who were not given dolls and who were given trucks, and found themselves saying to each other, look, daddy truck is carrying the baby truck, tells me something."[25] He never indicated what the "something" was; his little girls may have meant only that their daddy looked more like a truck to them than their mommy did. Summers also mentioned studies of identical twins separated at birth, which have demonstrated many remarkable similarities in the interests and achievements of twins raised apart. But that research rests on the biological fact that identical twins, unlike most humans, really *do* have an identical genetic heritage. Such studies provide a powerful argument for the influence of genetics on individual human beings, but they tell us little about the behavior, capacities, or attainments of large groups of people who do not share the same DNA — whether the groups being compared are women and men, blacks and whites, or Asians and Europeans.

What places Summers's speculative statements within the realm of junk thought is not the idea there might be some differences in aptitude between men and women but his unsupported conclusion that such disparities, if they exist, are more important than the very different cultural messages girls and boys receive about whether they can expect to succeed in science. Let us assume, for the sake of argument, that girls and boys receive an equal amount of encouragement when they display an interest in math or science and that even on a hypothetically equal playing field, boys are genetically destined to produce two thinkers on the level of Albert Einstein in the course of a century, while girls can be expected to produce only one Alberta Einstein. That the distribution of genius is predictable is, of course, a ridiculous proposition, but it is even more ridiculous to posit the existence of an equal playing field. Belief in differential aptitude offers a handy excuse for educators to do nothing more to stimulate girls' interest in science, and it also rules out any need for research institutes and businesses to make changes that would support rather than discourage the careers of scientists who are also mothers. Moreover, if women are less fitted by nature than men for the work of science, the lords of academia can skip all of those annoying diversity-promoting conferences and thereby avoid the irresistible temptation to put their feet in their mouths.

Female academics, especially scientists who got where they were by enduring and battling discrimination throughout the early and middle stages of their careers, were Summers's strongest critics. It must be especially galling for women scientists and doctors who have paid their dues to hear a Harvard president pontificating about the inborn scientific inadequacies of the female sex, because any woman over fifty who has succeeded in science or medicine has had to put up with more discrimination than men like Summers can ever imagine. Dr. Marcia Angell, editor in chief emerita of the *New England Journal of Medicine* (and the only woman editor in the history of that venerable publication), recalls having been told in college that she "thought like a man," and having so internalized stereotypes about the inferiority of female doctors that she "lacked enough sense to be offended by this compliment."[26] The most vociferous defenders of Summers were right-wing academics and journalists, who claimed that the Harvard president was being pilloried for having spoken a politically incorrect truth. The right-wingers found themselves in the unfamiliar and pleasant position of being able to bash the pinko–left–politically correct Harvard faculty while simultaneously demonstrating their fair-mindedness by supporting a Harvard president with a Clintonian past. The real reason for Summers's unpopularity with the faculty seems to have been his lack — perhaps due to a genetic deficit — of the ego-massaging skills essential to the success of any university president.

Summers's guesswork about a female

deficit in scientific and mathematical aptitude was presented against the ironic backdrop of a rising chorus of voices claiming that boys are the ones in real academic trouble at every stage of the educational process. The common theme, of course, is that male and female brains are different in ways that explain differential outcomes and even require differential treatment. On October 25, 2006, *The New York Times* published what should have been a startling front-page story under the relatively innocuous headline, "Change in Federal Rules Backs Single-Sex Public Education." The story revealed that the Bush administration had adopted a new policy allowing public school districts to create single-sex classes and even single-sex schools, as long as enrollment in such programs is voluntary and as long as classes of "substantially equal" quality are made available to students of the excluded sex. In other words, separate but equal. The policy contradicts a landmark law, Title IX of the education amendment act of 1972, that prohibits sex-segregated education in public schools except for physical education and sex education classes.

Education Secretary Margaret Spellings told the *Times* that research supported the benefits of single-sex education and that the policy change would somehow be managed in accordance with the law banning sex segregation in public schools. But a statement by Stephanie Monroe, head of the Education Department's Office of Civil Rights, acknowledged that the government's own research offers no unequivocal evidence of such benefits. "Educational research, though it's ongoing and shows some mixed results, does suggest that single-sex education can provide some benefits to some students, under certain circumstances," Monroe said.[27] *Mixed results . . . some benefits . . . under certain circumstances.* That hardly constitutes an airtight, or even a reasonable, case for a policy that would jettison not just thirty-five years of feminist efforts aimed at achieving equality for women in education but the pragmatic, commonsensical coeducation that has been the rule rather than the exception in public schools since the dawn of the republic. The little red schoolhouse was not a fiction, and there was no curtain dividing girls and boys: that they would all learn to read, write, and do their sums was taken for granted.

The push to spend tax dollars on single-sex education is a pet cause of political conservatives, many of whom believe that both boys and girls will do better in class if they are not distracted by the presence of the opposite sex, but it is also supported by many liberals taken in by the marketing of the so-called boy crisis. Predictably, the originators of the boy crisis are making money out of the newly discovered threat. The Gurian Institute, founded in 1997 by family therapist Michael Gurian, author of *The Wonder of Boys* (2006), sponsors pricy seminars designed to indoctrinate teachers in theories — and I use the word "theory" in its everyday nonscientific sense — about hardwired neurological differences between girls and boys. These half-baked ideas, put into practice by the Kentucky school principal lauded in *Newsweek,* lead to the conclusion that the education of boys and girls ought to be conducted in separate classes in order to address their supposedly different learning styles. Bruce Perry, a Houston neurologist who specializes in disruptive children, described the standard public school system, in which boys and girls attend coed classes beginning in kindergarten, as a "biologically disrespectful model of education."[28] Because most young girls are more verbally adept than most young boys, emphasis on reading and writing skills is said to place boys at a particular disadvantage in the early grades. Women — both feminists and anti-feminists — have also gotten into the act. Louann Brizendine, a neuropsychiatrist who calls herself a feminist and runs a hormone clinic for women in San Francisco, hit it big on talk shows in 2006 with her book *The Female Brain.* "Connecting through talking activates the pleasure centers in a girl's brain," she explains. "We're not talking about a small amount of pleasure. This is huge. It's a major dopamine and oxytocin rush, which is the biggest, fattest, neurological reward you can get outside of an orgasm."[29] Is it the mission of schools to coax their students into studying by offering neurological rewards second only to orgasm, and, in any case, isn't it more fun to sneak messages in a classroom where talking is theoretically forbidden?

The right wing, not to be outdone, blames the boy crisis on feminists who either hate real men or want to turn boys into girls. Cristina Hoff Sommers, a fellow with the American Enterprise Institute, encompasses the entire case in the title of her book, *The War Against Boys: How Misguided Feminism Is Harming Our Young Men* (2001). On the one hand, boys are said to have more natural aptitude than girls for science and math; on the other, the male of the species is losing out academically to a "biologically disrespectful" model of education, created by and for women. To pile on the illogic and contradictions, some feminists have long advocated single-sex education as a way of protecting girls from having their opinions stifled by verbally aggressive boys. Presumably, these are not the same boys labeled so verbally backward that they need to be protected from chatty Cathys in first and second grade.

The gaping hole in all of the talk about male problems in school is that the boy crisis is largely confined to poor and minority communities. Rich white boys are not falling behind rich white girls. There is, however, a crisis in the African-American community, and it begins in elementary school. At the high school level, the picture is especially grim. A study by the Urban Institute reported that in Boston schools, 104 white girls finish high school for every 100 boys — a gap but hardly a crisis. Among African Americans, the gap is 139 to 100. That is a real calamity, but it seems preposterous to attribute the gap to a "biologically disrespectful" school system that works quite well for upper-middle-class whites of both sexes. Nationwide, more than half of African-American boys drop out of high school — a statistic with deeply rooted social causes that have been explored by a host of black writers and scholars of varying political persuasions, including National Public Radio's Juan Williams, *Newsday*'s Les Payne, *New York Times* op-ed columnist Bob Herbert, the conservative author Shelby Steele, the sociologist Orlando Patterson, and the historian Henry Louis Gates. Unlike the whites enamored of the "boy crisis," none of these African-American commentators focuses on genetics or the supposedly different learning styles of girls and boys. Instead, they examine a street culture that glorifies violence as proof of manhood and denigrates learning, as well as the absence of a father in so many poor African-American homes. A similar pattern is evident in low-income Hispanic neighborhoods and among poor whites, for whom the divorce rate is also much higher than it is among more affluent white Americans. The reasons why girls do better than boys, even in subcultures permeated by violence and poverty, surely have something to do with the greater susceptibility of boys to malign influences — including drugs, gangs, and macho contempt for women — in the absence of positive, disciplined adult men in their lives. Yet (go figure!) white academics and members of the media are more interested in looking at the way boy brains and girl brains differ in "verbal processing." It seems that the portion of the brain, the amygdala, where emotions are processed is poorly connected in boys to the part of the brain that expresses emotions in words; ergo, boys need to be taught to read and write in different ways from girls. According to this logic, the amygdalas of women before the eighteenth century must also have had a screw loose, given that nearly all great writers were men. Or could it be that women in pre-Enlightenment societies were rarely taught to read and write and systematically discouraged from intellectual pursuits?

The top award for sounding the alarm in the silly season of the boy crisis must go to *New York Times* columnist David Brooks. Having charged both the Old Left and the New Left with the death of middlebrow culture, Brooks assigns the blame for boys' reading problems to "young adult" novels written by women. Boys hate reading because they "are sent home with these new-wave young adult problem novels, which all seem to be about introspectively morose young women whose parents are either suicidal drug addicts or fatally ill manic depressives."[30] To stimulate boys' interest in books, Brooks says, they must be assigned more Hemingway, Tolstoy, Homer, and Twain. Tolstoy? Surely not *Anna Karenina*. How could one expect any boy, with a brain improperly wired for verbal processing, to be interested in a novel with a woman's name as its title? And the entire argument is based on the dubious assumption that assigned school reading lists can turn children, whether male or female, into readers — or turn them off reading altogether. If that were true, no one who was taught to read with the Dick-and-Jane primers would ever have opened another book.

Memoirs of self-educated men and women of the nineteenth century show that they cut their teeth on the same books — the Bible and Shakespeare — because those were the only books available in many small communities. When today's American children fail to develop either the skills or the habit of reading, something has gone radically wrong long before the age when anyone is old enough to enjoy or comprehend one tenth of Tolstoy, Homer, Twain, and Hemingway. Even those banal young adult novels (yes, Judy Blume has a lot to answer for) would be beyond the reach of teenage girls unless they had developed the habit of reading in early childhood. Adult men, including those who grew up long before feminism supposedly wrecked education for boys, also read fewer books — especially fiction — than women, but the decline in reading for pleasure is an across-the-board phenomenon, evident among Americans of both sexes and every income and ethnic group. What does any of this have to do with brain differences? "Women use both sides of their brain more symmetrically than men," Brooks explains. "Men and women hear and smell differently (women are much more sensitive). Boys and girls process colors differently (young girls enjoy an array of red, green and orange crayons, whereas young boys generally stick to black, gray and blue). Men and women experience risk differently (men enjoy it more)."[31] Perhaps, in addition to pushing Twain and Hemingway, teachers should keep a stock of "boy books" with black, gray, and blue jackets, and save the brighter covers for girls.

It is almost too easy — rather like shooting quail with clipped wings — to make fun of this brand of junk thought. However, the truly disturbing element in the renewed emphasis on innate differences between boy brains and girl brains, regardless of the source, is that such beliefs are directly descended from the unscientific and anti-scientific assumptions of the past. There is nothing new about the idea that various groups of human beings are ill-suited by nature for certain kinds of learning: we have heard it all before, from ancient sages who declared women unfit for the study of philosophy; from plantation owners certain that Negroes were too weak-brained to learn to read (not weak-brained enough, though, for southerners to feel comfortable unless they passed laws prohibiting the teaching of reading to slaves); from nineteenth-century men who insisted that the female constitution was too fragile to withstand the rigors of higher education; and, last but not least, from white native-born American Protestants, one generation after another, who insisted that the Irish, the Chinese coolies, the East Europeans and Italians, would never be capable of educating themselves to do anything beyond manual labor. In fairness, it must be acknowledged that proponents of the boy brain–girl brain dichotomy insist that their theories do not imply the superiority or inferiority of one sex and that the only goal of single-sex education is to show respect for biology by teaching boys and girls in ways best suited to their gender-linked brain chemistries. This is a distinction without a difference: whatever the intent, separating boys and girls in school — and paying for the separation with public funds — amounts to an official endorsement of the idea that "men are from Mars, women from Venus." This assumption also lets the governing class, and citizens of all races, off the hook about their responsibility for the persistence of an American underclass in which boys and men are truly in a permanent state of crisis.

The boy brain–girl brain brouhaha has been created mainly by psychologists and social scientists. Junk thought is much more pervasive, and easier to promote, in sociology and psychology than it is in the physical sciences, because the endorsement of dubious social science does not require a wholesale rejection of expert opinion. Those who adamantly reject evolution are hard put to find serious scientists to support their position: instead, they must fall back on the occasional crank who opposes the scientific consensus and claim that dissent is being suppressed by a conspiracy of elitists who control universities and research institutes.

That there is considerable debate within the scientific community over the particulars at various stages of evolution is the most persuasive proof that no conspiracy exists. But no one can legitimately claim to be both a serious scientist and a serious opponent of evolutionism. In the social sciences, by contrast, there is no shortage of credentialed experts to endorse any position, however untethered from both common sense and scholarly evidence. The repressed memory movement could never have gained such traction in the nineties if there had not been a plethora of psychotherapists, with a string of degrees, using their professional authority to promote the idea that it was perfectly easy for a woman to forget having been sexually molested in childhood and to "recover" the memory — with sufficient therapy, of course — in adulthood. That there were also respected psychiatric authorities who opposed the recovered memory movement only encouraged the public to give more weight to emotion and opinion than to the contrary evidence set forth by hard-hearted scientists.

The proponents of separate educational approaches for boys and girls enjoy an extra advantage in the battle for public attention: they can claim scientific support for a social prescription by calling selectively on medical research findings. The vague citation of "medical studies" in support of one junk premise or another inspires as deep a faith, based on as little substance, as the Holy Grail. Junk thought marketers, in the press and academia, frequently bolster their arguments with studies based on such small samples that they have almost no scientific validity. Even when research on sex differences is scientifically respectable, the identification of such differences, whether cultural or genetic, does not necessarily mean that anything needs to be done to remedy them. There really is brain research highlighting many differences between girls and boys. It is intriguing, sometimes enjoyable, to receive scientific confirmation of what life experience has already taught most adults — that women are more sensitive than men to color and noise and that the male of the species has a keener appetite for risk than the female. Although the relative role of nature and nurture is far from clear, these differences may well have something to do with such curious phenomena as the overwhelmingly male enthusiasm for video games, and the corresponding indifference of most women to the same booming business. Here's an idea for parents who want to encourage their sons to read more: forget about brain wiring and place a limit of one hour a day on video gaming. If playing

Grand Theft Auto represents a uniquely male learning style, it is a style that should not be encouraged — and same-sex classrooms would likely reinforce rather than ameliorate the problem.

Finally, the simplistic slogans of junk thought are perfectly suited to modern mass media, which must fixate on novelty in order to catch the eyes and ears of a public with an increasingly short attention span. On the day the Bush administration announced its plans to promote sex-segregated classes in public schools, all of the evening television newscasts ran largely uncritical features, quoting experts who are already making money out of the budding "boy brain, girl brain" industry. Extra! Extra! The television producers were certainly capable of imagining the click of millions of remotes to another channel, had their newscasts run a bold segment proclaiming, "Boys, Girls, Still Learn in Pretty Much the Same Old Way."

Chapter Ten: The Culture of Distraction

In 1989, James D. Squires, then editor of the *Chicago Tribune,* invited the new chairman of the Gannett Corporation to discuss the future of journalism with members of the American Society of Newspaper Editors. Among the editors' concerns were the already sharp decline in newspaper reading among young Americans and the homogenizing impact of media conglomerates like Gannett on the content of local papers. According to Squires, the Gannett chairman, John Curley, laughed and said, "You mean, talk to a bunch of people like you? Squires, you're over."[1]

At age forty-six, Squires was not a grizzled, computer-illiterate survivor of old-time newspapering as depicted in *The Front Page,* but he was nevertheless being written off as a representative of values inimical to the bottom-line corporate mentality holding sway over a growing number of the nation's most venerable newspapers and magazines. Of course, the brusque Gannett executive was right, in the sense that control of print news media was already passing rapidly from those who believed that it was their responsibility to inform and sometimes educate the public, in as much depth as possible, to those who specialized in the truncation of text in a futile effort to compete with video. Try as they might — and they did and still do — the newspaper and magazine editors who followed Squires's generation could not possibly shorten their articles enough, and add enough jazzy color pictures, to lure younger audiences away from the more arousing split-second impressions and sensations to be gleaned from a passing glance at the television screen or an even quicker hit on the Internet's flashing, ever-changing cavalcade of images. The decline in newspaper reading after the early seventies was a miner's canary for an accelerating and relentless abbreviation of the public's attention span, now fragmented into millions of bits and bytes by the unlimited electronically and digitally generated distractions that make up our way of life.

One obvious objection to emphasizing the ill fortunes of newspapers in a discussion of the current wave of American anti-intellectualism is that the nation's newspapers, as well as mass-circulation magazines, have never been known for their high intellectual quality. Indeed, the popular press has generally treated intellectuals and their doings, except for celebrities like Ralph Waldo Emerson and Albert Einstein, with an attitude ranging from indifference to outright disdain. The intellectual shortcomings of past and present newspapers are, however, beside the point, because the real difference between today's video and yesterday's print is not content but context — a context in which the proliferating visual images and noises of the video/digital age permeate the minute-by-minute experience of our lives. Newspaper reading was a habit that accompanied the beginning or ending of each workday for millions; it did not constitute a continuous invasion of individual thought and consciousness. The most trashy newspaper and the most sublime work of literature share a crucial characteristic: each can be picked up, perused, contemplated, and put down at will. Printed works do not take up mental space simply by virtue of being there; attention must be paid or their content, whether simple or complex, can never be truly assimilated. The willed attention demanded by print is the antithesis of the reflexive distraction encouraged by infotainment media, whether one is talking about the tunes on an iPod, a picture flashing briefly on a home page, a text message, a video game, or the latest offering of "reality" TV. That all of these sources of information and entertainment are capable of simultaneously engendering distraction and absorption accounts for much of their snakelike charm. As Todd Gitlin observes, the common misuse of "the media" in the singular is more than a grammatical error.

Grammatical sticklers (like this writer) cringe when the media themselves or college students reared on them (or it) speak of "the media" as they might speak of "the sky" — as if there were only one. There is, however, a reason for this error other than grammatical slovenliness. Something about our experience makes us want to address media as "it." We may be confused about whether "the media" are or "is" technologies or cultural codes — whether "television" is an electronic system for bringing images into the home, or the sum of Oprah, Dan Rather, Jerry Springer, and MTV; whether "the media" includes alternative rock or the Internet. But through all the confusion we sense something like a unity at work. . . . Even as we click around, something *feels* uniform — a relentless pace, a pattern of interruption, a pressure toward unseriousness, a readiness for sensation, an anticipation of the next new thing. Whatever the diversity of texts, the media largely share a texture. . . .[2]

Media thus constitute *the* medium in an ecological sense, as the natural habitat of an organism — specifically, the human organism. Although this overarching medium includes many intellectually useful components, it is on balance an unfriendly habitat not only for serious high-level intellectual endeavor but also for the more ordinary exchanges of ideas that enliven and elevate culture at every level. That the medium was not designed, intelligently or otherwise, to be an anti-intellectual force only attests to its subliminal as well as its overt power. Many will object to the grouping of media products that appear on the interactive computer screen with products on essentially passive television and DVD screens, but the differences pale in comparison to an overwhelming commonality — the capability to deliver near-instant gratification through visual imagery.

Aggrieved eulogies for print culture, and railing against the domination of American culture by video-driven infotainment media, have become so common that almost no one, except those who still make a living from the printed word, pays any attention to critiques that could easily be titled, "The Decline and Fall of Everything." Those who take a dark view of the intellectual and political consequences of the eclipse of print are obliged to establish their bona fides by disclaiming any resistance to the proposition that the computer has effected not only a technological but an intellectual breakthrough in the march of human progress. It has now become more insulting to call someone a Luddite than to call her a cheat, a drug addict, or a slut. It is also important for the critic to forestall charges of elitism by acknowledging that she too enjoys mindlessly "vegging out" in front of the television set after a tough day. Better yet, there should be no quotation marks around vegging, because the quotes suggest a certain sense of superiority that smacks of forbidden elitism. Finally, there is the obligatory statement, before saying anything about the particularly adverse impact of the media on children, that every generation has always taken a dim view of the intellectual seriousness and attainments of young folks.

The easiest way to address the cultural ills propagated by the media without sounding like a crochety Luddite is to focus mainly on infotainment content and its most egregious manifestations, and that is the tactic adopted by most consumer groups dedicated to changing the media by changing the message. The assumption that content determines context, rather than vice-versa, is shared by the many diverse crusaders against relentless advertising on children's television shows; violence in all television programming; the brutish, misogynist lyrics and images of many pop music productions; kiddie porn Web sites proliferating on the Internet; and other pieces of broadcast and Webcast junk too numerous to mention. The basic idea is that by eliminating certain kinds of poison, the media can be made safe for children and all living things. It is of course important to mount such efforts, if only for the sake of being able to walk around with a clearer conscience about the world we are bequeathing to the next generation. But the media really do constitute a self-renewing, unified organism that cannot be contained or modified in any fundamental sense by lopping off some of the more malignant clusters of cells.

Consider relatively recent research findings indicating that the number of hours a television set is on in the average American home each day — seven — did not change measurably between the early 1980s and the turn of the millennium. What did change, however, was the proportion of Americans who watched "whatever's on," as distinct from a particular television program. In 1979, 29 percent of Americans said that they watched anything that happened to be on television. By 1995, the figure for indiscriminate television watchers had risen to 43 percent.[3] These statistics are probably an underestimate, given the absence of consciousness inherent in the reflexive consumption of anything. Among medical specialists who treat obesity, it is well known that people who "graze" — snack around the clock — not only consume more calories each day but are less likely to have any idea of how much they are eating than are people who sit down for regular meals.

What, then, is one to make of the reasonable-sounding proposition that all we have to do to control the influence of the media in our lives is to turn off the television set, the iPod, the computer? It is not so easy to turn off media that make up, as a once ubiquitous television commercial for cotton clothing proclaimed, "the fabric of our lives." In many homes, including the homes of those who consider themselves intellectuals, the television set is on regardless of whether anyone is watching. It feels more natural than not to half-see the light and half-hear the sound streaming from the television set, and that is as true for those raised before the television era as it is for the young. In 1985, Neil Postman described television as the paradigm for our dependency on all media. Writing at a time when everyone was beginning to talk about personal computers but few households actually had one, Postman made the point that television was largely responsible for informing the public that computers would soon be essential to everyone's life — that "our children will fail in school and be left behind in life if they are not 'computer literate.' "[4] Although the Internet has now taken over many of the informational and marketing tasks that used to be performed by television, magazines, and newspapers, the image of television as paradigm is still valid. Television differs from the computer in that the former is merely an entertainment medium, while the latter is both an infotainment medium and a tool, replacing, in far more efficient fashion, the functions of earlier single-use tools like the typewriter and the Yellow Pages. What computers and television share is their status as a way of life.

The computer way of life, which does include text as well as video and audio, exerts its most powerful pull through its instantaneousness. The advent of portable devices for viewing images and listening to music — often simultaneously — has expanded the reach of media even further, into the spaces in which people used to be alone, whether willingly or unwillingly, with their own thoughts. Ah, I hear the technophiles saying, but these new devices are *customized,* they offer endless choices geared to individual intelligence and interests, so they are nothing like the three-network "boob tube" of the fifties. In this view, the new digital forms of both video and audio are actually a boon to intellectual life because they do not require individual members of the audience to settle for lowest common denominator taste. Both the old and new video/audio media, however, impose the demand that everyone take his or her place as a member of the audience, and although many computer programs are interactive, they are interactive only within the universe defined by the software program. The more time people spend before the computer screen or any screen, the less time and desire they have for two human activities critical to a fruitful and demanding intellectual life: reading and conversation. The media invade, and in many instances destroy altogether, the silence that promotes reading and the free time required for both solitary thinking and social conversation. Above all, the media extend their domination of cultural life by lowering the age at which children's minds — boy brains and girl brains alike — are exposed to large and continuously increasing doses of packaged entertainment.

For several years, producers of children's video have been turning out products aimed not only at three- to five-year-olds already in preschool but at toddlers and infants too young to sit up. The year 2006 may one day be considered a turning point in the media drive for total penetration of the human market. The pretentious *Baby Einstein* video series — aimed at parents who want to give their babies an edge in the race for admission to prestigious preschools, which feed into prestigious elementary and secondary schools, which ultimately disgorge their charges into the Ivy League — was already well established. Early in 2006, however, the videos aimed at toddlers were joined by the first television channel, BabyFirstTV, aimed not at sophisticated two- and three-year-olds but at infants in the cradle.

Available on satellite and cable for $9.99 a month, BabyFirst marketed itself as commercial-free, but the entire project might properly be described as a commercial for television itself — a commercial that begins before the target audience is physically capable of turning its back to the screen. As always, there were some putative experts weighing in on both sides of the issue. "I was skeptical when I first heard about it," said Dr. Edward McCabe, physician in chief of the Mattel Children's Hospital at the University of California at Los Angeles. "But I became convinced that this is a major evolution in media for kids."[5] McCabe, whose quote to the Associated Press was reprinted in an article about "infantainment" on TV.com (where else?), is also a member of the advisory board of BabyFirst and is the most frequently quoted expert associated with the program. Dr. McCabe is an eminent geneticist, and he would be the first physician you would want to consult about glycerol kinase deficiency, a metabolic disorder caused by a chromosomal irregularity, but nothing in his medical background suggests that he knows any more than the Maytag repairman about the impact of television on the intellectual development of normal babies. Since nearly all of the medical professionals who have devoted their entire careers to ordinary child development are highly skeptical about exposing babies to more video, the marketers must make do with physicians whose medical expertise lies elsewhere.

Even more disturbing in certain respects was the introduction by the Sesame Workshop of a series of half-hour DVDs titled *Sesame Beginnings,* aimed at children between ages six months and two years. Creator and overlord of the beloved *Sesame Street* series for older preschoolers, Sesame Workshop is identified in the minds of Americans with quality and with educational benefits: how could anyone object to anything with the imprimatur of the Muppets? As it happens, a number of prominent pediatricians and child psychologists — including Dr. T. Berry Brazelton, successor to Dr. Benjamin Spock as America's unofficial parental adviser in chief; Dr. David Elkind, author of *The Hurried Child* (2001); and Dr. Alvin F. Poussaint, an African-

American psychiatrist who has focused on child rearing in the black community — did voice objections. In a strong critique of the push to expose babies to videos, they cited the American Academy of Pediatrics recommendation that children under two watch no television at all. Their statement unleashed the fury of just about everyone who makes a living from video, including consultants who stand to make a bundle from their participation in the production of the videos and media critics for newspapers and magazines.

The champions of infant videoland in the mainstream media, including print media, attacked the "elitism" of the highly regarded pediatricians and child development specialists who spoke out against the DVDs. Virginia Heffernan, a television critic for *The New York Times,* wrote a searing column about the arrogance of the "experts in Boston" — including Drs. Brazelton, Elkind, and Poussaint. The proper name "Boston" has become a substitute for "capital of the pointy-headed eastern intellectual establishment and home of 'the elites.'" The anti-video experts, according to Heffernan, were "more than a little Luddite in their opposition to 'Sesame Beginnings,' as if technology itself — a screen of any kind! —

would harm children, who ought presumably to gaze only at sunsets, shake wooden rattles and cuddle corn-husk dolls."[6]

In this view, the only possible reasons for opposing the exposure of infants to canned entertainment are intellectual snobbery, reflexive opposition to technology for anyone at any age, and, of course, lack of sympathy for the burdens of hardworking parents. In any case, video marketers need have no fear that their messages are failing to reach the very young. A pioneering 2003 study by the Kaiser Family Foundation correctly uses the term "screen media" to lump together all forms of children's video. In that year, 43 percent of children under age two already watched television every day, while a whopping 68 percent were exposed to some form of daily video on TV, DVD, or VCR. Approximately 30 percent of children under three have a TV set in their bedrooms, as do 43 percent of four- to six-year-olds.[7] Presumably, these media-savvy tots have forsaken their corn-husk dolls and wooden rattles and are more likely to see the sun go down on their personal video screens than over a real horizon.

The marketers insist that the wholesome baby DVDs are meant to promote interaction between parents and children: Mommy or Daddy is supposed to be watching *Sesame Beginnings* right along with Baby. Among the more revealing and saddening sequences in the videos are those focusing on mothers, some celebrities and some unknown, playing with their babies. Why would any parent, instead of cuddling and talking to his or her own baby, prefer to watch a DVD of another parent playing with another baby? The answer, whether parents admit it to themselves or not, is that Mom and Dad want the little ones to fall into their customary trance at the sight of a favorite video on the screen — yes, *any* screen. The grown-ups can then escape the nursery and enjoy a glass of wine and some adult conversation (if they aren't watching television themselves). And there would be nothing wrong with that, if video did not become a habitual pacifier. But it does become a habitual pacifier in most households and is designed to do so. There is no large body of research indicating that it is a bad idea to turn on the television set for infants in the cradle because, until now, there has never been a large enough group of infant subjects. The first serious study on the subject, released in 2007 by researchers at the University of Washington and Seattle Children's Hospital, suggested that videos like *Baby Einstein* and *Brainy Baby* may actually impede language development in children between the ages of eight and sixteen months. The researchers found that for every hour infants watched the videos, they understood an average of six to eight fewer words than babies who were not exposed to video at such an early age.[8] But if marketers have their way, there will soon be no control group of infants who have *not* become hooked on video long before they can walk or talk.

One particularly dismaying finding by the Kaiser Foundation is that children under six now spend an average of two hours a day viewing screen media, while they spend only thirty-nine minutes a day reading or listening to their parents read to them.[9] Is more research required to tell us what is already known from medical studies of drugs and from millennia of educational effort — that the impact of any substance or experience, good or bad, is magnified by the length of exposure and that the effect is strongest on immature and therefore more malleable organisms? Give us a baby, and we will give you a lifelong video consumer.

There is really no need to make a case for the proposition that video watching displaces reading for pleasure. When four out of ten adults read no books at all (fiction or nonfiction) in the course of a year, and more than half read no fiction, the facts speak for themselves. Between 1982 and 2002, according to a decennial survey by the National Endowment for the Arts (NEA), the proportion of Americans reading fiction declined by 10 percent overall, with the steepest decline — 28 percent — registered among those under age twenty-five. Even more ominously, the rate of decline in literary reading nearly tripled between 1992 and 2002, the decade during which personal computers and portable electronic devices entered the everyday lives of a majority of Americans.[10] Moreover, the NEA used the broadest possible definition of "literary reading" — applying the term to any work of fiction or poetry. Thus many among the minority of adult Americans who read any fiction for pleasure may be occupying themselves exclusively with romance novels or the new brand of raunchier female fantasy known as "chick lit" — a genre whose authors make the middlebrow writers of the fifties look like Shakespeare and Tolstoy.

These recent statistics are particularly important because they document the decreasing popularity of books in a largely literate society. Even if such figures had existed two centuries ago, it would be pointless to compare the proportion of readers in 2000 to the proportion in 1800, when only a small minority of the population could read at all. However, the decline of recreational reading during the past two decades can only be attributed to competition from other forms of entertainment. For admirers of the new video status quo, all that remains is the assertion that the decreasing popularity of serious reading, as serious reading has been understood for centuries, is not really a bad cultural development because other media simply provide another way of learning. In *Everything Bad Is Good for You,* technophile Steven Johnson argues that "yes, we're spending less time reading literary fiction, but that's because we're spending less time doing *everything* we used to do before. . . . We're buying fewer CDs; we're going out to movies less regularly. We're doing all these old activities less because a dozen new activities have become bona fide mainstream pursuits in the past ten years: the Web, e-mail, games, DVDs, cable on-demand, text chat. We're reading less because there are only so many hours in the day. . . . If reading were the only cultural pursuit to show declining numbers, there might be cause for alarm. . . . As long as reading books remains *part* of our cultural diet, as long as the new popular forms continue to offer their own cognitive rewards, we're not likely to descend into a culture of mental atrophy anytime soon."[11] The sorrow, the pity, and the unanswerability of this argument is embodied in the phrase "cognitive rewards." Of course different media and different activities provide different cognitive rewards by challenging different parts of the brain. Riding a bicycle, milking a cow, and reading a book require the services of different, as well as some of the same, neurons, but only reading is indispensable to intellectual life. The more sophisticated video games require intense concentration, but in the end, the cognitive reward for the master of the game amounts to little more than an improved ability to navigate other, more complex video games. Reading good books, by contrast, does little to improve reading skills — certainly not after the age of seven or eight — but it does expand the depth and range of the reader's knowledge and imagination in just about every area of conceivable interest to human beings. When Anna Karenina throws herself in front of the train, the reader is left with an endless series of questions about the nature of betrayal, the sexual double standard, the compromises of marriage, parental duty versus personal fulfillment, family loyalty, religion in nineteenth-century Russia — the great and the quotidian dilemmas of life in every era and the red meat of intellectual discourse. When a gamer overcomes the last video obstacle, there is little left to think about except the search for another, even more complicated game. Johnson is half-right. We are reading less because there are only so many hours in a day, but the other half of the explanation is that growing numbers of people, especially the young, prefer to spend those hours engaged in various forms of video entertainment, including completely passive forms on noninteractive screens, as well as the more cognitively challenging, interactive offerings of video games.

When dedicated gamers start talking about the virtues of video games that stimulate the creativity of players by requiring them to build cities rather than blow away their opponents, they sound like long-ago readers of *Playboy* who claimed that they bought the magazine for its high-quality articles. Nevertheless, the existence of devilishly sophisticated video games with low violence and sex quotients must be conceded, even if these serious intellectual games are not the ones on most teenage boys' wish lists. For the sake of argument, I will define a great video game as one that provides the maximum challenge to the neurological and psychological faculties of the human brain. There is also a system of rewards built in to every video game that has little to do with the general cognitive rewards touted by Johnson. These include experience points that enable the player to move to another level, "loot" that is the virtual equivalent of Monopoly money, and pats on the back reminiscent of "good dog." As Johnson rightly notes, "most games offer a fictional world where rewards are larger, and more vivid, more clearly defined, than life."[12] It has often been asserted that video games, because they demand so much trial-and-error experimentation from the participants, offer a perfect way to introduce young people to the scientific method. Real science, however, generally involves years of wrong turns and dead ends; the larger than life rewards, if and when they come at all, do not pop up with the regularity of icons in video games.

The short attention span that makes many children reject books as boring does not apply to video games, so there is now a major push to supplement books with "educational" games in the classroom. In theory, there is no reason why limited, carefully targeted educational video games could not be used as supplements to books; in practice, given the addictive nature of video gaming and the huge financial stakes, the technology is more likely to become a substitute for reading and other traditional ways of learning. Teenage boys will spend hours playing video games but would not dream of devoting the same amount of time to the novels that marked a teenage nerd of my generation as a potential *mensch* who might have more to offer than a book-disdaining jock. The question is why. I suspect that the rewards (idiotic as this may sound to someone who has never been caught up in a video game) account for a good deal of the attraction; there is no incentive to keep reading a novel, after all, other than the pull of the uninterrupted narrative. Moreover, in-game rewards do not merely offer encouragement; they also serve as interrupters, marking the end of one puzzle and the beginning of another: the reward itself is a distraction that provides novelty while allowing the player to remain within the game.

There will soon be no shortage of money

for research and development of educational video games designed to take advantage of the lure of rewards in the ostensible pursuit of learning. The John D. and Catherine T. MacArthur Foundation will spend $50 million over the next five years to study and underwrite new digital learning media. The Federation of American Scientists (FAS) — an organization best known for providing advice to U.S. government agencies on national security issues — has called for greater federal investment in games that teach "higher-order thinking skills such as . . . interpretive analysis, problem solving, plan formulation and execution, and adaptation to rapid change."[13] One can only wish, if the scientists are right, that government officials had been exposed to such video games before they launched the war in Iraq. FAS president Henry Kelly believes that educational gaming, which allows students to move at their own pace, is far superior to the typical classroom, in which the student-teacher ratio is seldom below 30 to 1. Video gaming is "like hiring an individual tutor for every student," Kelly declares.[14] If a student makes the correct decision within the game, he receives an in-game reward; and if he makes the wrong decision, he gets another chance — as opposed to a wrong answer on a test, which brings a lower grade and no second chance. The flaw in this logic is that neither the pass-fail logic of a traditional nonvideo classroom nor the reward-based system of the video game has much to do with the education of minds not only capable of adaptation to rapid change but also imbued with the combination of curiosity about both past and present that is the essence of true learning. Moreover, there has been almost no research conducted on the efficacy of teaching through video games, although the U.S. Army does make extensive use of "video simulations" for recruitment and certain kinds of training. I have little doubt, however, that within the next five to ten years, educational video games will become a classroom staple and reading will become even less popular among children who already prefer video to print. After all, the next generation of elementary school students will already have been primed, by the videos and DVDs they viewed as infants, for educational video games — and they will already, whether they know it consciously or not, find books less exciting and interesting than the moving images that have been their companions since the first months of life. Needless to say, there is a huge amount of money to be made by selling video games to schools. The FAS report, titled *Harnessing the Power of Video Games for Learning*, was released in conjunction with the Entertainment Software Association, a public relations group that promotes video games for companies that have cornered roughly 90 percent of the $7 billion gaming market. These facts were noted unapologetically in the FAS press release inviting reporters to attend a press conference summarizing the report, but the connection between the FAS report and a profit-making software PR firm was omitted from most news accounts. Only one sour note emerged in most of the stories. Charles E. Finn, president of the Thomas B. Fordham Foundation, a respected think tank that has produced reports documenting the deficiencies of American elementary and secondary schools, had the temerity to call the FAS recommendations "silly." He asked: "Are they next going to propose government-funded studies of the educational value of comic books, reality TV shows and instant messaging?" Finn is, no doubt, another of those nutty Luddites.

There is no reason to believe that the trend toward uncritical approval of "post-Gutenberg" education will ever be reversed, because the young receive not only cognitive rewards but other, more tangible rewards for video prowess. In the spring of 2006, I received a Distinguished Alumni Award from the College of Communications Arts at Michigan State University, where I overheard a revealing conversation between a dean and one of his associates on the stage at commencement. The dean mentioned that one of the best ways to separate "top gun" applicants from other talented high school seniors — those who already boast high SAT scores and high school grades — was the superior video-gaming skills of the "top guns." The night before, I had met an honor student at an awards dinner and happened to mention Franklin D. Roosevelt's fireside chats as a major innovation in political communication in the twentieth century. She looked absolutely blank, and I realized that even if she knew who FDR was, she had never heard about the fireside chats — which meant that she had reached her senior year in college without learning much about the New Deal or Roosevelt's place in American history. In a college of communications arts, one might expect the students to have heard something about both the fireside chats and the Kennedy-Nixon debates. But if proficiency at video games is the mark of a "top gun," knowledge of history may not be seen as important for success either in school or in a subsequent career working "in media." If students receive the biggest prizes for video gamesmanship and other forms of technological savvy, technology is surely what they will prize the most.

Moreover, the amount of free time devoted to a particular activity is an absolute measure of the cultural and personal value placed on that activity. For a clear-eyed look at American priorities, one need only watch the lines form at dawn (actually, at midnight) on the day after Thanksgiving, as customers vie — sometimes through fist-fights that must be broken up by police — to take advantage of the first holiday sales of flat-screen television sets, new video games, and elaborate iPods. Are Americans literally knocking each other's teeth out to be among the first customers to score a discounted book? Not unless the author signing books is a celebrity they have seen on television.

In the realm of new technologies that are displacing traditional reading, the concept of "enough" does not exist. The marketing triumph of Apple's iPhone in the summer of 2007 is the most recent example of the public's obsession with the acquisition of devices that provide instantaneous and continuous access to video and audio distraction, anywhere and at any time. Anyone who has not been in a coma for the past nine months knows that the iPhone is a powerful handheld computer, offering Internet access and combining most (though not all) of the functions of a telephone, a music-storing iPod, a camera, and many other audio and video devices that used to be tethered to large machines in one's home (or, at the very least, to a heavy laptop). As the temperature climbed into the nineties during the last week in June and New York City suffered through its first seasonal spate of power outages, people camped out on the sweltering sidewalks in front of Apple stores for up to three days in order to be first in line when the devices finally went on sale. The consensus of the technology wonks was that the iPhone was a great success because it goes where no phone has gone before. (For $500 to $600, plus monthly service charges, it should.) If you are so inclined, you can see almost anything that you can see on your computer on your 3.5-inch iPhone screen. The system does have a few glitches. Although users can access Word documents on the iPhone, they cannot edit them. And typing on a virtual keyboard is something of a problem, even with smart software that tries to finish your words if you tap the wrong letter (a system that offers even more possibilities for misunderstanding than ordinary e-mail). The whole point of the iPhone, however, is its comprehensiveness; the availability of more distraction that can literally be held in the palm of one's hand will surely reduce whatever part of personal time is still devoted to reading. You'll never walk alone.

It makes as little sense to suggest that there is no reason to fear for civilization as long as reading remains a part of our cultural diet as it would to assert that there is no reason to fear for children's physical fitness as long as exercise remains a part of their lives. A part can be huge, or it can be so small that it dwindles into insignificance. Like reading, the playtime children once devoted to physical activity has been steadily displaced by video. If American children continue to exercise less, even if physical activity remains a "part" of their day, they will inevitably become fatter. And if the slice of our cultural diet devoted to reading continues to shrink, intellectual life will inevitably become further impoverished.

■ ■ ■ ■

As both passive and active consumers of video become progressively more impatient with the process of acquiring information through written language, all providers of infotainment are under great pressure to deliver their messages and generate responses as quickly as possible — and quickness today is much quicker than it used to be. A widely publicized study by the cultural historian Kiku Adatto found that between 1968 and 1988, the average sound bite for a presidential candidate — featuring the candidate's own voice — dropped from 42.3 seconds to 9.8 seconds. By 2000, the daily candidate bite was down to just 7.8 seconds.[15]

During the past twenty-five years, all of the print media — including not only newspapers but magazines, and not only mass-circulation magazines but magazines aimed at well-educated readers — have followed the example of television by drastically cutting the length of their articles. When television news executives believe that they will lose their audience's attention if a sound bite lasts more than eight seconds, why should magazine editors believe that readers will sit still for a lengthy article that might take a half hour, or even fifteen minutes, to read? Anyone who has written for print media of any kind since the late 1980s has had to cope with relentless editorial demands to tell a story in one fourth to one half of the space allotted for similar articles in the sixties and seventies. In 1974, for one of the fiftieth-anniversary editions of the soon-to-be-deceased *Saturday Review,* I wrote a 3,000-word review of new translations from the Russian of the poetry of Anna Akhmatova, Joseph Brodsky, and Osip Mandelstam. It is impossible to imagine selling a piece of that length, on such an esoteric subject, to any publication today other than a tiny literary journal, *The New York Review of Books,* or *The New Yorker* — the latter now the only remaining general-circulation magazine to bridge the gap between middlebrow and highbrow and make money without foundation support.[*]

In the late seventies and even well into the

[*] *Vanity Fair,* another Newhouse publication, might also be said to fall into this category, but its celebrity orientation is much more pronounced than that of *The New Yorker,* as is its tendency to devote endless pages of coverage to people whose only claim to celebrity is their immense wealth.

eighties, I made quite a good living writing serious articles for women's magazines — most between 3,000 and 5,000 words — on topics ranging from domestic violence to the status of women in the Soviet Union. In 1988, the respected veteran editor of *Glamour* magazine, Ruth Whitney, sent me to Russia to explore the question of whether the political changes set in motion by Mikhail Gorbachev would mean change for Soviet women, and the resulting article was nearly 5,000 words long. It would be unthinkable for any women's magazine editor today to devote that amount of space to such a substantive topic. I also wrote for another legendary editor, Helen Gurley Brown of *Cosmopolitan,* and she too was partial to long articles: she assumed that her female readers were as interested in reading as they were in looking at pictures of sexy models. "Mrs. Brown" (as she was always called by her pampered writers) once wrote me a complimentary note about my use in an article of a Milton quote, "With thee conversing I forget all time,/All seasons, and their change; all please alike." Dwight Macdonald would certainly have sneered, because the *Cosmopolitan* equivalents of skating horses were endless pages of advice about how to seduce men, build a lucrative career, and perhaps land a husband. But there is no way that a quote from *Paradise Lost* — with the original seventeenth-century punctuation, no less — would make it into any magazine aimed at young women today. Like newspapers, women's magazines hardly represent the summit of intellectual life; but the change in their contents over the past two decades — like the decline of newspaper reading — is yet another testament to the lowering of the bar in popular culture.

When Brown was replaced as editor of *Cosmopolitan,* I had several articles in inventory, and one of the new editors informed me that my first task would be to cut the pieces in half. "Words, words, words," she said in an exasperated tone. The same woman who, for inexplicable reasons, seemed to want me to continue to write for the magazine, had a sizzling idea for my first assignment. She wanted to commission an article, filled with first-person interviews, on the subject of men who like to watch their girlfriends masturbate. At first I thought this was a bad joke — what would Diana Trilling say? — but I soon realized that it was time to say good-bye to what had been a steady source of income.

Longer does not necessarily mean better,

of course: the meaty reporting pieces in *The New Yorker* edited by David Remnick are enhanced rather than diminished because they are somewhat shorter (though still very long by present-day magazine standards) than they were under William Shawn. However, routine and extreme truncation of all text, based on editors' low expectations of themselves and the public, is a guarantee of coarse content fit only for coarse readers — brevity as the soul not of wit but of vulgarity. I doubt that it would ever have occurred to any old-time women's magazine editor to commission an article of any length on men watching women masturbate, not only because the subject would have been considered too vulgar for the average reader but because it is difficult to imagine what would constitute an "in-depth" exploration of the topic.

Once the vulgarity issue falls by the wayside, as it has in recent years in magazines aimed at young women, it is possible to imagine putting together enough prurient quotes, either wholly invented or gleaned from men foolish enough to agree to an interview, to produce a piece of no more than 1,000 words — and pieces of 1,000 words or less are what women's magazines want today. When print editors try to compete not with other newspapers and magazines but with YouTube, reality TV, and blogs with instant feedback, they *must* pick subjects that can be disposed of in a minimum of words. Print media constantly advertise their suitability for people with "on-the-go lifestyles." It is only a matter of time before a publication markets itself as "The Magazine for People Who Hate to Read."

Another symptom of the embattlement of print culture is the slash-and-burn approach of newspaper executives toward coverage of those arts — especially literature and classical music — considered minority tastes. The declining amount of newspaper space devoted to book reviews is a story dating from the late sixties, but the process has accelerated during the past decade for three related reasons. First, many venerable local newspapers once under family ownership, like the *Los Angeles Times,* have been taken over by corporations determined to cut jobs and indifferent to the stodgy notion of cultural coverage as a public duty. Stand-alone book review sections have never made a profit, but family-controlled papers like *The New York Times* and *The Washington Post* regard literary and arts criticism as a part of their cultural obligation. Second, all newspapers have aging, declining readerships, and de-emphasizing traditonal arts coverage while beefing up coverage of popular video and digital culture — both in print and online editions — is seen as a strategy for attracting younger readers. Finally, many aging baby boomers are less interested than their parents were not just in literary reading but in all performing arts, including classical music, that were rejected by the youth culture of the sixties. Newspaper publishers are betting that boomer readers now in their forties, fifties, and sixties will not miss book reviews and classical music criticism any more than readers (and hoped-for new readers) in their twenties and thirties. In 2007 alone, the *Los Angeles Times* folded its separate Sunday book review into an opinion section, cutting the number of book pages from twelve to ten, while the *San Francisco Chronicle* dropped its weekly book pages from six to four. The *Atlanta Journal-Constitution* eliminated the job of book editor altogether (erasing jobs in a bureaucratic "reorganization" rather than directly firing people is a favorite tactic of executives dedicated to bringing their arts pages in line with popular taste). Book review pages have also been sharply cut at *Newsday,* a Long

Island newspaper owned (like the *Los Angeles Times*) by the Tribune Company. According to the National Book Critics Circle (NBCC), smaller newspapers across the country are relying increasingly on sketchy wire service book reviews — when they make space for reviews at all.[16]

Of course, writers and critics lamenting the demise of newspaper book reviews strongly resemble the character in an old Jewish joke, usually set in a Lower East Side delicatessen, in which a customer complains incessantly to the waiter about the poor quality of the meal. The diatribe ends with the punch line: "Such terrible food — and such small portions!" It is true that book reviews in newspapers have a decidedly middlebrow tone, but their fading away offers yet another example of the value of middlebrow culture. The proliferating array of online literary blogs cannot take the place of regular newspaper reviews, although they would add more to literary discourse if the overall print culture itself were healthier. There are a few outstanding literary blogs, such as The Elegant Variation, which does run long reviews by writers who actually know something about the subject under discussion. Many book review blogs, however, are little more than the aggrieved ramblings of would-be writers whose work has been rejected by print editors and publishers. Such blogs feature a good deal of conspiracy theorizing (of the sort usually bandied about at cocktail parties in the literary world outside blogs) about why certain books get reviewed in *The New York Times* and *The New York Review of Books* and others are ignored. The democratic character of the Web, which allows almost anyone who wants to review a book his say, is an advantage for reviewers themselves but not necessarily for authors or consumers trying to figure out how they might like to spend their book dollars. If I read a review in a newspaper, I usually have a general idea of the qualifications of the reviewer and a sense of whether he or she has a political or personal ax to grind. But how am I to decide whether I ought to spend five minutes reading a review on bookslut.com (one of the livelier literary blogs)? I dip into bookslut's review of David Markson's *The Last Novel,* and I see that the reviewer is miffed at Markson for not appreciating Bob Dylan.[17] Then the reviewer writes, with a good deal of bravado, that he did not know who the distinguished American composer Ned Rorem was until he turned to Google for the answer. This tells me all I need to know about the reviewer's cultural bona fides, but I have already wasted several minutes of my time. (At the end of the piece, I learn that the reviewer is Justin Taylor, editor of *The Apocalypse Reader,* a collection of short stories about the end of the world.) It is not a mortal sin against culture to be ignorant of Rorem's résumé, but pride in one's ignorance is hardly a recommendation for a reviewer. Newspapers, as anyone who has ever labored over a 1,000-word review can attest, expect more out of their freelance contributors as well as their staff reviewers. By downgrading book review sections, the papers are becoming complicit in the very phenomenon that threatens their survival: the decline of print culture. As NBCC president John Freeman notes, "Newspapers fret and worry over the future of print while they dismantle the section of the paper which deals most closely with two things which have kept them alive since the dawn of printing presses: the public's hunger for knowledge and the written word."[18]

On the classical music front, the future of criticism appears even more grim. In Minneapolis and Chicago — cities with long-established music cultures and world-class orchestras — newspaper critics accepted forced buyouts and were replaced by freelancers. "They didn't fire me," said Michael Anthony, longtime music critic for *The Star-Tribune* in Minneapolis. "They fired my job."[19] In Atlanta, the *Journal-Constitution* tried to abolish the job of classical music critic just as it had abolished the job of book editor, but the paper backed down after receiving fierce protests from influential local patrons of the arts.

As the space shrinks for coverage of books and classical performing arts, newspapers are expanding their coverage, in print and online, of pop culture, infotainment, and everything connected with digital media. It is all too reminiscent of the doomed efforts of old middlebrow magazines like *Saturday Review* to attract a younger audience by latching on to the trends of the late sixties and early seventies. Of course pop culture and the digital world ought to be covered in depth by print media, but that coverage is unlikely to halt the decline in newspaper circulation. The problem is that the more obsessed people are with infotainment, the less likely they are to read anything. Editors may pack their arts sections with dissections of the newest trends in hip-hop, accounts of the latest video on YouTube, and (a sop to the older boomers) reviews of the latest concert or DVD by arthritic sixties rock stars who refuse to fade gracefully into the sunset, but those reviews will not necessarily lure anyone away from their iPods, i-Phones, computers, or DVD players. On digital toys, infotainment consumers can see or hear (or see and hear) the real thing instead of reading about it.

There is a school of thought that applauds the Internet as the Messiah come to save print culture, but this hope of salvation rests on a fundamental confusion between the availability of text and real reading and writing. The Internet surely does offer a text as well as a video highway, open to anyone who can use Google, but text and intellectually substantive reading matter are hardly identical. The coming years will undoubtedly witness the creation of an ever-expanding library of texts online — even if Google never reaches its hubristic goal of scanning the contents of every book in the world. I wish Google all the best (as if it needed my good wishes), even though I share the concerns of other authors about breach of copyright. But if Google wants to scan my first book about Russia, which sold no more than 2,000 copies back in 1972, and if someone in Uzbekistan wants to read the book online, well, more power to him.

However, reading in the traditional open-ended sense is not what most of us, whatever our age and level of computer literacy, do on the Internet. What we are engaged in — like birds of prey looking for their next meal — is a process of swooping around with an eye out for certain kinds of information. I almost never stop to think for any length of time about whatever I read online, however intrinsically interesting or well written the material may be, because my primary aim is to save time — not to lose my sense of time as I do when I read a compelling book in its old-fashioned form. If the information is important enough, I print it out and check it out with other, offline sources — a necessary precaution, since I found while fact-checking my last book that the error rate for online sources was triple the error rate for facts extracted from books. In any case, I am not really reading but gathering texts for highly specific purposes, and I have a feeling that it will be no different for future users of a universal virtual library. That hypothetical Uzbek reader will probably be a college student intent on snatching anecdotes for a term paper on the folkways of what used to be called the USSR, and it is highly unlikely that he will read my *Moscow*

Conversations from virtual cover to virtual cover. Consider the following description, written by a contributor to *Wired* magazine, of the possibilities for research in the digital library of the future:

Search engines are transforming our culture because they harness the power of relationships, which is all links really are. . . . The static world of book knowledge is about to be transformed by the same elevation of relationships, as each page in a book discovers other pages and other books. Once text is digital, books seep out of their bindings and weave themselves together. The collective intelligence of a library allows us to see things we can't see in a single, isolated book.

At the same time, once digitized, books can be unraveled into single pages or be reduced further, into snippets of a page. These snippets will be remixed into reordered books and virtual bookshelves . . . the universal library will encourage the creation of virtual "bookshelves" — a collection of texts, some as short as a paragraph, others as long as entire books, that form a library shelf's worth of specialized information. And as with music playlists, once created, these "bookshelves" will be published and swapped in the public commons. Indeed, some authors will begin to write books to be read as snippets or to be remixed as pages.[20]

I am certain that this ghastly prediction will be fulfilled, at least in part, within the next few decades, because the process is already well under way. The use of the term "remixed," recalling as it does the editing of both film and sound recordings, is highly suggestive. Many authors (to use the term loosely) of manuscripts, from college term papers to commercially published books, are already producing material suitable for nothing but remix. The process also has another name: plagiarism. In 2002, a national survey by the Management Education Center at Rutgers University found that more than half of high school students had plagiarized works found on the Internet.[21] But it would be a great mistake to paint the Internet as the sole or even the primary villain here. The history department of Vermont's Middlebury College, which created a flap by banning citations of Wikipedia in student research papers, missed the real point, which is that no encyclopedia (online or off) should be cited as a source in any research project. That encyclopedias were a no-no used to be taught at the high school level: one of the first things that Dale Brubaker, my high school government teacher, made clear to his annoyed students was that they could not use the *Britannica* to write their term papers. Who knew, back when the encyclopedia salesman came calling at the door with the siren song of handily available knowledge, that the children of the house would not be allowed to use the volumes to write their high school term papers? There is no surer sign of the degeneration of the print-based middlebrow culture than the fact that university professors are now obliged to teach their students research basics that used to be taught to high school freshmen.

The technology of the computer age has of course accelerated the decline of respect for literary originality: it is much easier and faster than it used to be to troll for "remix" material. Such technology is ideally suited to the purposes of "packaging" firms, which encourage authors to produce literary products bearing a strong resemblance to previous products that have already proved their commercial viability. These prepackaged products should not be called books, any more than text written to be packaged as snippets or remixed pages on the Internet should be considered a book. Indeed, the authors of such products should not be called writers; their work is better summed up in Joseph Stalin's unforgettable description of writers as "engineers of human souls." (Stalin is supposed to have uttered the phrase for the first time — it was originally coined by a minor Soviet novelist — in a toast at a writers' gathering in 1932. A few years later, writers who were insufficiently talented as engineers would disappear into the Gulag.)

The most notorious packaging-plagiarism furor in recent years erupted over a chick lit book, published by Little, Brown in 2006 and crafted by Kaavya Viswanathan, a nineteen-year-old Harvard sophomore. As the first chick lit book by and about an Indian American, *How Opal Mehta Got Kissed, Got Wild, and Got a Life* received an extraordinary amount of publicity and seemed destined for best-sellerdom when it was discovered that the author had plagiarized a good many passages from two other immortal chick lit novels — Megan McCafferty's *Sloppy Firsts* and *Second Helpings*. Viswanathan claimed that the "copying" had been unintentional because she has a photographic memory and had read McCafferty's novels so many times as a teenager.

Eventually, Little, Brown pulled *Opal Mehta* from the stores and canceled the Harvard prodigy's two-book contract.

But there is much more to the story than the dubious ethics of one ambitious young woman. It seems that Viswanathan, as a high school senior, had conceived of the project as the result of advice from a private counselor, hired by her parents to boost their daughter's chances of getting into an Ivy League school. The counselor, as it happens, was the author of a book on writing college applications, and she showed some of Viswanathan's writing to her own agent at the William Morris Agency. The agent referred Viswanathan to Alloy Entertainment, a book packager that produces proposals for publishers and hires engineers of girlish souls to produce books based on prepackaged plots and characters. *The New York Times* quoted Cindy Eagan, editorial director at Little, Brown Books for Young Readers, who said of packaging, "In a way it's kind of like working on a television show. We all work together in shaping each novel."[22] Little, Brown Books for Young Readers is the publisher of Clique, A-List, and Gossip Girl, three popular series of pseudobooks for preteens that are enough to make a feminist weep, since they are based on the premise that girls can do nothing but deceive, undermine, and compete with one another for boys.

Series like Gossip Girl are, in effect, the little sisters of more "mature" chick lit, produced by writers like Megan McCafferty and aimed at readers in their late teens and early twenties. In all of these series, packagers and publishers work together closely. Some of the packaged books are written to the packager's specifications, while in other instances, the writer is given more freedom to depart from the usual formula. In Viswanathan's case, that meant writing about an Indian-American woman instead of the white, African-American, and Hispanic women who already fill the pages of chick lit. The point about these books as a group, however, is that they all sound alike even if the words are not identical, because they all follow the same basic formula: it would be perfectly easy, as the Viswanathan episode demonstrates, to shift long passages from one of these books into another in a seamless remix. Another publishing executive acknowledged that there are "certain similarities across the board" in such series, adding that the "teenage experience is fairly universal."[23]

Packaging and writing according to formula is nothing new in publishing; both the Nancy Drew and the Hardy Boys series were produced, decade after decade, by different writers using the same pseudonym. The huge difference is that the earlier series were read almost entirely by children of elementary school age: Nancy Drew and the Hardy Boys were never intended to serve as a bridge and a model for similar books aimed at older teenagers or adults in their twenties. If a girl hadn't outgrown Nancy Drew by around age twelve, there was something wrong with her. When you were old enough to turn to books for an exploration of the mysteries of sex and adulthood, you turned to adult fiction by adult authors writing about adults. In the early sixties, girls headed for the Ivy League were reading Mary McCarthy and Philip Roth, not novels crafted by writers who were still in their teens or barely out of them. In their formulaic predictability, both "young adult" and chick lit pseudobooks resemble nothing so much as the endless offerings of new television programs that strive to imitate previously successful programs.

Kaavya Viswanathan may have been consigned to the public stocks, but her attitude toward literature is hardly unusual. The saddest part of her interview with the *Times* was her explanation that she had originally written a story modeled after Alice Sebold's best seller, *The Lovely Bones,* but the agent at William Morris thought the piece "too dark." Viswanathan was advised by the agent and book packager that "it would be better if I did a lighter piece. They thought that was more likely to sell."[24] Of course. Why would you hesitate to imitate a chick lit author if your imitation of another, more serious writer had less auspicious sales prospects?

The concept of "texts" as interchangeable commmodities flows naturally from the idea that reading itself is a facet of cultural life that can be swapped, with no individual or social harm, for other cultural commodities like video games — as long as reading books does not disappear altogether. As John Updike eloquently argues, "The printed, bound and paid-for book was — still is, for the moment — more exacting, more demanding, of its producer and consumer both. It is the site of an encounter, in silence, of two minds, one following in the other's steps but invited to imagine, to argue, to concur on a level of reflection beyond that of personal encounter, with all its merely social conventions, its merciful padding of blather and mutual forgiveness. Book readers and writers are approaching the condition of holdouts, surly hermits who refuse to come out and play in the electronic sunshine of the post-Gutenberg village."[25] Updike's address was delivered at the 2006 convention of the American Booksellers Association, an organization that is understandably less than joyful about the prospect of books being available as free remix fodder on the Internet. It might be argued that the opinions of authors and booksellers are tainted by the desire for personal profit from copyrighted books. It might also be argued that Google is not trying to assemble a free, universal online library out of charitable motives. I say that readers get what they pay for — in time as well as money.

If books are the first mighty and indispensable pillar of intellectual life, conversation is the second. In many respects, the mass media have been responsible for an even more formidable assault on conversation than on literature during the past forty years. Conversation took its first heavy hit in the fifties, when many families began turning on the television set while eating dinner. This practice was forbidden by my mother but permitted in many homes, and the lure of the black-and-white screen was so strong that I always looked forward to sleepovers at the homes of friends whose parents took a more permissive attitude about watching television during meals. Television programs did not end conversation, but they changed its nature: while watching a favorite program, we were likely to talk about what was happening on the screen rather than what was going on in our own lives. The past two decades, by contrast, have produced an explosion of what are called conversation avoidance devices.

Stephen Miller, in a lively history of conversation, points out that these devices include not only obvious conversation stoppers like video games and music players with headphones but, paradoxically, cell phones, e-mail, and text messaging. All of the messaging devices facilitate communication, but communication and conversation bear essentially the same relationship to each other as text and good books: there is no guarantee that the former will produce the latter. In a review of Miller's book, Russell Baker describes the family conversation that permeated his upbringing during the thirties.

One of my childhood memories, from

Depression days, is of lying in bed at the edge of sleep and hearing the murmur of people, grown-ups, talking, talking, talking into the night. Our house was small, intimate, and overcrowded with adults who had not worked for a long time, and money was scarce. So they talked, and talked, and talked. It seemed to be reminiscence mostly; they were brothers and sisters of a big family with memories that needed reexamining. They must have joked because there was a lot of quiet laughter, but they talked about serious matters too. Woodrow Wilson was discussed a lot. They wondered whether Wilson had been "an idealist." Was that why he has failed? And had he been gulled by the English, and hadn't the United States been tricked into pulling Europe's chestnuts out of the fire? It felt safe going off to sleep to the steady murmur of that conversation.[26]

For those struggling through the Depression, conversation had the great virtue of costing nothing. But my memories of the family conversation during the fifties, when life was much less of a financial struggle than it had been a generation earlier, are strikingly similar to Baker's. I too remember dozing off, when I was eight or nine, to the low hum of conversation in the next room — and trying not to fall asleep because I longed to overhear what the grown-ups had to say about subjects not considered fit for little pitchers with big ears (an expression I have not heard anyone use for decades). These included my parents' worries about the Bomb — which they tried to downplay whenever the subject came up, as it often did, in the news of the day; the executions of Julius and Ethel Rosenberg; and whether I should be cautioned against telling my little brother that there was no Santa Claus. When I was a few years older — old enough to participate in and understand adult talk but not old enough to find adults boring — I stayed up to join the grown-ups.

Today, preteens are alone in their rooms after dinner, doing the endless homework — another enemy of reading for pleasure — now required of children at every age; surfing the Internet, text-messaging on their cell phones, or playing video games. Parents, too, are often alone with their preferred forms of entertainment, although women, occupied with household chores even if they have been working all day in an office, generally have less time than men to surf the Web in the evenings.

At its heart, all intellectual and emotional

life is a conversation — and the conversation begins at birth. If the family dinner table once provided the first face-to-face setting for the semiformal pleasure of social conversation, it was quickly followed by the school lunchroom, sleepovers at friends' houses, late-night dormitory bull sessions, coffeehouses, bars — any setting that offered the chance for friends to exchange ideas and personal confidences. But personal social contact, outside as well as inside the family, is another casualty of the culture of distraction. Adults of all ages report that they have fewer friends, and fewer people with whom they discuss important matters, than they did twenty years ago. One in four Americans say that they have no one to talk to about important subjects — more than double the percentage in 1985. The greatest drop occurred in social contacts with non-family members: 43 percent of Americans talked about important matters with friends in 1985, but only 20 percent did so in 2004.[27]

There are undoubtedly many reasons for the decline in conversational friendships; Americans spend more time working than they used to, and the hectic schedules of families in which both parents work leave adults with much less free time to cultivate friendships and maintain a social life. The isolating effect of technology, however, is another important factor: headphones offer a convenient way to shut out not only the unwanted noises of strangers but the conversation, perhaps equally unwanted, of friends and family. In situations where people used to be forced to talk to one another — long car rides, a lazy afternoon on the beach, the school lunchroom — the young routinely shut out their elders and often their contemporaries. Anyone who graduated from college before 1980 is bound to be struck by the silence of student residences today; the late-night and all-night conversations that were such a staple of student life for generations have given way to whatever individual experiences are going on in rooms where everyone is online or in an iPod cocoon. I had to spend a night in a dormitory after delivering a lecture at a university last year, and, remembering the high level of noise and laughter that lasted well into the night when I was a student, I anticipated losing some sleep. Not to worry: the dorm was eerily quiet, and, when I encountered two students making coffee in a communal kitchen, we did not exchange a word because they were both jiggling their heads to the music of their iPods. Even at a school as politically apathetic and vocationally oriented as Michigan State was when I was a student there in the early sixties, I have no doubt that the presence of a real writer — albeit a noncelebrity — would have attracted a small group of students for some intense discussion.

If the proliferation of time-consuming conversation avoidance devices clearly discourages the development of conversational skills, another significant influence is the domination of the airwaves and Internet blogs by what Miller calls "ersatz conversation." These include the angry back-and-forthing characteristic of ideologically driven radio and television talk shows and the softer setup — scripted though live — favored by such icons as Oprah Winfrey. Hosts like Bill O'Reilly do not even make a pretense of being interested in what their guests have to say; they simply interrupt anyone who disagrees with their political views. I appeared on *The O'Reilly Factor* at the urging of my publisher, who correctly advised me that even though O'Reilly would be hostile to my ideas, my book would get a hearing from a certain percentage of viewers who turn on the show for the sole purpose of being roused to anger by whatever the right-wing host has to say that day.

O'Rielly set the tone by addressing me as "Madam" — a once polite convention that now has a pejorative ring — and I was told later that I had "scored points" by addressing him as "Sir." Maybe so, but what was taking place bore no resemblance to a real conversation.

On talk shows like *Oprah,* a different kind of ersatz conversation takes place. Winfrey is, of course, the queen of empathy, although she can turn into a stern judge on occasion, as she did when the author James Frey lied to her about his fictionalized memoir *A Million Little Pieces.* For the most part, though, guests know what is expected of them and stick to the emotional script, which decrees that the audience be told about trials and sorrows, a struggle to survive, and the ultimate triumph and renewal of the human spirit. That actually had been Frey's intent, but he was lying about the specifics of his trials and apparently about the renewal of his spirit. The *Oprah* script is not a conversation but a condensed version of *Pilgrim's Progress,* in which it is Winfrey's role to keep guests, and the audience, from falling too far into the Slough of Despond. On the rare occasions when someone does depart from the formula, as Tom Cruise did when he began jumping up and down on the studio couch to announce his infatuation with Katie Holmes, Winfrey becomes visibly disconcerted.

The millions of so-called conversations conducted each day on blogs are equally ersatz. Even when bloggers are engaged in what is supposedly direct dialogue with one another, the exercise is usually distinguished by the absence of any relationship between comments and responses. Blogs spew forth, in largely unedited form, the crude observations of people who are often unable to express themselves coherently in writing and are as inept at the virtual conversational skills required for online exchanges as they must be at face-to-face communication. The point of blogging is self-expression, not dialogue. I am a regular panelist for a blog, "On Faith," published by *The Washington Post* and *Newsweek,* and I am bemused, though rarely amused, by the non sequiturs that my essays frequently elicit. A typical exchange ensued after I noted, in my weekly commentary, that public opinion polls consistently indicate that women, as a group, are more religious than men. One response, simply signed "Me," argued straightforwardly that women are more religious than men because women are stupider than men. Mr. Me then went into a rant about women turning to faith because they want God to send them a man who will provide money for child support — presumably one of the perks of religiosity.

"The most common prayer," he wrote, "is, 'Dear God, please don't let 'him' lose his job for I can't make it without the 'child support' check." The peculiar punctuation and solipsistic tone, like the moniker "Me," are characteristic of chat in the blogosphere. Whether the comments are reasonable or obviously loony, they bear no resemblance to a real conversation, in which identifiable people are held responsible for what they say and are even, on occasion, asked for facts to back up their opinions. Of course, real-life discussions also involve a great many bores and boors who have never learned that the art of conversation demands listening as well as talking, but such people are eventually penalized by the avoidance or outright disappoval of others. Nothing like that happens in the virtual world, unless the blogger violates a specific rule, such as a prohibition of personal attacks or obscenities.

As the art of live conversation continues its decline, it is saddening to discover that some of the best examples of old-fashioned, discursive, passionate intellectual conversation can be found today only in books. For a glimpse of the way intellectuals used to talk, not only to one another but to anyone else who happened to be within range, one might consult a splendid, concise 1988 portrait of the maverick journalist I. F. Stone, compiled from taped conversations between Stone and the author, Andrew Patner. (Patner's responses are omitted.) Stone, an autodidact who dropped out of college in his junior year, was talking about his research for a book about the trial of Socrates.

I've often said that nobody has ever gotten away with so much egregious nonsense out of sheer charm as Plato. It's nonsense — absolute nonsense. And the devout Platonists — it's like a cult, they're like Moonies. I mean, Plato is a fascinating thinker, and a marvelous writer, and a man of comic genius. Olympiodorus says that he wanted to be a writer of comedy, of plays and comedy — he's supposed to have had a copy of Aristophanes on his bed when he died — but when he met Socrates he gave that up. . . . And you have to read him, too, not just for his system or ideas, but for the way he gets at it, for all the by-products, the joy, and the wrestle, so to speak. No other philosopher turned his philosophies into little dramas. That gives them part of their continual charm. . . . The *Phaedo* is just — I was reading the *Phaedo* at American University, and I came to the end. I just burst into tears. The kids must have thought I'd gone wacky. It's very moving. A great drama.

. . . And so, you understand the Greek theater and its wellsprings of freedom much better when you look at the Roman theater and comedy. And with the Greek law and the Roman law, the procedure and laws of the Greek Assembly and the Roman Assembly. . . . I don't care much for Rome. Cicero is a big tub of crap. Typical corporation lawyer and ass-kisser of the rich and powerful. But he studied in Athens, a few centuries after the great days, and his philosophical treatises, while they're not profound, are very valuable. You consult what he has to say in the *De natura deorum, De divinatione,* and the *Tusculan Disputations.* . . . I agree with Caesar, though. He called the prose style Asianic, by which he meant overadorned, and I think his speeches are a little too flowery.[28]

That is what a passionate intellectual conversation sounds like — the genuine learnedness, the intensity, the sense of communion with people who lived and died thousands of years ago. I wish I had been on the other end of that conversation. It's been a long time since I've heard anyone call Plato a purveyor of egregious nonsense, and Cicero *was* a big ass-kisser. One need look no further for a perfect example of the connection between the decline of reading and the decline of intellectual conversation.

Another form of conversation — the kind that used to take place in letters — is not merely in decline but for all practical purposes dead. E-mail, often cited as the savior of written communication and as a worthy successor to obsolete snail mail, has delivered the coup de grâce to the traditional letter. While reorganizing my home office, I recently came across a thick file of letters from 1968, when I was still working as a reporter in Washington and my fiancé, the Africa correspondent of *The Washington Post,* was stationed in Nairobi, Kenya. Newly engaged and in love, we wrote each other long letters — two to five pages, single-spaced — at least twice a week. Holding the thin, crinkly sheets of airmail paper for the first time in decades, I was reminded of the excitement I felt each time I opened the mailbox and saw that it contained a thick envelope. My letters provide a portrait of my younger self, but also a mini-history of many of the traumatic events of 1968. In one sequence of letters, I was attempting to convey to Tony what it felt like to watch flames and smoke rise over Washington as violence and looting erupted in the city's poorest black neighborhoods after Martin Luther King's assassination. How could I have forgotten my fear when a cop pointed a gun at me before he saw the press pass entitling me to be in the riot zone? Or my sense of utter despair when, the morning after King's death, a black cab driver turned around and said, "I want you to know that if I could afford *not* to pick up white people today, I'd leave you standing on the corner."

Tony's letters provided vivid snapshots of apartheid in South Africa; of the tragic, pointless civil war between Nigeria and Biafra, where he too had found himself on the business end of guns; of his fear that the end of colonialism would not bring about social and economic justice for poor Africans but would instead give rise to a new class of corrupt African dictators. Letters like these are not just repositories of personal memory; they have also, throughout the ages, served as important primary sources for historians and biographers.

I have no idea how biographers will go about reconstructing the lives of people born after, roughly, 1950, in the absence of a paper trail of personal correspondence that used to be conducted not only by intellectuals but by large numbers of literate men and women. Like the decline of newspaper reading, the decline of letter writing — which began long before e-mail — was an early sign of the enfeeblement of print culture. By the early 1970s, as long-distance telephone rates continued to drop, letter writing was already becoming an unusual rather than a routine activity and was increasingly considered a burden — especially by my own generation. Had my exchanges with my fiancé been conducted by e-mail, I am certain that the rich content and lively style of letters would have been altered for the worse. Although we would have been in touch more frequently, the total length of our exchanges would have been much shorter. Even if I had saved all of our e-mails (and I might have, given that we were about to be married), I know that there would have been less to ponder thirty-five years later.

I know this because of the haste and inattentiveness with which my close friends and I approach the reading and writing of our own e-mail today. Neither I, nor anyone I know, turns to e-mail with anything like the sense of anticipation and pleasure that used to accompany my opening of the mailbox. How could we? The daily glut of spam and business communications — even when some of the messages are welcome — is a constant annoyance. When I receive an e-mail from someone dear to me, I am happy. But the contents usually amount to, "Hi, I was thinking about you when I read this article the other day," followed by a link. And I answer in the same nondiscursive way. When I first went online, I was excited about e-mail because I thought it would replace the long letters I used to send and receive, but I soon found that lengthy e-mails elicited very brief responses — even when the sender was someone who liked me or loved me. So I started replying in kind.

There undoubtedly are a few people who save their e-mail correspondence with good friends and who write e-mails as interesting as the letters many of us used to write during the snail-mail era. For the most part, though, e-mail as a medium really is the message — and the message is short. Future historians will look in vain for the kinds of letters that passed between John Adams and Thomas Jefferson; Gustave Flaubert and George Sand; Johannes Brahms and Clara Schumann; Hannah Arendt and Mary McCarthy; Lord Byron and everyone in his world. They will look in vain for traces of an intellectual life in which reading, writing, and conversing face-to-face are seamlessly linked in a way that facilitates deep connections among people who love ideas.

Shortly after I found my letters to my fiancé from the sixties, I stumbled across one final treasure-trove of correspondence, ranging from the early eighties to the mid-nineties and containing evidence of what will surely be my last full-blown epistolary friendship. My correspondent was Philip Vellacott, a great British translator of Euripides and Aeschylus, who died, at age ninety, in 1997. I first read Philip's translations in the early 1980s, when I was reading all of the Greek tragedies for my book *Wild Justice: The Evolution of Revenge*. He possessed the gift of rendering ancient texts in language at once timeless and contemporary, elevated but never inflated, and his work excited me as much as if I were reading the plays for the first time. In fact, as the result of a spotty higher education, I *was* encountering Euripides for the first time. I intended to write Philip a fan letter, telling him how much I admired his style of translation, but — having already become accustomed to receiving no responses to letters — I never followed through. With astonished pleasure, I opened an envelope one morning in 1984 and found a spidery handwritten note from Philip, with his return address in Wales. He began: "I have just read your remarkable *Wild Justice,* which I came across in a London bookstore, and I was so enthralled by your arguments that I was instantly impelled to write you a fan letter."

Thus began our epistolary relationship, which would turn us into real friends before we met face-to-face for the first time. I finally embarked on the education in Greek tragedy, with a brilliant teacher as my guide, that I had missed in college. Philip and I also wrote each other about our love of Bach; our enjoyment of the impersonal comfort of American motels; and our detestation of the ascendant right-wing politics of the eighties on both sides of the Atlantic. Philip loathed Margaret Thatcher but preferred her to Ronald Reagan because, as he put it, "Mrs. Thatcher looks as mean as her social policies." Most of all, we talked about books. He introduced me to William Empson's *Milton's God,* and I introduced him to Alfred Kazin's *A Walker in the City* and *New York Jew.* One of Philip's passions — something else we shared — was feminism. His views on Euripidean tragedy as a commentary on women's wrongs antedated feminist literary criticism by two decades. Until he became too frail to travel, Philip looked forward with the keenest anticipation to regular stints as a visiting professor of classics at the University of California at Santa Cruz. He felt entirely at home in what he described as "a cauldron, or if you will, a hot tub of revisionist scholarship" — even though he was dismayed by the corruption of language in American academia. He gleefully recounted a polite scrap with a feminist literary critic, noted for her dogmatism, who approvingly ascribed Medea's murders of her children to "a passion for gender justice." Philip replied, "Surely justice is androgynous, rather like the Holy Spirit."

Philip talked about the greatest writers who ever lived as if they were his personal friends — and of course they were. The last time I saw him, we were on our way to meet a mutual acquaintance but found ourselves trapped in the subway for a half-hour because a man had jumped onto the tracks as the train was pulling into the Eighty-sixth Street station. Philip managed to distract me from my claustrophobia and the subway suicide with a passionate disquisition on the advantages of a belated education.

"I quite envied you, being thirty-five when you first met Euripides," he said, as if we were on our way to meet the playwright for a drink. "Why, it would be like falling in love for the first time when you are actually old enough to understand another human being. What a wonder! I speak with authority, because I was thirty-two when I met the love of my life and the woman I was most fortunate to marry." A scruffy teenager, fanning himself with the shirt he had removed in the stifling car, was listening intently to the fiery old man with the cultivated, turn-of-the-century English diction. When subway workers finally led us out of the car, the teenager turned around to Philip and said, "Man, hearing you talk was a blast."

It was. That subway ride took place at some point in the late eighties, before the proliferation of headphones and personal listening devices, or Philip's young admirer would probably have been walled off in a private world of noise. With the triumph of the culture of distraction, conversations that begin with the printed word and end with a world of knowledge are becoming a blast from the past.

CHAPTER ELEVEN:
PUBLIC LIFE:
DEFINING DUMBNESS
DOWNWARD

On April 4, 1968, Robert F. Kennedy had just arrived to deliver a campaign speech in Indianapolis when he learned that Martin Luther King had been assassinated in Memphis. Kennedy's aides urged him to cancel the speech, but he decided to deliver the tragic news himself to a predominantly black crowd. He began by addressing the members of the audience as "ladies and gentlemen" and asking them to lower their campaign signs. What followed was a small masterpiece of extemporaneous American public rhetoric — perhaps the last of its kind in a long political tradition. Speaking in a choked voice, Kennedy turned naturally to the lines from Aeschylus that had consoled him after the assassination of his brother:

Even in our sleep, pain which cannot forget falls drop by drop upon the heart,

until, in our own despair,
against our will,
comes wisdom
through the awful grace of God.*

Then Kennedy went on to declare, "What we need in the United States is not division; what we need in the United States is not violence and lawlessness, but is love, and wisdom, and compassion toward one another, and a feeling of justice toward those who still suffer within our country, whether they be white or whether they be black." He concluded with the hope that Americans would dedicate themselves "to what the Greeks wrote so many years ago: to tame the savageness of man and make gentle the life of this world. Let us dedicate ourselves to that, and say a prayer for our country and for our people."[1]

What is striking about this speech, apart from its unscripted nature, is its elevated tone and language. Kennedy assumed that an audience of ordinary men and women — ladies and gentlemen — would respond to words written thousands of years ago by a Greek dramatist. He used a quotation that

* The quotation, from Aeschylus's *Agamemnon,* has been rendered in slightly different versions by different translators.

arose spontaneously from his own tastes and emotions, and it did not occur to him to patronize his audience by looking for a more easily recognizable allusion drawn from popular culture. Another striking aspect of this address is the humility of its concluding sentence. In the sixties, that ghastly, malignant decade of right-wing myth, it had not yet become obligatory for politicians to conclude their speeches with a triumphalist "God bless America." To suggest that we say a prayer for our country and our people is to acknowledge error — the fault that lies within Americans and must not be ascribed to alien, un-American influences.

It is not my intention to evoke nostalgia for Camelot, to sentimentalize Robert Kennedy, or to suggest that, because he could quote ancient poetry, he was a true intellectual. However, Kennedy's 1968 speech now sounds almost as archaic as the language of Aeschylus himself. I cannot imagine a popular politician making such a speech in the current cultural climate — even if his own literary tastes led him to turn naturally to Greek tragedy — because he would fear being branded a snob and an elitist. Had Kennedy been subject to the forces that constrain political speech today, he would have turned not to Aeschylus but to Bob Dylan, the Beatles, or Peter, Paul, and Mary for words to express his grief. The shunning of unfamiliar allusions and figures of speech by those who aspire to leadership offers highly visible evidence of the extent to which dumbness has been defined downward in American public life during the last forty years.[*]

Politicians, like members of the media, are both the creators and the creatures of a public distrustful of complexity, nuance, and sophisticated knowledge. It is almost impossible for people accustomed to hearing their president comment on complicated policy issues with such statements as "I'm the decider" to imagine the pains taken by Franklin Roosevelt, in the dark early months after the nation's entry into the Second World War, to explain why the armed forces were suffering one defeat after another in the Pacific. Roosevelt's first fireside chat after Pearl Harbor came in February 1942, and he had asked Americans to spread out a map during his radio address so that they could follow and comprehend the geography of battle. *The New York Times* quoted one

[*] When Senator Daniel Patrick Moynihan coined the phrase "defining deviancy downward" in the 1970s, he was referring to crime.

E. O. Schmidt, sales manager of a Manhattan bookstore, about the public response to the president's request. Schmidt had rounded up 2,000 copies of a new atlas to meet the expected demand, and, by the night of the fireside chat, every map had been sold. Roosevelt told his listeners — who included 80 percent of all American adults — that he had asked them to use maps so that they might better understand a war being waged, unlike previous wars, on "every continent, every island, every sea, every air-lane in the world." In explaining the strategic situation to the public, Roosevelt was able to draw on his own extensive knowledge of geography, acquired early in life through his well-known hobby of stamp collecting. He had told his speechwriters that he was certain if Americans understood the immensity of the distances over which supplies must travel to the armed forces, "if they understand the problem and what we are driving at, I am sure that they can take any kind of bad news right on the chin."

This is a portrait not only of a different presidency and president but of different Americans, without access to satellite-enhanced Google maps but with a much greater receptivity to learning than today's public. According to a 2006 survey of geographic literacy conducted by National Geographic–Roper, nearly half of Americans between ages eighteen and twenty-four do not think it necessary to know the location of other countries in which important news is being made. More than a third consider it "not at all important" to know a foreign language, and only 14 percent consider it "very important." In the same young adult age group, two thirds of those surveyed in December 2005–January 2006 — after more than three years of combat and 2,400 American deaths in Iraq — were unable to find Iraq on a map. The results were no aberration: when the same survey was conducted in 2002, Americans ranked second to last among participating countries; the United States trailed Canada, France, Germany, the United Kingdom, Italy, Japan, and Sweden.

Moreover, the age of those polled points clearly to a massive failure of American education at both the high school and college levels: people used to know more, not less, about geography when they were young, because classroom lessons were still fresh in their minds. One bit of "good news" cited in the report is that Americans with some college experience were four times as likely as those with only a high school education to be able to locate Iraq, Saudi Arabia, Iran, and Israel on a map. The bad news: the actual figures of those who successfully identified those Middle Eastern countries were just 23 percent in the college group and 6 percent for high school graduates. To put it another way, nearly eight out of ten young Americans with at least a high school education have no idea of the location of four countries intimately linked to American interests.

As for the much touted educational value of the Internet, using the Web to get the news of the day has limited value: young adults who read news on the Web would have scored about 69 — in traditional grading terms — on the National Geographic–Roper test, while those who did not use the Internet would have scored 59. (Fifty-three questions were asked. The college group correctly answered an average of 36.8 questions, while the high school group averaged 31.2.) Thus, both groups flunked — but the Internet users had a higher failing grade than those who did not use the Web. That such news is cited as a bright spot in an otherwise grim picture is itself a testament to lowered expectations. In a stunning understatement, the authors of the study concluded that "these results suggest that young people in the United States . . . are unprepared for an increasingly global future."[2] The title of the report might as well have been "Ignorant and Proud of It."

Public ignorance and anti-intellectualism are not identical, of course, but they are certainly kissing cousins. Both foster the rise of candidates who regard a broad knowledge of history, science, and culture, and a decent command of their native language as political liabilities rather than assets — and who frequently try to downplay these qualities, even if they possess them, in order to pander to a public that considers conspicuous displays of learning a form of snobbery. One measure of the conscious degradation of standards for political self-presentation and discourse during the past fifty years is the contrast between the presidential campaigns of John Kerry and John Kennedy, both scions of wealth and privilege, both recipients of the best possible American and international educations, both epitomizing cosmopolitanism — from their taste for travel and interest in world history to their choice of exotic-looking, elegant, multilingual wives. Kerry spent much of his campaign in a doomed effort to make himself look and sound more like an average Joe, and he only managed to humiliate himself by pulling stunts like donning camouflage clothes for a goose hunt clearly intended to impress rural sportsmen. It turned out that the hunting outfit and the twelve-gauge double-barreled shotgun wielded by Kerry for photographers were borrowed from an Ohio farmer who also offered up his geese as a political sacrifice. Kerry tried to jettison his educated East Coast diction on the campaign trail, where he started dropping his g's, t's, and n's, and took care to make the obligatory references to folks.

John Kennedy, by contrast, played up the sophisticated qualities that set him apart from but also gripped the imagination of ordinary voters. He famously balked at donning cowboy hats, Indian headdresses, baseball caps, or any headgear designed to show that he was just an ordinary guy, and he would surely have been appalled by the suggestion that he put on a phony southern or rural midwestern accent. Whether Kennedy was as cultivated as he seemed, whether he really was an omnivorous reader who could have been a historian — or, at the very least, a high-middlebrow journalist like his admirers Walter Lippmann and Richard Rovere — was less important than his desire to be seen and admired for his intellectual qualities. His favorite contemporary novelist seems to have been Ian Fleming, but he made sure to inform potential biographers that his favorite novel of all time was Stendhal's *The Red and the Black.* One of the most intriguing aspects of the Kennedy persona, Alfred Kazin observed, was "how eagerly his bookishness, his flair and sophistication, his very relish for the company of intellectual specialists, have been advertised to the public without any fear that it might dismay a people so notoriously suspicious of these qualities in others."[3]

Whatever the reality, there is no question that the image of Kennedy as a cosmopolitan polymath — someone who represented what Americans might aspire to for themselves or, more likely, for their sons — was a vital part of his appeal. Cultural literacy in a presidential candidate was seen as a desirable trait by the public, and the culturally sophisticated image that the Kennedys presented to the world only enhanced their domestic appeal. Yet forty years later, when college graduates made up a much larger proportion of the American population than they had in the early sixties, voters entrusted the nation's highest office to a man whose most distinctive personal trait has always been an absolute lack of intellectual curiosity. The son, grandson, and great-grandson of rich and powerful men, George W. Bush is the living embodiment of the gentleman's C: there cannot be anyone in the country who believes that Bush's brain would have gotten him anywhere near Yale, Harvard Business School, or the ownership of a baseball team — much less the presidency — without his family name and connections. Nevertheless, this walking testament to unearned privilege somehow managed to convince voters that he was just an ordinary guy and did not belong to the detested "elites."

How did he do it? I think that he was able to pull it off simply by being himself, as evinced most obviously by his bumbling use of his native language. Unlike Kerry and Al Gore, Bush did not have to work at sounding like a regular guy with a less than elite education; despite summers in Kennebunkport and stints at Ivy League institutions, the words "nuclear" and "government," which presidents must use with considerable frequency, will always roll trippingly off his tongue as "nuculer" and "guv'mint." Bush's presidential demeanor has been characterized by a sneering, aggressive provincialism, which he displays not just at home but abroad, for the edification of foreign leaders. The American public — at least before it turned decisively against the Iraq War — was either charmed by or indifferent to oafish performances that would have mortified middle-class citizens of other developed nations. At a joint press conference with President Jacques Chirac in Paris, for example, Bush responded petulantly when NBC correspondent David Gregory posed a question to Chirac in fluent French. "Very good," snapped the president of the United States. "The guy memorizes four words, and he plays like he's intercontinental." An amazed Gregory started to reply, "I could go on . . . ," but Bush cut him off and said, "I'm impressed — *que bueno*. I'm literate in two languages."

The implication that any American who addresses a foreign leader in his own language must be putting on an act was clear. Bush is also prone to referring to Spanish as "Mexican," as he did at the 2001 Summit of the Americas in Quebec City, where he refused to answer questions from reporters — "neither in French nor in English nor in Mexican." The issue is not whether Bush is as stupid as he sounds but that he, like so many of the young Americans surveyed in the National Geographic–Roper Poll, is unashamed of — and even seems quite proud of — his own parochialism and intellectual limitations.

If Bush's election was not a measure of conscious anti-intellectualism on the part of voters, it was certainly a measure of the public's indifference to demonstrable mental acuity and knowledge as standards for the presidency. In this context, it is important to note that most members of the media rarely raise questions, even in a roundabout way, about the intellect of a major party presidential candidate — much less about a man who actually occupies the Oval Office. A president may be described as stubborn, or as impatient, or as a sexual libertine — even, on rare occasions, as a liar — but it would be unthinkable for "objective" reporters, in print or on television, to bluntly raise the question, "Is this man smart enough to be in charge of the country?" It is a question that ought to be asked openly about every man and woman who seeks high office. Opinion columnists with well-known political views do feel free to question the intelligence of government leaders, but the very fact that issues involving intellect and learning are generally relegated to op-ed pages tends to downgrade their importance in the public eye. If NBC's Tim Russert — whose only identifiable opinion is his enthusiasm for fatherhood — were to raise questions about a candidate's intellectual qualifications, it would carry more weight than anything a well-known liberal or conservative commentator had to say. Competence has resurfaced as a political issue in the current campaign, but the media generally address the subject within the context of executive skills; the relationship between incompetence and sheer stupidity is almost never discussed. The time for the press to home in on Bush's educational, cultural, and intellectual limitations was during his first campaign for the presidency. Why should anyone have been surprised that a man who had never displayed any interest in seeing the rest of the world would one day advise Russian president Vladimir Putin, "You know, sometimes when you study history you get stuck in the past"?[4] Or that a former frat boy satisfied with the gentleman's C would respond to a hurricane-devastated New Orleans by alluding to the wild weekends he had spent there in his youth? This is not to say that the smartest boy or girl in the class would necessarily make the best president, but that there ought to be a higher threshold of intellect, as well as a higher standard of cultural and scientific literacy, than that currently required for political candidates.

Intelligence itself has not yet become a disqualifier for the modern American presidency, but the electability of an intelligent candidate often seems to depend on his ability to soften and downplay his "egghead" side. Bill Clinton, as has been noted by his enemies as well as his supporters, was one of the smartest and best educated presidents of the twentieth century, and he strongly resembled John Kennedy in the catholicity of his interests. Many political observers believe that Clinton, had he been eligible to run for a third term, would have defeated Bush overwhelmingly. But Clinton — like both Kennedys but unlike Al Gore and John Kerry — possesses immense personal charm and a common touch that overshadows what, in a less seductive personality, would be perceived as intellectual arrogance and elitist taste. Moreover, Clinton came from a rural, working-class background and wound up at Oxford and Yale Law School entirely as a result of his own hard work: his was a story of *earned* privilege, and he was able to present it that way in his campaigns. Gore's seriousness and studiousness, by contrast

— including his longtime concern about global warming, which the public did not yet share in 2000 — were perceived as arrogant and patronizing after his debates with Bush. Facing off against both Gore and Kerry, Bush was seen by a majority of voters as more of a "real person." Perhaps Kerry's fate was already sealed weeks before the election, when a majority of undecided voters told pollsters that Bush was the kind of man they would rather have a beer with (if Bush could stop at just one) than Kerry.

Is it possible that American voters have learned something about the consequences of choosing an intellectually challenged chief executive on the basis of a beer test? Whatever one thinks of their respective political views, the most active candidates for the presidential nomination in both parties over the past year cannot be accused of being dumb. Hillary Clinton, John Edwards, Barack Obama, Rudolph Giuliani, John McCain, and Mitt Romney — even though they come from very different backgrounds, ranging from near poverty to immense wealth — can all form intelligible and grammatical English sentences. Each of them pronounces the word "nuclear" correctly. It is a safe bet that all of them read newspapers and that none of them waits for a staff briefing each day in order to avoid being exposed to "opinions" from the outside world. It remains to be seen, as the campaign heats up and comes down to the final two, whether "elitism" will resurface as a political negative. One wonders whether any candidate, instead of trying to prove that he or she is just one of the folks, would dare to tell voters that the nation needs not an ordinary but an extraordinary person as president and that one crucial qualification for the nation's highest office is the intellectual ability to distinguish, in times of crisis and on a daily basis, between worthwhile and worthless opinions.

One of the true ironies of American public life today is that although politicians have become increasingly determined to downplay any telltale signs of intellectualism or elitism while running for office, intellectuals play an increasingly important role in the conduct of government. Since John Kennedy turned to liberal academia to staff his White House, intellectuals have filled many key official jobs, as well as unofficial but highly influential advisory roles, in every Democratic and Republican administration. During the past thirty years, the old liberal intellectual establishment, based primarily in academia, has been joined by, and in certain crucial respects outsmarted by, a conservative intellectual establishment with a permanent base in right-wing think tanks and foundations underwritten by the fortunes of conservative businessmen. The right-wing egghead establishment cut its teeth during the Reagan administration and achieved immeasurably greater influence under George W. Bush, who is even more committed to the right's foreign policy and economic agenda than Reagan was. The success of conservative strategists in masking their own elite class status, at least for the general public, and defining "the elites" as liberals has been the critical factor in their outsmarting of the intellectual left.

When Richard Hofstadter was completing *Anti-Intellectualism in American Life* in the early sixties, twentieth-century American intellectualism was considered synonymous with political liberalism — an analysis that, although exceptions could be cited, was largely justified at that time. While there were a few prominent conservative intellectual gadflies like Bill Buckley, there had been no conservative intellectual "establishment" in the United States since the influential social Darwinists of the late nineteenth century. It is fair to say that the entire left-of-center intellectual community was devastated by Adlai Stevenson's defeat in 1952, particularly because Dwight Eisenhower's running mate was Richard Nixon, the man liberal intellectuals loved to loathe. *Time* magazine, that barometer of conventional wisdom, reported that Eisenhower's drubbing of Stevenson had revealed the existence of a "wide and unhealthy gap between the American intellectuals and the people." After Stevenson's defeat, Arthur Schlesinger, Jr., writing in the highbrow *Partisan Review,* said flatly that intellectuals were now "on the run in American society."[5] As it turned out, of course, liberal intellectuals (Schlesinger included) did not have to run very long or very far and would, in less than a decade, be having the time of their lives as advisers to and cultural middlemen for the Kennedy administration.

Liberal intellectuals who came of age before the Second World War — at least those who did not succumb fully to the seductive charm of the Kennedy White House — regarded the propinquity of their scholarly peers to power as a mixed blessing. They were generally more concerned about the corruption of intellectuals by power than about the potential corruption of government policy by intellectuals whom no one had elected. Most liberal intellectuals shaped by the Depression had simply assumed that they would always remain at the economic as well as the social margins of American life and that their position as outsiders was a necessary condition of their role as independent thinkers. As postwar America confounded the low economic and professional expectations of the prewar intellectuals, the unease of that generation about becoming insiders only intensified during the Kennedy years. The visible presence of so many intellectuals near the seat of political power elicited criticism and soul-searching from many of their peers — some of whom had been excluded from the charmed circle by the Kennedys and some of whom had deliberately chosen to exclude themselves from the power loop. A portion of this criticism was surely rooted in envy, but much of it was based on serious concerns about the growing entanglement of intellectuals with the military and foreign policy establishments. The more liberal academics in the Kennedy administration, including Schlesinger, were rarely taken seriously when it came to matters of national defense and security, but the real influence wielded by the more hawkish intellectuals was already clear in the early sixties and became even more pronounced after Kennedy's assassination.

Kazin's catty observation that "power from Washington seemed to be stored up in the cells of Kennedy's executive assistants and advisers even on a weekend romp in Wellfleet among their old colleagues" was founded on a serious concern about potentially dangerous conflicts between the life of the mind and access to governmental clout, even or perhaps especially when the latter was exercised only through influence over elected officials. In an essay written shortly after the 1961 Bay of Pigs debacle, Kazin noted that Cold War liberal intellectuals had not covered themselves with glory and had in fact proffered quite stupid advice, divorced from any sense of what the military or social realities on the ground might be, to the president. "The only defense that I have heard against the frightening impatience displayed in the Cuban adventure," Kazin observed, "has been that so-and-so wasn't in on the decision and that intellectuals on the outside never recognize how many important decisions are improvised and uncalculated. Where, then, is the meaningful relation of intellectuals to power? Is it only to write memoranda, to 'educate' the decisions that others make? History will not absolve them that cheaply."[6]

That generalization applies just as strongly to the intellectual hawks, some of them the same people whose misjudgments led to the Bay of Pigs fiasco, who helped draw the Kennedy administration into a military commitment in Vietnam and exercised even greater influence during Lyndon Johnson's presidency. Yet nearly all of the simmering populist anti-intellectualism of the late sixties focused not on the Cold War hawkish intellectuals but on left-wing antiwar intellectuals, who resided not within the Johnson West Wing but on university campuses. This period provided the basis for the right's long and successful attempt to pin the elitist label only on liberal intellectuals, even as real liberal influence diminished in government. The right was never opposed to the intellectual rationalizations for the Vietnam War provided by McGeorge Bundy and Walter and Eugene Rostow during the Johnson years or, during the Nixon administration, to Henry Kissinger's Machiavellian rationales for extending the carnage into Cambodia and prolonging the violence.

By 1980, popular identification of intellectualism with the left was such that the right-wing intellectuals who provided much of the ideology for the Reagan administration were able to advance the fiction — so important first to Reagan and, twenty years later, to the election of Bush the younger — that the so-called elites consist entirely of liberals opposed to old-fashioned American values of traditional religion, unquestioning patriotism, and pulling oneself up by one's own bootstraps. Conservative intellectuals mastered an art that liberals never did: they somehow managed to present themselves as an aggrieved minority even while feasting, as liberals had during the Kennedy administration, at the government trough.

In 1985, when Mikhail Gorbachev was beginning to shake things up in the Soviet Union but American conservatives were warning against taking Gorbachev's calls for reform at face value, the flourishing but still not entirely triumphant neocon establishment held a conference in Washington's Madison Hotel. This right-wing intellectual elite had assembled at one of the capital's most expensive hotels for the explicit purpose of warning ordinary, working-class Americans against a new betrayal being prepared by elitist, Gorby-loving liberal intellectuals — those who presumably held forth at conferences in expensive hotels owned by Marxists. The neocons' intent was not only to sound the alarm against any softening toward the Soviet Union but also to remind everyone of the by then fifty-year-old weakness of American intellectuals for communism. One of the more unintentionally hilarious speeches at the conference was delivered by the novelist Tom Wolfe. As Sidney Blumenthal, who would later become an aide to Bill Clinton, recounts:

> When the main course of polemics was cleared away and only dessert remained, the writer Tom Wolfe was served up. He wore pastels, the crowd wore gray. None dared call it chic. The ideological spoilsmen — conservative intellectuals with think-tank sinecures, foundation executives, political operatives, and federal jobholders, were congratulated on their "courage" for appearing at this lush affair in Reagan's Washington, incidentally funded in part by the State Department. Then came the rote attack on the New Class, those who really have power, "a class of ruling intellectuals trained to rule a country," Wolfe declared. The appeal of Marxism, he explained, was due to its "implicit secret promise . . . of handing power over to intellectuals." . . . The conservatives applauded, dispersed into the Washington night, and showed up at

their New Class jobs the next morning.[7]

One darkly humorous aspect of this speech was the notion that anyone in 1985, given awareness of the bloody fate of so many intellectuals, including Marxists, under various Communist regimes in the preceding fifty years, might still believe in the existence of an "implicit secret promise" that Marxists would hand over power to intellectuals.

The use of popular anti-intellectualism by one group of intellectuals to attack another group of intellectuals is hardly unique on the world stage — the Bolsheviks were masters of the art — but it is something relatively new in America, where attacks on intellectuals as a class have generally been launched from outside the intellectual community. The bitter political battles over communism among intellectuals in the thirties were chiefly an internal affair: none of the Old Leftists possessed enough broad public influence, much less real power, to inflame popular anti-intellectualism or use it against other intellectuals. Even during the McCarthy era, when intellectuals were called on to name names, the attack on intellectuals *as liberals,* and on liberals as Communist fellow travelers, was spearheaded chiefly by nonintellectual and anti-intellectual right-wing politicians (although aided by former Communist and fellow-traveling intellectuals-turned-informers).

Only since the 1980s has there been a full-blown battle between two heavyweight intellectual establishments that regard each other with an antipathy as fierce as that between the Communists and anti-Communist liberals of the thirties. Unlike the battling intellectuals of the thirties, today's intellectuals really do possess a fair amount of influence within the larger culture. The right-wing intellectuals have managed to frame their battle with liberal intellectuals as a conflict between "ordinary" Americans and those who look down on them from a lofty perch. That the Heritage Foundation, the American Enterprise Institute, the Hoover Institution, et al., are also lofty perches for eggheads, that these right-wing think tanks have as incestuous a relationship to conservative government officials as Harvard ever did to the Kennedy administration, is largely unknown to the general public. During the Reagan administration, when Irving Kristol charged intellectuals with the crime of alienation from the American way of life, he also described neoconservatives as the representatives of a heretofore inarticulate "bourgeois popu-lism." Kristol was certain that the American people — those "bourgeois populists" — were free of the alienation that infected liberal intellectuals foolish enough to con-sider Social Security, Medicare, laws against racial discrimination, and even nuclear arms control an essential part of the American way of life.[8] As an ex-Trotskyist, Kristol could hardly call himself a "bourgeois intel-lectual" — though that is a fairly accurate description of the intellectual refugees from the Old Left who found a new spiritual home in foundations established by capital-ist plutocrats.

Right-wing intellectuals have also proved much more adept than their left-of-center counterparts at keeping their heads below the mainstream media radar; most shun the kind of celebrity that might draw public at-tention to their role as a permanent un-elected establishment serving at the pleasure of conservative politicians. The pedigree of today's right-wing brain trust — the web of family and professional connections that form America's substitute for inherited wealth (although the neocons now have plenty of money themselves) is largely invis-ible to the vast numbers of Americans who rely on television for whatever they know about influences on government policy. The success of the older neoconservatives in raising so many children who fully accepted their family values is a source of envy for many graying liberals; no doubt the unpredictability of liberal offspring has something to do with the pernicious and permissive influence of Dr. Spock on their parents' child-rearing practices.

Kristol and his wife, the historian Gertrude Himmelfarb, succeeded in begetting William Kristol, editor of *The Weekly Standard,* who apparently imbibed contempt for liberalism with his mother's milk and his father's spleen and eventually followed in Dad's footsteps by painting the sixties as the most iniquitous period in the nation's history. Norman Podhoretz and Midge Decter produced John Podhoretz, who will soon take over the *Commentary* editorship held by his dad for thirty-five years. Neo-nepotism, it seems, is a powerful neoconservative family value. The elder Podhoretzes also acquired an influential son-in-law, Elliott Abrams, now Bush's deputy national security adviser for "global democracy strategy" and one of those undead intellectual bureaucrats who seem impervious to every effort to drive stakes through their hearts. As assistant secretary of state for

Latin American affairs under Reagan, Abrams became a major force in promoting American support for the Nicaraguan contras. Convicted on charges related to the Iran-contra affair, he was pardoned by President George H. W. Bush, which left him free to return to the government payroll when the younger Bush entered the Oval Office.

Like his neocon contemporaries who came of age in the sixties, Abrams hates everything about the decade. Anything emanating from liberals, especially intellectuals, can only be a conspiracy. "I'm sorry, but John Lennon was not that important a figure in our times," Abrams declared a week after Lennon's murder in 1980. "Why is his death getting more attention than Elvis Presley's? Because Lennon is perceived as a left-wing figure politically, anti-establishment, a man of social conscience with concern for the poor. And therefore, he's being made into a great figure. Too much has been made of his life. It does not deserve a full day's television and radio coverage. I'm sick of it."[9] Someone should have unearthed this old quote, if only for a reality check, when Abrams was tapped for an influential State Department post at the beginning of the Reagan administration in 1981. Does anyone belong in a responsible government job if he seriously believes that Elvis Presley — who, in the fifties, was viewed by many traditionalists as a greater threat than communism to the morals of American youth — was ever ignored by the media?

The current generation of right-wing intellectuals, young when they entered government during the Reagan administration, have matured into the more powerful, full-grown ideologues who have guided the Bush administration. Paul Wolfowitz, Richard Perle, and Kristol *fils* are among the most important intellectual architects of the Iraq War, yet their hands were largely invisible at the outset — except to their own conservative intellectual constituency; to primarily liberal readers of publications like *The New Yorker, The Atlantic, The Nation,* and *The New Republic;* and to politically astute viewers of programs like PBS's *Frontline* and Bill Moyers's documentaries. The influence of the intellectual right over a president who rarely set foot outside the United States before deciding to run for the nation's highest office deserves much more mainstream press and public attention than it has received.

There is certainly a valuable and legitimate

role to be played by intellectuals — both liberal and conservative — in public life, and presidents and other politicians will naturally draw on the intellectual community most closely allied with their own views. But the relationship of intellectuals to power is more problematic today than it was forty years ago precisely because of the decline in cultural literacy on the part of the public and the public's elected representatives. I do not know whether, had John Kennedy lived and been elected to a second term, he would have turned against the intellectual hawks who were pushing for more military involvement in Vietnam; that hope has always seemed to me to belong more to the Camelot myth than to the real world. There is much more solid evidence that Robert Kennedy, had he run on an antiwar platform and defeated Nixon, would have gotten rid of the leftover Ivy League cold warriors from his brother's administration as well as those hired by Johnson. But there is no question that both Kennedys, unlike Bush, had the brains and the intellectual background to understand what the eggheads were talking about.

Even Ronald Reagan, whose views about history seem to have been shaped primarily by the movies — and the roles he played in them — did not always listen to the voices of his most conservative intellectual advisers. Although greatly beholden to the intellectuals of the New Right and in general agreement with their views on foreign affairs, Reagan, despite the perorations of the neocons at the Madison Hotel, rejected the hard right position on the crucial issue of relations with the Soviet government of Mikhail Gorbachev. Warned by many of his right-wing advisers that Gorbachev was nothing but a Bolshevik wolf in the sheep's clothing of a reformer, Reagan nevertheless treated the Soviet premier's advocacy of *glasnost* as the real deal and was rewarded by being given the credit, at least by much of the American public, for the end of the Cold War and the subsequent dissolution of the Soviet Union.

There is nothing in George Bush's record to suggest that he has ever questioned the expertise or the judgment of his most conservative house intellectuals — or that he would ever hire or keep anyone on staff who disagreed with his views. When other twentieth-century presidents, Republican and Democratic, drew on the resources of the intellectual community, they hired staff members who represented a relatively broad spectrum of opinion within either liberalism or conservatism. Bush, by contrast, chose only those intellectual — and nonintellectual — advisers who came from the extreme right fraction of the conservative spectrum. The exception was Secretary of State Colin Powell, who resigned after Bush's first term. The value of intellectuals' contribution to government depends entirely on the capacity of their elected boss to absorb and assess not only the ideas but the quality of the evidence presented to him by people who, although they may well possess more information than he does about a particular topic, have not been elected to represent anyone.

The one-sidedness of intellectual participation in the Bush administration has been evident in domestic as well as foreign policy, in matters of scientific expertise as well as political philosophy. One exemplary specimen is the President's Council on Bioethics, composed mainly of philosophers, lawyers, and scientists who agree with the president's strong, religiously based anti-abortion views, disagree with the scientific and medical consensus favoring embryonic stem cell research, and have provided elaborate rationales for the administration's opposition to federal funding for most research involving embryonic cells. Systematically excluded from the panel were distinguished bioethicists and scientists — by far the majority in their professions — who have supported embryonic stem cell research and whose general ideas on the ethical boundaries of scientific inquiry are derived from sources other than the most conservative teachings of the Roman Catholic Church, fundamentalist Protestantism, and ultra-Orthodox Judaism. Both government officials and the public would have benefited from a lively intellectual debate airing all points of view on controversial issues at the intersection of science and ethics, but the real purpose of the bioethics advisory group was not to advise but to provide academic cover for the administration's religiously and politically motivated policies.

Hofstadter envisioned an America in which intellectuals would include specialized experts and "perhaps also critics capable of stepping mentally outside their society and looking relentlessly at its assumptions, in sufficient number and with sufficient freedom to make themselves felt." He warned that although it "would be tragic if all intellectuals aimed to serve power . . . it would be equally tragic if intellectuals who became associated with power were driven to believe they no longer had any connection with the intellectual community; their conclusion would almost inevitably be that their responsibilities are to power alone."[10] The relationship between intellectuals and power in the Bush administration, particularly regarding the war in Iraq, suggests that America is much closer to Hofstadter's worst-case scenario than to his best-case outcome.

The older generation's concern about the corruption of intellectuals by power seems utterly quaint in an era when a Paul Wolfowitz can move seamlessly from the Johns Hopkins University School of Advanced International Studies (as dean of SAIS, he transformed the school into a center of right-wing political thought) to the Department of Defense to the presidency of the World Bank. At the World Bank, Wolfowitz even succumbed to the most banal form of corruption — using his power to bolster his female companion's career and salary. Some liberals argue that right-wing functionaries like Wolfowitz cannot be considered intellectuals at all because they are completely caught up in the exercise of political power. That seems to me a misjudgment, based largely on animus toward the politics represented by the right-wing intellectual establishment. If the grown-up Reagan neocons were stupid — if they did not have command of an intellectual vocabulary that makes wishful thinking sound rational — they would be less dangerous.

Americans have historically been suspicious of intellectuals as political ideologues, but they had far less reason to worry about Depression-era scholars who debated the merits of Stalin and Trotsky in the City College lunchroom than they do today about intellectuals who have actually influenced presidential decisions on war and peace — whether from inside or outside the government. One can only wish that Bill Kristol, instead of being received respectfully at the White House as an expert on foreign affairs, was, like his father, a New York intellectual whose fulminations circulated mainly among other New York intellectuals and never attracted the attention of anyone with the power to implement his ideological schemes.

Out-of-power (in Washington) liberal intellectuals also have a good deal to answer for, and one of their most serious failures of vision has been a reluctance to acknowledge the political significance of public ignorance. Liberals have tended to define the Bush administration as the problem and the source of all that has gone wrong during the past eight years and to see an outraged citizenry, ready to throw the bums out, as the solution. While an angry public may be the short-term solution, an ignorant public is the long-term problem in American public life. Like many Democratic politicians, left-of-center intellectuals have focused on the right-wing deceptions employed to sell the war in Iraq rather than on the ignorance and erosion of historical memory that make serious deceptions possible and plausible — not only about Iraq but about a vast array of domestic and international issues.

The general decline in American civic, cultural, and scientific literacy has encouraged political polarization because the field of debate is often left to those who care most intensely — with an out-of-the-mainstream passion — about a specific political and cultural agenda. Every shortcoming of American governance, in foreign relations and domestic affairs, is related in some fashion to the knowledge deficit of the American public — if only because there is no widespread indignation at policies shaped by elected officials who suffer from the same intellectual blind spots as their constituents. The Iraq Study Group's report on the multi-layered failure of America's war in Iraq, released at the end of 2006, revealed that of more than 1,100 employees at the U.S. Embassy in Baghdad, only thirty-two spoke Arabic at all, and just six were fluent in the language. It may be shocking, but it is hardly surprising, that the United States government would staff an embassy almost entirely with diplomats who literally cannot understand what local people are talking about. We are, after all, citizens of a nation in which five out of six young adults do not consider it particularly important to know any foreign language. Most Americans do not cringe when their president mocks an American correspondent who is fluent in another language, so why should anyone be surprised when the president's administration does not make it a priority to hire Arabic speakers or send them to Baghdad?

As both dumbness and smartness are defined downward — among intellectuals and nonintellectuals alike — it becomes much easier to convince people of the validity of extreme positions. Not only basic knowledge but the ability to think critically are required to understand the factual errors (as distinct from differences of opinion) that generally provide the foundation for policies at the far ends of the political spectrum. Take the question of high-end tax cuts advocated by the free market absolutists on the political right. Democrats and moderate Republicans have repeatedly explained that 90 percent of the benefits from the tax cuts during the past eight years have gone to just 1 percent — the top 1 percent — of Americans. To understand that argument, however, voters must understand what those percentages mean — and in which part of the population their own income falls. And those international math tests on which U.S. students do so badly show that percentages and fractions are a particular source of confusion for American high school graduates. In similar fashion, the right wing's relentless attack on "unelected activist judges" feeds on public ignorance about the Constitution's separation of powers and the reasons why the framers established an independent, unelected federal judiciary in the first place. Two thirds of Americans cannot name the three branches of government or come up with the name of a single Supreme Court justice. Voters who rate the judiciary as an important issue are in a distinct minority, and many of them are on the far right.

Americans who get their news primarily from television rather than newspapers know much less about the judicial system than newspaper readers. Two thirds of newspaper readers, but only 40 percent of television news watchers, know that the primary mission of the Supreme Court is to interpret the Constitution.[11] When people are ignorant of the high court's constitutional mandate, it is much easier to convince them that justices are supposed to reflect public opinion — and that something has gone wrong when a court hands down a decision that contradicts popular wisdom. More than half of adults do not even know that there are nine Supreme Court justices. Without that basic bit of knowledge, citizens were hardly likely to be excited by the change in the balance of power represented by the elevation of two highly conservative judges, John G. Roberts and Samuel A. Alito, to the high court in a single year. And there was plenty to be excited about, as demonstrated during the past year by the high court's sharp turn to the right on cases involving school desegregation, First Amendment rights, and government regulation of business. The replacement of the moderate Sandra Day O'Connor by Alito has made the critical difference, altering the stance of the court in ways that will directly affect the lives of Americans for decades (assuming that Alito and Roberts, now in their early fifties, will share the longevity of so many Supreme Court justices). It seems unlikely that the majority of Americans — those who do not even know how many justices are on the court — realize that apart from leading the nation into war, a president's most enduring mark on American society is made by his appointments to the federal judiciary.

Memory has been the greatest civic casualty of the past fifty years, but before people can be expected to remember anything, they must have absorbed certain basic facts and ideas worth remembering. Americans, including many graduates of the nation's most prestigious universities, have a shaky grasp not only of basic mathematics and science but of the milestones of their nation's history and the fundamental ideas and structures on which their government rests. Surveys conducted by the National Constitution Center show that while Americans hold the Constitution in high esteem, they know relatively little about the nation's founding document. Asked whether they could recall any of the rights guaranteed by the First Amendment, a majority could name only freedom of speech. After that, only four in ten could name freedom of religion and one in three freedom of the press. More than a third were unable to list any First Amendment rights; 42 percent think that the Constitution explicitly states that "the first language of the United States is English"; and 25 percent believe that Christianity was established by the Constitution as the official government religion. The young are even more ignorant than their parents and grandparents. About half of adults — but just 41 percent of teenagers — can name the three branches of government. Only four in ten adults — but just two in ten teenagers — know that there are one hundred U.S. senators. The vast majority of both adults and teens have no idea of when or by whom the Constitution was written. Among the teenagers, nearly 98 percent cannot name the Chief Justice of the United States.[12]

This is our civic present and, if nothing is done to stem the rising tide of ignorance among the young, our even more disturbing civic future. In 1981, in a speech to the graduating class of Notre Dame University, Ronald Reagan expressed the hope that "when it's your time to explain to another generation the meaning of the past and thereby hold out to them the promise of their future, that you'll recall the truths and traditions . . . that define our civilization and make up our national heritage. And now, they're yours to protect and pass on."[13] Reagan was referring specifically to his sunny version of the American past, in which, although "sad episodes exist, any objective observer must hold a positive view of American history, a history that has been the story of hopes fulfilled and dreams made into reality."[14]

However citizens interpret the past, and however strongly they may disagree on what the past reveals about the present, it is impossible to recall "truths and traditions" that were never learned in the first place. Secular liberals and religious conservatives, for example, disagree on many issues connected with the role of religion in public life today. Participants in that dialogue may and do argue about exactly how high the wall of church-state separation should rise. But there can be no meaningful discussion if both sides do not know what the First Amendment actually says — that Congress "shall make no law respecting an establishment of religion, or prohibiting the free exercise thereof." The election of the first Muslim member of the House of Representatives in 2006, for example, became the occasion for a know-nothing debate about whether he could take his oath of office on the Koran rather than the Bible. Anyone, liberal or conservative, who actually knows what the First Amendment says knows the answer: it would clearly be unconstitutional to prevent a representative from taking an oath on the religious book of his choice. It would be equally unconstitutional, for that matter, to require a public official to take an oath on any sacred book, since Article VI of the Constitution explicitly prohibits all religious tests for public office. But the large percentage of Americans who do not understand the First Amendment have certainly never heard of the less publicized Article VI. The newly elected representative Keith Ellison, a Democrat from Minnesota, ended the controversy by taking his oath on a copy of the Koran, borrowed from the National Archives and believed to have been owned by Thomas Jefferson. Ellison, it seems, has read not only the Koran and the Constitution but a biography that mentions the contents of Thomas Jefferson's library.

One might think that the promotion of basic civic literacy could provide common ground for intellectuals of opposing political views, but that has not happened. Right-wing intellectuals, particularly those involved in government, constantly bleat about the lamentable state of cultural literacy in America, but what they mean is *their* version of cultural literacy and American history. They want American children to be taught more about the Constitution in school, but they do not want lessons that contradict their political agenda — say, an American history class that discusses the framers' deliberate omission of any reference to God or limitations on the president's power to wage war without formal congressional approval. Liberal intellectuals, especially those in academia, tend to gloss over the importance of basic facts in favor of multicultural issues that, however important they may be today, cannot be understood or examined coherently by young people who do not know that the Constitution was written in 1787 and that it took the Civil War, fought more than seven decades later, to bring an end to the formula for slavery written into the blueprint for a federal government. The importance of chronology has been downplayed at all levels of the educational system for the past fifty years, and that is largely the work of those who fail to understand that students can hardly be expected to comprehend why things happened — the frequently stated mantra of progressive educators — if they do not know what happened and when.

In the early 1990s, a brouhaha over an attempt to develop national standards for the teaching of history offered an exemplary and depressing demonstration of the politically motivated pigheadedness shared by many hard-line conservative and left-wing multiculturalist intellectuals. Lynne Cheney, chair of the National Endowment for the Humanities during the administration of President George H. W. Bush (and the wife of Dick Cheney), approved a grant to the National Center for History in the Schools, based at the University of California at Los Angeles, for the development of voluntary national history standards. When the standards were released in 1994, many distinguished conservative and liberal historians were appalled. The results were a fair-minded historian's nightmare, seemingly crafted by a collective composed of all of the politically correct purveyors of junk thought in academia. The Constitution itself received short shrift. Such was the level of political correctness that the guidelines continually referred to "the American peoples" — as if that had been customary language at any point in American history and the framers had begun the Preamble with "We the Peoples . . . in order to form a more perfect Union."

In the 1994 standards, the McCarthy era received much more attention than the revolutionary period and the Constitution. An angry Mrs. Cheney, who had egg on her face for having approved the grant in the first place, led the charge against the standards, criticizing them for emphasizing American shortcomings and downgrading American heroes and achievements. Politicians were even angrier, and the Senate passed a motion censuring the standards — a strange concept in itself — by a vote of 99 to 1. President Bill Clinton, who should have known better and probably did, jumped on the bandwagon to declare that all efforts to develop national history standards were misguided and that only the states should determine what was taught in their schools. In doing so, Clinton ignored the fact that the absence of national standards is one of the main reasons why American children know so much less about their history than European children know about the history of their native lands.

But that was not the end of the controversy, because many educators and historians realized that national curriculum standards were still a good idea even if this particular set of standards was a specimen of junk thought. The Council for Basic Education, a nonprofit foundation for the promotion of innovation in schools, brought together panels of professional historians, who decided that the standards could be rescued from the doghouse of the culture wars. The UCLA Center modified its orginal recommendations, based on the historians' advice, and in 1996 released a new suggested curriculum that pleased nearly everyone but the lunatic fringe of the academic far left and the hard-core right.

Diane Ravitch, an educational historian and a political conservative, and the staunchly liberal Arthur Schlesinger, Jr., collaborated on an unusual article, originally published in *The Wall Street Journal*, praising the new national standards and urging that the original misbegotten recommendations not stand as an obstacle to a national effort to improve the teaching of history. The article was widely circulated because it was a rare example of public intellectuals collaborating, in spite of their different political views, on an important effort attempting to address the grave shortcomings of American civic education. The authors state unequivocally:

> The revised standards arrive at a critical juncture. Our children know too little about our history (or any other). In recent years, the teaching of history has been submerged in a shapeless mass of "social studies" aiming to teach children "social dynamics," "interpersonal relations," the improvement of "self-esteem," and all sorts of other non-historical considerations. We have no doubt that the American people want their children — and the entire rising generation — to be well informed about who we are, where our institutions came from, and how we have confronted the discrepancy between our behavior and our ideals.

Both Schlesinger and Ravitch (who, while working for the Department of Education, had, like Cheney, signed off on the original grant application) criticized the first set of standards "for their failure to balance *pluribus* and *unum* and to place the nation's democratic ideals at the center of its history."

The authors went on to praise the revised standards as "rigorous, honest, and as nearly accurate as any group of historians could make them. They do not take sides, and they pose the most fundamental questions about our nation's history." Among the changes: The term "peoples" was jettisoned; more space was devoted to the Constitution and the Bill of Rights; and, as the authors noted, although "attention is rightly directed to our nation's troubled history of racial, ethnic, and religious tension, these issues are now placed within the context of the nation's ongoing quest to make our practices conform to our ideals." In addition, the new standards eliminated "references to obscure people whose main credential seemed to be that they were not dead white males."[15] Translation: although the 1996 standards would not satisfy those who want American history to be taught as one long and unbroken record of injustice, neither would they satisfy those, like Reagan, who want children to learn a prettied-up version of history in which slavery, to cite just one example, is treated not as a central and terrible American reality but as merely one of those trifling "sad episodes in our past." The new standards were made widely available, on a voluntary basis, to school districts intent on improving the teaching of history. Unfortunately, the problem with voluntary attempts to improve academic standards is that the changes are seldom embraced by local school districts most in need of remediation.

One person who would not give the national history standards a second chance was Lynne Cheney. Mrs. Cheney became so incensed over the very phrase "national history standards" that in 2004 she used her clout as the wife of the vice president (although she no longer had an official government job) to bully the Department of Education into destroying 300,000 copies of a revised edition of a pamphlet, *Helping Your Child Learn History,* intended to complement the 1996 standards. The Department of Education originally claimed that the pamphlets were recalled because of "typographical errors" but eventually had to confess that it was responding to Mrs. Cheney's objections to the very mention of national standards.[16] Mrs. Cheney is clearly one of those intellectuals who have concluded that their responsibilities are to power alone — and to the expansion of their own power. (In her case, exercising her responsibilities led her to call upon the derivative power she possessed as her husband's wife.)

It speaks badly for intellectuals as a group that Schlesinger and Ravitch's collaboration was such a noteworthy event — that so many prominent conservative and liberal scholars are more interested in bashing one another than in setting aside some of their disagreements in an effort to arrest the tide of ignorance that threatens the very foundations of American democracy. Too many intellectuals are simply feathering their own nests — like those who did not stand up for the core curriculum at universities in the sixties and early seventies — and thereby contributing to the deterioration of what used to be our common civic culture. Like the politicians so many of them are eager to serve, such intellectuals are making their own contribution to the dumbing down of public discourse.

Finally, too many proprietors of threatened print media are also taking the path of least resistance in discussions of vital public issues. Unlike the old middlebrow merchants of self-improvement, the new media lords are trying to meet readers at their own level of cultural and civic literacy — as demonstrated by the cutbacks in book reviews and classical music coverage — instead of attempting to raise the level of public knowledge and discourse. *Time,* in its annual Person of the Year issue at the end of 2006, slapped a glossy Mylar reflector on its cover and named "YOU — Yes, You" as the winner. Actually, "You" did not encompass everyone but only those Americans who either used the Internet or created new content for the World Wide Web. *Time's* Person of the Year, a citizen of "the new digital democracy," could be anyone who ordered a DVD from Netflix; posted a profile on MySpace; visited TIME.com (for that you get extra points); sent an e-mail; posted an image of himself or herself throwing up on YouTube; contributed a barbed obituary, cleverly designed to reveal the previously concealed sins of the deceased, to Legacy.com; googled a potential lover for a background check; or contributed to a political blog.

"America loves its solitary geniuses . . . ," *Time* intoned, "but those lonely dreamers may have to learn to play with others. Car companies are running open design contests. Reuters is carrying blog postings alongside its regular news feed. Microsoft is working overtime to fend off user-created Linux. We're looking at an explosion of productivity and innovation, and it's just getting started, as millions of minds that would otherwise have drowned in obscurity get backhauled into the global intellectual economy." As for the minds that richly deserve obscurity — minds responsible for the digital world's exponential growth of junk thought and bile — *Time* assures its shrinking number of readers that everything on the Internet is part of a "massive social experiment, and like any experiment worth trying, it could fail." Nevetheless, the Web offers a chance "to build a new kind of international understanding, not politician to politician, great man to great man, but citizen to citizen, person to person . . . a chance for people to look at a computer screen and really, genuinely wonder who's out there looking back at them. Go on. Tell us you're not just a little bit curious."[17]

Here's the best part: citizens of the "new digital democracy" do not have to vote, or read books, or spend any waking part of their days without the combination of hypnotic comfort and artificial stimulation offered on screen media by the infotainment industry. It apparently never occurred to the frightened executives who run *Time* that none of their pandering is likely to persuade digital addicts to turn off the screen and pick up a copy of the magazine. Like most politicians, most media opinion makers choose to pretend that dumbness is not being defined downward and to flatter Americans by telling them that they and their children are really the smartest, best educated generations ever to inhabit this nation. Some members of the political and media elite, offering what is arguably the most compelling evidence of the decline of cultural literacy in America, actually believe what they are saying.

Conclusion: Cultural Conservation

"The mind of this country, taught to aim at low objects, eats upon itself." In 1837, Emerson struck that note mainly as a rhetorical device, in a young nation obviously engaged in building up its intellectual capital. But Emerson's straw man has come to life in America's new age of unreason, and the inescapable theme of our time is the erosion of memory and knowledge. Memory loss has made us bad stewards of our intellectual inheritance, and the dissipation of our cultural storehouse gives rise in turn to new cycles of forgetting. Anti-rationalism and anti-intellectualism flourish in a mix that includes addiction to infotainment, every form of superstition and credulity, and an educational system that does a poor job of teaching not only basic skills but the logic underlying those skills.

It has become something of a literary convention for an author, at the end of a nonfiction book with an essentially pessimistic outlook, to propose solutions that, at least in theory, offer some basis for hope. But America's current cultural predicament resists amelioration precisely because so many of the customarily proffered remedies have themselves become formidable problems. Daniel Webster, in an 1826 eulogy for John Adams and Thomas Jefferson (both of whom, in one of the more poignant coincidences in American history, died on the fiftieth anniversary of the Declaration of Independence), declared that the young republic, as Jefferson and Adams had hoped, was already distinguished by "a newly awakened, and an unconquerable spirit of free inquiry, and by a diffusion of knowledge throughout the community, such as has been before altogether unknown and unheard of." The future of America, Webster argued, "is inseparably connected, fast bound up, in fortune and by fate, with these great interests. If they fall, we fall with them; if they stand, it will be because we have upholden them."[1]

Free inquiry and the diffusion of knowledge — inevitably involving more education for more people — have always been the secular rays of hope in every vision of America's future, but they will not suffice in an era when, despite the steady rise in the formal educational level of the population, so many Americans seem to know less and less. Science — how deep a faith it inspired in the Enlightenment rationalists of America's founding generation and their freethinking late nineteenth-century heirs! — can by itself provide no remedy for those who, out of ignorance or in servitude to an anti-rational form of faith, know little and care less about the basic principles that constitute the scientific method. Technology, our servant, has also become our master, as the information highway — potentially the greatest tool for the diffusion of learning ever devised — has, for too many, become a highway to the far-flung regions of junk thought.

It is difficult to suppress the fear that our expanding "digital democracy," coupled with the decline of reading, is imposing what Alexis de Tocqueville called a "new physiognomy of servitude." Concerned that unchecked majority rule might reward conformity rather than individuality, Tocqueville observed, "I very clearly discern two tendencies; one leading the mind of every man to untried thoughts, the other prohibiting him from thinking at all."[2] His cautionary statement is just as pertinent to a society in which technology transmits the same information and ideas instantaneously to millions, thereby encouraging conformity while offering a theoretically unlimited array of choices.

Yet there are countervailing forces, as there always have been even when the voices of ignorance, anti-rationalism, and anti-intellectualism have resounded most loudly in the public square. As the 2008 presidential campaign began, a strange and welcome locution was heard in the land: critics of the war in Iraq, in both parties, began calling themselves "reality-based" candidates. In the triumphalist fervor of President Bush's first term, a White House aide had spoken contemptuously of scholars, scientists, and journalists — all those who "believe that solutions emerge from judicious study of discernible reality." Now, it seems, Americans have lost their patience with politicians who ignore reality — at the very least, with those who boast about ignoring reality — and many ordinary voters are at last making a connection between disdain for evidence and the loss of American lives. Call it the revenge of the reality-based world. Evidence-based science is also looking better and better to much of the public. In Kansas, voters have removed anti-evolutionists from the state board of education, and in state after state, the public continues to reject faith-based restrictions on embryonic stem cell research. Public support for the research is growing even as Bush continues to keep faith with his right-wing religious base by blocking congressional efforts to expand federal support for embryonic studies. We might have arrived at what psychologists call a "teachable moment" — a point at which citizens are attuned, as a result of events that cannot be ignored, to the perils of making decisions based on faith and emotion rather than facts and logic. At such times, people are willing to consider ideas, and even make changes in behavior, that they generally prefer to avoid.

To seize the moment, however, Americans must recognize that we are living through an overarching crisis of memory and knowledge involving everything about the way we learn and think. Such a recognition would have to come from ordinary citizens as well as their elected representatives, from nonintellectuals and intellectuals alike. The first essential step is a negative: we must give up the delusion that technology can supply the fix for a condition that, however much it is abetted by our new machines, is essentially nontechnological. In 2007, when Bill Gates announced the launch of Microsoft's Windows Vista operating system, he spoke earnestly about the ways in which the new software program, unlike the old Windows, allows him and his wife to limit the number of hours their preteen children spend on the computer. I had no sense that Gates was dissembling in order to sell his latest product, which we will all have to buy eventually anyway; he was simply indulging himself in the pleasant parental and, in his case, entrepreneurial delusion that there is a technological means of controlling the hunger for technologically generated sensation.

On the one hand, the founder of Microsoft knows that a bright twelve-year-old will surely figure out, and probably in short order, how to get around a system that supposedly enables Mom and Dad to control his screen time. On the other hand, rather like the Lord placing the fruit tree in Eden and warning Adam and Eve to stay away, the parent Bill Gates wants to believe that there is a way of shielding children from over-exposure to the tempting wares he has helped to create. The pretense that there is some mechanical, relatively simple means of breaking the intergenerational cycle of addiction to infotainment is just one example of our failure, as a society, to acknowledge the profundity and breadth of our cultural loss.

When the dumbing down of culture is seen as a collection of largely unrelated problems, concerned leaders in business, government, and education can only offer solutions that nibble at the edges. The crisis in contemporary American education, as suggested by the title of the No Child Left Behind Act, is treated by politicians, on the left and the right, as an affliction confined to a disadvantaged minority of the young, who can be helped by a concerted effort to raise standardized test scores. The testing prescription is, in fact, the educational equivalent of Microsoft's parental controls: both are reasonable, decent ideas, and they will do almost nothing to alleviate the cultural malaise that is leaving a majority, not a minority, of children behind — if the bar is set higher than a pitifully low checklist of basic skills. The low bar is the real issue, and the failure of so many poor blacks and Hispanics to meet the most minimal standards attests only to the vast racial, class, and economic disparities in American society. That children from more affluent homes can pass undemanding standardized tests does not mean that they are learning what citizens of a functional democracy need to know.

What might help alert the public to the deeper significance of our nation's intellectual shortcomings? Real political leadership, comparable to Franklin Roosevelt's effort to educate Americans in the late 1930s about their stake in the future of Europe and the threat posed by Nazism, could take advantage of the public anger about the war in Iraq to make this a truly teachable moment instead of a simple repudiation of a failed policy. But it would take awesome courage for a candidate to say to voters: "The problem isn't just that you were lied to. The real problem is that we, as a people, have become too lazy to learn what we need to know to make sound public decisions. The problem is that two thirds of us can't find Iraq on a map, and many members of Congress don't know a Shiite from a Sunni. The problem is that the public doesn't know enough or care enough about culture to be outraged when a United States secretary of defense, informed that some of the oldest artifacts of Western civilization are being looted from a Baghdad museum on our watch, says dismissively, 'Stuff happens.' The problem is that most of us don't bother to read newspapers or even watch the news on television. Our own ignorance is our worst enemy." It is so much easier, so much safer politically, to simply say, "You were the victims of a lie," than to suggest that both voters and their elected representatives, in both parties, must shoulder much of the blame for their willingness to be deceived. It is easy to imagine the chorus of sneers from ignorant talking heads on cable news if a presidential candidate dared to use the word "ignorance" in public. Al Gore, who really did try to educate the public about global warming, was mocked unceasingly and called a bore and a pedant during his vice presidency and throughout his presidential campaign; only when he left the political stage, or was assumed to have left the political stage, did he find a voice that made Americans pay attention.

The public's growing concern about global warming is one more indication of the renewal of interest in the pesky, reality-based world and offers yet another teachable moment. Given the losing track record of politicians who have tried to educate voters about complicated issues during the past twenty years, it is certainly a long shot, even during this potentially receptive period of national self-doubt, to bet on the emergence of leadership that aspires to a higher standard of reason and knowledge. But it has happened before — and not only in the Enlightenment dawn of the republic. John Kennedy's famous 1963 speech at American University, calling for negotiations with the Soviet Union on a nuclear test-ban treaty, is generally regarded today as the beginning of détente. In a masterful invocation of reason and its power for good, Kennedy described peace as "the necessary rational end of rational men," and asserted that human "reason and spirit have often solved the seemingly unsolvable — and we believe they can do it again." Drawing a distinction between attainable goals and unattainable dreams, Kennedy said, "I am not referring to the absolute, infinite concept of universal peace and goodwill of which some fantasies and fanatics dream. I do not deny the value of hopes and dreams, but we merely invite discouragement and incredulity by making that our only and immediate goal." I can imagine such a speech about any number of life-and-death issues today, and I can imagine an American audience eager to hear a politician speaking in the voice of reason rather than the voice of fantasy.

Intellectuals could also make a much greater contribution to public understanding than they have over the past few decades. Luminaries in the world of science have recently shown that genuine experts can make a genuine difference in the quality of public debate and public knowledge about scientific matters. For decades, top-level scientists stood aloof from the battle over the teaching of evolution in public schools, in part because they felt that answering the arguments of creationists and intelligent design proponents would afford greater respectability to anti-evolutionists. For the past few years, though, many scientists and scientific organizations have done an about-face and entered the battle by speaking about evolution in a wide variety of public forums and testifying in court to keep intelligent design and creationism out of public school biology classes. As Judge John E. Jones III said explicitly in his *Kitzmiller v. Dover* opinion, extensive scientific testimony played a critical role in building the case that intelligent design was not a scientific theory but a religiously based argument for the existence of a supernatural creator. In 2006, Scientists and Engineers for America, a nonpartisan group with sixteen Nobel laureates on its board, was formed for the explicit purpose of endorsing candidates who support mainstream scientific positions and providing "pro-science" candidates with background material on issues ranging from energy policy to stem cell research. There is no such thing as right-wing or left-wing science — although there are certainly left-wing and right-wing scientists — but respected researchers generally agree on what separates real science, dedicated to the search for truth in the natural world, from pseudosciences designed to serve political, religious, or social ends. There could be no more important task today than the communication of that distinction to the public, and scientifically accomplished intellectuals — or, to put it another way, scientists who are intellectual generalists — are uniquely equipped for the task.

In the humanities and social sciences, a similar consensus is urgently needed if intellectuals are to serve as a force for the improvement of public education and the elevation of public discourse. The reason why Arthur Schlesinger and Diane Ravitch were able to cooperate in an appeal for national history standards is that neither was beholden to a political master or an inflexible political ideology. Ravitch is nonpartisan enough to have served in the U.S. Department of Education under the administrations of both George H. W. Bush and Bill Clinton. Schlesinger, who died in 2007 at age eighty-nine, stood out for decades, long after his political involvement with the Kennedy brothers, as a voice of reason and lucidity in the culture wars over the nation's history. He may have been the last remaining public intellectual, in the sense that the term was used decades ago, and it would have been much more difficult, if not impossible, for him to play that role had he retained the close ties to power that he enjoyed during the Kennedy administration. In an essay titled "History and National Stupidity," Schlesinger poignantly observed:

Sometimes, when I am particularly depressed, I ascribe our behavior to stupidity — the stupidity of our leadership, the stupidity of our culture. Thirty years ago we suffered military defeat — fighting an unwinnable war against a country about which we knew nothing. . . . Vietnam was bad enough, but to repeat the same experiment thirty years later in Iraq is a strong argument for a case of national stupidity.

In the meantime, let a thousand historical flowers bloom. History is never a closed book or a final verdict. It is always in the making. Let historians not forsake the quest for knowledge, however tricky and full of problems that quest may be, in the interests of an ideology, a nation, a race, a sex, or a cause. The great strength of the practice of history in a free society is its capacity for self-correction.[3]

This is the voice of a genuinely civic-minded intellectual, using his scholarly gifts in an effort to encourage his countrymen to consider their behavior from a different perspective. It should be the goal of all public intellectuals to exert their influence, insofar as it exists, as Schlesinger and Ravitch did in their passionate appeal for emphasis on a common civic culture in the teaching of history. Similar efforts are needed, by true scholars who have not taken up residence on the wilder shores of political dogma, to combat the epidemic of junk thought in every area of the humanities and social sciences.

One problem that cries out for collaboration between liberal and conservative intellectuals is the pandering of higher education institutions to students who apparently want to major in infotainment. Anyone who takes more than a cursory look at the vast array of college curriculum offerings on popular culture, from "fat studies" to in-depth examinations of television sitcoms, knows how far standards have been lowered to accommodate both students and their teachers — many of the latter having cut their teeth on the worst aspects of sixties and seventies pop culture.

A sorry insight into the kinds of courses offered at countless universities throughout the nation was a by-product of the immense publicity surrounding the shooting of thirty-two people on the Virginia Tech University campus in 2007. A few days after the massacre, front-page stories revealed that professors and students in the English department had been especially concerned about the behavior and writings of the gunman, Cho Seung-Hui. It seems that Cho was a student in an English course in contemporary horror films and literature, in which the class studied such immortal English-language works as the movie *Friday the 13th* and the best-selling novels of Stephen King and Patricia Cornwell, whose heroine happens to be a Virginia forensic pathologist. The existence of such a class tells us nothing about the shooter or his motives, but it says a good deal about what passes for higher education today. The works of both

Cornwell and King are excellent aids in getting through transcontinental airline flights, their chief virtues being their length and an impressive amount of suspense and gore, sufficient to distract the reader from the real horrors of flying coach. In the Virginia Tech class, students were also required to keep "fear journals," in which they wrote about their reactions to the works covered in class and even their private bogeymen. How can it be that American culture has so debased itself that institutions calling themselves universities, and academic bodies calling themselves English departments, actually give course credit for writing "fear journals"? The job of higher education is not to instruct students in popular culture but to expose them to something better. Genuine intellectuals — some of whom still exist on college campuses — ought to make a crusade out of ridding their institutions of such pap. Courses in popular culture are extremely popular with students, and the faculty members who teach them argue that such classes enable students to "deconstruct" and think critically about mass entertainment. Those faculty members are wrong. What classes in popular culture really do is allow students to continue aiming their minds at low objects. Offer a course in which students are required to read *Crime and Punishment* and *Wuthering Heights,* and they may come to understand why *Friday the 13th* and Stephen King's novels are not worthy objects for deconstruction.

In the social sciences, experts who have nothing to gain by promoting social pseudoscience must make their voices heard in the nonacademic public square. Proposals to instruct boy brains and girl brains in separate classes, for example, have been advanced primarily by educational gurus and psychologists who stand to make a profit from the implementation of a retrograde idea presented in a new pseudoscientific package. We need to hear from distinguished educators, historians of education, and sociologists who understand and can explain to the public the inadvisability of embarking on such a radical departure from our nation's best traditions regarding the "diffusion of knowledge." We need to hear more, not less, from reality-based intellectuals about all of the social problems that have been exacerbated by public ignorance — that is, all social problems. But we also need political leaders smart and sophisticated enough to recognize that intellectuals — whether they are sitting in think tanks, universities, or the West Wing — are as capable as anyone else of spouting reckless nonsense.

It is possible that nothing will help. The nation's memory and attention span may already have sustained so much damage that they cannot be revived by the best efforts of America's best minds. I too am nibbling at the edges by talking about the need for political leaders who address Americans as thinking adults; for intellectuals willing to step up and bring their knowledge, instead of a lust for power, to the public square; for educators devoted to teaching and learning rather than to the latest fads in pop psychology. None of these suggestions addresses the core problem created by the media — the pacifiers of the mind that permeate our homes, schools, and politics. There is little evidence to indicate that Americans have either the desire or the will to lessen their dependency on the easy satisfactions held out by the video and digital world; on the contrary, the successful marketing of infant videos suggests that many parents are eager to draw their children into the infotainment snare before they have any chance to explore the world on their own. At the end of his 2007 State of the Union address, President Bush followed the ancient custom (dating from the Reagan administration) of introducing "ordinary citizens" who have "made a difference" in American life. Among the honorees was Julie Aigner-Clark, the brain behind the *Baby Einstein* video series.

Aigner-Clark, according to her riches-to-megariches story, launched her business out of a desire to share her own love of music and art with her baby daughter and started out by producing videos in her basement. Singing, dancing, or playing an instrument *in vivo* apparently weren't good enough. By 2001, the business was worth more than $20 million, and then — as Bush said in a breathless tone that might have been used to describe the miracle of the loaves and fishes — "Julie sold Baby Einstein to the Walt Disney Company." Although Aigner-Clark originally marketed her videos as a tool for producing smarter babies, she switched gears last summer after the publication of a University of Washington study indicating that infants who watch *Baby Einstein* may actually lag behind their videoless peers in language development. The videos were never designed to make babies smarter, Aigner-Clark told the Associated Press, but were intended to make babies happier by exposing them to "beautiful things" like art, music, and poetry. Happy babies must learn early that the beautiful things in life aren't free. If this is truly the new American dream for the upbringing of future generations, it is painful to think about what the cultural landscape will look like a generation from now.

If there is to be an alternative to the culture of distraction, it can only be created one family at a time, by parents and citizens determined to preserve a saving remnant of those who prize memory and true learning above all else. Adult self-control, not digital parental controls, is the chief requirement for the transmission of individual and historical memory. A parent who sits down in front of a television after dinner every night, while monitoring children's computer use to make sure that their homework is done before they go online, is sending not a mixed message but a thoroughly negative message about books: screen time, of whatever sort, is the reward for children who have done all of their boring Gutenberg-era chores. I know that I became a reader in childhood because my parents were constantly reading. They watched television too, of course, but books always seemed like the passports to the adult world. The endless warnings about the dangers of too much screen time for the young evade the fact that children are simply following in their parents' footsteps — or, more to the point, sinking into the spreading round indentations their parents have left on the couch. It is unrealistic to expect people simply to turn off their television sets, computers, or iPods, because infotainment addiction resembles compulsive eating rather than alcoholism or smoking: alcohol and nicotine can be eliminated, but both food and the media supply essential nutrients as well as nonessential junk.

A few years ago, I decided to gauge the extent of my own media dependency by participating in an annual week without television sponsored by a quixotic nonprofit organization called the TV-Turnoff Network. Turning off the television actually meant turning off all screen entertainment for a video-free week, and what an uncomfortable week it turned out to be for me — as it apparently does for most people who sign on for the experiment. There is real pain involved in forbidding ourselves, even for a limited period, from flipping on the remote: the pain is called withdrawal. Given that 80 percent of American homes have at least two television sets — and more than half have at least three — nearly all of us, whatever our level of education or age, are lying if we say that we rarely watch TV. And it is shaming to admit, especially within the privacy of our minds, how often we choose video toys to block out our own thoughts or the demands of those we love as well as to avoid more active forms of entertainment — from reading a book to attending a concert. Turning off the television made me admit how much time I was habitually losing to the infotainment maw, yet I also discovered, after the initial withdrawal pangs passed, that it was both easy and enjoyable to cut that time in half. It was a revelation to realize how much I had been missing in the books I was supposedly reading while the television flickered in my peripheral vision. Anyone who values self-reliance will be changed for the better by limiting screen time, and for parents — who literally hold the future in their hands — there is no way, apart from the force of example, to raise children whose minds are not absolutely in thrall to commercially generated images.

Like all conservationists, a cultural conservationist in today's America can only act in hope while living with amply justified fear. "What is the remedy?" Emerson asked so many years ago. ". . . Is it not the chief disgrace in the world, not to be a unit; — not to be reckoned one character; — not to yield that peculiar fruit which each man was created to bear, but to be reckoned in the gross, in the hundred, or the thousand . . . Not so, brothers and friends — please God, ours shall not be so."

NOTES

CHAPTER ONE: THE WAY WE LIVE NOW

1. Franklin Delano Roosevelt, *Fireside Chats* (New York, 1995), pp. 48–49, 62–63.
2. George Orwell, "Politics and the English Language," *Horizon,* 76 (London, 1946); www.orwell.ru/library/essays/politics/english/e_polit.
3. Robert Wright, "Shock Talk Without Apologies," *New York Times,* April 14, 2007.
4. Russell Baker, "Talking It Up," *New York Review of Books,* May 11, 2006.
5. Richard Hofstadter, *Anti-Intellectualism in American Life* (New York, 1963), p. 22.
6. Ron Suskind, "Without a Doubt," *New York Times Magazine,* October 17, 2004.
7. Neil Postman, *Amusing Ourselves to Death* (New York, 1985), p.16.
8. In "HBO Criticized for Pushing TV to Infants," Associated Press, May 12, 2005.

9. Steven Johnson, *Everything Bad Is Good for You* (New York, 2005), p. 181.

10. Ibid., p. 183.

11. See Nancy Gibbs, "Apocalypse Now," *Time,* July 1, 2002.

12. "The Religious and Other Beliefs of Americans 2003," Harris Interactive Poll, February 26, 2003.

13. Gibbs, "Apocalypse Now."

14. Frederick Lewis Allen, *Only Yesterday* (New York, 1931), p. 171.

15. "Public Divided on Origins of Life," August 30, 2005, Pew Forum on Religion and Public Life; www.pewforum.org.

16. "Good Science, Bad Science: Teaching Evolution in the States," Thomas B. Fordham Foundation, September 1, 2000, figure 1; www.edexcellence.net.

17. Cornelia Dean, "Evolution Takes a Back Seat in U.S. Classes," *New York Times,* February 1, 2005.

18. George E. Webb, *The Evolution Controversy in America* (Lexington, Ky., 1994), p. 254.

19. George Gallup, *The Role of the Bible in American Society* (Princeton, N.J., 1990), p. 17; Genesis reference in Stephen Prothero, *Religious Literacy* (San Francisco, 2007), p. 12.

20. Michael Medved, "March of the Con-

servatives: Penguin Film as Political Fodder," *New York Times,* September 13, 2005.

21. *Kitzmiller v. Dover School District,* U.S. District Court for the Middle District of Pennsylvania, case no. 04cv.2688.

22. Bill Moyers, "The Delusional Is No Longer Marginal," *New York Review of Books,* March 24, 2005.

CHAPTER TWO: THE WAY WE LIVED THEN

1. Many details of the setting are drawn from Bliss Perry, "Emerson's Most Famous Speech," in *The Praise of Folly and Other Papers* (New York, 1923), pp. 81–113.

2. *"The American Scholar" Today: Emerson's Essay and Some Critical Views,* ed. C. David Mead (New York, 1970), pp. 29–30.

3. James Russell Lowell, "Thoreau," *My Study Windows* (Boston, 1885), pp. 197–98.

4. Alexis de Tocqueville, *Democracy in America* (1840; New York, 1960), vol. 2, p. 35.

5. Ibid., pp. 36–37.

6. Henry Adams, *A History of the United States* (1891–96; New York, 1962), vol. 1, p. 184.

7. See Merle Curti, *American Paradox: The Conflict of Thought and Action* (New Brunswick, N.J., 1956), p. 16.

8. James Madison, "Preface to Notes on Debates," in *The Record of the Federal Convention of 1787,* ed. Max Farrand (New Haven, Conn., 1937), vol. 3, p. 94.

9. George Washington, *The Writings of George Washington,* ed. Jared Sparks (Boston, 1834), vol. 1, p. 572, quoted in Adolphe E. Meyer, *An Educational History of the American People* (New York, 1957), p. 103.

10. *"The American Scholar" Today,* p. 14.

11. Bayard Rush Hall (under pseudonym Robert Carlton), *The New Purchase, or, Seven and a Half Years in the Far West* (New York, 1843), vol. 2, p. 85.

12. Sidney E. Mead, *The Lively Experiment: The Shaping of Christianity in America* (New York, 1963), p. 129.

13. Ellen D. Larned, *History of Windham County, Connecticut* (Worcester, Mass., 1880), vol. 2, pp. 220–21, in G. Adolf Koch, *Republican Religion* (New York, 1933), p. 245.

14. See Hofstadter, *Anti-Intellectualism in American Life,* pp. 81–82.

15. See Susan Jacoby, *Freethinkers: A His-*

tory of American Secularism (New York, 2004), pp. 15–34.

16. Russell Nye, *The Cultural Life of the New Nation: 1776–1830* (New York, 1960), pp. 74–75.

17. Lyman Beecher, *Autobiography, Correspondence, Etc.,* ed. Charles Beecher (New York, 1865), vol. 1, p. 43.

18. See Jon Butler, *Awash in a Sea of Faith* (Boston, 1990), p. 220.

19. William Bentley, *The Diary of William Bentley* (Salem, Mass., 1905), vol. 3, p. 442.

20. Tocqueville, *Democracy in America,* vol. 2, p. 25.

21. Ibid., pp. 35–36.

22. W. J. Cash, *The Mind of the South* (New York, 1941), p. 17.

23. Quoted in H. C. Barnard, *Education and the French Revolution* (Cambridge, 1969), p. 82.

24. Meyer, *An Educational History of the American People,* p. 105.

25. Horace Mann to Frederick Packard, March 18, 1838, in Jonathan Messerli, *Horace Mann: A Biography* (New York, 1972), p. 310.

26. Mann to Packard, June 23, 1838, in ibid., p. 311.

27. Scott Baier, Sean Mulholland, Chad Turner, and Robert Tamura, *Income and Education of the States of the United States, 1840–2000,* Working Paper 2004-31, November 2004, Federal Reserve Bank of Atlanta, Working Papers Series.

28. See Meyer, *An Educational History of the American People,* p. 210.

29. *The Case of Thomas Cooper . . . Submitted to the Legislature and the People of South Carolina, December 1831* (Columbia, S.C., 1831), pp. 14–15, in Richard Hofstadter and Walter P. Metzger, *The Development of Academic Freedom in the United States* (New York, 1955), pp. 266–67.

30. Carl Bode, *The American Lyceum: Town Meeting of the Mind* (New York, 1956), p. 101.

31. Ibid., p. 48.

32. See Jacoby, *Freethinkers,* pp. 74–77.

33. Bode, *The American Lyceum,* p. 156.

34. Doris Kearns Goodwin, *Team of Rivals: The Political Genius of Abraham Lincoln* (New York, 2005), p. 51.

35. *"The American Scholar" Today,* pp. 17–18.

Chapter Three: Social Pseudoscience in the Morning of America's Culture Wars

1. See Richard Hofstadter, *Social Darwinism in American Thought* (Boston, 1992), pp. 51–66.
2. William Graham Sumner, "The Concentration of Wealth: Its Economic Justification," in *The Challenge of Facts and Other Essays* (New Haven, Conn., 1914) p. 89.
3. Merle Curti, *The Growth of American Thought* (New York, 1943), p. 601.
4. Ibid.
5. Henry Miller Lydenberg, *History of the New York Public Library* (New York, 1923), p. 419.
6. *New York Tribune*, December 18, 1869.
7. Joan Shelley Rubin, *The Making of Middlebrow Culture* (Chapel Hill, N.C.), 1992, p. 18.
8. Richard Ohmann, *Selling Culture: Magazines, Markets, and Class at the Turn of the Century* (New York, 1996), p. 29, in Todd Gitlin, *Media Unlimited* (New York, 2001), p. 29.
9. *New York Times*, September 2, 1876.
10. Andrew Carnegie, *Autobiography of Andrew Carnegie* (Boston, 1924), p. 339.
11. Hofstadter, *Social Darwinism in American Thought*, p. 32.

12. See Charles A. Beard and Mary R. Beard, *The American Spirit: A Study of the Idea of Civilization in the United States* (New York, 1942), vol. 4, p. 347.

13. William Graham Sumner, "Reply to a Socialist," in ibid., p. 57.

14. Henry Ward Beecher, "Communism Denounced," *New York Times,* July 30, 1877.

15. Charles Darwin, *The Origin of Species* and *The Descent of Man* (1859, 1871; New York, 1948), p. 501.

16. Quoted in Mead, *The Lively Experiment,* p. 95.

17. William James, "Great Men and Their Environment," *Atlantic Monthly* (October 1880); www.cscs.umich.edu/~crshalizi/James/great_men.html.

18. Thorstein Veblen, *The Theory of the Leisure Class* (1899; New York, 1995), p. 210.

19. William English Walling, *The Larger Aspects of Socialism* (New York, 1913), pp. 81–82.

20. Michael Kazin, *A Godly Hero: The Life of William Jennings Bryan* (New York, 2006), p. 289.

21. Robert W. Cherny, *A Righteous Cause: The Life of William Jennings Bryan* (Boston,

1985), p. 172.

22. Theodore Roosevelt, "History As Literature," in *History As Literature and Other Essays* (London, 1914), p. 12.

23. "Americans' Bible Knowledge Is in the Ballpark, But Often Off Base," Barna Group, July 12, 2001.

CHAPTER FOUR: REDS, PINKOS, FELLOW TRAVELERS

1. Dan T. Carter, *From George Wallace to Newt Gingrich* (Baton Rouge, La.), pp. 118–19, in Glenn Feldman, ed., *Politics and Religion in the White South* (Lexington, Ky.), p. 308.

2. Emma Goldman, *My Disillusionment in Russia* (1923; Gloucestor, Mass., 1983), p. 262.

3. Clarence Darrow, *The Story of My Life* (New York, 1932), p. 218.

4. Lawrence W. Levine, *Defender of the Faith: William Jennings Bryan: The Last Decade, 1915–1925* (New York, 1965), p. 279.

5. See Irving Howe, *A Margin of Hope* (New York, 1982), pp. 61–89, and Irving Kristol, *Reflections of a Neoconservative* (New York, 1983), pp. 4–13.

6. Howe, *A Margin of Hope,* p. 65.

7. Irving Howe and Lewis Coser, *The American Communist Party: A Critical History* (New York, 1974), p. 419.

8. Diana Trilling, *The Beginning of the Journey* (New York, 1993), pp. 180–81.

9. Ellen W. Schwecker, *No Ivory Tower: McCarthyism and the Universities* (New York, 1986), p. 9.

10. Marshall Frady, *Billy Graham: A Parable of American Righteousness* (Boston, 1979), p. 292.

11. Quoted in David Caute, *The Great Fear* (New York, 1978), p. 421.

12. Arthur Miller, *Timebends* (New York, 1987), pp. 341–42.

13. "Elia Kazan," *American Masters,* http://www.pbs.org/wnet/americanmasters/database/kazan_e.html.

Chapter Five: Middlebrow Culture from Noon to Twilight

1. Virginia Woolf, "Middlebrow," in *The Death of the Moth* (New York, 1942), p. 182.

2. Van Wyck Brooks, *America's Coming of Age* (1915; New York, 1975), pp. 28–29.

3. Classical music figures in Julie Lee, "A Requiem for Classical Music," *Regional Review,* Federal Reserve Bank of Boston,

Quarter 2, 2003. Other cultural statistics in Dwight Macdonald, "Masscult and Midcult" (1960), in *Against the American Grain: Essays on the Effects of Mass Culture* (New York, 1962), p. 59.

4. John Hope Franklin, *Mirror to America* (New York, 2005), p. 28.

5. Norman Podhoretz, *Making It* (New York, 1967), pp. 10–11.

6. Joan Shelley Rubin, *The Making of Middlebrow Culture* (New York, 1992), p. 160.

7. H. G. Wells, *The Outline of History,* 2nd ed. (New York, 1926), pp. 1–2.

8. Ibid., pp. 7–8.

9. See Rubin, *The Making of Middlebrow Culture,* p. 233.

10. Harry Golden, *The World of Haldeman-Julius* (New York, 1960), p. 5.

11. Dwight Macdonald, "Book-of-the-Millennium Club," *The New Yorker,* November 29, 1952.

12. Ibid.

13. See Rubin, *The Making of Middlebrow Culture,* p. 191.

14. Milton Mayer, "Great Books," *Life,* October 28, 1946.

15. Rubin, *The Making of Middlebrow Culture,* p. 100.

16. See Al Silverman, ed., *The Book of the*

Month: Sixty Years of Books in American Life (New York, 1986), "Decade Three" and "Decade Four," pp. 93–180.

17. Ingrid D. Rowland, "The Titan of Titans," *New York Review of Books,* April 27, 2006.

18. Ibid.

19. Podhoretz, *Making It,* p. 169.

20. Trilling, *The Beginning of the Journey,* p. 346.

21. A. M. Sperber, *Murrow: His Life and Times* (New York, 1986), p. 426.

22. David Brooks, *New York Times,* June 16, 2005.

23. Macdonald, "Masscult and Midcult," in *Against the American Grain,* pp. 12–13.

24. Ibid., pp. 54–55.

CHAPTER SIX: BLAMING IT ON THE SIXTIES

1. Irving Kristol, *New York Times Magazine,* January 23, 1977.

2. Susan Jacoby, "We *Did* Overcome," *New York Times Magazine,* April 10, 1977.

3. Philip Roth, "Imagining Jews," *New York Review of Books,* September 29, 1974.

4. Robert Bork, *Slouching Towards Gomorrah: Modern Liberalism and American Decline* (New York, 1996), p. 53.

5. Norman Podhoretz, *Breaking Ranks*

(New York, 1979), p. 306.

6. Allan Bloom, *The Closing of the American Mind* (New York, 1987), pp. 323–24.

7. See Mark Kurlansky, *1968: The Year That Rocked the World* (New York, 2004), p. 203.

8. Staughton Lynd, "Non-Violent Alternatives to American Violence," in Louis Menash and Ronald Radosh, eds., *Teach-ins: USA* (New York, 1967), p. 54.

9. Quoted in Kurlansky, *1968,* p. 180.

10. Bloom, *The Closing of the American Mind,* p. 334.

11. Ibid., p. 320.

12. A. O. Scott, "In Search of the Best," *New York Times Book Review,* May 21, 2006.

13. W. E. B. DuBois, *The Souls of Black Folk* (Cambridge, Mass., 1903); Great Books Online (Bartleby.com, 1999); http://www.bartleby.com/114/6.html.

14. Sheldon Wolin, "The Destructive Sixties and Postmodern Conservatism," in Stephen Macedo, ed., *Reassessing the Sixties: Debating the Political and Cultural Legacy* (New York, 1996), pp. 150–51.

15. Maurice Isserman, *If I Had a Hammer* (New York, 1987), p. 116.

16. Kurlansky, *1968,* p. 286.

17. Richard Lemon, *The Troubled Americans* (New York, 1970), pp. 235–36.

18. Ibid., p. 35.

19. Timothy George, "The 'Baptist Pope'," *Christianity Today,* March 11, 2002, p. 54.

20. David Stricklin, "Fundamentalism," *Handbook of Texas Online,* General Libraries at the University of Texas at Austin and the Texas State Historical Association; http://www.tsha.utexas.edu/handbook/online/articles/FF/itfl.html.

21. "Southern Baptists Bar Liberal Treatise on Bible," *New York Times,* June 4, 1970.

22. Ibid.

23. Maurice Isserman and Michael Kazin, *America Divided: The Civil War of the 1960s* (New York, 2004), p. 254.

24. Ibid.

25. Andrew M. Greeley, "Children of the Council," *America,* June 7, 2004.

26. Lowell D. Streiker and Gerald S. Strober, *Religion and the New Majority: Billy Graham, Middle America, and the Politics of the Seventies* (New York, 1972), p. 70.

27. Reinhold Niebuhr, "The King's Chapel and the King's Court," *Christianity and Crisis,* August 4, 1969.

28. Sydney E. Ahlstrom, *A Religious History of the American People* (New Haven, Conn., 1972), p. 1087.

29. Ibid., p. 1095.

Chapter Seven: Legacies

1. Dan Wakefield, *Going All the Way* (New York, 1970), p. 190.
2. "Demographic Profile: American Baby Boomers," MetLife Mature Market Institute Analysis, Populations Projection Project, 2003; www.metlife.com.
3. Susan Jacoby, "We Love You, Slava," *New York Times Magazine,* April 18, 1976.
4. Harvey Mansfield, *Reassessing the Sixties* (New York, 1997), p. 36.
5. Josh Greenfeld, "For Simon and Garfunkel All Is Groovy," *New York Times Magazine,* October 13, 1968.
6. Donald MacLeod, "Christopher Ricks: Someone's Gotta Hold of His Art," *The Guardian* (London), July 13, 2004.
7. Allan Kozinn, "Interpreting the Beatles Without Copying," *New York Times,* January 13, 2007.
8. William O'Neill, *Readin, Ritin, and Rafferty!: A Study of Educational Fundamentalism* (Berkeley, 1969), p. 61.
9. Kurlansky, *1968,* p. xviii.
10. Jerry Rubin, *Growing (Up) at 37* (New York, 1976), p. 93.
11. See Leo Braudy, *The Frenzy of Renown*

(New York, 1986), pp. 19–28.

12. Michael Rossman, "Letter to Jerry Rubin," in Todd Gitlin, *The Whole World Is Watching: Mass Media in the Making and Unmaking of the New Left* (Berkeley, 2003), p. 173.

13. Susan Jacoby, "Howard University: In Search of a Black Identity," *Saturday Review,* April 20, 1968.

14. See Gitlin, *The Whole World Is Watching,* pp. 150–53.

15. Arthur Schlesinger, Jr., "History and National Stupidity," *New York Review of Books,* April 27, 2006.

Chapter Eight: The New Old-Time Religion

1. Fred M. Heckinger, "Challenges Are Predicted — 30% of All Schools Use Some Rite," *The New York Times,* June 26, 1962.

2. Walter Russell Mead, "God's Country," *Foreign Affairs* (September–October 2006).

3. Nancy Ammerman, "The New South and the New Baptists," *The Christian Century,* May 14, 1986.

4. "Many Americans Uneasy with Mix of Religion and Politics," Pew Forum on

Religion and Public Life, August 24, 2006; www.pewforum.org.

5. Data on belief in Bible from August 24, 2006, Pew Forum survey. Figures on evolution from August 30, 2005, survey, "Public Divided on Origins of Life: Religion a Strength and Weakness for Both Parties," Pew Forum; www.pewforum.org.

6. Baier, et al., *Income and Education of the States of the United States, 1840–2000.*

7. Hanna Rosin, "God and Country," *The New Yorker,* June 27, 2005.

8. "Many Americans Uneasy with Mix of Religion and Politics," Pew Forum.

9. Maureen Dowd, "Awake and Scream," *New York Times,* September 16, 2006.

10. Mead, "God's Country."

11. "Many Americans Uneasy with Mix of Religion and Politics," Pew Forum.

12. Patricia Zapor, "End of 'Catholic Vote'?", Catholic News Service, November 9, 2004.

13. Chris Suellentrop, "The Rev. John Mc-Closkey: The Catholic Church's K Street Lobbyist," *Slate,* August 9, 2002; http://www.slate.com/id/2069194.

14. Antonin Scalia, "God's Justice and Ours," *First Things: The Journal of Religion and Public Life* (May 2002).

15. Graduate Center, City University of

New York, *American Religious Identification Survey, 2001,* exhibits 1, 3.

16. "Public Divided on Origins of Life," Pew Forum.

17. Sam Harris, *The End of Faith: Religion, Terror, and the Future of Reason* (New York, 2004), p. 20.

18. Harold Jacoby, *Practical Talks by an Astronomer* (New York, 1902), p. 48.

19. See Susan Jacoby, *Freethinkers,* p. 343.

20. 410 US 113.

21. "God and American Diplomacy," *The Economist,* February 6, 2003.

22. Quoted in Stephen Phelan, "Oh Come All Ye Faithless," *Sunday Herald* (London), January 8, 2006.

23. Carson Holloway, "The Public-Intellectual Menace," *National Review,* June 19, 2006.

24. "Spirit and Power: A 10-Country Survey of Pentecostals," October 5, 2006, Pew Forum on Religion and Public Life.

25. Jeffery L. Sheier, "Faith in America," *U.S. News & World Report,* May 6, 2002.

CHAPTER NINE: JUNK THOUGHT

1. Carl Sagan, *The Demon-Haunted World* (New York, 1996), p. 21.

2. US05-380, *Gonzales v. Carhart.*

3. See N. F. Russo, and K. L. Zierk, "Abortion, Childbearing, and Women's Well-Being," *Professional Psychology: Research and Practice,* 23 (1992), pp. 269–80 and N. Stotland, "The Myth of the Abortion Trauma Syndrome," *Journal of the American Medical Association,* 268 (October 1992), p. 15.

4. Peg Tyre, "Boy Brains, Girl Brains: Are Separate Classrooms the Best Way to Teach Kids?", *Newsweek,* September 19, 2005.

5. Herbert Benson, et al., "Study of Therapeutic Effects of Intercessory Prayer (STEP)," *American Heart Journal,* 151 (April 2006), pp. 762–64.

6. Quoted in Benedict Carey, "Long-Awaited Medical Study Questions the Power of Prayer," *New York Times,* March 31, 2006.

7. Christopher Lee, "Family Planning Chief Seen as Political Pick," The Washington Post–Los Angeles Times News Service, in *San Francisco Chronicle,* November 17, 2002.

8. "Religious Identification in the United States," Ontario Consultants on Religious Tolerance, December 15, 2001; www.religious tolerance.org/chr_prac2.htm.

9. Atul Gawande, "Annals of Medicine: The Score," *The New Yorker,* October 9, 2006.

10. "A Population-Based Study of Measles, Mumps, and Rubella Vaccination and Autism," *New England Journal of Medicine,* 347 (November 7, 2002), p. 1477. See also http://www.pubmedcentral.nih.gov/articlerender.fcgi?artid=112634.

11. Jake Paul Fratkin, "The Treatment of Pertussis (Whooping Cough) Chinese Herbal Medicine. Part Two: Risks and Benefits of Vaccinations," *Acupuncture Today* (September 2006); www.acupuncturetoday.com.

12. *New York Times Magazine,* May 6, 2001; interview conducted by Arthur Allen.

13. Josh Goldstein, "Report: Autism Rate Higher Than Thought," *Philadelpia Inquirer,* February 9, 2007.

14. Paul J. Shabtuck and Maureen Durkin, "A Spectrum of Disputes," *New York Times,* June 11, 2007.

15. E. Sue Blume, *Secret Survivors: Uncovering Emotional Incest and Its Aftereffects in Women* (New York, 1990), p. xiv.

16. Judith Herman Lewis, *Trauma and Recovery* (New York, 1992), p. 1.

17. Abby Ellin, "Big People on Campus," *New York Times,* November 26, 2006.

18. Steven Milloy, "Polar Bear Meltdown?" December 28, 2006, www.FOXNews .com.

19. See John Tierney, "The Kids Are All Right," *New York Times,* October 14, 2006.

20. "U.S. Students Continue to Lag Behind Their International Counterparts in Math," American Psychological Association Online, vol. 36, March 3, 2005.

21. "Outcomes of Learning: Results from the 2000 Program for International Student Assessment of 15-Year-Olds in Reading, Mathematics, and Science Literacy," Organization for Economic Cooperation and Development; http://www.site selection.com/ssinsider/snapshots/ sf011210.htm.

22. Quoted in Marcia Angell, *Science on Trial: The Clash of Medical Evidence and the Law in the Breast Implant Case* (New York, 1986), p. 180.

23. Sandra Harding, *The Science Question in Feminism* (Ithaca, N.Y., 1986), p. 113.

24. Susan McClary, *Feminine Endings: Music, Gender, and Sexuality* (Minneapolis, 1991), pp. 128–29.

25. Lawrence H. Summers, "Remarks at NBER Conference on Diversifying the Science & Engineering Workforce," January 14, 2005, http://www.president

.harvard.edu/speeches/2005/nber/html.

26. Angell, *Science on Trial*, p. 189.

27. Diana Jean Schemo, "Change in Federal Rules Backs Single-Sex Education," *New York Times*, October 25, 2006.

28. Peg Tyre, "The Trouble with Boys," *Newsweek*, January 30, 2006.

29. See Joe Garofoli, "Femme Mentale," *San Francisco Chronicle*, August 6, 2006.

30. David Brooks, "The Gender Gap at School," *New York Times*, June 11, 2006.

31. Ibid.

CHAPTER TEN: THE CULTURE OF DISTRACTION

1. James D. Squires, *Read All About It: The Corporate Takeover of America's Newspapers* (New York, 1993), p. 208.

2. Gitlin, *Media Unlimited*, p. 7.

3. Ibid., p. 16.

4. Postman, *Amusing Ourselves to Death*, p. 78.

5. Colin Mahan, "Babies Get Some Infantainment," May 12, 2006, http://www.tv.com/story/4511.html.

6. Virginia Heffernan, "The Evil Screen's Plot to Take Over the 2-and-Under World," *New York Times*, April 14, 2006.

7. "Zero to Six: Electronic Media in the

Lives of Infants, Toddlers and Preschoolers," Kaiser Family Foundation and the Children's Digital Media Centers, October 28, 2003.

8. Jeneen Interlandi, "Are Educational Videos Bad for Your Baby?", August 7, 2007, *Newsweek,* http://www.msnbc.msn.com/id/20167189/site/newsweek/page/2/.

9. Ibid.

10. "Reading At Risk," July 8, 2000, National Endowment for the Arts.

11. Johnson, *Everything Bad Is Good for You,* p. 184.

12. Ibid., p. 36.

13. *Harnessing the Power of Video Games for Learning,* Federation of American Scientists, October 17, 2006.

14. Nick Summers, "Videogames in the Classroom?", *Newsweek,* October 19, 2006; http://www.msnbc.msn.com/id/153361/site/newsweek.

15. Kiko Adatto, *Sound Bite Democracy: Network Evening News Presidential Campaign Coverage, 1968 and 1988,* Research Paper R-2, Joan Shorenstein Barrone Center for Press, Politics, and Public Policy, June 1990. Thomas L. Patterson, *Diminishing Returns: A Comparison of the 1968 and 2000 Election Night Broadcasts,*

Harvard University Faculty Research Working Papers Series, RWP03-050, December 2003.

16. John Freeman, "The National Book Critics Circle's Campaign to Save Book Reviews," http://www.bookcritics.org/?go=saveBookReviews.

17. Justin Taylor, "The Last Novel by David Markson," http://www.bookslut.com/fiction/2007_06_011196.php.

18. Freeman, "The National Book Critics Circle's Campaign."

19. Quoted in Daniel J. Wakin, "Newspapers Trimming Classical Music Critics," *New York Times,* June 9, 2007.

20. Kevin Kelly, "What Will Happen to Books?", *New York Times Magazine,* May 14, 2006.

21. "New Study Confirms Internet Plagiarism Is Prevalent," Office of Media Relations, Rutgers University; http://urwebsrv.rutgers.edu/medrel/viewArticle.html?ArticleID=3408.

22. Motoko Rich and Dinitia Smith, "First, Idea, Plot and Characters. Then, a Book Needs an Author," *New York Times,* April 27, 2006.

23. Ibid.

24. Ibid.

25. John Updike, "The End of Authorship,"

New York Times Book Review, June 25, 2006.

26. Russell Baker, "Talking It Up," *New York Review of Books,* May 11, 2006.

27. Lynn Smith-Lovin, Miller McPherson, and Matthew E. Brashears, "Core Discussion Networks of Americans," *American Sociological Review* (June 2006).

28. Andrew Patner, *I. F. Stone: A Portrait* (New York, 1988), pp. 23–24.

CHAPTER ELEVEN: PUBLIC LIFE

1. Robert F. Kennedy speech, Indianapolis, April 4, 1968, John F. Kennedy Library; http://www.cs.umb.jfklibrary/r040468.htm.

2. 2006 National Geographic–Roper Survey of Geographic Literacy, May 2, 2006; http://www.nationalgeographic.roper.com/roper2006/findings.html.

3. Alfred Kazin, "The President and Other Intellectuals," in *Contemporaries* (Boston, 1962), pp. 453–54.

4. Interview with Peggy Noonan, "A Chat in the Oval Office," *Wall Street Journal,* December 12, 2001.

5. Quoted in Hofstadter, *Anti-Intellectualism in American Life,* p. 4.

6. Kazin, "The President and Other Intel-

lectuals," p. 463.

7. Sidney Blumenthal, *The Rise of the Counter-Establishment: From Conservative Ideology to Political Power* (New York, 1986), p. 7.

8. Kristol, *Reflections of a Neoconservative,* p. xv.

9. Quoted in Blumenthal, *The Rise of the Counter-Establishment,* pp. 161–62.

10. Hofstadter, *Anti-Intellectualism in American Life,* pp. 429–30.

11. "Public Understanding, Media, and Communication," Annenberg Public Policy Center, 2006 public opinion poll; http://www.annenbergpublicpolicycenter .org/Releases/Release_Courts20060928 Courts_Summary _20060928.

12. 1997 National Poll, National Constitution Center; 1998 Teens Poll; www .constitutioncenter.org.

13. Ronald Reagan, Address at Commencement Exercises at the University of Notre Dame, May 17, 1981; http://www.reagan .utexas.edu/archives/speeches/1981/ 51781a.htm.

14. Ronald Reagan, Remarks at the Annual Convention of the National Association of Evangelicals, March 8, 1983; http:// www.ronaldreagan.com/sp_6htm.

15. Diane Ravitch and Arthur Schlesinger,

Jr., "The New, Improved History Standards," *Wall Street Journal,* April 3, 1996.
16. Richard Alonso-Zaldiver and Jean Merl, "Booklet That Upset Mrs. Cheney Is History," *Los Angeles Times,* October 8, 2004.
17. Lev Grossman, "*Time's* Person of the Year: You," *Time,* December 13, 2006.

CONCLUSION: CULTURAL CONSERVATION

1. Lester J. Cappon, ed., *The Adams-Jefferson Letters* (Chapel Hill, 1959), vol. 1, pp. l–li.
2. Tocqueville, *Democracy in America,* vol. 2, pp. 11–12.
3. Arthur Schlesinger, Jr., "History and National Stupidity," *New York Review of Books,* April 27, 2006.

SELECTED BIBLIOGRAPHY

Adams, Henry. *History of the United States,* vols. 1–2. New York: Antiquarian Press, 1962.

Adams, John, and Thomas Jefferson. *The Adams-Jefferson Letters,* vols. 1-2, ed. Lester J. Cappon. Chapel Hill: University of North Carolina Press, 1959.

Ahlstrom, Sydney E. *A Religious History of the American People.* New Haven: Yale University Press, 1972.

Allen, Frederick Lewis. *Only Yesterday.* New York: Harper & Bros., 1931.

Angell, Marcia. *Science on Trial: The Clash of Medical Evidence and the Law in the Breast Implant Case.* New York: W. W. Norton, 1986.

Avrich, Paul. *The Haymarket Tragedy.* Princeton: Princeton University Press, 1984.

Bagdikian, Ben H. *The New Media Monopoly.*

Boston: Beacon Press, 2004.

Barnard, H. D. *Education and the French Revolution.* London: Cambridge University Press, 1969.

Beard, Charles A., and Mary B. Beard, *The American Spirit: A Study of the Idea of Civilization in the United States,* vol. 4. New York: Macmillan, 1942.

Beecher, Lyman. *Autobiography, Correspondence, Etc.,* ed. Charles Beecher. New York: Harper, 1865.

Bell, Daniel, ed. *The Radical Right.* New Brunswick, N.J.: Transaction Publishers, 2002.

Bentley, William. *The Diary of William Bentley,* vols. 1–4. Salem, Mass.: Essex Institute, 1905.

Blumenthal, Sidney. *The Rise of the Counter-Establishment.* New York: Times Books, 1986.

Bode, Carl. *The American Lyceum: Town Meeting of the Mind.* New York: Oxford University Press, 1956.

Bork, Robert H. *Slouching Towards Gomorrah: Modern Liberalism and American Decline.* New York: HarperCollins, 1996.

Braudy, Leo. *The Frenzy of Renown: Fame and Its History.* New York: Oxford University Press, 1986.

Brennan, Mary C. *Turning Right in the Six-ties: The Conservative Capture of the Re-publican Party.* Chapel Hill: University of North Carolina Press, 1995.

Burton, David H. *The Learned Presidency: Theodore Roosevelt, William Howard Taft, Woodrow Wilson.* Rutherford, N.J.: Fair-leigh Dickinson University Press, 1988.

Butler, Jon. *Awash in a Sea of Faith.* Cam-bridge, Mass.: Harvard University Press, 1990.

Carnegie, Andrew. *The Autobiography of Andrew Carnegie.* Boston: Houghton Miff-lin, 1924.

Cherny, Robert W. *A Righteous Cause: The Life of William Jennings Bryan,* ed. Oscar Handlin. Boston: Little, Brown, 1985.

Clancy, Susan A. *Abducted: How People Come to Believe They Were Kidnapped by Aliens.* Cambridge, Mass.: Harvard Uni-versity Press, 1995.

Crews, Frederick. *The Memory Wars.* New York: New York Review of Books, 1995.

Curti, Merle. *American Paradox: The Conflict of Thought and Action.* New Brunswick, N.J.: Rutgers University Press, 1956.

————. *The Growth of American Thought.* New York: Harper, 1943.

————. *Human Nature in American Thought:*

A History. Madison: University of Wisconsin Press, 1980.

Decter, Midge. *An Old Wife's Tale.* New York: Regan Books, 2001.

Emerson, Ralph Waldo. *Selected Essays,* ed. Larzer Ziff. New York: Penguin, 1982.

Farrand, Max, ed. *The Records of the Constitutional Convention of 1787,* vol. 1. New Haven: Yale University Press, 1937.

Feldman, Glenn, ed. *Politics and Religion in the White South.* Lexington: University Press of Kentucky, 2005.

Fiske, John. *Essays Historical and Literary.* New York: Macmillan, 1907.

Frank, Thomas. *What's the Matter with Kansas?* New York: Metropolitan Books, 2004.

Gilligan, Carol. *In a Different Voice: Psychological Theory and Women's Development.* Cambridge, Mass.: Harvard University Presss, 1982.

Gitlin, Todd. *Media Unlimited.* New York: Metropolitan Books, 2001.

———. *The Whole World Is Watching: Mass Media in the Making and Unmaking of the New Left.* Berkeley: University of California Press, 2003.

Goldman, Emma. *My Disillusionment in Russia* (1923). Gloucester, Mass.: Peter

Smith, 1983.

Goodwin, Doris Kearns. *No Ordinary Time: Franklin and Eleanor Roosevelt: The Home Front in World War II.* New York: Simon & Schuster, 1994.

Griffith, Robert. *The Politics of Fear: Joseph R. McCarthy and the Senate.* Lexington: University Press of Kentucky, 1970.

Hall, Bayard Rush (under pseudonym Robert Carlton), *The New Purchase: or, Seven and a Half Years in the Far West,* vols. 1–2. New York: D. Appleton & Co., 1855.

Handy, Robert T. *A Christian America: Protestant Hopes and Historical Realities.* New York: Oxford University Press, 1983.

Harding, Sandra. *The Science Question in Feminism.* Ithaca, N.Y.: Cornell University Press, 1986.

Harris, Sam. *The End of Faith: Religion, Terror, and the Future of Reason.* New York: W. W. Norton, 2004.

Herman, Judith Lewis. *Trauma and Recovery.* New York: Basic Books, 1992.

Hill, Samuel S., ed. *Religion in the Southern States.* Macon, Ga.: Mercer University Press, 1983.

Hofstadter, Richard. *Anti-Intellectualism in American Life.* New York: Knopf, 1963.

———. *Social Darwinism in American*

Thought. Boston: Beacon Press, 1992.

———, and Walter P. Metzger. *The Development of Academic Freedom in the United States.* New York: Columbia University Press, 1955.

Howe, Irving. *A Margin of Hope: An Intellectual Autobiography.* New York: Harcourt Brace Jovanovich, 1982.

———, and Lewis Coser. *The American Communist Party.* New York: Da Capo Press, 1974.

Isserman, Maurice. *If I Had a Hammer.* New York: Basic Books. 1987.

———, and Michael Kazin. *America Divided: The Civil War of the 1960s.* New York: Oxford University Press, 2004.

Jacoby, Harold. *Practical Talks by an Astronomer.* New York: Charles Scribner's Sons, 1902.

Jacoby, Susan. *Freethinkers: A History of American Secularism.* New York: Metropolitan Books. 2004.

———. *Half-Jew: A Daughter's Search for Her Family's Buried Past.* New York: Scribner, 2000.

James, William. *Collected Essays and Reviews.* New York: Longmans, Green, 1920.

Jefferson, Thomas. *Basic Writings of Thomas Jefferson,* ed. Philip Foner. New York:

Wiley Book Co., 1944.

————. *The Life and Selected Writings of Thomas Jefferson,* ed. Adrienne Koch and William Peden. New York: Modern Library, 1944.

Kazin, Michael. *A Godly Hero: The Life of William Jennings Bryan.* New York: Knopf, 2006.

Ketcham, Ralph. *James Madison: A Biography.* New York: Macmillan, 1971.

Koch, G. Adolf. *Republican Religion: The American Revolution and the Cult of Reason.* New York: Henry Holt, 1933.

Kristol, Irving. *Reflections of a Neoconservative.* New York: Basic Books, 1983.

Kurlansky, Mark. *1968: The Year That Rocked the World.* New York: Ballantine Books, 2004.

Lemon, Richard. *The Troubled American.* New York: Simon & Schuster, 1970.

Loftus, Elizabeth, and Katharine Ketcham. *The Myth of Repressed Memory.* New York: St. Martin's Press, 1994.

Lowell, James Russell. *My Study Windows.* Boston: Houghton Mifflin, 1885.

Lydenberg, Henry Miller. *History of the New York Public Library.* New York: New York Public Library, 1923.

Macedo, Stephen, ed. *Reassessing the Six-*

ties: Debating the Political and Cultural Legacy. New York: W. W. Norton, 1997.

Marcus, Daniel. *Happy Days and Wonder Years: The Fifties and Sixties in Contemporary Cultural Politics.* New Brunswick, N.J.: Rutgers University Press, 2004.

Matheson, Terry. *Alien Abductions: Creating a Modern Phenomenon.* Buffalo: Prometheus Books, 1998.

Mead, Sidney E. *The Lively Experiment: The Shaping of Christianity in America.* New York: Harper & Row, 1963.

Messerli, Jonathan. *Horace Mann: A Biography.* New York: Knopf, 1972.

Meyer, Adolphe E. *An Educational History of the American People.* New York: McGraw-Hill, 1957.

Miller, Arthur. *Timebends: A Life.* New York: Grove Press, 1987.

Miller, Stephen. *Conversation: A History of a Declining Art.* New Haven: Yale University Press, 2006.

Navasky, Victor S. *Naming Names.* New York: Viking Press, 1980.

Nye, Russell Blaine. *The Cultural Life of the New Nation: 1776–1830.* New York: Harper, 1960.

———. *Society and Culture in America,*

1830–1860. New York: Harper & Row, 1974.

———. *The Unembarrassed Muse: The Popular Arts in America.* New York: Dial Press, 1970.

O'Neill, William. *Readin, Ritin, and Rafferty!: A Study of Educational Fundamentalism.* Berkeley: Glendessary Press, 1969.

Patner, Andrew. *I.F. Stone: A Portrait.* New York: Pantheon Books, 1988.

Perry, Bliss. *The Praise of Folly, and Other Papers.* Boston: Houghton Mifflin, 1923.

Podhoretz, Norman. *Breaking Ranks.* New York: Harper & Row, 1979.

———. *Making It.* New York: Random House, 1967.

Radway, Janice A. *A Feeling for Books: The Book-of-the-Month Club, Literary Taste, and Middle-Class Desire.* Chapel Hill: University of North Carolina Press, 1997.

Rand, Ayn. *The Fountainhead.* New York: Bobbs-Merrill, 1943.

Roosevelt, Theodore. *History As Literature and Other Essays.* London: John Murray, 1913.

Sagan, Carl. *The Demon-Haunted World.* New York: Random House, 1996.

Saunders, Robert M. *In Search of Woodrow Wilson: Beliefs and Behavior.* Westport,

Conn.: Greenwood Press, 1998.

Schlesinger, Arthur, Jr. *The Disuniting of America.* New York: W. W. Norton, 1992.

Silverman, Al, ed. *The Book of the Month: Sixty Years of Books in American Life.* Boston: Little, Brown, 1986.

Sperber, A. M. *Murrow: His Life and Times.* New York: Bantam Books, 1986.

Squires, James D. *Read All About It: The Corporate Takeover of America's Newspapers.* New York: Times Books, 1993.

Streiker, Lowell D., and Gerald S. Strober. *Religion and the New Majority.* New York: Association Press, 1972.

Sumner, William Graham. *Challenge of Facts and Other Essays.* New Haven: Yale University Press, 1914.

Talmadge, Irving DeWitt, ed. *Whose Revolution?: A Study of the Future Course of Liberalism in the United States.* New York: Howell, Soskin, 1941.

Tocqueville, Alexis de. *Democracy in America,* vol. 2 (1840). New York: Knopf, 1960.

Trilling, Diana. *The Beginning of the Journey.* New York: Harcourt Brace, 1993.

———. *We Must March My Darlings.* New York: Harcourt Brace Jovanovich, 1977.

Trilling, Lionel. *The Liberal Imagination.*

New York: Viking Press, 1950.

Veblen, Thorstein. *The Higher Learning in America.* New York: Sagamore Press. 1957.

————. *The Theory of the Leisure Class* (1899). New York: Modern Library, 1995.

Wallace, Mike. *Mickey Mouse History and Other Essays on American Memory.* Philadelphia: Temple University Press, 1993.

Walling, William English. *The Larger Aspects of Socialism.* New York: Macmillan, 1913.

Walters, Kerry S. *Elihu Palmer's "Principles of Nature."* Wolfeboro, N.H.: Longwood Academic, 1990.

Ward, Lester Frank. *The Psychic Factors of Civilization.* New York: Johnson Reprint Corp., 1970.

ACKNOWLEDGMENTS

As always, I owe a debt that I can never repay to the New York Public Library. This book was written in the Frederick Lewis Allen Room, a haven for nonfiction writers in the main research library at Fifth Avenue and Forty-second Street. My special thanks go to Wayne Furman, head of the library's Office of Special Collections, for not expelling me from this writer's Eden even after my allotted time had expired.

Bob and Blaikie Worth provided financial grants and personal encouragement at critical points during the four years it took to complete the book. Bob also made a number of valuable editorial suggestions.

Aaron Asher, my longtime editor, now retired from publishing, was my first reader.

Pantheon's publisher, Dan Frank, not only gave me the idea for *The Age of American Unreason* but made tactfully phrased, invaluable editorial suggestions at every stage of the work.

Special thanks go to Pantheon's Fran Bigman, who seems to do just about everything to make things go more smoothly. Here's a special message for Fran's younger siblings — Abby, Jenny, Maura, Hillary, Matthew, and Jeffrey: listen to your big sister about books.

Credit for the elegant original cover design belongs to Barbara DeWilde. Ann Adelman was responsible for the meticulous copy editing of the original edition. And I can't thank Elisabeth Calamari and Katie Freeman enough for putting up with my long memos about publicity of that same edition.

I also wish to express my gratitude to the Center for Inquiry Transnational, a rationalist think tank with headquarters in Buffalo, New York. I am a consultant on public programming to the organization's New York branch, the Center for Inquiry–New York City, and I owe special thanks to my colleagues Austin Dacey, the organization's representative to the United Nations, and Derek Araujo, executive director, for their flexibility about work assignments and hours. Dr. Paul Kurtz, the founder of CFI Transnational, is a genuine inspiration — a tireless advocate of secularism, free inquiry, and science and a battler against every form of unreason.

My literary agents and friends, Georges and Anne Borchardt, have supported my work for the past thirty years.

ABOUT THE AUTHOR

Susan Jacoby is the author of seven books, including *Freethinkers: A History of American Secularism* and *Wild Justice,* a Pulitzer Prize finalist. A frequent contributor to national magazines and newspapers, she is also a consultant on programming for the Center for Inquiry–New York City, a rationalist think tank. She lives in New York City.